The Legal Position of Intergovernmental Organizations

Legal Aspects of International Organizations

VOLUME 65

The titles published in this series are listed at *brill.com/laio*

The Legal Position of Intergovernmental Organizations

A Functional Necessity Analysis of Their Legal Status and Immunities

SECOND REVISED EDITION

By

Peter H.F. Bekker

BRILL | NIJHOFF

LEIDEN | BOSTON

Cover illustration: Oscar Bekker (for: Peter H.F. Bekker, *The Legal Position of Intergovernmental Organizations*)

The first edition of *The Legal Position of Intergovernmental Organizations: A Functional Necessity Analysis of Their Legal Status and Immunities*, 9780792329046, was published by Kluwer Academic Publishers in 1994, with the help of the T.M.C. Asser Institute.

The Library of Congress Cataloging-in-Publication Data is available online at https://catalog.loc.gov
LC record available at https://lccn.loc.gov/2025014275

Typeface for the Latin, Greek, and Cyrillic scripts: "Brill". See and download: brill.com/brill-typeface.

ISSN 0924-4883
ISBN 978-90-04-72420-4 (hardback)
ISBN 978-90-04-72421-1 (e-book)
DOI 10.1163/9789004724211

This book is printed on acid-free paper and produced in a sustainable manner.

To Henry Schermers (1928–2006)
and Ignaz Seidl-Hohenveldern (1918–2001),
two international institutional law pioneers

Contents

Foreword

It was the late Judge Sir Hersch Lauterpacht who said: "once we approach at close quarters practically any branch of international law, we are driven, amidst some feeling of incredulity, to the conclusion that although there is as a rule a consensus of opinion on broad principle – even this may be an overestimate in some cases – there is no semblance of agreement in relation to specific rules and problems". That was some forty years ago (see 49 AJIL 17 (1955)), and things have greatly improved since that time, thanks not least to the codification work of the International Law Commission; and Lauterpacht was indeed writing about the contribution that codification could make to the progressive element of the law. Nevertheless there remain areas of international law where there are no doubt 'broad principles' but an inadequacy of generally accepted hard law. One such area is that of the legal position of intergovernmental organizations, their legal status and immunities. It is with some enthusiasm therefore that one can commend Mr. Bekker's able excursion into that difficult area.

It should be said at the outset that a major complication of these problems of legal status and immunities is that they are not merely questions of public international law; in virtually all practical cases they involve questions not only of public international law, but also of private international law and of municipal law. As I had occasion to observe some four years ago, "... the former boundaries between public international law and private international law and municipal law have become less clearly defined, and in their place are grey, often puzzling, boundary zones. New terms such as 'transnational' law have appeared in order to recognize if not to explain one such grey area. It is no longer always obvious whether, at a given moment, one is dealing with public international law, private international law or municipal law." (39 ICLQ 522 (1990)).

But this makes the subject not only one of difficulties and complexities, but also of opportunity. For the very complication of these relationships is the consequence of the expansion of public international law to govern new areas of human activity. This is well illustrated by the question of jurisdictional immunities. Whereas in the older books this was a one of the more straightforward parts of international law, the emergence of the commercial exceptions to the general rule has meant that the law about immunity is now a most important part of any law, international or domestic, concerned with international commerce, trade and indeed banking.

The broad juridical provenance of these problems, as they may appear in the domestic fora, is well illustrated by the spate of cases before the High Court in England and eventually the House of Lords (there was also litigation before the courts in Malaysia, New York and the Court of Justice of the European Communities) and which arose from the announcement, in October 1985, by the International Tin Council that it was unable to meet its commitments, leaving debts estimated at £750 million. The central question was inevitably the legal status of the Tin Council; or to put the same question in more practical terms, whether the debtor plaintiffs could now have recourse against the States members of that international organization. It was these problems raised by the Tin Council cases which evidently inspired Mr. Bekker to undertake this study.

The like problems arise constantly not only in domestic courts but also in international commercial arbitrations and indeed before the International Court of Justice itself. In commercial arbitration there is, for example, the very lengthy matter of Westland Helicopters and the Arab Organization for Industrialization (see 23 ILM 1071 (1984) for an Interim Award; the final award on the merits of this case was handed down in July 1993 but has not yet been published). As to the International Court of Justice, there is the *Mazilu* Advisory Opinion of 15 December 1989 (1989 ICJ Rep. 177): the only case in which a principal organ of the United Nations, other than the General Assembly and the Security Council, has requested an Opinion from the Court; and more recently still, there have been the *Lockerbie* cases which may yet raise difficult and very important questions about the relationship of the Court and the Security Council.

It is in relation to a branch of law such as this one that the systematization that results from good academic work comes into its own. Rigorous exposition and analysis of the materials can, of itself, be an important contribution to our understanding. But the best work goes further; it discerns principles and patterns, consistencies rather than incompatibilities, and thus is able to make a positive contribution to both the general apprehension of the law, and to its practical usefulness.

This essentially intellectual task of the legal scholar has been well understood by Mr. Bekker. At the outset he tackles one source of confusion: much of the law about the privileges and immunities enjoyed by States and governments, and indeed diplomats, is driven by the notion of sovereignty. But intergovernmental organizations, insofar as they may indeed have a juridical status of their own, by the same token cannot be said to be sovereign. Questions therefore arise how far stock concepts, such as even the well-known distinction between acts *jure imperii* and acts *jure gestionis* can properly be applied, even by analogy, to intergovernmental organizations. Courts have not been consistent in their answers to these sorts of question. Mr. Bekker finds a solution to these problems in the two-fold principle of 'functional necessity', which is an appropriate and practical criterion for intergovernmental organizations, and which makes recourse even by analogy to the legal position of sovereigns, wholly unnecessary and illogical. This general principle of functional necessity is again usefully qualified by "the principle of the *speciality* of the international organization" concerned. These principles Mr. Bekker works out in a three-stage scheme of first, the identification of the functions and purposes of a particular organization; second, the consequent appropriate selection of immunities and privileges; and third, the scope and extent of those immunities and privileges, having regard to that organization's 'official activity.'

In the course of this survey and analysis, Mr. Bekker deals with the relevant work of the International Law Commission, with the views of commentators (he acknowledges a special debt to the work of the late Professor Virally), and the jurisprudence of case law.

After these chapters setting out his general thesis on this area of law, Mr. Bekker then turns to the exposition and analysis of the decisions of the English Courts in the *International Tin Council* cases, thus using those practical problems to illustrate and confirm his own thesis. Finally there is a chapter of conclusions concerning the functional necessity approach, in which the author identifies some of its disadvantages, as well as its advantages which he concludes to be preponderant.

The essentially practical, as well as theoretical importance of this kind of work needs to be stressed. It is by no means as fully understood as it should be, that the gap in our juridical understanding of international organization is a serious weakness of modern international law. The institutionalisation of curial settlement and decision is already quite well developed, as a glance at the volumes of the *International Law Reports* will demonstrate. What is still in a relatively underdeveloped stage is the machinery for political and administrative decision. To deal with that is an urgent task; for courts of justice cannot stand on their own. And what is lacking is still much of the theoretical basis for such organisations and their relationships with States and with one another. As the author himself says: "the concept of the international organization in its modem form is a relatively new one and the problems posed by the legal status, privileges and immunities of international organizations are, consequently, also of recent date."

The present work of Mr. Bekker is an important contribution to the filling of that gap.

His Excellency Sir Robert Yewdall Jennings, April 1994
Judge of the International Court of Justice and its President during 1991–1993

Preface

The basis for the present study of the law of international organizations was created on the occasion of a visit to London in the Spring of 1989. There, I discussed with Professor Henry G. Schermers, a specialist on international institutional law from Leiden University in The Netherlands, a case which at that time was pending before the English courts and which concerned the International Tin Council, headquartered in London. The idea was raised to investigate that case and to embody it by way of a case-study in a general work on the legal position of intergovernmental organizations. It was decided to tackle in this study the question of the legal status, privileges and immunities of intergovernmental organizations as distinct legal entities, and to leave to a later date research on the specific question of the responsibility under international law of these subjects of international law.

The present book is the result of approximately four years of research into the legal position of intergovernmental organizations, with a particular emphasis on the United Nations. The United Nations was chosen as the prime object of study because of the ready availability of resources, combined with the present author's personal experience inside this organization. Consequently, other intergovernmental organizations, especially those operating in Europe such as the European Union, receive relatively little consideration in this study. Although the European Union is an intergovernmental organization, its unique nature as a supranational organization with its own court, the Court of Justice of the European Union, which is the competent organ to hear cases in which the EU is in any way involved, sets it aside from other international organizations. The study was started at Leiden University, The Netherlands, in the Fall of 1989, under the supervision of Professor Henry G. Schermers. After a three-month stay at the Office of Legal Affairs, Office of the Legal Counsel (Dr. Carl-August Fleischhauer), United Nations Headquarters in New York during the Summer of 1990, I continued my research during 1990–91 as a graduate student at the Harvard Law School in Cambridge, Massachusetts, U.S.A., and as an associate in the Amsterdam law firm of Houthoff. The study was finalized between 1992 and early 1994 during my tenure as a legal assistant to Registrar Eduardo Valencia-Ospina of the International Court of Justice in The Hague. It was submitted as a doctoral thesis at Leiden University Law School, The Netherlands, on 20 June 1994. I wish to thank the supervisors and examiners of my thesis, Prof. Henry G. Schermers (Chairman; Leiden University), Prof. Leo J. Bouchez (Utrecht University), H.E. Judge George

H. Aldrich (Iran-U.S. Claims Tribunal, The Hague), H.E. Prof. Peter H. Kooijmans (Minister for Foreign Affairs of The Netherlands), Prof. Detlev F. Vagts (Harvard Law School; Co-Editor-in-Chief, AJIL) and Dr. Niels M. Blokker (Leiden University), for their support in the preparation of this book.

I hope the reader will find traces of my combined civil law/common law education and international experience described above, in both the style, approach and resources used for the present work.

By giving a compact review of some of the fundamental questions relating to the legal position of international organizations, I hope to provide a better understanding of the operation of these important subjects of international law.

I gratefully acknowledge my debt of gratitude to Professor Ignaz Seidl-Hohenveldern for his expert comments on an early draft of this study and for providing me with updated information on the subject-matter. I am also grateful to Professor Sompong Sucharitkul, formerly ILC Special Rapporteur on 'Jurisdictional immunities of States and their property,' who offered his expert advice in the preparation of the early research stages.

A special debt of gratitude is extended to Dr. Carl-August Fleischhauer, The Legal Counsel of the United Nations Secretariat at the time of my stay at the Office of Legal Affairs of the United Nations in 1990, for providing me with an opportunity to gain first-hand knowledge of the practice of the United Nations relating to the subject-matter of the present study. The able supervision of Ralph Zacklin and Serguei Tarassenko, of the Office of the Legal Counsel, is gratefully remembered. The stay at United Nations Headquarters was made possible through grants from the Leyden University Fund and the Mordenate College Foundation, Leiden, The Netherlands.

The assistance of Conor McAuliffe, legal officer in the Registry of the International Court of Justice, in providing invaluable comments on the final manuscript is acknowledged with keen appreciation.

Finally, I am grateful for the excellent – word-processing and other – assistance of the staff of the T.M.C. Asser Institute and for the trust put in me by Martinus Nijhoff Publishers.

Peter H.F. Bekker
The Hague, Spring 1994

Preface to the Second Revised Edition

The 30-year anniversary of the original publication date of this book constituted an opportune time to prepare a substantially revised and updated edition of the original 1994 version of the book. The second edition aims to describe relevant developments that have occurred during the intervening three-decade period, profiting from my experience working with, and representing, intergovernmental organizations in a variety of settings, both contentious and non-contentious, as well as my experience in teaching the law of intergovernmental organizations, or international institutional law, since leaving the staff of the International Court of Justice in late 1994, most recently as a professor and Chair in International Law at the University of Dundee's Centre for Energy, Petroleum and Mineral Law and Policy (CEPMLP). It is hoped that the revised and updated second edition of the book will be welcomed as an improvement over the original version of this work, which, as odd as it may sound writing in the third decade of the twenty-first century, was prepared without the benefit of electronic sources available through the internet. All the sources used in preparing the original version of this book stemmed from "manual" research and reviewing hard copies of sources, mostly obtained from libraries located in the United States and The Netherlands. It was written during a time that was fundamentally different from today's "age of the internet," characterized by its sheer limitless availability of online information and sources.

The revised and updated second edition of this book, which has greatly profited from the development of the internet since 1994 and the emergence of specialist journals such as the *International Organizations Law Review* (published since 2004) and other specialist literature, does not seek to replace the essentially scholarly nature and generalized analytical approach of the original version of the book with a more practice-oriented monograph, even though it incorporates many references to the relevant practices of international organizations and it includes practical tips for dealing with international organizations, including in settling disputes to which international organizations are parties. The theoretical framework set forth in the original version of this book can be said to have stood the test of time, with functional necessity remaining the foundation-stone for the legal position of intergovernmental organizations, including their immunities. The principal goal in updating the book was to capture relevant case law, both national and international, as well as relevant scholarly writings and practices within intergovernmental organizations with a view to providing the reader with the pertinent sources that will enable further analysis of issues relating to the legal position of intergovernmental organizations. Some of these post-1994 developments caused the re-writing or re-phrasing of certain parts of this book or the addition of sentences, paragraphs or (sub-) sections where appropriate. As a result, the book has grown considerably in size, by one-third, or some 80 pages of new text.

The original text of this book included a number of quotes in non-English languages from the literature, especially sources in the French and German languages. In order to keep the revisions to a manageable scope, it was decided to leave those original quotes unchanged, without an English translation—any reader who is unable to read those foreign-language excerpts nowadays will be able to use quick-translation internet sources to translate the excerpts into English.

Among the most noteworthy, and in some sense transformational, developments arising from the period between 1994 and 2024 are the introduction and fine-tuning of methods of counterbalancing organizational immunities, particularly through the instrument of independent accountability mechanisms, or grievance systems, within intergovernmental organizations, and the adoption of the Articles on the Responsibility of International Organizations (ARIO) by the International Law Commission of the United Nations in 2011. While an in-depth discussion of the aforementioned developments goes beyond the scope of this book, it was considered important to touch upon certain aspects of these developments in the second revised edition of the book, particularly in the discussion of Step Three in Chapter 2 of the book. Another welcome development, albeit one that is still in its early stage at the time of preparing the second revised edition of this book, is the ILC's decision to include the topic of settlement of disputes to which international organizations are parties in its current program of work in 2022. The ILC's work on this topic, especially the input from (host) States and intergovernmental organizations through their replies to relevant questionnaires and through contributions to debates, undoubtedly will enrich our understanding of the legal position of intergovernmental organizations, especially their legal position in a contentious setting, and will assist in settling disputes involving international organizations in a way that satisfies all parties concerned and that meets the needs of justice, including access to justice for those dealing with intergovernmental organizations cloaked with immunity.

While intergovernmental organizations have not escaped criticism and calls for reform in recent years, they undoubtedly remain an essential part of the rules-based global order, as was highlighted by the crucial role played by the World Health Organization in coordinating an effective response to the COVID-19 pandemic that severely disrupted life on Earth from early 2020 onwards. The challenges posed by climate change and cross-border (armed) conflicts between two or more States can only be met by States effectively collaborating with and within intergovernmental organizations, as opposed to resorting to unilateralism. In order to make intergovernmental organizations succeed in exercising their functions in fulfilment of their purposes in an effective and efficient way, it is important to continue contributing to our understanding of their unique nature, needs and limitations, which remains the aim of this book.

Reflecting on the origins of this book, I realize how fortunate I was to have had the opportunity to discuss this work originally in person with international law giants such as Carl-August Fleischhauer, Sir Robert Jennings, Peter Kooijmans, Henry Schermers, Ignaz Seidl-Hohenveldern, Sompong Sucharitkul, Paul Szasz and Detlev Vagts, all of whom have passed away in recent years. I will forever cherish the memory of my conversations with each of them in preparing the original text of this book during stints in Cambridge (Massachusetts), Leiden, New York (United Nations) and The Hague (ICJ).

The second revised edition of this book, which was prepared in New York, is dedicated to the memory of two pioneers of international institutional law, who passed away after the original publication date of this book: Professor Henry (Hein) Schermers (1928–2006), an internationally renowned Dutch scholar in international institutional law who served as my Ph.D. supervisor and academic mentor during my law studies at Leiden University, and Professor Ignaz Seidl-Hohenveldern (1918–2001), an Austrian pioneer in the subject-matter of this book with whom I was working in an expert role on a case before the United Nations Compensation Commission at the time of his death in 2001. Their mentorship, support and friendship are fondly remembered and constitute an enduring source of inspiration to me.

I am grateful to Ms. Marie Sheldon, Ms. Ingeborg van der Laan and the able staff at Brill for assisting me with the publication of the revised and updated second edition of this book, thereby ensuring that my magnum opus remains relevant and useful 30 years after its original publication, and to the University of Dundee for granting me a special research leave enabling me to prepare the second edition of this book.

Finally, a special thanks to my son Oscar Bekker (15), a native New Yorker with dual Dutch-US citizenship, for lending his artistic talents to produce the United Nations Headquarters illustration that appears on the cover of this book.

Peter H.F. Bekker
New York, December 2024

Abbreviations

Add.	Addendum
AFDI	*Annuaire français de droit international*
AJIL	American Journal of International Law
All E.R.	All England Law Reports, 1936-date
Am. U.L. Rev.	American University Law Review
Annuaire	*Annuaire de l'Institut de Droit International*
App.	Application
App.Cas.	Appeal Cases (U.K.), 1875-date
ASEAN	Association of Southeast Asian Nations
BG. BL.	*Bundes Gesetz Blatt* (Ger.)
BYBIL	British Year Book of International Law
Chinese J. Int'l L.	Chinese Journal of International Law
CJEU	Court of Justice of the European Union
C.L.J.	Cambridge Law Journal
CMLR	Common Market Law Review
Cmnd.	Command Papers (U.K.), 1956-date
Comm. Mkt. L. Rep.	Common Market Law Reports
Const.	Constitution
Dep't St. Bull.	Department of State Bulletin (U.S.)
Doc(s).	Document(s)
EC	European Communities
ECOSOC	Economic and Social Council of the United Nations
ECHR	European Convention on Human Rights
ECR	Reports of the Court of Justice of the European Communities (European Court Reports)
ECSC	European Coal and Steel Community
EEC	European Economic Community
EFTA	European Free Trade Association
ELDO	European Launcher Development Organization
EMBL	European Molecular Biology Laboratory
EPO	European Patent Organization
ESA	European Space Agency
ESRO	European Space Research Organization
EU	European Union
FAO	Food and Agriculture Organization of the United Nations
F.2d	Federal Reporter, Second Series, 1925–1993 (U.S.)
F.3d	Federal Reporter, Third Series, 1993–2021 (U.S.)

F.4th	Federal Reporter, Fourth Series, 2021-date (U.S.)
F.R.D.	Federal Rules Decisions, 1941-date (U.S.)
F.Supp.	Federal Supplement, First Series, 1933–1998 (U.S.)
F.Supp. 2d	Federal Supplement, Second Series, 1938–2014 (U.S.)
F.Supp. 3d	Federal Supplement, Third Series, 2014-date (U.S.)
GAOR	General Assembly Official Records
GATT	General Agreement on Tariffs and Trade
Ger.	Germany
GYIL	German Yearbook of International Law
Harv. Int'l L.J.	Harvard International Law Journal
Harv. L.R.	Harvard Law Review
H.L.	House of Lords (U.K.)
H.R.	House of Representatives (U.S.)
IAEA	International Atomic Energy Agency
IAM	Independent accountability mechanism
IBRD	International Bank for Reconstruction and Development
ICAO	International Civil Aviation Organization
ICCPR	International Covenant on Civil and Political Rights
ICJ	International Court of Justice
ICJ Rep.	ICJ, *Reports of Judgments, Advisory Opinions and Orders*
ICLQ	International and Comparative Law Quarterly
IDA	International Development Association
IFAD	International Fund for Agricultural Development
IFC	International Finance Corporation
ILC	International Law Commission of the United Nations
ILM	International Legal Materials
ILO	International Labour Organization
ILR	International Law Reports
IMF	International Monetary Fund
IMO	International Maritime Organization
Indian J. Int'l L.	Indian Journal of International Law
INTERPOL	International Criminal Police Organization
Int'l L.Q.	International Law Quarterly
IOLR	International Organizations Law Review
IRO	International Refugee Organization
ITA	International Tin Agreement
ITC	International Tin Council
ITO	International Tin Organization
ITU	International Telecommunication Union

J.W.T.L.	Journal of World Trade Law
LJIL	Leiden Journal of International Law
L.N.T.S.	League of Nations Treaty Series
Mich. J. Int'l L.	Michigan Journal of International Law
Mich. L. Rev.	Michigan Law Review
MIGA	Multilateral Investment Guarantee Agency
n.	note
NAFO	North Atlantic Fisheries Organization
NATO	North Atlantic Treaty Organization
Neth.	Netherlands
N.I.L.R.	Netherlands International Law Review
NJ	*Nederlandse Jurisprudentie* (Neth.), 1913-date
NJW	*Neue Juristische Wochenschrift*
N.Y.I.L.	Netherlands Yearbook of International Law
N.Y.S.2d	West's New York Supplement, Second Series
NYU J. Int'l L. & Pol.	New York University Journal of International Law and Politics
OAS	Organization of American States
OJZ	*Oesterreichische Juristen Zeitung*
OPEC	Organization of the Petroleum Exporting Countries
para.	Paragraph
paras.	Paragraphs
PCA	Permanent Court of Arbitration
PCIJ	Permanent Court of International Justice
PCIJ (ser. B)	PCIJ, Collection of *Advisory Opinions* (before 1931)
P.L.	Public Law (U.S.)
PLO	Palestine Liberation Organization
Pol. Y.B. Int'l L.	Polish Yearbook of International Law
Proc. Am. Soc'y Int'l L.	Proceedings of the American Society of International Law
Q.B.	Queen's Bench Law Reports (U.K.)
RdC	*Recueil des Cours de l'Académie de droit international*
R.E.D.I.	*Revue Egyptienne de Droit International*
REV ARB	*Revue de l'arbitrage*
R.G.D.I.P.	*Revue général de droit international public*
RvdW	*Rechtspraak van de Week* (Neth.)
RIW	*Recht der internationalen Wirtschaft*
S	section
S. CT.	West's Supreme Court Reporter (U.S.)

S.I.	Statutory Instrument (U.K.)
Sol. J.	Solicitors Journal (U.K.)
Suff. Transnat'l L.R.	Suffolk Transnational Law Review
Suff. Transnat'l L.J.	Suffolk Transnational Law Journal
Supp.	Supplement
TIAS	Treaties and Other International Acts Series (U.S.)
U.K.	United Kingdom
UN	United Nations Organization
UNAT	United Nations Administrative Tribunal (until 2009); United Nations Appeals Tribunal (2009–)
U.N.C.I.O.	United Nations Conference on International Organization (San Francisco, 1945)
UNCTAD	United Nations Conference on Trade and Development
UNDP	United Nations Development Programme
UNDT	United Nations Dispute Tribunal
UNESCO	United Nations Educational, Scientific and Cultural Organization
UNIDO	United Nations Industrial Development Organization
UN Jurid. Y.B.	United Nations Juridical Yearbook
U.N.T.S.	United Nations Treaty Series
UNYB	United Nations Year Book
UPU	Universal Postal Union
U.S.	United States of America
U.S.C.	United States Code
USTS	United States Treaty Series
Va. J. Int'l L.	Virginia Journal of International Law
WHO	World Health Organization
WIPO	World Intellectual Property Organization
W.L.R.	Weekly Law Reports (U.K.)
WMO	World Meteorological Organization
WTO	World Trade Organization
Yale L.J.	Yale Law Journal
Y.B. Int'l L. Comm'n	Yearbook of the International Law Commission
ZaöRV	*Zeitschrift für ausländisches öffentliches Recht und Völkerrecht*

CHAPTER 1

Introduction

1 Purpose and Scope of This Study

As a prominent European jurist once stated: "Depuis quelques décades, les Organisations Internationales jouent un rôle éminent dans les relations internationales au point qu'on peut voir dans cette 'institutionalisation' des rapports internationaux, *l'une des caractéristiques essentielles de notre époque.*" (emphasis added)[1] The present study examines the new-found role of international organizations by addressing their external relations with sovereign States and with other subjects of international law as well as other entities, with a particular emphasis on the legal status, privileges and immunities of intergovernmental organizations.

The concept of the international organization in its modern form is a relatively new one and the problems posed by the legal status, privileges and immunities of international organizations are, consequently, also of recent date.[2] In contrast to the considerable body of law concerning diplomatic and sovereign/State immunities – a body that stems from age-old bilateral diplomatic activities – the question of the status and immunities of international organizations attained prominence only in the second-half of the twentieth century.[3] As one authority has summarized, "[h]istorically, the present content of international immunities derives from the experience of the League of Nations as developed by the International Labour Organisation when submitted to the test of wartime conditions ... and subsequently reviewed by the General Assembly of the United Nations at its First Session

---

1 P. Pescatore, *Les relations extérieures des Communautés européennes: Contribution à la doctrine de la personnalité des Organisations internationales*, 103 RdC 1, 198 (1961 II).

2 For a review of the evolution of the concept of the international organization, see C. Archer, International Organizations 3–33 (2nd. ed. 1992)[hereinafter: ARCHER]; *see also* ILC Special Rapporteur El-Erian, *First Report on* 'Relations between States and Inter-governmental Organizations (First Part of the topic),' UN Doc. A/CN.4/161 and Add. 1 (1963) *reprinted in* [1963] 2 Y.B. Int'l L. Comm'n 159, paras. 13–60, UN Doc. A/CN.4/SER.A/1963/Add. 1; [1985] 1 Y.B. Int'l L. Comm'n 283, paras. 4–6, UN Doc. A/CN.4/SER.A/1985.

3 For a historical survey of the immunities of international organizations, see J.L. Kunz, *Privileges and Immunities of International Organizations*, 41 AJIL 828 (1947)[hereinafter: Kunz].

 | DOI:10.1163/9789004724211_002

in 1946."[4] Before the creation of such general international organizations, however, constituent instruments establishing international river commissions[5] and administrative unions were concluded in the first half of the nineteenth century; these documents already contained provisions which give evidence of the origin of the legal position of international organizations.[6] There are now over 300 intergovernmental organizations, which have their headquarters or have operations in the territory of some State which may or may not be a member of the organization.[7]

As the legal issues involved in today's multilateral framework become more and more interwoven, there is an increased risk of blurring specific institutional law concepts with those developed in general public international law, in particular that part of the law that deals with inter-State relations. This may even lead to neglect of the special nature of international organizations. At the same time, in order not to overreach, one must take into account the legitimate needs of those whom this part of international law addresses. The emerging practice of international organizations carrying out quasi-commercial activities calls for a re-examination of the legal status, privileges and immunities of international organizations. But this re-examination should not be a rote application of the terminology and concepts of related yet different and inapposite branches of international law.[8] The exigencies of modern multilateral diplomacy with and within international organizations has led to a *new* category of privileges and immunities, influenced by, but in essence quite distinct from, the already existing

4 C.W. Jenks, International Immunities 12 (1961)[hereinafter: JENKS].

5 Thus, the Central Commission for the Navigation of the Rhine was originally granted "independence and neutrality" under Article 231 of the German-French Treaty of 15 August 1804. *See* Kunz, at 828.

6 *See* El-Erian, *Preliminary Report* on 'Relations between States and International Organizations (Second Part of the topic),' UN Doc. A/CN.4/304 (1977) *reprinted in* [1977] 2 Y.B. Int'l L. Comm'n 139, 142–143, UN Doc. A/CN.4/SER.A/1977/Add. 1 (Part 1).

7 For an extensive treatise on international organizations law, see H.G. Schermers and N.M. Blokker, International Institutional Law: Unity within Diversity (6th ed. 2018)[hereinafter: SCHERMERS]. Dutch scholar Henry G. Schermers (1928–2006) has been described as "arguably, the leading post-war representative of the school of thought that has come to be known as functionalism" and as "the Linnaeus of international organizations law." J. Klabbers, *Schermers' Dilemma*, 32 EJIL 565, 565, 582 (2020).

8 *See also* Illueca, in [1983] 1 Y.B. Int'l L. Comm'n 247, para. 43, UN Doc. A/CN.4/SER.A/1983: "The increasing number of international organizations and the variety of their activities and fields of competence called for specific rules which must be sought elsewhere than in the usual sources in order to solve the problems relating to the functioning of such organizations."

international law concerning immunity. As an eminent French international lawyer has stated:

> On ne saurait mettre en doute, pensons-nous, que l'analyse des organisations internationales ait besoin aujourd'hui, pour progresser, de s'appuyer sur une théorie solide .... Mais, parce que l'observation démontre que l'organisation internationale constitue un phénomène d'organisation politique irréductible au phénomène étatique, nous croyons que *cette théorie doit être conçue sans idées préconçues, c'est-à-dire sans références explicites ou implicites à la théorie de l'Etat, de façon totalement indépendante, à partir des seules observations faites sur les organisations existantes.*[9] (emphasis added)

Observations were made to similar effect on behalf of the Austrian Government at the Sixteenth Session of the UN General Assembly:

> ... the traditional norms of international law can be applied only to a limited degree, because they were created by the practice of States and therefore fit the organizational structure of *States*. Although a new practice is slowly being developed by and in respect of *international organizations*, it is still embryonic and, above all, multiform. To ameliorate the situation, traditional norms need to be adjusted, new norms to be created.[10] (emphasis added)

The present study does not furnish a comprehensive commentary on the complex question of the legal status of international organizations in general, nor does it review each and every privilege and immunity of a given international organization. Rather, the purpose of this study is to approach the question from a different angle and to clear the field under consideration from the confusion that may be caused by simply adopting the terminology and basic concepts of other branches of public international law – especially sovereign/State immunity law. While it is true that the law of the immunities of international organizations shares some of the principles developed in sovereign and diplomatic immunity law, especially

---

9 M. Virally, *De la classification des organisations internationales, in* Miscellanea Ganshof van der Meersch 365, 370–371 (Vol. 1, 1972)[hereinafter: Virally, Classification].

10 16 GAOR, Annexes (Agenda Item 70), at 16, para. 2 *quoted in* [1964] 1 Y.B. Int'l L. Comm'n 207, para. 27, UN Doc. A/CN.4/SER.A/1964.

that of functional necessity, their wholesale application to international organizations should be avoided for reasons which will become apparent in the course of this book. The approach suggested here – the functional necessity concept – which has a basis-element and an extent-element, may be summarized as follows in its application to international organizations:

> An international organization shall be entitled to (no more than) what is strictly necessary for the exercise of its functions in the fulfilment of its purposes.

The functional necessity approach explains the existence and extent of the legal status, privileges and immunities of international organizations by focusing on an organization's functions and purposes, thereby developing a theory that is characterized by the consistent use of terminology proper to international organizations and that does justice to the principle of the *speciality* of the international organization.[11] This approach is tailored to the special functional needs of international organizations, which makes the functional necessity test in essence a relative and not an absolute one: what is necessary for the functions and purposes of one international organization may not be so for another.[12] Hence, the functional necessity concept is a useful starting-point for an analysis which is in closest conformity with the special characteristics of international organizations.

Against this general background, the present study endeavors to separate from the confusion surrounding the issues of the legal status, privileges and immunities of intergovernmental organizations some basic principles and problems by establishing a *functional typology* of the legal position of intergovernmental organizations.[13] It presents a general concept of functional necessity in its application to the issues of legal status and privileges and

---

11 *See Legality of the Use by a State of Nuclear Weapons in Armed Conflict*, Advisory Opinion, 1996 ICJ Rep. 66, at 78–79, para. 25 ("International organizations are governed by the 'principle of speciality', that is to say, they are invested by the States which create them with powers, the limits of which are a function of the common interests whose promotion those States entrust to them."); *Pulp Mills on the River Uruguay* (*Argentina v. Uruguay*), Judgment, 2010 ICJ Rep. 14, at 53, para. 89. *See also* R.-J. Dupuy, in 55 *Annuaire* 214, 254 (1973); Salmon, *id.* at 401; Mahiou, in [1983] 1 Y.B. Int'l L. Comm'n 245, para. 32, UN Doc. A/CN.4/SER.A/1983.

12 *See* McCaffrey, in [1990] 1 Y.B. Int'l L. Comm'n 218, para. 39, UN Doc. A/CN.4/SER.A/1990; Al-Qaysi, in *id.* at 222–223, para. 15.

13 *See* ILC Special Rapporteur Díaz González, in [1985] 1 Y.B. Int'l L. Comm'n 284, para. 12, UN Doc. A/CN.4/SER.A/1985.

immunities by way of a simple three-step approach.[14] Step One concerns the *identification* of the entity concerned, by studying its legal status, i.e., its personality, capacity and competence (powers) by reference to an organization's purposes and functions, in order to assess whether it has a functional need and justification for protection by way of privileges and immunities. Step Two applies the basis-element of functional necessity in monitoring and *selecting* privileges and immunities for a given organization, having regard to its purposes and functions as identified in Step One. Step Three examines the value of the functional necessity concept as a yardstick for determining the scope or *extent* of selected immunities. It addresses the question as to what kind of activities of an international organization are deserving of protection. It determines how far a selected immunity should be stretched in a particular case, having regard to the nature of the activities carried out by the international organization. Finally, Chapter 3 applies the theoretical framework of Chapter 2 to a practical example, by examining certain legal issues involved in the landmark English proceedings involving the International Tin Council. The emphasis will be on the immunity aspects of these cases, rather than on the main legal issue involved, the responsibility of an intergovernmental organization. In this we follow the distinction made in 1963 by ILC Special Rapporteur El-Erian between the legal status, privileges and immunities of international organizations, and the other aspects of relations between States and international organizations, such as the responsibility of international organizations.[15] The latter aspect, as distinct from the privileges and immunities of international organizations, was not included in the program of work of the International Law Commission until 2002, and draft articles addressing the responsibility of international organizations were not adopted by the ILC until 2011.[16] One must be careful not to cast one's net too wide lest the subject become

14 *See* M. Egger, Die Vorrechte und Befreiungen zugunsten internationalen Organisationen und ihrer Funktionäre 147 (1954)[hereinafter: EGGER].

15 *See* El-Erian, in [1963] 1 Y.B. Int'l L. Comm'n 298, para. 110, UN Doc. A/CN.4/SER.A/1963.

16 *See* Section 3.6.5 of Chapter 2 of this book. As early as 1961, Austria suggested that the topic of the responsibility of international organizations be referred to the ILC, but this proposal did not receive sufficient support at the time. *See* 16 GAOR Annex 15 (Agenda Item 70), at 17, UN Doc. A/4796/Add. 6 (1961). *See also* I. Seidl-Hohenveldern, *Responsibility of Member States of an International Organization for Acts of the Organization, in* International Law at the Time of its Codification – Essays in Honour of Roberto Ago 415 (Vol. III, 1987)[hereinafter: Seidl-Hohenveldern, Responsibility].

unmanageable, and hence the responsibility of international organizations is mostly left outside the scope of the present study. As has been pointed out within the ILC, the rules pertaining to the topic of the relations between States and international organizations are continually evolving with the development of international organizations, rendering it difficult to determine which questions properly pertain to this dynamic topic and which should be left aside.[17] This explains why topics such as the responsibility of international organizations and that of the settlement of disputes to which international organizations are parties only have featured in the more recent program of work of the ILC.

Moreover, the scope of the present work is confined to intergovernmental organizations *as distinct legal entities*, and the status, privileges and immunities of *individuals* who, as executive agents of international organizations, are "charged by an organ of the Organization with carrying out, or helping to carry out, one of its functions,"[18] will not be discussed in detail.

In short, this study concerns the subject-matter covered by Articles 104 and 105, paragraph 1, of the Charter of the United Nations and corresponding articles of the constituent instruments of certain other intergovernmental organizations, as studied by the International Law Commission from 1976 until 1992, when the topic was removed from the ILC's agenda. The researcher of the United Nations system of organizations is able to profit from several extensive studies of the practice concerning this topic.[19] But a study of a more conceptual kind on the general role of functional necessity

17 *See* Tunkin, in [1963] 1 Y.B. Int'l L. Comm'n 299, para. 119, UN Doc. A/CN.4/SER.A/1963; Al-Baharna, in [1987] 1 Y.B. Int'l L. Comm'n 203, para. 38, UN Doc. A/CN.4/SER.A/1987.

18 *Reparation for Injuries Suffered in the Service of the United Nations*, Advisory Opinion, 1949 ICJ Rep. 174, 177.

19 *See, e.g., Repertory of United Nations Practice*, UN Sales No. 1955.V.2 (Vol. V, 1955) and its *Supplements 1–5*; '*Legislative Texts and Treaty Provisions concerning the Legal Status, Privileges and Immunities of International Organizations*,' UN Docs. ST/LEG/SER.B/10 (1959) & ST/LEG/SER.B/11 (1961); '*The Practice of the United Nations, the specialized agencies and the International Atomic Energy Agency concerning their status, privileges and immunities*,' UN Doc. A/CN.4/L.118 and Add. 1–2 *reprinted in* [1967] 2 Y.B. Int'l L. Comm'n 154–324, UN Doc. A/CN.4/SER.A/1967/Add 1, *Id., supplementary study prepared by the Secretariat*, UN Doc. A/CN.4/L.383 and Add. 1–3 *reprinted in* [1985] 2 Y.B. Int'l L. Comm'n 145, UN Doc. A/CN.4/SER.A/1985/Add. 1 (Part 1/Add.1). The annual volumes of the UN Jurid. Y.B, the UNYB, and the reports of the UN Committee on Relations with the Host Country also provide useful information; *see also 'Economic co-operation and integration among developing countries: Compilation of the principal legal instruments*,' UNCTAD doc. TD/B/609/Add. 1 (5 Vols.). In addition, the relevant Yearbooks of the ILC will be discussed below.

in the legal position of intergovernmental organizations has so far been lacking, despite the fact that scholars have been referring to the need to analyze the relationship between the scope of the legal position of international organizations and their particular functions and purposes.[20] Although the great majority of the leading authorities on the legal status and immunities of international organizations accept and make reference in their writings to functional necessity, they do so mostly in the context of a discussion of the material contents of specific immunities, rather than inversely projecting the functional principle on the broader issue of the legal position of international organizations, as is done in the present study. In other words, this study sets up an *analytical framework* of the broader issue of the legal position of intergovernmental organizations from the perspective of functional necessity. In contrast to most existing surveys on the immunities of international organizations, this book concentrates on some of the more general fundamental concepts *applicable to* the study of the legal status and immunities of intergovernmental organizations rather than describing certain immunities which evidence the *application of* functional necessity in a particular case and at the same time borrowing the terminology of different branches of immunity law. As Fedder posited in 1960:

> Having originated pragmatically, the [functional] concept has not achieved the status of being well-formulated or consistently applied; however, sufficient consistency has been demonstrated to permit systematic study. Considering the size and scope of operations of international organizations today and the fact that such organizations require and receive special protection to perform their peculiar functions, the need for systematic study pointing the way to refinement of practice is evident.[21]

The present work endeavors to fill this gap, by providing, in a nutshell, the tools for a re-examination of the legal status, privileges and immunities of international organizations in the light of developments since 1945. It is a

20 *See, e.g.*, [1985] 2 Y.B. Int'l L. Comm'n 104, para. 6, UN Doc. A/CN.4/SER.A/1985/Add. 1 (Part 1).

21 E.H. Fedder, *The Functional Basis of International Privileges and Immunities: A New Concept in International Law and Organization*, 9 AM.U.L. REV. 60 (1960)[hereinafter: Fedder].

study of some of the fundamental issues of "a topic which had not yet been studied as intensively as it deserved."[22]

2 The Work of the International Law Commission on Relations between States and International Organizations (1962–1992)[23]

2.1 *The Early Stages*

This section describes the history, development and current status of the study of the legal position of international organizations by the International Law Commission (ILC), an advisory body established, pursuant to Article 13, paragraph 1, of the UN Charter, by the General Assembly of the United Nations in 1947.[24]

The history of this topic within the ILC dates back to 1957. The first discussions on the subject can be found in the summary record of its 383rd meeting held on 24 April 1957, during the general debate on a draft for the codification of the law relating to diplomatic intercourse and immunities, which at that time was on the ILC's agenda.[25]

---

22 ILC Chairman Jagota, in [1985] 1 Y.B. Int'l L. Comm'n 286, para. 25, UN Doc. A/CN.4/SER.A/1985.

23 For a summary and assessment of the ILC's work on the topic see P.H.F. Bekker, *The Work of the International Law Commission on 'Relations between States and International Organizations' Discontinued: an Assessment*, 6 LJIL 3 (1993)[hereinafter: Bekker].

24 The ILC was established by GA Res. 174(II) of 21 Nov. 1947. The Statute of the ILC, annexed to Res. 174(II), most recently amended by Res. 36/39 of 18 Nov. 1981 (*see* UN Doc. A/CN.4/4/Rev.2 (1982)), regulates the organization, functions and methods of work of the ILC. The ILC consists of 34 members, who are "persons of recognized competence in international law" reflecting the main forms of civilization and the principal legal systems of the world, and who are elected for a renewable term of five years. According to Art. 1, para. 1, of the ILC's Statute, the object of the ILC is to promote the progressive development of international law and its codification. For a detailed analysis of the history and the activities of the ILC, see THE WORK OF THE INTERNATIONAL LAW COMMISSION, UN Sales No. E.88.V.1 (10th ed. 2023); *see also* B. Ramcharan, The International Law Commission – Its Approach to the Codification and Progressive Development of International Law (1977); S. Sucharitkul, *The Role of the International Law Commission in the Decade of International Law*, 3 LJIL 15 (1990); B. Graefrath, *The International Law Commission Tomorrow: Improving its Organization and Methods of Work*, 85 AJIL 595 (1991)(giving further references at nn.1 and 8) [hereinafter: Graefrath].

25 *See* [1957] 1 Y.B. Int'l L. Comm'n 2, 3, paras. 16–17 (Bartos), 20–22 (Garcia Amador), 31 (El-Erian), 33 (Seelie), 37 (Tunkin), 41 (Liang), 45 (Seelie), 47 (Fitzmaurice), UN Doc. A/CN.4/SER.A/1957.

The ILC also referred to the topic in its report to the General Assembly covering the work of its tenth session held in 1958.[26] In Chapter III of this report, dealing with the topic 'Diplomatic Intercourse and Immunities,' it was pointed out that, apart from diplomatic relations between States, there were also relations between States and international organizations, including the question of the privileges and immunities of the organizations themselves.[27]

On 5 December 1958, during its regular thirteenth session, the General Assembly adopted Resolution 1289(XIII), entitled 'Relations between States and inter-governmental organizations.'[28] The resolution refers to the observations made by governments of member States at the twelfth and thirteenth sessions of the Assembly. The records of these sessions reveal that the French delegate, Mr. Chaumont, had introduced the idea of the ILC taking up the subject of relations between States and international organizations after the completion of its studies on consular intercourse and immunities and *ad hoc* diplomacy. This idea was actively supported by, *inter alia*, the representative of Egypt to the Sixth (Legal) Committee of the General Assembly.[29] On 12 November 1958, the Sixth Committee adopted by 60 votes to none, with two abstentions, a draft resolution submitted by France and thus endorsed Mr. Chaumont's idea.[30] Based on this recommendation

26 *See* UN Doc. A/3859 reprinted in [1958] 2 Y.B. Int'l L. Comm'n 78, UN Doc. A/CN.4/SER.A/1958/Add. 1.

27 *Id.*, at 89, para. 52. For a discussion of the differences between inter-State diplomatic relations and relations between States and international organizations, see UN Doc. A/CN.4/304 (1977) *reprinted in* [1977] 2 Y.B. Int'l L. Comm'n 139, 152, paras. 63–64, UN Doc. A/CN.4/SER.A/1977/Add. 1 (Part 1); [1967] 2 Y.B. Int'l L. Comm'n 141, paras. 51–53, UN Doc. A/CN.4/SER.A/1967/Add. 1. *See also* A. El-Erian, *International Organizations and International Relations, in* A Handbook on International Organizations 625 (R.-J. Dupuy ed. 1984)[hereinafter: El-Erian, DUPUY].

28 *See* 13 GAOR Supp. (No. 18) at 54, UN Doc. A/4090 (1959).

29 The Egyptian delegate, Mr. Abdullah El-Erian, later became the ILC's first Special Rapporteur on this topic and was among the first delegates to refer to the topic. In his capacity as the Representative of Egypt to the Sixth Committee at the twelfth session of the General Assembly, he expressed the hope that in due time the ILC would deal with the questions of the status, privileges and immunities of international organizations. *See* 12 GAOR Sixth Comm. (513th mtg.) at 22, para. 14, UN Doc. A/C.6/SR.513 (1957); *see also* the comments made by him during the thirteenth session, 13 GAOR Sixth Comm. (580th mtg.), at 144, paras. 8 and 17, UN Doc. A/C.6/SR.580 (1959).

30 *See* UN Doc. A/C.6/L.427/Rev. 1 and Corr. 1, as amended; 13 GAOR Sixth Comm. (580th mtg.) at 145, para. 27, UN Doc. A/C.6/SR.580 (1958); 13 GAOR Sixth Comm. (569th mtg.) at 91, para. 22, UN Doc. A/C.6/SR.569 (1958); 13 GAOR Sixth Comm. (571st mtg.) at 101, paras. 15–17, UN Doc. A/C.6/SR.571 (1958).

of the Sixth Committee, the General Assembly, in Resolution 1289(XIII), invited the ILC:

> to give further consideration to the question of relations between States and inter-governmental international organizations at the proper time, after study of diplomatic intercourse and immunities, consular intercourse and immunities and *ad hoc* diplomacy has been completed by the United Nations and in the light of the results of that study and of the discussion in the General Assembly.

The ILC took note of Resolution 1289(XIII) at its eleventh session in 1959 and it resolved to give consideration to the matter in due course.[31] Subsequently, Austria and The Netherlands officially proposed that the topic of the status of international organizations and the relations between States and international organizations be considered by the ILC as part of its codification program.[32]

At its fourteenth session held in 1962, the ILC decided to place the consideration of the relations between States and intergovernmental organizations on the agenda of its next session.[33] The ILC reached this decision after having taken note of the suggestions put forward by delegations in the Sixth Committee at the sixteenth session of the General Assembly, and having considered that codification of this part of the law of international organizations would meet a growing need in the light of the complex legal issues raised by a continually increasing number of organizations.[34] This was a

31 *See Report of the International Law Commission covering the work of its eleventh session*, UN Doc. A/4169 (1959) *reprinted in* [1959] 2 Y.B. Int'l L. Comm'n 87, 123, para. 48, UN Doc. A/CN.4/SER.A/1959/Add. 1.

32 *See* 16 GAOR Annex 15 (Agenda Item 70) at 14, 17, UN Doc. A/4796/Add. 6 (1961) (Austria); 16 GAOR Annex 16 (Agenda Item 70) at 17, UN Doc. A/4796/Add. 7 (1961)(Netherlands). Observations by these governments had been received pursuant to the General Assembly's invitation to member States, by Res. 1505(XV) of 12 Dec. 1960, to submit in writing to the Secretary-General, before 1 July 1961, any views or suggestions they might have on the question of the future work of the ILC in the field of the codification and progressive development of international law: *see* 15 GAOR Supp. (No. 16) at 59–60, UN Doc. A/4684 (1961). *See also* El-Erian, in [1964] 1 Y.B. Int'l L. Comm'n 207, para. 27, UN Doc. A/CN.4/SER.A/1964.

33 *See* [1962] 2 Y.B. Int'l L. Comm'n 97, paras. 170–176, UN Doc. A/CN.4/SER.A/1962/Add. 1.

34 *See* in particular the statements made by the representatives of the United Arab Republic (the later Egypt) and Indonesia, 16 GAOR Sixth Comm. (723rd and 726th mtgs.)

unique initiative by the ILC in that it represented its first attempt to codify a subject within the field of international institutional law proper; it had hitherto confined its codification efforts to relations between the traditional subjects of international law, namely, States.

At its 669th meeting held on 27 June 1962, the ILC appointed Mr. Abdullah El-Erian of Egypt as *Special Rapporteur* on the topic and requested him to submit a first report to the next session of the ILC.[35]

2.2 *The First Part of the Topic*

2.2.1 The Work of Special Rapporteur El-Erian

Pursuant to the ILC's request at its fourteenth session, the Special Rapporteur submitted his *First Report* at the fifteenth session of the ILC in 1963.[36] This document, including the debate on it within the ILC, merits some consideration, because of its general, preliminary character and its bearing upon the subsequent treatment of the topic. The First Report described the evolution of the concept of the international organization, tracing the historical development of the conference system and the international administrative unions established during the second half of the nineteenth century and their final transformation into international organizations endowed with political, economic, social and technical missions. It also reviewed earlier attempts to codify international law pertaining to the legal status of international organizations, and presented a preliminary survey of the scope of the subject of the legal status of these organizations. The Special Rapporteur also submitted a Working Paper on the scope and order of future work on the subject.[37] This one-page document classified the subject into three groups of related questions, which according to the Special Rapporteur should be studied in the order he proposed. The first group would

---

at 167, para. 3 and 190, para. 10, UN Docs. A/C.6/SR.723 and A/C.6/SR.726 (1962), respectively.

35 *See* [1962] 2 Y.B. Int'l L. Comm'n 192, para. 75, UN Doc. A/CN.4/SER.A/1962/Add. 1. At the time of his appointment, Mr. El-Erian, of Egyptian nationality, was Director of the Department of Legal Affairs and Treaties of the Egyptian Ministry of Foreign Affairs. Later in his career he served as Ambassador to France, as well as to several UN bodies. He was a member of the International Court of Justice from 6 Feb. 1979 until his death in office on 12 Dec. 1981. For his bibliography see *ICJ Yearbook 1980–1981*, at 29–30. On the system of 'Special Rapporteurs,' see Graefrath, at 604.

36 *See* UN Doc. A/CN.4/161 and Add. 1 *reprinted in* [1963] 2 Y.B. Int'l L. Comm'n 159, UN Doc. A/CN.4/SER.A/1963/Add. 1.

37 *See* UN Doc. A/CN.4/L. 103 (1963) *reprinted in* [1963] 2 Y.B. Int'l L. Comm'n 186, UN Doc. A/CN.4/SER.A/1963/Add. 1.

concentrate on general principles of juridical personality of international organizations, including their legal capacity, treaty-making capacity and capacity to espouse international claims. The second group of questions would deal with international privileges and immunities. Within this second group the Special Rapporteur proposed a further distinction between the privileges and immunities of: (1) international organizations as bodies corporate; (2) officials of international organizations; and (3) representatives to international organizations. Finally, Mr. El-Erian proposed that the consideration of the third group of "special" questions, including the law of treaties with respect to international organizations and their responsibility, should be deferred to a future stage in the work of the ILC.

At its 717th and 718th meetings held on 9 and 10 July 1963, the ILC held a preliminary discussion of the First Report, designed to give those members who already had a settled opinion on the matter an opportunity of stating their views.[38] At its sixteenth session held in 1964, the ILC continued its consideration of the Report, the Working Paper, and, in connection therewith, examined a list of specific questions submitted by the Special Rapporteur as a basis of discussion for defining the scope and mode of treatment of the subject.[39] Declining to follow the three-tier order of priorities that Mr. El-Erian had recommended in his Working Paper, the ILC decided to divide its work on the topic into two separate parts. The first part would concentrate on the status, privileges and immunities of *representatives of States* to international organizations, while the second part would deal with the *international organizations* themselves, reflecting their status, privileges and immunities, as well as that of their agents, namely, officials, experts on mission, and other persons having official business with the organization, not being representatives of States.[40] The ILC thus decided that priority should be given to the third sub-group of the second group of questions concerning the legal position of representatives to international organizations. The Special Rapporteur was given a new mandate to continue his work and to prepare a Second Report, which was to contain a first set of

38 *See* [1963] 1 Y.B. Int'l L. Comm'n 297–307, 717th-718th mtgs., UN Doc. A/CN.4/SER.A/1963.

39 *See* UN Doc. A/CN.4/L. 104 (1963). For the discussions that took place within the ILC see [1964] 1 Y.B. Int'L L. Comm'n 206–223, 755th-757th mtgs., UN Doc. A/CN.4/SER.A/1964. See also [1964] 2 Y.B. Int'l L. Comm'n 226–227, paras. 41–42, UN Doc. A/CN.4/SER.A/1964/Add. 1.

40 The study was also intended to extend to resident representatives and observers who represent an international organization to a State or who are sent by one international organization to another. On this question, see El-Erian, DUPUY, at 635–642.

draft articles on the status, privileges and immunities of representatives of States to international organizations.[41]

The first part of the topic was designed to complete the codification of the law of diplomatic relations, which had already resulted in conventions on (inter-State) diplomatic and consular intercourse.[42] Between 1963 and 1971, Mr. El-Erian submitted a total of six reports on this topic. Since the first part of the topic has no direct bearing on the subject-matter of the present study, which deals with questions related to the *second* part of the ILC's work on the legal position of international organizations as separate legal entities, its consideration within the ILC will be discussed only briefly. The dual aim of this concise review is to provide the reader with the necessary references for a more detailed examination of the first part of the ILC's study, as well as to facilitate a greater understanding of the second part with which the present study is directly concerned.

It must first be realized that diplomatic intercourse within the framework of international organizations is of a somewhat different character than inter-State diplomatic relations. The close relationship which a 'permanent mission,' i.e., a State's embassy to an international organization, maintains with the organization is of a *tripartite* nature, involving the host State, the sending State and the organization.[43] The scope and nature of the work of representatives of States to organizations also differ from those of diplomats accredited to States, in that the former interact with a particular entity, namely, an international organization that operates in a specific limited field, unlike sovereign States which are not limited to any specific areas or functions.[44]

The legal status, privileges and immunities of the representatives of States are regulated by many existing international agreements and domestic arrangements of a wide variety.[45] As concerns their status within the United

---

41 *See Report of the Commission to the General Assembly covering the work of its fifteenth session*, UN Doc. A/5509 (1963) reprinted in [1963] 2 Y.B. Int'l L. Comm'n 187, 225, para. 66, UN Doc. A/CN.4/SER.A/1963/Add. 1; [1963] 1 Y.B. Int'l L. Comm'n 297–307, UN Doc. A/CN.4/SER.A/1963.

42 *See* 1961 Vienna Convention on Diplomatic Relations, 500 U.N.T.S. 95; 1963 Vienna Convention on Consular Relations, 596 U.N.T.S. 261; and 1969 Convention on Special Missions, 24 GAOR Supp. (No.30) at 99, UN Doc. A/7630 (1970).

43 *E.g.*, The Netherlands (sending State) sends its diplomats to its Permanent Mission to the United Nations (organization) in New York, U.S.A. (host State).

44 *See* SCHERMERS, at 1213–1214, paras. 1812–1815.

45 For a compilation of legislative texts of over 30 States and treaty provisions concerning the legal position of the representatives of States see UN Docs. ST/LEG/SER.B/10 (1959) & ST/LEG/SER.B/11 (1961). *See also* Restatement (Third) of Foreign Relations Law of the United States §470, at 518–524 (1987)[hereinafter: Restatement (Third)];

Nations, Article 105, paragraph 2, of the UN Charter[46] merely provides as follows:

> Representatives of the Members of the United Nations and officials of the Organization shall similarly enjoy such privileges and immunities as are necessary for the independent exercise of their functions in connexion with the Organization.

Although representatives of States are mentioned in paragraph 2 on a par with officials of the organization, the legal régime which governs their respective status differs in both extent and nature. This emerges from the *Convention on the Privileges and Immunities of the United Nations*, adopted by the General Assembly on 13 February 1946,[47] the legal basis for which is found in Article 105, paragraph 3, of the Charter.[48] The General Convention devotes a set of separate articles, consisting of several 'Sections,' to the representatives of member States and to officials.[49] Article IV, which consists of six Sections, spells out the legal position of the "Representatives of Members to the principal and subsidiary organs of the United Nations and to conferences convened by the United Nations." Unlike officials, representatives enjoy immunity from personal arrest or detention and from seizure of their personal baggage.[50] Although Section 16 of Article IV provides that "the

---

M.M. Whiteman, Digest of International Law, Vol. 13, at 111–142 (1968)[hereinafter: WHITEMAN, 13 DIGEST].

46 For the preparatory work in connection with Art. 105, para. 2, of the UN CHARTER, see 13 U.N.C.I.O. Docs. (1945).

47 *See* 1 U.N.T.S. 15 and 90 U.N.T.S. 327 (corr.) [hereinafter: General Convention]. The General Convention will be discussed below when the legal bases of organizational immunities are addressed.

48 Paragraph 3 reads as follows: "The General Assembly may make recommendations with a view to determining the details of the application of paragraphs 1 and 2 of this Article or may propose conventions to the Members of the United Nations for this purpose." For an explanation of the relationship between the various paragraphs of Art. 105, see 13 U.N.C.I.O. Doc. 933, IV/2/42(2), at 704 (1945). *See also Repertory of United Nations Practice*, at 366–368, paras. 167–175, UN Sales No. 1955.V.2 (Vol. V, 1955).

49 GA Res. 76(1) (1946) defines "officials," whose legal position is covered by Article V of the General Convention, as "all members of the staff of the United Nations, with the exception of those who are recruited locally and are assigned to hourly rates." *See Resolutions adopted by the General Assembly during the first part of its first session*, UN Doc. A/64 (1946), at 139. *See also Repertory of United Nations Practice*, at 351–352, paras. 98–103, UN Sales No. 1955.V.2 (Vol. V, 1955).

50 *Compare* Art. IV, S. 11(a) with Art. V, S. 18(a). *See also* Restatement (Third) § 470, Comment (c), at 519.

expression 'representatives' shall be deemed to include all delegates, deputy delegates, advisers, technical experts and secretaries of delegations,"[51] the term "*permanent* representative" is not used in the General Convention and no reference at all is made to observers from non-member States or from other international organizations or bodies. By contrast, although it does not deal with observers, the *Agreement between the United Nations and the United States of America regarding the Headquarters of the United Nations*[52] expressly regulates the position of resident or permanent representatives of member States to the United Nations, and it stipulates in Article V, Section 15(4), that they shall "be entitled in the territory of the United States to the same privileges and immunities, subject to corresponding conditions and obligations, as it accords to diplomatic envoys accredited to it."[53] But even this bilateral agreement left open a number of issues, such as the legal status of mission premises,[54] which was one of the many gaps to be addressed by the Special Rapporteur in his reports.

The Special Rapporteur submitted his *Second Report* to the ILC at its nineteenth session in 1967,[55] and a *Third Report* at the twentieth session

51 The expression "secretaries" of delegations refers to the secretaries of diplomatic rank and not to the service personnel of delegations. *See Repertory of United Nations Practice*, at 346, para. 80, n.85, UN Sales No. 1955.V.2 (Vol. V, 1955).

52 11 U.N.T.S. 11. This Headquarters Agreement entered into force on 21 Nov. 1947, by an Exchange of Notes, in accordance with Section 28. For a background note, see *Repertory of United Nations Practice*, at 369, paras. 178–180 and n.156, UN Sales No. 1955.V.2 (Vol. V, 1955).

53 Note that, pursuant to Section 26 of the Headquarters Agreement, the provisions of that Agreement prevail over the General Convention in any case of absolute conflict. *See also* GA Res. 257 A(III) of 3 Dec. 1948 on "Permanent Missions," UN Doc. A/810 (1948), at 171–172. For an explanation of the expression "resident representative to the United Nations" as used in the Headquarters Agreement, see *Repertory of United Nations Practice*, at 346–347, paras. 82–84, UN Sales No. 1955. V.2 (Vol. V, 1955) and *Supplement No. 3*, at 229, para. 68, UN Sales No. E.73. V.2 (Vol. IV, 1973). In general, a comparison of the UN Charter, the General Convention and special bilateral agreements reveals a gradual movement from a legal position drafted in *functional* terms (U.S. International Organizations Immunities Act) to one of almost full *diplomatic* privileges and immunities (UN-U.S. Headquarters Agreement). *See also* Fedder, at 68–69.

54 *See Repertory of United Nations Practice, Supplement No. 3*, at 231, para. 83, UN Sales No. E.73.V.2 (Vol. IV, 1973).

55 *See* UN Doc. A/CN.4/195 and Add. 1 *reprinted in* [1967] 2 Y.B. Int'l L. Comm'n 133, UN Doc. A/CN.4/SER.A/1967/Add. 1.

in 1968.[56] Owing to the pressure of work on other topics, it was decided to consider both Reports in 1968.[57]

The *Second Report* submitted by the Special Rapporteur addressed general problems relating to the diplomatic law[58] of international organizations, such as the status of representatives of member States and that of observers from non-member States to international organizations. It also explained the evolution of the institution of permanent missions of member States to international organizations.[59] In the same Report, the Special Rapporteur addressed some preliminary questions and introduced a first set of draft articles of an introductory nature, with commentaries, on general provisions pertaining to the scope and nature of the articles.[60]

The *Third Report* contained a full set of fifty-six draft articles on the legal position of representatives of States to international organizations.[61] Draft articles 1–20, concerning general provisions and permanent missions, constituted a self-contained set of articles and dealt with all the general aspects of the first part of the topic. These articles were adopted unanimously by the ILC, were referred to the Drafting Committee at its 986th meeting held

56 *See* UN Doc. A/CN.4/203 and Add. 1–5 *reprinted in* [1968] 2 Y.B. Int'l L. Comm'n 119, UN Doc. A/CN.4/SER.A/1968/Add. 1, which contains further references to the topic at 187 and 193–213, paras. 9–28.

57 Also, the Special Rapporteur was absent "due to events in the Middle East," *see Letter dated 1 December 1967 from Sir Humphrey Waldock, Chairman of the International Law Commission, to the Director of Legal Affairs, European Committee on Legal Co-operation,* UN Doc. A/CN.4/L.126 (1968) reprinted in [1968] 2 Y.B. Int'l L. Comm'n 187–188, UN Doc. A/CN.4/SER.A/1968/Add. 1.

58 For an explanation of this term in the present context see [1967] 2 Y.B. Int'l L. Comm'n 146, para. 80, UN Doc. A/CN.4/SER.A/1967/Add. 1.

59 *See id.*, at 143. A member State of an international organization has a right, not an obligation, to have a *permanent mission* to that organization, which is bound by the organization's constituent instrument and internal rules. For a description of the nature of a permanent mission see *id.* at 140, para. 42. *See also* J.G. Fennessy, *The 1975 Vienna Convention on the Representation of States in their Relations with International Organizations of a Universal Character,* 70 AJIL 62, 68 (1976)[hereinafter: Fennessy]; El-Erian, DUPUY, at 627–631.

60 For the text of the draft articles, with Commentary, see [1967] 2 Y.B. Int'l L. Comm'n 152, UN Doc. A/CN.4/SER.A/1967/Add. 1.

61 The 56 draft articles were divided into four main Parts: (I) General Provisions (Arts. 1–4); (II) Permanent Missions to international organizations (Arts. 5–46); (III) Delegations to organs of international organizations or to conferences convened by international organizations (Arts. 47–52); (IV) Permanent observers of non-member States to international organizations (Arts. 53–56).

on 31 July 1968,[62] and, through the Secretary-General, were transmitted to Governments of UN member States for their observations.[63] It is noteworthy that draft article 2, paragraph 2, was designed to bring together the differing opinions expressed by ILC members on one important point. Some members, including the Special Rapporteur,[64] favored a restrictive approach that would focus solely on international organizations of a universal character, whereas others thought regional organizations should be included in the study.[65] These differences, which had already arisen at the fifteenth session, were reconciled, on the surface at least, at the ILC's twentieth session by the adoption of draft article 2, which, following a general statement in paragraph 1 that the articles would apply to representatives of States to international organizations of a universal character, added that the articles could equally apply to representatives of States to other international organizations, in spite of their apparent application to universal organizations only.[66]

In connection with the adoption by the ILC of Part I of the draft articles, concerning "General Provisions," the word 'inter-governmental' in the topic's title was changed to 'international.' As such it appeared for the first time in the records of the ILC's twenty-first session held in 1969.[67]

---

62 *See* [1968] 1 Y.B. Int'l L. Comm'n 249, para. 90, UN Doc. A/CN.4/SER.A/1968. For the plenary discussions on the respective Reports, see *id.*, 943rd–956th, 958th–960th, 968th–975th, and 980th–986th mtgs. The 21 draft articles, with a commentary on each article, have been reproduced in [1968] 2 Y.B. Int'l L. Comm'n 196–213, UN Doc. A/CN.4/SER.A/1968/Add. 1. The ILC elects a Drafting Committee for each session which normally consists of fifteen members, *see* Graefrath, at 609.

63 *See* ILC Statute, Arts. 16 and 21, UN Doc. A/CN.4/4/Rev.2 (1982); [1968] 2 Y.B. Int'l L. Comm'n 195, para. 22, UN Doc. A/CN.4/SER.A/1968/Add. 1.

64 *See* UN Doc. A/CN.4/L. 103 (1963) *reprinted in* [1963] 2 Y.B. Int'l L. Comm'n 186, 186, para. 2, UN Doc. A/CN.4/SER.A/1963/Add. 1.

65 *See* [1964] 1 Y.B. Int'l L. Comm'n 206–207, UN Doc. A/CN.4/SER.A/1964; [1968] 2 Y.B. Int'l L. Comm'n 195, paras. 26–28, UN Doc. A/CN.4/SER.A/1968/Add. 1.

66 *See* [1968] 2 Y.B. Int'l L. Comm'n 197, UN Doc. A/CN.4/SER.A/1968/Add. 1. Draft article 2 did, however, not end the discussion on this point, which appeared time and again in the ILC's consideration of the topic, see, e.g., Mr. El-Erian's *Second Report* on the second part of the topic submitted in 1978, UN Doc. A/CN.4/311 and Add. 1 *reprinted in* [1978] 2 Y.B. Int'l L. Comm'n 263, at 267–268, UN Doc. A/CN.4/SER.A/1978/Add. 1 (Part 1), and the discussions on the *Third Report* submitted by his successor in 1987, [1987] 1 Y.B. Int'l L. Comm'n 187–216, UN Doc. A/CN.4/SER.A/1987.

67 This change of title had no impact upon the scope or treatment of the topic. The use of the word 'inter-governmental' related back to GA Res. 1289(XIII), 13 GAOR Supp. (No. 18) at 54, UN Doc. A/4090 (1959), which employed the rather unusual term 'inter-governmental international organizations,' following an amendment that had been

The year 1967 marked an important milestone in the study of the topic. In that year, a document prepared by the UN Secretariat entitled '*The Practice of the United Nations, the Specialized Agencies and the International Atomic Energy Agency concerning their Status, Privileges and Immunities*' was published.[68] This study, which covered in general the period through 31 December 1965, summarized the practice which had developed in this sphere since the organizations concerned, belonging to the so-called United Nations Family, were founded.[69] It did so by dividing between the practice relating to the legal position of the representatives of States to different organizations, on the one hand, and that of these organizations as such, on the other. The survey thus followed the distinction that had been made by the ILC in its initial study of the topic. The UN Office of Legal Affairs has followed up on its promise to publish a series of studies containing similar information, which can be found in, *inter alia*, Part One entitled 'Legal Status of the United Nations and related intergovernmental organizations' of the annual *United Nations Juridical Yearbook*.

The *Fourth Report*, submitted in 1969, contained a revised text of draft articles 26–49 covering the subjects of privileges and immunities of permanent missions to international organizations, conduct of the permanent mission and its members, and ending of the function of the permanent representative. In addition, it proposed several new provisions.[70] The ILC

---

proposed by the representative of Greece in 1958. *See* 13 GAOR Sixth Comm. (580th mtg.) at 145, paras. 24–26, UN Doc. A/C.6/SR.580 (1959). It was, however, deemed preferable to use the term 'international organization,' since this was the term used in Art. 2, para. 1(1), of the 1969 Vienna Convention on the Law of Treaties (signed on 23 May 1969, entry into force on 27 Jan. 1980, UN Doc. A/CONF.39/27, 4th Annex *reprinted in* 8 ILM 679 (1969)).

68 *See* UN Doc. A/CN.4/L.118 and Add. 1–2 *reprinted in* [1967] 2 Y.B. Int'l L. Comm'n 154, UN Doc. A/CN.4/SER.A/1967/Add. 1.

69 Already in 1957, Mr. Liang, who served as Secretary of the ILC in his capacity as Director of the Codification Division of the UN Office of Legal Affairs, had pointed at the desirability for the ILC to analyze the text of Arts. 104 and 105 of the UN Charter, the Conventions on the privileges and immunities of the UN and of the Specialized Agencies and related instruments, and to study the way in which they had worked in practice. *See* [1957] 1 Y.B. Int'l L. Comm'n 5, para. 41, UN Doc. A/CN.4/SER.A/1957. The representative of Egypt to the thirteenth session of the General Assembly in 1958, Mr. El-Erian, suggested that, instead of the ILC being requested to consider the question, the UN Secretariat should be entrusted with the preparation of a study in the light of the statement by Mr. Liang. See 13 GAOR, Sixth Comm. (580th mtg.) at 145, para. 18, UN Doc. A/C.6/SR.580 (1959).

70 *See* UN Doc. A/CN.4/218 and Add. 1 *reprinted in* [1969] 2 Y.B. Int'l L. Comm'n 1, UN Doc. A/CN.4/SER.A/1969/Add. 1.

considered the Fourth Report at its twenty-first session in 1969[71] and it adopted a second group of twenty-nine articles.[72]

The Special Rapporteur presented his *Fifth Report* in 1970.[73] It contained a series of draft articles concerning permanent observer missions[74] and delegations[75] to organs of international organizations and to conferences convened by them. The ILC considered the Fifth Report at its twenty-second session in 1970.[76]

At its twenty-third session held in 1971, the ILC had before it the Sixth and final Report, together with three working papers prepared by the Special Rapporteur.[77]

At its 1147th meeting held on 29 July 1971, the ILC adopted a final set of 82 consolidated draft articles and an Annex thereto. This final draft was submitted to the General Assembly, accompanied by a recommendation to

---

71 *See* [1969] 1 Y.B. Int'l L. Comm'n 4, 991st-999th and 1014th-1036th mtgs., UN Doc. A/CN.4/SER.A/1969.

72 *See Report of the International Law Commission on the work of its twenty-first session*, UN Doc. A/7610/Rev. 1 (1969) *reprinted in* [1969] 2 Y.B. Int'l L. Comm'n 206, 206, para. 13, UN Doc. A/CN.4/SER.A/1969/Add. 1.

73 *See* UN Doc. A/CN.4/227 and Add. 1–2, incorporating UN Doc. A/CN.4/227/Corr.2 *reprinted in* [1970] 2 Y.B. Int'l L. Comm'n 1, UN Doc. A/CN.4/SER.A/1970/Add. 1.

74 A non-member State of an international organization, or another organization or body, may have a *permanent observer mission* representing it before the organization, which performs a rather independent and informal role. On the status of non-Member observers, see [1967] 2 Y.B. Int'l L. Comm'n 142, paras. 58–60, UN Doc. A/CN.4/SER.A/1967/Add. 1. *See also* El-Erian, DUPUY, at 633–635. For the position of the United Nations with respect to permanent observers of non-member States, see *Repertory of United Nations Practice, Supplement No. 3*, at 231–232, paras. 85–87, UN Sales No. E.73.V.2 (Vol. IV, 1973). On status-related questions concerning the permanent observer mission of the Palestine Liberation Organization (PLO) to the United Nations, see *Applicability of the Obligation to Arbitrate under Section 21 of the United Nations Headquarters Agreement of 26 June 1947*, Advisory Opinion, 1988 ICJ Rep. 12. *See also* Note, *International Agreements: United Nations Headquarters Agreement – Dispute over the United States' Denial of a Visa to Yasir Arafat*, 30 Harv. Int'l L.J. 536 (1989) (authored by S. Sadiq Reza).

75 (Observer) delegations are in principle of a temporary, *ad hoc* character. *See* [1967] 2 Y.B. Int'l L. Comm'n 149–152, paras. 95–117, UN Doc. A/CN.4/SER.A/1967/Add. 1.

76 *See* [1970] 1 Y.B. Int'l L. Comm'n 3, 1043rd–1045th, 1047th–1065th, 1069th, 1073rd, and 1077th–1078th mtgs., UN Doc. A/CN.4/SER.A/1970.

77 *See* UN Doc. A/CN.4/241 and Add. 1–6 *reprinted in* [1971] 2 Y.B. Int'l L. Comm'n 1, UN Doc. A/CN.4/SER.A/1971/Add. 1 (Part 1). The Sixth Report contained a summary of the written comments of States and international organizations and the views expressed in the UN General Assembly. For the working papers, see UN Docs. A/CN .4/L .166, A/CN.4/L .171, and A/CN.4/L. 173 *reprinted in* [1971] 2 Y.B. Int'l L. Comm'n 101, 105 and 106, UN Doc. A/CN.4/SER.A/1971/Add. 1 (Part 2).

convene an international conference of plenipotentiaries with a view to concluding a multilateral convention on the representation of States in their relations with international organizations.[78]

In sum, it may be said that the draft articles presented a rather liberal régime of provisions on the representation of States to international organizations, conferring broad immunities upon representatives (including their families) to international organizations, to the extent of virtually equating permanent missions of member States and permanent observer missions of non-member States to international organizations with traditional diplomatic missions to States.[79] The immunity provisions of the draft reflect a mixture of immunity régimes: some are absolute, while others are restrictive in that commercial activities are kept outside the realm of protection. Yet others are functional, being confined to acts performed in the exercise of official duties. The influence of the immunity régime contained in the 1961 Vienna Convention on Diplomatic Relations is apparent.

2.2.2 Codification and Progressive Development of International Law: The 1975 Vienna Convention

Subsequent to the adoption by the General Assembly of a number of resolutions of a preparatory nature,[80] the *United Nations Conference on the Representation of States in Their Relations with International Organizations* was held in Vienna, Austria, from 4 February 1975 to 14 March 1975.[81] It was the first codification conference held under the aegis of the United Nations in which all States of the world were invited to participate.[82] In the end,

---

78 *See* ILC Statute, Art. 23, sub-para. 1(d), UN Doc. A/CN.4/4/Rev.2 (1982). *Report of the International Law Commission on the work of its twenty-third session*, UN Doc. A/8410/Rev .1 (1971) *reprinted in* [1971] 2 Y.B. Int'l L. Comm'n 275, 278, UN Doc. A/CN.4/SER.A/1971/Add. 1 (Part 1). For the discussion that took place within the ILC, see [1971] 1 Y.B. Int'l L. Comm'n 4, 1088th–1127th, 1130th–1140th, 1142nd and 1146th-l 147th mtgs., UN Doc. A/CN.4/SER.A/1971.

79 *See* Fennessy, at 64.

80 *See* GA Res. 2780(XXVI), 26 GAOR Supp. (No. 29) at 136, UN Doc. A/8429 (1972); 2966 (XXVII), 27 GAOR Supp. (No. 30) at 116, UN Doc. A/8730 (1973); 3072(XXVIII), 28 GAOR Supp. (No. 30) at 140, UN Doc. A/9030 (1974); and 3247(XXIX), 29 GAOR Supp. (No. 31) at 142, UN Doc. A/9631 (1975).

81 This was almost four years after the ILC had submitted its final Draft to the UN General Assembly.

82 *See* GA Res. 3247(XXIX), para. l, 29 GAOR Supp. (No. 31) at 142, UN Doc. A/9631 (1975).

representatives of 80 States as well as observers of various organizations and bodies were present at the Conference.[83]

The Official Records of the Conference reveal that, from the very start, the Conference suffered from a basic bipolarized division of interests between *sending* States, mainly from the Communist Block and the developing world, and *host* States, mostly being Western developed countries. Representing the majority, the sending States favored an expansion of the ILC Draft, which, as mentioned before, could already be considered somewhat liberal. By contrast, because they concerned more the progressive development of international law rather than its codification, the host States sought to limit the broad régime of privileges and immunities proposed in the ILC Draft, especially with regard to permanent observer missions and delegations.[84] Thus, heated debates arose over the régime which should govern the establishment and functions of permanent observer missions, temporary observers and observer delegations.[85] In the end, the sending States were able to secure equality between permanent missions and permanent observer missions, and between observer delegations and other delegations, but the latter only at the expense of a draft article on the inviolability of premises of delegations, which was successfully blocked by the group of host States. The Convention thus includes a gap in this respect. In general, it seems that the exceptional pace of work, within a limited period of six weeks, did not encourage constructive negotiations and was unfavorable to compromise, meetings being poorly attended, with inconsistent and sometimes conflicting voting patterns.

---

83 *See* Official Records of the United Nations Conference on the Representation of States in Their Relations with International Organizations, Vienna, 4 February-14 March 1975, vol. i (Summary records of the plenary meetings and of the meetings of the Committee of the Whole), UN Doc. A/CONF.67/18 (1976); *id.*, Vol. II (Documents of the Conference), UN Doc. A/CONF.67/18/Add. 1 (1976).

84 *See* Fennessy, at 65; H.F. Köck, *Multinational Diplomacy and Progressive Development of International Law, The Vienna Convention of March 14, 1975*, 28 ZaöRV 51, 60–61 (1977)[hereinafter: Köck]. On the special position of the host State, see [1967] 2 Y.B. Int'l L. Comm'n 142, paras. 54–55, UN Doc. A/CN.4/SER.A/1967/Add. 1; A. El-Erian, *La Conference et la Convention sur la Representation des Etats dans leurs relations avec les organisations Internationales (un aperçu général)*, 21 AFDI 445, 461–469 (1975)[hereinafter: El-Erian, AFDI]; *id.*, DUPUY, at 631.

85 *See also* Köck, at 68–81; J.-P. Ritter, *La Conférence et la Convention sur la représentation des états dans leurs relations avec les organisations internationales - Quelques questions particulières*, 21 AFDI 471, 475–478 (1975)[hereinafter: Ritter].

In spite of these differences of opinion, the Conference managed to adopt, on 14 March 1975, the *Vienna Convention on the Representation of States in Their Relations with International Organizations of a Universal Character.*[86] The Convention regulates the matter of (member and non-member) State representation before universal organizations of an intergovernmental nature.[87] The organizations covered by the Convention are, however, not themselves parties to it: in essence, it is a Convention between host States and sending States.[88] The structure of the Convention is as follows: a preamble is followed by 92 articles, which are divided into six parts, the first, introductory part being devoted to the use of terms and the Convention's relationship to other international agreements. The main body of rules promulgated by the Convention is found in Parts II–IV. Part II regulates the establishment, functions, facilities and privileges and immunities of missions to international organizations (covering both permanent missions of member States and permanent observer missions of non-member States). Part III deals with delegations of member States to organs and conferences held under the auspices of the organization, while

86 Hereinafter: 1975 Vienna Convention. The voting was: 57 in favor to one (Belgium) against, with 15 abstentions (including the United States of America, Switzerland, France and the United Kingdom). For the text see UN Doc. A/CONF.67/16, *reprinted in* United Nations Conference on the Representation of States in their Relations with International Organizations – Vienna, 4 February-14 March 1975, Official Records, Vol. II (Documents of the Conference), at 207, UN Doc. A/CONF.67/18/Add. 1 (1976), *reprinted in* 25 ILM 543 (1986) and 69 AJIL 730 (1975). In addition to the Convention, the Conference also adopted five resolutions, which are annexed to the Final Act of the Conference. Two of these resolutions were designed to provide for the situation, not covered by the Convention, of representatives of entities other than States (such as national liberation movements) who might participate in the work of international organizations. *See* Official Records of the United Nations Conference on the Representation of States in their Relations with International Organizations, Vol. II, 204–205 *reprinting* UN Doc. A/CONF.64/15 (Final Act), annex.

87 According to Art. 1, para. 1(2), "'international organization of a universal character' means the United Nations, its specialized agencies, the International Atomic Energy Agency and any similar organization whose membership and responsibilities are on a world-wide scale."

88 *See* Ritter, at 473–475. The Convention creates certain rights and obligations for international organizations, such as the obligation, under Article 22, to assist the sending State in respect of privileges and immunities which its mission enjoys under the Convention. The international organization has an interest in the observance and protection of the privileges and immunities of representatives of States to it because these representatives enjoy them to ensure the independent exercise of their functions in connection with the organization. *See also* [1968] 2 Y.B. Int'l L. Comm'n 122, para. 11, UN Doc. A/CN.4/SER.A/1968/Add. 1; El-Erian, DUPUY, at 632.

Part IV addresses the legal position of observer delegations to organs and conferences. Parts V–VI contain general provisions and final clauses.[89]

As Special Rapporteur El-Erian, who served as Expert Consultant to the Conference, explained in a commentary,[90] the Convention mainly attempts to provide uniform standards and common denominators to regulate the law on diplomatic relations between States and international organizations, without prejudice to existing agreements covering this field. Other commentators' assessments of the Convention range from "fully satisfactory"[91] to "a regrettable failure."[92]

As a result of the circumstances described above, in particular the fundamental clash of positions referred to, it should not come as a surprise that the ratification process has been slow. Thus, the Convention has not yet entered into force as of this writing. As of 1 December 2024, the Convention still fell one ratification short of the total of 35 ratifications necessary for the Convention to enter into force.[93] The fact that States remained unenthusiastic from the moment of the conclusion of the Convention had an adverse effect on the subsequent work of the ILC on the (second part of the) topic, and partly accounts for its eventual discontinuance.

2.3 *The Second Part of the Topic*

2.3.1 The Work of Special Rapporteur El-Erian Continued

Whereas the first part of the topic had concerned the agents of States, the second part was scheduled to deal with the status, privileges and

89 For a concise survey of the provisions of the 1975 Convention see J. Sette-Camara, *U.N. and International Law-Making: the Vienna Convention on the Representation of States in their Relations with International Organizations*, in UN Law/Fundamental Rights – Two Topics in International Law 91 (A. Cassese ed. 1979)[hereinafter: Sette-Camara]; *see also* Köck; P. Cahier, *La Convention de Vienne de 1975 sur la représentation des Etats dans leurs relations avec les organisations internationales de caractère universel* (Zaragoza, 1973–1974, cited in El-Erian, DUPUY, at 632 n.11).

90 *See* A. El-Erian, *Vienna Convention on the Representation of States in Their Relations with International Organizations of a Universal Character*, [Installment] 5 Encyclopedia of Public International Law 392 (1983)[hereinafter: El-Erian, ENCYCLOPEDIA]; *id.*, AFDI, at 452.

91 Sette-Camara, at 109; notice incidentally that Sette-Camara was the Conference's President.

92 Fennesy, at 72.

93 Pursuant to Art. 89, para. 1, the Convention will enter into force on the thirtieth day following the date of deposit of the thirty-fifth instrument of ratification or accession. As of 1 December 2024, the online treaty database accessible on the UN website listed 20 Signatories (*i.e.* States having signed but not ratified) and 34 Parties (*i.e.*, States having signed and ratified) to the Convention.

immunities of international organizations and their 'agents,' that is to say their officials, experts on mission, and other persons engaged in their activities not being representatives of States.[94] The ILC considered the second part of the topic between 1976 and 1992. From 1976 to 1979, Special Rapporteur El-Erian submitted two Reports and his successor Díaz González subsequently produced a further six Reports on this part of the topic.

At its twenty-eighth session in 1976, the ILC requested Special Rapporteur El-Erian to prepare a Preliminary Report to enable it to take the necessary decisions and to define its course of action on the second part of the topic.[95]

The Special Rapporteur submitted his *Preliminary Report* at the ILC's twenty-ninth session in 1977.[96] It traced the evolution of legal norms which govern the legal status and immunities of universal and regional organizations and described certain developments in other related subjects studied by the ILC which had a bearing on the subject-matter of the study. In addition, it examined a number of general questions of a preliminary character with a view to defining and identifying the course of action and method of work which the ILC should follow. The Special Rapporteur concluded that the elaborate and varied network of treaty law and practice in this field needed concretization, harmonization and consolidation, which the ILC could achieve by pursuing an empirical method and a pragmatic approach and by concentrating on practical and concrete issues instead of engaging in theoretical discussions.

The ILC discussed the Preliminary Report at its twenty-ninth session held in 1977, and it endorsed the conclusions of the Special Rapporteur.[97] The discussions centered around such issues as the advisability and form of codifying the second part of the topic, its scope and subject-matter, and the theoretical basis of the immunities of international organizations. While the form of the eventual outcome of the project was left open,[98] the vast

94 Thus, whereas the first part of the ILC's study dealt with the relationship between host States and sending States, the second part focused on the relationship between host States and international organizations.

95 *See* [1976] 2 Y.B. Int'l L. Comm'n 164, para. 173, UN Doc. A/CN.4/SER.A/1976/Add. 1 (Part 2).

96 *See* UN Doc. A/CN.4/304 (1977) *reprinted in* [1977] 2 Y.B. Int'l L. Comm'n 139, UN Doc. A/CN .4/SER.A/1977/Add. 1 (Part 1).

97 *See* [1977] 1 Y.B. Int'l L. Comm'n 201, 1452nd-1454th, and 1470th mtgs., UN Doc. A/CN.4/SER.A/1977. *See also* GA Res. 32/151, para. 6, 32 GAOR Supp. (No. 45) at 214, UN Doc. A/32/45 (1978).

98 For a summary of the views expressed by some ILC members on this question, see [1978] 2 Y.B. Int'l L. Comm'n 271, paras. 59–63, UN Doc. A/CN.4/SER.A/1978/Add. 1

majority of ILC members were of the opinion that the topic was ripe for codification and that in principle all international organizations should be considered and not only those of a universal character. It was, however, deemed practicable to start with a study of the practice within the United Nations system of organizations. The members seemed to agree also that while the ultimate aim should be a codification and unification of existing rules, at the same time the ILC should not shy away from progressive development on certain points where such was necessary to fill any gaps or to harmonize existing practice.

The Special Rapporteur submitted his *Second Report* in 1978.[99] It examined a number of general questions concerning the impact of institutional evolution and functional expansion in the sphere of international organizations, the contribution of domestic law to the legislative sources of organizational immunities and the place of regional organizations in, and the case for codification of, organizational immunity law. Contrary to the position he had taken with regard to the study of the *first* part of the topic, the Special Rapporteur took, for the purposes of the study, a broad approach covering international organizations of both a universal and a regional character. He argued that the final decision on whether to include regional organizations in the eventual codification could be taken only when the study was completed. Moreover, he recommended that the first stage should concentrate on the position of the organizations themselves and that problems relating to individual persons be left until later. The Special Rapporteur interpreted his mandate as one aimed at producing a common denominator, i.e., general rules that would play a residuary role when there was no law to govern a particular situation.[100]

(Part 1); *see also* El-Erian, in [1977] 1 Y.B. Int'l L. Comm'n 204, para. 21, UN Doc. A/CN.4/SER.A/1977; Sinclair, in [1983] 1 Y.B. Int'l L. Comm'n 242, para. 7, UN Doc. A/CN.4/SER.A/1983; Mahiou, in *id.*, at 245, para. 33; Njenga, in *id.*, at 251, para. 28; Rao, in [1987] 1 Y.B. Int'l L. Comm'n 204, para. 50; [1990] 1 Y.B. Int'l L. Comm'n 201, para. 7 (Hayes), 208, para. 19 (Rao), 220, para. 56 (Solari Tudela), 221, para. 4 and 222, para. 9 (Beesley), 223, para. 18 (Al-Qaysi), UN Doc. A/CN.4/SER.A/1990. The options left open are, *inter alia*, a convention, a general framework agreement laying down residual rules, an additional protocol to the general conventions, a code, a restatement, a declaration, model rules, and recommendations by the UN General Assembly.

99 *See* UN Doc. A/CN.4/311 and Add. 1 *reprinted in* [1978] 2 Y.B. Int'l L. Comm'n 263, UN Doc. A/CN.4/SER.A/1978/Add. 1 (Part 1).

100 *See* [1978] 1 Y.B. Int'l L. Comm'n 268, para. 46, UN Doc. A/CN.4/SER.A/1978.

At its thirtieth session held in 1978, the ILC reviewed the Second Report and it approved the conclusions and recommendations set out therein.[101] In particular, it decided that the first stage of the second part should concentrate on the position of the organizations themselves and that legal issues relating to individual persons should be studied at a later date.

2.3.2 Díaz González: A New Special Rapporteur – A New Approach?

The thirty-first session of the ILC, held in 1979, had a certain impact upon the approach taken in the ILC's study of the second part of the topic.

Following Mr. El-Erian's resignation from the ILC on his election, on 31 October 1978, to the International Court of Justice, the ILC, at its 1580th meeting held on 31 July 1979, appointed Mr. Leonardo Díaz González of Venezuela to succeed Mr. El-Erian as Special Rapporteur for the topic 'Relations between States and International Organizations (second part of the topic).'[102]

During its thirty-first to thirty-fourth sessions, covering the years 1979–1982, the ILC did not devote any substantial discussions to the topic, owing to the backlog on its agenda of draft articles on other, more advanced topics.

Following a change of membership of the ILC, the work was resumed at its thirty-fifth session held in 1983. In that year, the new Special Rapporteur submitted a *Preliminary Report* aimed at eliciting the views of the (new) members of the ILC.[103] The Special Rapporteur took as his point of departure the fact that both the ILC and the General Assembly had approved the conclusions and recommendations of the previous Special Rapporteur.[104] This Preliminary Report was the subject of discussions at the ILC's thirty-fifth session.[105] The change in membership, together with

---

101 *See* [1978] 1 Y.B. Int'l L. Comm'n 260–269, 1522nd–1524th mtgs., UN Doc. A/CN.4/SER.A/1978.

102 *See* [1979] 1 Y.B. Int'l L. Comm'n 240, paras. 49–50, UN Doc. A/CN.4/SER.A/1979. Mr. Díaz González was an Ambassador to, *inter alia*, China and worked in the Secretariat of UNESCO. He was also a Representative of Venezuela to the Fourth Committee of the UN General Assembly.

103 *See* UN Doc. A/CN.4/370, incorporating UN Doc. A/CN.4/370/Corr.1 *reprinted in* [1983] 2 Y.B. Int'l L. Comm'n 227, UN Doc. A/CN.4/SER.A/1983/Add. 1 (Part 1).

104 *See* [1983] 2 Y.B. Int'l L. Comm'n 228, para. 11, UN Doc. A/CN.4/SER.A/1983/Add. l (Part 1); see also [1986] 2 Y.B. Int'l L. Comm'n 165, para. 18, and 166, para. 25, UN Doc. A/CN.4/SER.A/1986/Add. 1 (Part 1).

105 *See* [1983] 1 Y.B. Int'l L. Comm'n 237–256, 1796th–1799th mtgs., UN Doc. A/CN.4/SER.A/1983.

the appointment of a new Special Rapporteur, led once again to extensive discussions about the scope and subject-matter of the study rather than its content. Ultimately, the members agreed to "proceed with great caution, endeavouring to adopt a pragmatic approach to the topic in order to avoid protracted discussions of a doctrinaire, theoretical nature."[106] As evidence of its decision to take a pragmatic approach, the ILC reached the conclusion that "[f]or the purposes of its initial work on the second part of the topic, the Commission should adopt a broad outlook, since the study should include regional organizations. The final decision on whether to include such organizations in a future codification could be taken only when the study was completed."[107]

A *Second Report* appeared in 1985.[108] It dealt with the notion of an international organization and with the questions of the legal personality and capacity of international organizations, on which it presented a draft article comprising two alternatives.[109] The Report also considered possible approaches to the scope of the future draft articles on the topic. The ILC held a brief discussion on the Report at its thirty-seventh session.[110] It did not vote on the draft article but decided to resume the discussion at its thirty-eighth session, and it requested the Special Rapporteur to prepare a schematic outline of the subject-matter to be covered by the various draft articles that he intended to prepare on the topic, together with his concrete suggestions.[111]

In 1985, the UN Secretariat issued a supplementary study on '*The Practice of the United Nations, the Specialized Agencies and the International Atomic Energy Agency concerning their Status, Privileges and Immunities,*' which

106 *See* [1983] 2 Y.B. Int'l L. Comm'n 80, para. 276, UN Doc. A/CN.4/SER.A/1983/Add. 1 (Part 2). The ILC decided to adopt a pragmatic approach so that it could formulate specific draft articles on the topic without getting entangled in doctrinal issues.

107 *See* [1983] 2 Y.B. Int'l L. Comm'n 80, para. 277(c), UN Doc. A/CN.4/SER.A/1983/Add. 1 (Part 2).

108 *See* UN Doc. A/CN.4/391 and Add. 1 reprinted in [1985] 2 Y.B. Int'l L. Comm'n 103, UN Doc. A/CN.4/SER.A/1985/Add. 1 (Part 1).

109 For a review of this draft article see this study's section on Legal Status (Step One) below.

110 *See* [1985] 1 Y.B. Int'l L. Comm'n 283, 1925th-1927th, and 1929th mtgs., UN Doc. A/CN.4/SER.A/1985.

111 *See* [1985] 2 Y.B. Int'l L. Comm'n 67, para. 267, UN Doc. A/CN.4/SER.A/1985/Add. 1 (Part 2).

updated the previous 1967 study.[112] The Secretariat had prepared the study at the ILC's request[113] on the basis of replies received to questionnaires addressed in 1978 and 1984 by the UN Legal Counsel to his colleagues of the Specialized Agencies and the International Atomic Energy Agency (IAEA), on the practice of these organizations relating to their status, privileges and immunities.[114] The 1985 study revised and updated the 1967 version in the light of these replies and the new material which had emerged from 1 January 1966. Both studies have proved to be invaluable tools for the offices of legal affairs of various international organizations in tackling questions related to the legal position of these organizations.

In compliance with the ILC's wishes expressed in 1985, the *Third Report*, submitted by the Special Rapporteur in 1986, contained a tentative schematic outline of the subject-matter to be covered by the draft.[115] The outline, besides referring to definitions and legal personality, distinguished between three categories, namely, the non-fiscal and financial-fiscal privileges and immunities of (i) the organization, (ii) those of officials, and (iii) those of experts on mission for, and persons having official business with, the organization. Finally, the outline referred to certain other questions such as *laissez-passer* travel documents, abuse and withdrawal of immunities, and settlement of disputes. Due to lack of time, the ILC was again unable to discuss the topic at its thirty-eighth session and it had to defer the consideration of the Third Report to its thirty-ninth session.

In 1987, discussions on the Third Report were held within the plenary of the ILC,[116] with particular focus on the question of the scope of immunities to be covered by future draft articles, and the relevance of the schematic

112 *See* UN Doc. A/CN.4/L.383 and Add.1–3 *reprinted in* [1985] 2 Y.B. Int'l L. Comm'n 145, UN Doc. A/CN.4/SER.A/1985/Add. 1 (Part 1/Add. 1).

113 *See* [1983] 1 Y.B. Int'l L. Comm'n 256, paras. 10–11, UN Doc. A/CN.4/SER.A/1983.

114 The text is *reprinted in* [1983] 2 Y.B. Int'l L. Comm'n 227, paras. 6–7, UN Doc. A/CN.4/SER.A/1983/Add. 1 (Part 1). At its thirty-eighth session in 1986, the ILC had before it a document prepared by the UN Secretariat which set out, on a question-by-question basis, the replies received by the Secretariat from international organizations in response to the Legal Counsel's 1984 questionnaire, see UN Doc. ST/LEG/17.

115 *See* UN Doc. A/CN.4/401 reprinted in [1986] 2 Y.B. Int'l L. Comm'n 163 (outline at 167, para. 34), UN Doc. A/CN.4/SER.A/1986/Add. 1 (Part 1). The Report took account of the replies to the various questionnaires sent between 1965 and 1984 by the UN Legal Counsel to the UN specialized agencies, to IAEA and to certain regional organizations. These replies are contained in the studies of 1967 and 1985 prepared by the UN Secretariat, referred to above, and in UN Doc. ST/LEG/17 (1987), relating to regional organizations.

116 *See* [1987] 1 Y.B. Int'l L. Comm'n 187, 2023rd–2027th, 2029th mtgs., UN Doc. A/CN.4/SER.A/1987.

outline for the drafting of these articles.[117] It appeared that a number of ILC members were after all inclined to confine not only the eventual draft but also the prior study to international organizations of a universal character. But it was decided that the final decision on this matter would be left until the draft had been completed. The hope was expressed that a set of draft articles would be submitted in due course, and it was agreed that the Special Rapporteur should proceed with his study of the topic on the basis of both the schematic outline proposed by him and the discussion in the ILC.[118] In his concluding remarks following the general debate, the Special Rapporteur stated that his intention was not to harmonize existing provisions on the topic, but to seek to co-ordinate, to concretize and to identify any gaps in the law so as to clarify certain privileges and immunities. According to him, the goal was to supplement the rules in force and to elaborate a new set of rules to help resolve the problems that international organizations faced in their relations with States.[119]

The *Fourth Report*, which appeared in 1989, contained 11 draft articles covering general provisions (Articles 1–4), legal personality (Articles 5–6),[120] and property, funds and assets (Articles 7–11), the latter reflecting the organization's jurisdictional immunities, the status of its premises and freedom to transfer funds and other assets.[121] The ILC had the Fourth Report before it at its forty-first session in 1989, but it was again unable to consider it owing to lack of time.[122] Thus, no consideration was given to the topic during the period 1988–1989.

117 This prompted ILC member Mahiou to point out that the "topic had been on the agenda for 10 years, yet the Commission was still discussing its scope and field of application." *See* [1987] 1 Y.B. Int'l L. Comm'n 195, para. 20; *see also* Barsegov, id. at 199, para. 12 and 200, para. 17, and Calero Rodrigues, *id.* at 202, para. 31.

118 *See* [1987] 1 Y.B. Int'l L. Comm'n 216, para. 25, UN Doc. A/CN.4/SER.A/1987.

119 *See* [1987] 1 Y.B. Int'l L. Comm'n 215, para. 15, and 216, para. 19, UN Doc. A/CN.4/SER.A/1987.

120 For a review of these draft articles, see also under Step One, *infra*, of this study.

121 *See* UN Doc. A/CN.4/424 and Corr.1 *reprinted in* [1989] 2 Y.B. Int'l L. Comm'n 153–168, UN Doc. A/CN.4/SER.A/1989/Add. 1 (Part 1). The Special Rapporteur stated that he would, for the time being, confine his study to organizations of a universal character. *See id.* at 156, para. 18. Some of these draft articles will be reviewed under Step Two, *infra*, of our analysis.

122 *See* [1989] 1 Y.B. Int'l L. Comm'n 281–284, 2133rd mtg., UN Doc. A/CN.4/SER.A/1989; *see also* [1989] 2 Y.B. Int'l L. Comm'n 131–136, UN Doc. A/CN.4/SER.A/1989/Add. 1 (Part 2). It should be noted, incidentally, that the Special Rapporteur, Mr. Díaz González, was elected Chairman of the ILC at its 2042nd meeting held on 9 May 1988. *See* [1988] 1 Y.B. Int'l L. Comm'n 2, para. 8, UN Doc. A/CN.4/SER.A/1988.

Special Rapporteur Díaz González submitted a *Fifth Report* at the forty-second session of the ILC in 1990.[123] It contained six draft articles constituting Part III of the draft, on archives (Article 12), and Part IV, relating to publications (Article 13), and communications facilities (Articles 14–17). At this session, the ILC examined the *Fourth Report*.[124] In his Fourth Report, the Special Rapporteur had referred to various issues of a more conceptual nature, stressing that functional necessity governed the field covered by the draft.[125] Of the 24 members of the ILC who participated in the debate on this Report, no fewer than 17 explicitly applied the functional approach to the question of the legal position of international organizations, while stressing that requirements of their functions and purposes dictate the legal régime applicable to them. Several members availed themselves of the term 'functional necessity.'[126] Subject to certain drafting suggestions, draft articles 1–11 met with general agreement, and it was therefore decided to refer them to the Drafting Committee.[127]

A *Sixth Report*, which completed the study of the first stage of the draft concerning the legal position of international organizations themselves, was submitted at the forty-third session of the ILC held in 1991.[128] It introduced five draft articles constituting Part V of the Draft, on fiscal immunities (Articles 18–19, and 21) and exemption from customs duties (Article 20), as well as one article of a definitional nature (Article 22).[129] The ILC considered

---

123 *See* UN Doc. A/CN.4/432 (1990), reissued as UN Doc. A/CN.4/438 and Corr. 1 (1991) *reprinted in* [1991] 2 Y.B. Int'l L. Comm'n, UN Doc. A/CN.4/SER.A/1991/Add. 1 (Part 1).

124 *See* UN Docs. A/CN.4/SR.2176–2180 (1990) *reprinted in* [1990] 1 Y.B. Int'l L. Comm'n 200–233, 2176th-2180th mtgs., UN Doc. A/CN.4/SER.A/1990. For a summary of the comments and observations by the members of the ILC see *Report of the International Law Commission on the work of its forty-second session*, 45 GAOR Supp. (No. 10) at 227–241, paras. 424–463, UN Doc. A/45/10 (1990).

125 *See* [1989] 2 Y.B. Int'l L. Comm'n 161, para. 56, UN Doc. A/CN.4/SER.A/1989/Add. 1 (Part 1). The first Special Rapporteur, Mr. El-Erian, was an advocate of the functional theory himself. He also called it the "demands of the office" theory. See [1957] 1 Y.B. Int'l L. Comm'n 4, para. 31, UN Doc. A/CN.4/SER.A/1957.

126 *See* [1990] 1 Y.B. Int'l L. Comm'n 204, para. 28 (Al-Baharna), 205, para. 37 (Shi); 213, para. 4 (Ogiso), 217, para. 34 and 218, paras. 39 and 41 (McCaffrey), UN Doc. A/CN.4/SER.A/1990.

127 *See* [1990] 1 Y.B. Int'l L. Comm'n 233, para. 15, UN Doc. A/CN.4/SER.A/1990.

128 *See* UN Doc. A/CN.4/439 (1991) *reprinted in* [1991] 2 Y.B. Int'l L. Comm'n, UN Doc. A/CN.4/SER.A/1991/Add. 1 (Part 1).

129 Art. 22 states that "[f]or the purposes of the foregoing articles, the terms 'official activity' or 'official use' shall mean those relating to the accomplishment of the purposes of the international organizations."

both the Fifth and Sixth Reports at its forty-third session held in 1991.[130] Besides the Special Rapporteur, who introduced his two Reports, seven members of the ILC made comments on these Reports which, as one member pointed out, "dealt with relatively easy questions that had not given rise to serious controversy."[131] All members who participated in the debate referred to the functional criterion, and two used the term 'functional necessity.'[132] There was broad support for the contents of the two Reports and the draft articles contained in them, the latter subject to some suggestions as to their text. At the conclusion of the debate, on 5 July 1991, it was decided to refer the remaining draft articles 12–22 to the Drafting Committee, which would be responsible for including them in texts to be submitted for approval to the plenary session of the ILC.[133]

The work of the ILC on the second part of the topic had been proceeding during all this time in accordance with the successive resolutions adopted by the UN General Assembly under the item concerning the report of the ILC.[134]

2.4 *Current Status: The 1992 Report of the ILC's Planning Group*

On 9 December 1991, the General Assembly adopted Resolution 46/54, by which it requested the ILC, *inter alia*:

> (a) To consider thoroughly:
>
> (i) The planning of its activities and programme for the term of office of its members bearing in mind the desirability of achieving as much progress as possible in the preparation of draft articles on specific topics; ...[135]

---

130 *See* [1991] 1 Y.B. Int'l L. Comm'n 166, 167 (Special Rapporteur), 172 (Hayes), 173 (Jacovides), 174 (Roucounas), 175 (Njenga), 177 (Pellet), 178 (Pawlak), 179 (Al-Baharna), and 186 (Special Rapporteur), 2232nd-2236th mtgs., UN Doc. A/CN.4/SER.A/1991.

131 *See* Roucounas, in [1991] 1 Y.B. Int'l L. Comm'n 174, para. 2, UN Doc. A/CN.4/SER.A/1991.

132 *See* [1991] 1 Y.B. Int'l L. Comm'n 172, para. 28 (Hayes) and 176, para. 16 (Njenga), UN Doc. A/CN.4/SER.A/1991.

133 *See id.*, at 186, paras. 6–7.

134 *See* GA Res. 33/139 of 19 Dec. 1978, 34/141 of 17 Dec. 1979, 35/163 of 15 Dec. 1980, 36/114 of 10 Dec. 1981, 37/111 of 16 Dec. 1982, 38/138 of 19 Dec. 1983, 39/85 of 13 Dec. 1984, 40/75 of 11 Dec. 1985, 41/81 of 3 Dec. 1986, 42/156 of 7 Dec. 1987, 43/169 of 9 Dec. 1988, 44/35 of 4 Dec. 1989, 45/41 of 28 Nov. 1990 and 46/54 of 9 Dec. 1991.

135 GA Res. 46/54 (1991), para. 6 sub (a)(i), 46 GAOR Supp. (No. 49) at 286, UN Doc. A/46/49 (1992).

Subsequent to this request, the ILC agreed to take it up under item 7 of its agenda entitled 'Programme, procedures and working methods of the Commission, and its documents.' The Planning Group of the ILC's Enlarged Bureau established a Working Group,[136] which was to review, *inter alia*, the progress so far achieved on the topic 'Relations between States and international organizations (second part of the topic),' and to make a recommendation as to whether the ILC should continue with it and, in case it should, what direction it should follow.

In its report, which was submitted to the Planning Group on 7 July 1992, the Working Group issued a negative recommendation, to the effect that the ILC should decide not to pursue any further, during the term of office of its then-members,[137] its consideration of the topic. This recommendation received the approval of the Planning Group,[138] and was endorsed by the plenary meeting of the ILC at its forty-fourth session held in 1992,[139] over a strong plea by Special Rapporteur Díaz González who stressed the usefulness of systematizing and organizing the existing rules on the topic and filling the many gaps in the instruments in force.[140]

As the basis for its decision, the ILC referred to the following considerations raised by the Planning Group.

States had been slow to ratify or adhere to the 1975 Vienna Convention. The passage of time had failed to bring any sign of increased acceptance of the Convention by UN member States. Any convention on the second part of the topic was bound to meet the same lack of enthusiasm. Consequently,

---

136 The Working Group was established at the ILC's 2262nd meeting held on 19 May 1992, see *Draft Report of the International Law Commission on the work of its forty-fourth session*, Ch. V, at 4, para. 6, UN Doc. A/CN.4/L.474 of 21 July 1992.

137 This term expired on 31 Dec. 1996.

138 *See Report of the Planning Group on Programme, procedures and working methods of the Commission, and its documentation*, at 3, para. 11, UN Doc. A/CN.4/L.473/Rev.1 of 15 July 1992.

139 *See Report of the International Law Commission on the work of its forty-fourth session*, 47 GAOR Supp. (No. 10) at 132–133, para. 362, UN Doc. A/47/10 (1992).

140 *See Report of the International Law Commission on the work of its forty-second session*, 45 GAOR Supp. (No.10) at 228, para. 427, UN Doc. A/45/10 (1990); see also the earlier comments by then ILC Chairman Jagota, who stated: "As to the usefulness of the topic, although it was admittedly already partly covered by existing conventions, the draft articles would not be dealing with any specific organization, but would be laying down general principles in regard to the privileges and immunities of international organizations of a universal character: regional organizations and other new bodies could consult these general principles for guidance." *See* [1985] 1 Y.B. Int'l L. Comm'n 299, para. 41, UN Doc. A/CN.4/SER.A/1985. *See also* Al-Qaysi's warning in [1987] 1 Y.B. Int'l L. Comm'n 215, para. 11, UN Doc. A/CN.4/SER.A/1987.

doubts had arisen as to the advisability of continuing the work undertaken in 1976 on the second part of the topic, both by members of the ILC and by delegations in the Sixth Committee of the General Assembly.

At the ILC's forty-second and forty-third sessions in 1990–1991, it appeared that a number of its members displayed a certain lack of enthusiasm for the topic.[141] They expressed uncertainty about the purpose of, and need for, the study and they questioned the usefulness of proceeding with this part of the topic.[142] It was argued that the subject-matter had already been regulated by many existing agreements, such as conventions on privileges and immunities, headquarters and conference agreements, exchanges of notes, domestic laws, etc., and that, consequently, any codification would be redundant, or at least premature. Similar concerns were voiced within the Sixth Committee of the General Assembly, as well as within the secretariats of various international organizations.[143] Most importantly, the fact that the number of ratifications of the 1975 Convention had remained rather limited raised severe doubts within the ILC as to whether a convention on the second part of the topic would not encounter similar problems.[144] Even before the forty-second session, a tendency had developed within the ILC to

141 *See*, for the forty-second session held in 1990, *e.g.*, [1990] 1 Y.B. Int'l L. Comm'n 209, para. 28 (Rao), 210, para. 47 (Calero Rodrigues), 213, para. l (Ogiso), 217, para. 32 (McCaffrey) and 223, para. 19 (Eiriksson); for the forty-third session held in 1991, see, *e.g.*, Pellet, in [1991] 1 Y.B. Int'l L. Comm'n 177, paras. 2–3, UN Doc. A/CN.4/SER.A/1991.

142 *See* S. McCaffrey, *Current Developments: The Forty-Second Session of the International Law Commission*, 84 AJIL 930, 941 (1990); *id.*, *Current Developments: The Forty-Third Session of the International Law Commission*, 85 AJIL 703, 708 (1991). *See also* 46 GAOR Sixth Comm.(37th mtg.) at 7, para. 32, UN Doc. A/C.6/46/SR.37 (1991).

143 *See* UN Doc. A/CN.4/L.456, at 106, paras. 412–413 and 107, para. 415 (1991); *see also Topical summary of the discussion held in the Sixth Committee of the General Assembly during its forty-seventh session, prepared by the Secretariat*, at 78, para. 297, UN Doc. A/CN. 4/446 (1993). During the earlier debates on the topic 'Question of Treaties Concluded between States and International Organizations or between Two or More International Organizations,' Sette- Camara had stressed that an element of stability and generality could be introduced by a successful codification effort, which the organizations themselves, however, were not always anxious to have, because existing uncertainties sometimes suited them better than a system of specific and rigid rules. *See* [1973] 1 Y.B. Int'l L. Comm'n 201, para. 36, UN Doc. A/CN.4/SER.A/1973; similarly El-Erian, *id.* at 205, para. 27. During the forty-second session, ILC member Bennouna pointed out that international organizations were not complaining about the *status quo* that had been achieved in practice, but that they might do so if any attempt was made to change the system in force. *See* [1990] 1 Y.B. Int'l L. Comm'n 220, para. 63, UN Doc. A/CN.4/SER.A/ 1990.

144 *See also* H. Fox and Ph. Webb, The Law of State Immunity (3rd ed. 2013), at 586 ("any convention on the immunities of international organizations would necessarily be too

assign low priority to the second part of the topic. Certainly the topic was treated more favorably when Mr. El-Erian was still Special Rapporteur.[145] It is recalled that in 1964, the ILC decided to accord top priority to its work on relations between States and intergovernmental organizations from among those topics that were new on the ILC's agenda.[146] In stark contrast, the ILC did not even consider the topic during the years 1979–1982, 1988–1989 and 1992–1993, which was later explained by pointing out that the international community's needs had changed in a way that could not have been foreseen at the time when the topic had been included in the ILC's program of work.[147]

The decision to discontinue the project still came as a relative surprise, considering the broad support in the ILC for the path charted for the topic by the Special Rapporteur in his Fourth Report submitted in 1988.[148]

On 25 November 1992, the General Assembly adopted Resolution 47/33, by which it, *inter alia*, endorsed the decision of the ILC not to pursue its study of the topic under consideration.[149] The effect of Resolution 47/33 is that this topic no longer forms part of the ILC's program of work.

---

general to be useful in solving contentious disputes and establishing best practices") [hereinafter: FOX-WEBB].

145 It cannot be said, though, that Mr. El-Erian's successor was to blame for this situation. To the contrary, Mr. Díaz González was himself a victim of the lack of speed with which the plenary of the ILC considered his reports. *See* Pellet, in [1991] 1 Y.B. Int'l L. Comm'n 177, para. 1, UN Doc. A/CN.4/SER.A/1991. This lack of speed had more to do with other topics on the ILC's agenda, such as that on State responsibility, in which a backlog had developed or which were more pressing by their nature. *See* Hayes, in [1990] 1 Y.B. Int'l L. Comm'n 202, para. 17, UN Doc. A/CN.4/SER.A/1990.

146 *See* [1964] 2 Y.B. Int'l L. Comm'n 226, para. 36, UN Doc. A/CN.4/SER.A/1964/Add. 1. Notice incidentally that at that time even the important topic 'State responsibility' was scheduled for consideration after the topic 'Relations between States and intergovernmental organizations' had been completed. In 1992, however, 'State responsibility' appeared on top of the Drafting Committee's agenda, *see Report of the International Law Commission on the work of its forty-fourth session*, 47 GAOR Supp. (No. 10) at 4, para. 9, UN Doc. A/47/10 (1992). As early as 1958, the Greek delegation to the Sixth Committee had stressed that the matter was not an urgent one and that it accordingly called for no priority at all, *see* 13 GAOR Sixth Comm. (569th mtg.) at 91, para. 23, UN Doc. A/C.6/SR.569 (1959). *See also* Schwebel, in [1978] 1 Y.B. Int'l L. Comm'n 268, para. 36, UN Doc. A/CN.4/SER.A/1978.

147 *See* UN Doc. A/CN.4/SR.2295 of 12 May 1993, at 5.

148 *See Report of the International Law Commission on the 'work of its forty-second session*, 45 GAOR Supp. (No. 10) at 227, para. 424, UN Doc. A/45/10 (1990).

149 GA Res. 47/33, 47 GAOR Supp. (No. 49) at 287, 288, para. 7, UN Doc. A/47/49 (Vol. I) (1993). Action by the General Assembly was required since the ILC, in its study of the

Despite the fact that the ILC referred all of the 22 draft articles to the Drafting Committee on 5 July 1991,[150] the Committee did not take any action on them.[151] It follows that, despite the Special Rapporteur's announcement in 1989 that the Draft Articles would be immediately followed by a part relating to the privileges and immunities of the *officials* of international organizations,[152] that stage was never reached.

Even though the ILC's decision to discontinue the topic met with wide approval in the Sixth Committee in late 1993, one delegate expressed the hope that the question of the legal status, privileges and immunities of international civil servants would shortly be considered, explaining that the application in practice by analogy of the Vienna Convention on Diplomatic Relations had led to the commission of legal errors by national authorities which could have been avoided had specific norms on the matter existed.[153] In sum, the legal status, privileges and immunities of officials, experts on mission for, and persons having official business with, the organization, including such subjects as *laissez-passer* travel documents, abuse, waiver and settlement of disputes, remain still to be considered by the ILC.[154] Two officials from the UN Office of the Legal Counsel, which has the responsibility for the oversight of privileges and immunities within the United Nations system, have described certain unresolved contemporary questions concerning the independence of international civil servants and the observation in practice of their privileges and immunities.[155] Among the issues

---

topic, had been complying with the mandate assigned to it by the Assembly and reaffirmed in annual resolutions approving the report of the ILC.

150 *See* [1991] 1 Y.B. Int'l L. Comm'n 186, para. 7, UN Doc. A/CN.4/SER.A/1991.

151 *See* UN Doc. A/CN.4/L.473 (1992), at 9.

152 *See* [1989] 1 Y.B. Int'l L. Comm'n 283, para. 18, UN Doc. A/CN.4/SER.A/1989.

153 *See Report of the International Law Commission on the work of its forty-fourth session (1992) – Topical summary of the discussion held in the Sixth Committee of the General Assembly during its forty-seventh session*, prepared by the Secretariat, at 78, para. 297, UN Doc. A/CN.4/446 (1993).

154 These subjects appeared in the Special Rapporteur's original schematic outline submitted in 1986: *see* UN Doc. A/CN.4/401 *reprinted in* [1986] 2 Y.B. Int'l L. Comm'n 163, 167, UN Doc. A/CN.4/SER.A/1986/Add. 1 (Part 1). For an assessment of the contribution by the ILC to this field of international institutional law, employing the two statutory functions of the ILC, namely the codification of international law and the progressive development of international law, see Bekker, at 14–16.

155 S. Tarassenko & R. Zacklin, *Independence of International Civil Servants (Privileges and Immunities)*, *in* International Administration – Law And Management Practices In International Organisations iii.1/1–15 (C. de Cooker ed. 1990)[hereinafter: Tarassenko & Zacklin].

which according to these officials are in need of clarification is the exact status of locally recruited officials who fall outside the scope *ratione personae* of privileges and immunities enjoyed by internationally recruited 'officials' of the United Nations, as defined by General Assembly resolution 76(I).[156] In this connection, they have pointed to a persistent pattern of incidents concerning this category of officials, which has already prompted an institutional response on the part of organizations by way of administrative and legislative measures, such as formal reporting mechanisms and annual reports submitted by the UN Secretary-General.[157] The same authors have also pointed to the need for clarification of issues concerning the levying by certain States of special taxes or 'contributions' for development and exit and work permit taxes, in addition to the special questions raised by the increased activities of international organizations in the area of peacekeeping and peace-making.[158] These issues, which have arisen in practice, demonstrate that the ILC's continued study could have made useful concrete observations on the subject rather than attracting the criticism that its review might be "a purely academic exercise."[159]

---

156 *See, e.g.*, 1990 UN Jurid. Y.B 306–307, 309, UN Doc. ST/LEG/SER.C/28 (1993). *See also* A.J. Miller, *Privileges and Immunities of United Nations Officials*, 4(2) IOLR 169 (2008).

157 *See* Tarassenko & Zacklin, at 9.

158 *See id.*, at 10; Pellet, in [1991] 1 Y.B. Int'l L. Comm'n 177, para. 2, UN Doc. A/CN.4/SER.A/1991.

159 *See* Tomuschat, in [1990] 1 Y.B. Int'l L. Comm'n 202–203, para. 18, UN Doc. A/CN.4/SER.A/1990.

CHAPTER 2

A Three-Step Functional Necessity Analysis

1 Step One: Identification. Functional Necessity in Legal Status: Subject-Matter and Scope *Ratione Personae*

1.1 *Introduction*

According to the functional necessity concept in its most general pronouncement, *an entity shall be entitled to (no more than) what is strictly necessary for the exercise of its functions in the fulfilment of its purposes.*[1] Behind this general characterization lie a number of elements which form the focus of the present study. They will be dealt with separately, so that a step-by-step analysis will emerge.

Before entering into a discussion of the rights and duties of a legal entity, the initial assignment should be to *identify* the entity.

It is important not to become bogged down by the task of giving an exact definition of the object of functional necessity, namely, *international organizations.*[2] More particularly, this study is confined to *intergovernmental* organizations (IGOs) which are established by an agreement between or among sovereign States (and possibly other entities) governed by international law and whose membership consists entirely or principally of States.[3]

---

1 One commentator has referred to this "statement of the law" as "[t]he starting point for properly understanding functional necessity." J.D. Fry, *Rights, Functions, and International Legal Personality of International Organizations*, 36 Boston University International Law Journal 221–248, 238 (2018)[hereinafter: Fry]. The statement is in line with the UN General Assembly's 1946 resolution on the co-ordination of the privileges and immunities of the United Nations and the specialized agencies, which considered that "no privileges and immunities which are not really necessary should be asked for." Res. A/RES/22(I)D, adopted at the thirty-first plenary meeting on 13 Feb. 1946.

2 *See* Calle Y Calle, in [1977] 1 Y.B. Int'l L. Comm'n 207, para. 42, UN Doc. A/CN.4/SER.A/1977; Restatement (Third) §221; *see also* Shi, in [1990] 1 Y.B. Int'l L. Comm'n 204, para. 33, UN Doc. A/CN.4/SER.A/1990, pointing out that the problem is that no two organizations have identical purposes and functions. For a bibliography of international organizations in general see ARCHER, at 188–198.

3 *See* Art. 2, sub (a), of the 'Draft articles on the responsibility of international organizations.' adopted by the International Law Commission at its sixty-third session, and submitted to the UN General Assembly as part of the ILC's report covering the work of that session, UN Doc. A/66/10 (2011) ("'international organization' means an organization established by a treaty or other instrument governed by international law and possessing its

 | DOI:10.1163/9789004724211_003

It follows that non-governmental organizations (NGOs), which are established by individuals or other entities based on domestic law as opposed to international law, are excluded from the scope of the present study.[4]

Article 2, paragraph 1(i), of the 1969 *Vienna Convention on the Law of Treaties*[5] identifies an international organization as an 'intergovernmental' organization, without providing a detailed definition of the term. Article 1, paragraph 1(1), of the 1975 *Vienna Convention on the Representation of States in their Relations with International Organizations of a Universal Character*[6]

---

own international legal personality. International organizations may include as members, in addition to States, other entities"). *See also* Restatement (Third) §221, at 134; International Law Commission, First report on the settlement of international disputes to which international organizations are parties, by August Reinisch, Special Rapporteur, at 15–36, UN Doc. A/CN.4/756 (2023)(discussing defining elements of international organizations and previous relevant work of the ILC). While scholars such as Michel Virally have suggested that the term 'inter-state' organization is a more appropriate term to use, the term "intergovernmental" organizations is the one commonly employed in conventions, in practice and in the literature. *See* M. Virally, *La notion de fonction dans la théorie de l'organisation Internationale, in* Mélanges Offerts à Charles Rousseau – La Communauté Internationale 277 (1974)[hereinafter: Virally, Fonction]. *See also* C.W. Jenks, *Some Constitutional Problems of International Organizations*, 22 BYBIL 11, 18 (1945); De Luna, in [1963] 1 Y.B. Int'l L. Comm'n 301, para. 14, UN Doc. A/CN.4/SER.A/1963; [1967] 2 Y.B. Int'l L. Comm'n 147, para. 86, UN Doc. A/CN.4/SER.A/1967/Add. 1; ARCHER, at 1–2. According to ECOSOC Res. 288 (1950), "[e]very international organization which is not created by means of inter-governmental agreements shall be considered as a non-governmental international organization." It should be pointed out with Reuter, that certain organizations whose members are not States are recognized as having some international personality, that some intergovernmental organizations admit as members with reduced rights non-State territorial units, and that some organizations are not run entirely by State representatives. *See* P. Reuter, International Institutions 217–218 (1958)[hereinafter: REUTER, INSTITUTIONS].

4 Examples of NGOs are Greenpeace and Amnesty International. Schermers has pointed out that there is no generally recognized definition of non-governmental organizations, and simply defines them as all organizations established by individuals, as opposed to IGOs which are created by sovereign States. *See* H.G. Schermers, *The International Organizations, in* International Law: Achievements and Prospects 67–68, paras. 4–5 (M. Bedjaoui ed. 1991)[hereinafter: Schermers, Organizations]. *See also* Reuter, in [1987] 1 Y.B. Int'l L. Comm'n 189, para. 4, UN Doc. A/CN.4/SER.A/1987; J.E. Alvarez, International Organizations as Law-makers 1–16 (2005).

5 Signed on 23 May 1969, entered into force on 27 Jan. 1980, UN Doc. A/CONF.39/27, 4th. Annex, *reprinted in* 8 ILM 679 (1969). *See also* M.E. Villiger, Commentary on the 1969 Vienna Convention on the Law of Treaties 95 (2009).

6 *See* Official Records of the United Nations Conference on the Representation of States in their Relations with International Organizations, Vol. ii, Documents of the Conference, at 207, UN Sales No. E.75.V.12 (1975).

and Article 2, paragraph 1(i), of the 1986 *Vienna Convention on the Law of Treaties between States and International Organizations or between International Organizations*[7] employ the same wording, which is consistent with the terminology adopted in Article 57, paragraph 1, of the UN Charter, where international organizations are referred to as being established by intergovernmental agreement.

The *identification* of an entity as an intergovernmental organization is different from its *classification within* this group of organizations. Intergovernmental organizations can be divided into such categories as universal or regional, general or specialized, political or technical, etc. The present study avoids an excursion into the intricacies of such classifications, mainly caused by the many different (often subjective) criteria which may be employed in this exercise, and which have been thoroughly explored by other writers.[8] Most important, an analysis of the legal position of intergovernmental organizations by way of an analysis based on the functional necessity concept is essentially about *identification* of organizations and can be carried out without having to classify them, because this concept may be applied, to a degree determined by the specific nature of their purposes and functions, to every intergovernmental organization.[9] In the end, it is their nature and mission that determine whether their activities merit protection and to what extent, as will be demonstrated in Step Three of our analysis.[10]

---

7 *See* The Work of the International Law Commission, UN Sales No. E.88.V.1 (10th ed. 2023); *see also* [1989] 2 Y.B. Int'l L. Comm'n 155, paras. 15–16, UN Doc. A/CN.4/SER.A/1989/Add. 1 (Part 1).

8 *See, e.g.*, El-Erian, *First Report*, UN Doc. A/CN.4/161 and Add. 1 (1963) *reprinted in* [1963] 2 Y.B. Int'l L. Comm'n 159, 167–169, paras. 61–81, UN Doc. A/CN.4/SER. A/1963/Add. 1; Díaz González, *Fourth Report*, UN Doc. A/CN.4/424 and Corr. 1 (1989) *reprinted in* [1989] 1 Y.B. Int'l L. Comm'n 153, 158–160, paras. 34–49, UN Doc. A/CN.4/SER.A/1989; Virally, Classification, at 365–382; *id.*, *Definition and Classification of International Organizations: A Legal Approach*, *in* The Concept of International Organization 50 (G. Abi-Saab ed. 1981); REUTER, INSTITUTIONS, at 219–226; SCHERMERS, at 54–64, paras. 48–65; ARCHER, at 38–70. According to ILC-member Rao, "a classification would be not only impossible, but also irrelevant from the ... legal perspective, especially in respect of privileges and immunities." See [1990] 1 Y.B. Int'l L. Comm'n 208, para. 18, UN Doc. A/CN.4/SER.A/1990.

9 What is labelled 'identification' here seems to correspond, however, to Virally's second principle of classification of international organizations, for which he employs the criterion of "la nature propre et les caractéristiques de leurs fonctions." *See* Virally, Classification, at 373.

10 *See also* Reuter, in [1977] 1 Y.B. Int'l L. Comm'n 209, para. 11, UN Doc. A/CN.4/SER.A/1977.

As ILC Special Rapporteur Díaz González has pointed out,[11] the definitions proposed in the many legal and political publications all refer to three important constitutive elements of intergovernmental organizations, namely:

(1) the (conventional) *basis* element, in most cases consisting of a treaty, which is the constituent instrument of the organization, expressing the political will of sovereign States to co-operate in certain specified areas in order to attain certain purposes;[12]

(2) the element of *institutional structure*, represented by the constitutional set-up of the organization, guaranteeing a measure of permanence and stability in its functioning; and

(3) the *means* element, consisting of the functions and powers of the organization, i.e., the tools by which it is to pursue its purposes, as a separate entity, independently from the member States.

While intergovernmental organizations may have these basic characteristics in common, it is important to realize that there is an indefinite variety of such organizations which are extremely diverse in both nature and size. It may even be said that there are as many kinds of legal status as there are international organizations.[13] This diversity has an impact upon both the legal status of intergovernmental organizations and the immunities they require.[14] With this in mind, it may nonetheless be said that even though

---

11 *See* [1989] 1 Y.B. Int'l L. Comm'n 283, para. 11, UN Doc. A/CN.4/SER.A/1989; *id.*, *Second Report*, [1985] 2 Y.B. Int'l L. Comm'n 103, 106, UN Doc. A/CN.4/SER.A/1985/Add. 1 (Part 1); *see also* El-Erian, *First Report*, UN Doc. A/CN.4/161 and Add. 1 (1963) *reprinted in* [1963] 1 Y.B. Int'l L. Comm'n 159, 167, para. 60, UN Doc. A/CN.4/SER.A/1963/Add. 1; [1956] 2 Y.B. Int'l L. Comm'n 108, UN Doc. A/CN.4/SER.A/1956/Add. 1.

12 *See* Sucharitkul, in [1983] 1 Y.B. Int'l L. Comm'n 252, paras. 42–43, UN Doc. A/CN.4/SER.A/1983. It should be pointed out with M.K. Yasseen that "les traitées ne sont plus en général des traités formels sujets à ratification, mais qu'ils sont souvant des accords en forme simplifiée obtenus même par un échange de notes." Yasseen, *La personnalité juridique des organisations internationales*, *in* A Handbook on International Organizations 43, 51 (R.-J. Dupuy ed. 1988)[hereinafter: Yasseen]. In other words, there exist agreements establishing organizations different from the meaning of 'treaty' as defined in Article 2, paragraph 1(a), of the 1969 and 1986 Vienna Conventions, labelled as "acte non 'instrumenté'" by Reuter, in 55 *Annuaire* 214, 323 (1973). Thus, some organizations are established in some other way than by a treaty, e.g., UNICEF: *see* Rosenne, in 55 *Annuaire* 214, 329–330 (1973); Sucharitkul, in [1983] 1 Y.B. Int'l L. Comm'n 239, para. 17, UN Doc. A/CN.4/SER.A/1983.

13 *See* Mahiou, in [1983] 1 Y.B. Int'l L. Comm'n 245, para. 31, UN Doc. A/CN.4/SER.A/1983; *see also* Virally, Classification, at 371 ("le phénomène d'organisation internaţionale est caractérisé, entre autres, par son polymorphisme.").

14 *See* Sucharitkul, in [1983] 1 Y.B. Int'l L. Comm'n 239, para. 16, U.N. Doc. A/CN.4/SER.A/1983. At the same time, it follows that "the meaning to be attached to the privileges and immunities of international organizations could not be studied without taking

there might be considerable diversity among international organizations, there is sufficient similarity to justify a general treatment of these entities under the functional necessity analysis.[15]

The focus will first be on the role which functional necessity plays in the legal status of an international organization. To identify an international organization's legal status is to examine its purposes and functions, or "to look at what they are supposed to do and what they actually do."[16] In a functional necessity analysis, it becomes an identification *of the functional needs* of international organizations. Step One serves this purpose and hence will be dealt with first by way of an initial step of an introductory kind in our step-by-step functional necessity analysis.[17]

1.2 *The Concept of Function*

The notion of 'function' is at the core of the functional necessity concept and we shall for the most part follow Virally's ideas on this notion. The usefulness of the functional necessity criterion lies in its combining indissolubly the element of necessity with that of function, a combination which will emerge in particular from the discussion of Step Three of our analysis. Also, the criterion has very similar consequences whatever the nature and size of the international organization concerned.[18] To quote Virally's words:

> Les organisations internationales ne sont créées, dans la pratique, que sur la pression des besoins et en vue d'objectifs bien définis, sinon bien délimités. Cela est vrai aussi bien des organisations à compétences générales, comme l'ONU ou le Conseil de l'Europe, que des organisations à compétences limitées, comme l'Organisation météorologique mondiale. La structure et les pouvoirs dont elles sont dotées sont mesurés aussi exactement que possible sur ce qui est requis pour leur permettre de s'acquitter avec une efficacité raisonnable ces fonctions. *L'élément déterminant pour chaque organisation, celui qui*

---

account of what the actual concept of an international organization covered." Díaz González, in [1987] 1 Y.B. Int'l L. Comm'n 216, para. 20, UN Doc. A/CN.4/SER.A/1987.

15 At the same time, we realize that any conclusions which may in the subsequent pages be drawn from such similarity among international organizations, may not necessarily hold true for each and every organization, conform Reuter's warnings, in 55 *Annuaire* 214, 323, 325 (1973).

16 *See* Archer, at 51 (but that writer uses this description for *classifying* international organizations, rather than 'identifying' them).

17 *See also* El-Erian, in [1963] 1 Y.B. Int'l L. Comm'n 307, para. 85, UN Doc. A/CN.4/SER.A/1963.

18 *See* Njenga, in [1983] 1 Y.B. Int'l L. Comm'n 250, para. 24, UN Doc. A/CN.4/SER.A/1983.

> *commande tous les autres, c'est donc sa fonction,* et celle-ci apparaît comme d'autant plus importante en tant que principe de classification qu'elle varie d'organisation à organisation: elle est aussi principe d'individualisation.[19] (emphasis added)

Before we start our consideration of the functional element of our analytical framework, Virally's observation should be borne in mind:

> Le choix du concept de fonction comme base de la théorie de l'Organisation internationale n'entraine nullement l'adoption des *thèses fonctionnalistes*. Il est utilisé ici, en effet, de façon *neutre*. Il fait apparaître le caractère fondamentalement *instrumental* de *toute* Organisation internaţionale ....[20] (emphasis added)

The present study does not advocate a 'one-size-fits-all' approach to explaining the functional necessity concept underlying the legal status and immunities of intergovernmental organizations. The differences between international organizations, in terms of their purposes and functions, call for tailor-made solutions, as the discussion of the meaning of the key notion of 'official activity' and of methods of counterbalancing organizational immunities in Chapter 2 (Step Three) of this book highlights. As such, the present study is more in line with "an approach more sensitive to the economic and organizational aspects of international organizations," as advocated by certain scholars.[21] This study is neither 'pro-organization' nor 'anti-organization.' If anything, it is 'pro-international law,' in that it seeks to contribute, in an objective way, to finding solutions to issues and dilemmas confronted in the practice of intergovernmental organizations based on public international law. In doing so, it seeks to disprove the criticism that 'functionalist'-type approaches are deficient, and are in need of replacement, because of their perceived 'one-size-fits-all' trait. This study also should not be mischaracterized as being 'apologetic' in nature, in the sense that it seeks to shield international organizations from any and all forms of scrutiny in connection with their activities. It must be remembered that, when it comes to immunities, even according to the

19 Virally, Classification, at 373–374.

20 Virally, Fonction, at 281.

21 J. Klabbers, *Towards a Political Economy of International Organizations Law*, 20 IOLR 82–101, 82 (2023).

strictest régimes—for example, the Foreign Sovereign Immunities Act of the Uni-ted States of America[22]—the immunity of the entity concerned still is presumed by law and it can be overcome only if the party claiming that the other party does not enjoy immunity is able to prove, through convincing evidence, that certain exceptions to immunity recognized in statutory law or case law apply in a given situation or that the immunity was waived by the international organization concerned.

The UN General Assembly cautioned against a 'one-size-fits-all" approach in one of its earliest resolutions adopted in 1946, stating as follows:

> While recognizing that not all specialized agencies require all the privileges and immunities which may be needed by others, and that certain of these may, *by reason of their particular functions*, require privileges of a special nature which are not required by the United Nations itself, the General Assembly considers that the privileges and immunities of the United Nations should be regarded, as a general rule, as a maximum within which the various specialized agencies should enjoy such privileges and immunities *as the appropriate fulfilment of their respective functions require*, and that *no privileges and immunities which are not really necessary should be asked for.*[23] (emphasis added)

As ILC member Eiriksson once remarked, 'functional' means different things to different people[24] and the same can be said about 'necessity.'[25] The present study employs the term 'function' as understood by an institutional lawyer. It follows that the term 'function' is used in this study in a sense that significantly differs from the theory of 'functionalism' which is of a socio-political nature, presenting an external, ideological view of international co-operation and organization. This socio-political approach to international affairs, which flourished in the interwar period and the years following the Second World War,[26] has been described as being "essentially an assertion

22 *See* 28 U.S.C. § 1604. The presumption of immunity is subject to statutory exceptions set forth in the FSIA.

23 A/RES/22(I)D, adopted at the thirty-first plenary meeting of the General Assembly held on 13 Feb. 1946.

24 *See* Eiriksson, in [1990] 1 Y.B. Int'l L. Comm'n 224, para. 24, UN Doc. A/CN.4/SER.A/1990.

25 *See*, e.g. *Amaratunga v. Northwest Atlantic Fisheries Organization*, Supreme Court of Canada, judgment of 29 Nov. 2013, 2013 SCC 66, [2013] 3 SCR 866, at paras. 34–45.

26 *See* A.A. Fatouros, *On the Hegemonic Role of International Functional Organization*, 23 GYIL 9, 14 (1980)[hereinafter: Fatouros].

and defense of the proposition that the development of international economic and social cooperation is a major prerequisite for the ultimate solution of political conflicts and elimination of war."[27] One outside commentator has summarized the theory of functionalism as follows:

> According to it, a 'working peace system' can, and should, be brought about through a shifting of individual loyalties from national to international values, which will come about through a gradual process of continuing collaboration across national borders among persons working within international organizations engaged in serving particular human needs.[28]

Our approach, on the other hand, studies the concept of function from *within* operating organizations, being part of the established internal mechanism of a given international organization.[29] Here it is used in an objective and neutral sense, as an institutional element that has been created and can be observed as part of the organization's record.[30] While the theory of functionalism is at the 'macro' level and addresses the concept of the international organization, i.e., what instrumental value international organizations in general should have in society, functional necessity is more akin to a 'micro' concept related to the identifiable purposes and functions of any given organization; it is at a stage which has passed that of the underlying considerations leading to the creation of an organization, although it is true that, with a view to interpreting the proper

---

27 *See* I.L. Claude, Jr., Swords into Plowshares – The Problems and Progress of International Organization 345 (3d ed. 1964)[hereinafter: CLAUDE]. One of the modern founders of the theory of functionalism is David Mitrany, see, *e.g.*, his A Working Peace System (1943, republished in 1966), and The Functional Theory Of Politics (1975); *See also* A.J.R. Groom & P. Taylor, eds., Functionalism: Theory and Practice in International Relations (1975). For a sketch of functionalism, see J. Klabbers, *The EJIL Foreword: The Transformation of International Organizations Law*, 26 EJIL 9–82 (2015). *See also* J. Klabbers, *The Emergence of Functionalism in International Institutional Law: Colonial Inspirations*, 25 EJIL 645–675 (2014); SCHERMERS, at 10–11, para. 13A ("Even though the function or functions of international organizations are addressed in one way or another by all studies of the law of international organizations, it is difficult to see one all-embracing theory of functionalism in this field").

28 Fatouros, at 14. For a summary of the beliefs and assumptions behind the functionalist position see that same writer, at 15–17; CLAUDE, at 344–351; ARCHER, at 88–94.

29 In other words, this book offers an internal approach to the law of international organizations, which forms part of the broader field of public international law. *Compare* D.W. Kennedy, International Legal Structures 7, 287 (1987)[hereinafter: KENNEDY],

30 *See* ARCHER, at 2.

purposes and functions of an organization, recourse may have to be had to the broader, socio-political phenomena that lay behind its creation. Aspects of the theory of functionalism as described above may be reflected in the structure and mode of operation of international organizations, especially those belonging to the United Nations Family, and accordingly may be material for interpretative purposes.[31] Since international organizations are often created as a response to, and are affected in their daily operation by, certain developments in society, be it in science or in politics or in any other field, these outside developments also cannot be ignored in studying international organizations.[32]

As to its ordinary meaning, the Concise Oxford Dictionary describes 'function' as "activity proper to person or institution; mode of action or activity by which thing fulfils its purpose." Black's Law Dictionary indicates that 'function' denotes the nature and proper action of anything, the "fulfillment of a definite end or set of ends by the correct adjustment of means."[33] The word has also been defined as "une activité spécifique orientée vers la poursuite d'une finalité déterminée et extérieure à celui qui en est chargé"[34] or, more broadly, as "an organizational task devoted to the service of particular needs."[35]

A study of functions thus coincides with a study of organizational activities. As one author has stated, "[f]unctions relate to the subject matter of the activity and stand, therefore, close to the tasks of the organization."[36] In legal terminology, a function is a tool for the accomplishment of purposes, the two being intertwined. An international organization exercises functions to accomplish purposes. In order to demonstrate the relationship between the purposes and functions of an international organization, reference may

31 *See* Fatouros, at 19; ARCHER, at 3.

32 *See* KENNEDY, at 287–288. For the foregoing reasons, this study should not be mischaracterized as belonging to 'functionalism' literature. As Wellens has stated, "[i]n a functional approach the emphasis is on the operational functioning of the international organization requiring a large degree of autonomy and independence; a reluctant acceptance of the need for and the modalities of an accountability regime for international organization being put in place, including its remedial aspects, is frequently inherent in this approach." WELLENS, at 3, n.2. There is no such "reluctant acceptance" in the present study.

33 Black's Law Dictionary 463 (abr. 6th ed. 1991).

34 Virally, Fonction, at 281.

35 Fatouros, at 16.

36 K. Skubiszewski, *Implied Powers of International Organizations, in* International Law at a Time Of Perplexity – Essays in Honour of Shabtai Rosenne 855, 858 (1989)[hereinafter: Skubiszewski].

be made to some practical examples from the constituent instruments of existing organizations.

One may begin by asking whether functions are clearly discernible in practice. Some constituent instruments distinguish clearly between the purposes and functions of a given organization. Examples of this category are the treaties establishing UNESCO,[37] WHO[38] and WMO,[39] which all devote separate articles, or separate paragraphs within an article, to purposes and functions. Other documents do not separate them out and merely incorporate functions in a provision addressing the purposes of the organization. Examples of this last category are the constituent instruments of ILO,[40] IBRD[41] and IMF,[42] where functions can still be recognized from the use of

37 *See* 4 U.N.T.S. 275. The purposes of UNESCO are set forth in both the Preamble and in Article I, paragraph 1, of its Constitution. Its functions are spelled out in paragraph 2 of Article I, after the opening words "To realise this purpose the Organisation will: [(a)–(c)]."

38 *See* 14 U.N.T.S. 185. The 'objective' of WHO is spelled out in the Preamble of its Constitution and in Art. 1 (Chapter I). Its rather elaborate functions are summed up in Art. 2 (Chapter II) after the introductory words "In order to achieve its objective, the functions of the Organization shall be: [(a)–(v)]."

39 *See* 77 U.N.T.S. 144. The Convention on the World Meteorological Organization spells out the purposes of the WMO in Part II, Art. 2 sub (a)–(e). Art. 7 sub (a)–(l) of Part VI, entitled 'Functions', follows with an enumeration of the various functions of the WMO's supreme body, the Congress, which are created in order to achieve the purposes set out in Part II.

40 *See* 15 U.N.T.S. 35. The Constitution of the International Labour Organization contains some broad objectives in its Preamble and in an annexed document entitled 'Declaration Concerning the Aims and Purposes of the International Labour Organization.' *See* 15 U.N.T.S. 104. The Declaration incorporates some of the functions assigned to ILO in order to achieve its purposes, *e.g.*, sub III "... to further ... programmes," and sub IV "... by ... measures" (such as adopting international standards).

41 *See* 2 U.N.T.S. 134. The purposes of the World Bank are set out in Art. I sub (I)–(V) of its Articles of Agreement, incorporating the Bank's functions as follows: the IBRD is to, *inter alia*, assist its Members in the reconstruction and development of productive facilities and resources [purpose] by facilitating the investment of capital for productive purposes [function], to encourage private foreign investment [purpose] by means of guarantees or by participating in loans and investments [functions], and to promote the long-range balanced growth of international trade and the maintenance of equilibrium in balances of payments [purpose] by encouraging international investment [function].

42 *See* 2 U.N.T.S. 40. While not containing a clear distinction between purposes and functions, the Articles of Agreement of the IMF are, very generally, geared toward the promotion of international monetary co-operation by being assigned the function of providing a framework for consultation on international monetary issues.

the words "to this end," "to realize this purpose," or simply "by," indicating that specific functions are assigned to an organization in order to achieve more generally drafted purposes. Especially in the case of the specialized agencies referred to above, purposes are drafted in more general political-ideological terms, such as the attainment of lasting peace and security, social justice, higher standards of living and health, more efficient means of communication, financial development, etc. On the other hand, the functions of an organization are, generally speaking, the adoption of policies and international standards, the dissemination of information and the promotion of international action and technical assistance.[43] In general, it may be said that the broader the nature and area of operation of the organization, the more general and succinct its statement of purposes and the less clear a distinction between the purposes and functions of the organization. In any event, for the purpose of the discussion of the role of functional necessity, a clear distinction is not of the essence, since what functional necessity refers to is, in the final analysis, the achievement of purposes *through* the exercise of functions, the two being intertwined in this respect.[44] The element of the purposes of an international organization, i.e., the objective that the member States have in common and which prompted them to create the organization, is thus included in '*functional* necessity.' 'Functions' is a more workable term than 'purposes,' which are at a higher hierarchical level in the concept of international organization, being the ultimate *raison d'être* of the existence of these legal entities.[45] By exercising certain functions, through the carrying out of such specific activities as the adoption of international standards, an organization is seeking to accomplish certain higher goals, such as the attainment of lasting peace and security.

---

43 ARCHER, at 55, provides a useful table which sets out the aims and activities of 10 different IGOs by functional area. *See also id.* at 69.

44 *See* Seyersted, in 55 *Annuaire* 214, 403–404 (1973)("I wonder whether it is necessary to maintain both 'l'exercise de ses fonctions et' and 'la réalisation de son objet,' as cumulative conditions."). In legal doctrine, the terms purposes and functions are often used interchangeably to refer to the objectives of an international organization. Draft article 1(1)(c) proposed by Special Rapporteur Díaz González referred to "responsibilities" and it was argued by at least one member of the ILC that this term should be replaced by another one, possibly "functions." *See* Barsegov, in [1990] 1 Y.B. Int'l L. Comm'n 218, para. 45, UN Doc. A/CN.4/SER.A/1990.

45 *See also* Fry, at 239 ("Indeed, there might be one single *raison d'être* for *all* international organizations—all international organizations must exist as an international organization and international legal person in the first place, or else no purposes whatsoever can be realized").

In order to clarify the role that 'function' plays within international organizations, and to better understand the nature of their functioning in the international community, it may be instructive to have a closer look at the operational mechanics and background of these entities. In general, international organizations are created in order to fulfill purposes relating to values or interests which their member States have in common. States set up these bodies mainly to accomplish goals which they cannot attain themselves or which they believe an international organization can accomplish more efficiently at the international level. As Virally has stated, functions are characterized by their *purpose- or goal-orientedness*, which gives the function its dynamic character.[46] *Functions* serve *purposes*; international organizations exercise functions for the advancement of purposes. This advancement is ultimately carried out through the *powers* with which the organization is vested, as will be shown later in this study. The goal-orientedness of the functions which an international organization is to exercise constitutes the *raison d'être* of every international organization.[47]

All international organizations have in common the element of international co-operation between sovereign States, which Virally broadly defines as "toute action menée en commun par plusieurs Etats."[48] According to Virally, the notion of international co-operation in reality translates into that of functions, whereby he distinguishes among four stages, the borders of which may, however, overlap.[49]

First, there is the stage at which the organization's functioning is limited to the *harmonization* of policies and modes of conduct of individual member States, by providing them with a forum at which they can exchange their views on certain matters that come within the realm of the organization's mandate. At this stage, international organizations function as "organisations de concertation."[50] The next stage is that of the *co-ordination* of policy and conduct, in which States submit to common rules in their mutual relations. At this stage, co-operation manifests itself at two levels: that of the development of rules, and that of the inspection of compliance

46 Virally, Fonction, at 281.

47 *See* Díaz González, in [1985] 1 Y.B. Int'l L. Comm'n 284, para. 12, UN Doc. A/CN.4/SER.A/1985; Kunz, at 847.

48 Virally, Fonction, at 283; *compare* his earlier exposé on the classification of international organizations: Virally, Classification, at 368.

49 Virally, Fonction, at 284–288; *id.*, Classification, at 381, adding that "[i]l est bien clair, cependant, que peu d'organisations existantes, s'il en est, représentent un type pur" and that it instead concerns a process of evolution.

50 Virally, Classification, at 379.

with these rules.[51] The third stage is constituted by the realization of joint operations. At this stage, it is still sovereign States that furnish the means to implement agreed common objectives. The function of the international organization is limited to taking the necessary decisions in preparing joint operations to be carried out by the member States. This stage is characterized by the existence of *decision-making power* on the part of the international organization.[52] Accordingly, Virally describes the organizations that belong to this category as "organisations décisionnelles."[53] The fourth and final stage, and the most elevated one in terms of international co-operation, is that of the carrying out of operations by the international organization itself, which is no longer confined to decision-making but includes *executing* power. One leaves here the stage of inter-State co-operation properly so-called, since this stage concerns activities developed and implemented by the organization itself, with States being no more than suppliers of means for the carrying out of such operations by the organization. Accordingly, *inter-State co-operation* is replaced by *organizational operation*, decisions being taken independently by organs of international organizations, whose functions extend beyond mere inter-State co-operation.[54] Virally labels such organizations as "organisations opérationnelles."[55]

From a legal point of view, according to Virally, the functional goal-orientedness of an organization has a triple quality. Functional necessity is not only a tool of *authorization*, it also sets a *standard* or measure and it entails certain *obligations*.[56]

---

51 Virally, Fonction, at 285–286. Virally's stages 1–2 seem to correspond to the roles of 'instrument' and 'arena' in Archer's description of the role and function of international organizations. *See* ARCHER, at 135–147.

52 Virally, Fonction, at 286–287. Virally gives here the example of the power of the UN Security Council to take action under Art. 42 of Chapter VII of the UN Charter.

53 Virally, Classification, at 379–380.

54 Virally, Fonction, at 287–288. At its 3217th meeting held on 25 May 1993, the UN Security Council adopted, unanimously, Res. 827 (1993), establishing an 'International Tribunal for the Prosecution of Persons Responsible for Serious Violations of International Humanitarian Law Committed in the Territory of the Former Yugoslavia since 1991,' acting on the basis of Chapter VII of the UN Charter. *See* UN Doc. S/25704 of 3 May 1993 for a discussion of the legal basis for the establishment of this International Tribunal. This is an example of an organ of an international organization creating an institution which will be financed from the organization's regular budget. Virally's stages 3–4 may be said to correspond to the role of independent actor which Archer assigns to certain international organizations. *See* ARCHER, at 147.

55 Virally, Classification, at 379–380.

56 Virally, Fonction, at 291.

As to the first two attributes of function, that is to say those of authorization and standard, the purposes and functions of an international organization constitute its justification, its *ratio* and *raison d'être*, and that of every activity carried out by it: in exercising its functions an international organization is working toward the fulfilment of the fundamental purposes for which it was created. This can best be seen from the organization's *structure*. Once an organization is seen as an instrument, its organic framework can be understood as having been designed in order to enable it to exercise its functions in achieving, in the most effective way, certain objectives. It follows that its legal and organizational structure must provide it with the means that capture, and unite, the forces favorable to the successful accomplishment of the organization's purposes.[57] Because functional goal-orientedness is determinative of this organic construction, Virally proposes to call it a structuralizing goal-orientedness.[58] According to him, this explains the difference between, on the one hand, the constituent instruments of international organizations, in which the 'object and purpose' is of paramount importance, because it identifies the organization's 'mission,' and simple dispositive treaties between States, on the other. For when States sign a constituent instrument, they are concluding an agreement with a very specific object and purpose, namely, to entrust an organization with the task of accomplishing certain agreed purposes through the exercise of specific functions, the terms of which have been agreed between the parties.[59] The organic apparatus of an international organization only makes sense if seen in relation to its functional goal-orientedness. According to Virally, this is demonstrated by the fundamental role accorded in

57 Virally, Fonction, at 291. *Cf.* the analysis by the International Court of Justice of the structure of the United Nations in determining the international personality of that organization, in *Reparation for Injuries Suffered in the Service of the United Nations*, Advisory Opinion, 1949 ICJ Rep. 174, 178.

58 Virally, Fonction, at 291 ("une finalité 'structurante'.").

59 *Cf. Arbitral Award of 31 July 1989 (Guinea-Bissau v. Senegal)*, Judgment, 1991 ICJ Rep. 53, at 70, para. 49. *See also* R. Monaco, *Le caractère constitutionnel des actes institutifs d'organisations internationales*, *in* Mélanges offerts à Charfes Rouseau – La Communauté Internationale 153–172 (1974)[hereinafter: Monaco]. *But see* E. Lauterpacht, *The Development of the Law of International Organization by the Decisions of International Tribunals*, 152 RdC 377, 414–416 (1976 IV)[hereinafter: Lauterpacht, Development]. For the impact which this special characteristic of constituent instruments may have on the interpretation of such instruments, see M. Bos, A Methodology of International Law 159–165 (1984)[hereinafter: Bos, Methodology].

practice to the purposes and principles of Chapter 1 of the UN Charter.[60] The element of functional goal-orientedness also plays an important role in explaining the often unpredictable results of a certain action taken in satisfaction of the requirements of a purpose. In this respect there is a continuous evolution, according to new functional needs arising in practice. Moreover, these functional needs differ according to the type of organization: there are 'general' organizations, such as the United Nations, which operate in a field that is not restricted to one or more special areas and their functions accordingly extend to all aspects of international (co-)operation, in contrast with others whose activities are delimited by specialization.[61] While the need to make "analytical distinctions between regional and universal organizations, specialized or general organizations, or technical or not-so-technical organizations" has rightly been pointed out in the literature,[62] the functional necessity analysis laid out in the present study is presented in a manner that can be applied to any type of intergovernmental organization. In other words, the mode of analysis is a generalized one that relies on both doctrinal sources and a comparative analysis of intergovernmental organizations.[63]

Besides those of authorization and standard, there is another quality that functional goal-orientedness possesses according to Virally, which is that of *obligation*.[64] A function is not simply an authorized activity. The entrustment with functions comes with attendant duties and responsibilities, as the International Court of Justice stipulated in a landmark advisory opinion rendered in 1949.[65] Because international organizations are not vested with functions in their own interest, but in order to pursue 'external' goals which their member States have in common or have agreed upon, the accomplishment of these functions is a service, and consequently, an obligation.[66]

---

60 *See* Virally, Fonction, at 292.

61 *Id.*

62 J. Klabbers, *Book Review*, 17 IOLR 683 (2020).

63 *Id.*, at 684.

64 Virally, Fonction, at 293, 299.

65 *Reparation for Injuries Suffered in the Service of the United Nations*, Advisory Opinion, 1949 ICJ Rep. 174, 179. For a detailed discussion of this advisory opinion see below, where the element of international legal personality is discussed.

66 *See* Virally, Fonction, at 299; ILC Special Rapporteur Díaz González has pointed out that unlike sovereign States, which are political entities pursuing their own interests, international organizations are service agencies acting on behalf of all their member States. *See Report of the International Law Commission on the work of its forty-first*

This obligation falls especially to the international organization, through its various organs and in accordance with their internal competences. This entails two consequences.

First, the organs, and notably their heads of secretariat, are subject to functional duties and obligations, which at the same time confer upon them a certain authority in relation to the member States. To these obligations correspond rights, namely the right of the member States to the actual accomplishment of the organization's purposes, including the right of these States to insist that the organization does not assume functions connected with purposes other than those for which it was created, and to actually prevent any departure from those purposes.[67]

Second, functions also create obligations for member States. These are *negative* obligations inasmuch as the member States must refrain from pursuing activities of a kind which may hamper the accomplishment of the organization's purposes.[68] These negative obligations give birth to immunities: to these negative obligations on the part of States correspond positive rights of international organizations, which are entitled to functional immunities in carrying out their activities, as will be demonstrated in Step Two of our analysis.[69] In this area, the functional concept dictates *positive* obligations also which arise out of the creation of the organization, namely, that of co-operation with the organization, of the participation in its organs, of making financial contributions to it,[70] or, generally speaking, of

---

session, 44 GAOR Supp. (No. 10) at 379, para. 725, UN Doc. A/44/10 (1989); *see also* Pellet, in [1990] 1 Y.B. Int'l L. Comm'n 215, para. 18, UN Doc. A/CN.4/SER.A/1990.

67 *See* F. Seyersted, *International Personality of Intergovernmental Organizations. Do Their Capacities Really Depend upon Their Constitutions?*, 4 Indian J. Int'l L. 1, 31–32 (1964) [hereinafter: Seyersted, Personality]; Pawlak, in [1987] 1 Y.B. Int'l L. Comm'n 190, para. 16, UN Doc. A/CN.4/SER.A/1987. As Reuter has explained, "international organisations are not free to decide whether or not to carry out their functions: they have a legal obligation to do so." REUTER, INSTITUTIONS, at 230.

68 Virally, Fonction, at 299.

69 *Id.*, at 300.

70 Seyersted, Personality, at 24, has argued that it is doubtful whether an organization can oblige its member States to contribute to the budget of the organization if no such duty follows expressly (such as in UN Charter Art. 2, para. 5, Art. 17, para. 2, and Art. 19) or by implication from the constituent instrument or from another undertaking on the part of the member States concerned, the existence and extent of such an obligation being dependent upon an interpretation of the constituent instrument of the organization and the intention of its drafters. But in practice, this obligation will almost always be easily established by implication, and would ultimately be dictated by reasons of functional necessity to the effect that non-payment of contribution would undermine, or preclude, the fulfilment of the organization's purposes.

vesting the organization with the necessary resources for the accomplishment of its objectives.

1.3 *The Elements of Legal Status*

1.3.1 Introduction

In this section more specific consideration will be given to some of the basic aspects of the legal status properly so-called of international organizations. The term legal status has a narrower meaning than 'legal position.' 'Legal *position*' covers an organization's legal status, its privileges and immunities, and its responsibility, in other words an organization's rights and duties, whereas 'legal *status*' is restricted to the questions of the legal personality, capacity and powers of international organizations.[71]

At the outset, we note the words of caution expressed by such eminent international lawyers as Ago, Gros, Lachs and Rosenne,[72] who have all doubted the wisdom of starting with a detailed study of the status of international organizations. In the words of Rosenne, notions such as international legal personality are merely "convenient academic expressions for conveying certain ideas."[73] While we admit that personality is "more in the nature of a concept arrived at by scientific observation,"[74] the study of the legal status of international organizations, which includes more than just 'personality' issues, has nevertheless considerable merit and can be useful for the analysis of legal principles, in particular organizational immunities, provided one takes the following, restrictive approach. In studying some of the aspects of the fundamental question of the legal status of international organizations, several goals can be met.

---

71 *See generally* Restatement (Third) § 223, at 140–143. This distinction is justified by the records of the ILC, which reveal that in its study of the relations between States and international organizations, a distinction was made between the personality and privileges and immunities, on the one hand, and other aspects such as the responsibility of international organizations, on the other. See El-Erian, in [1963] 1 Y.B. Int'l L. Comm'n 298, para. 110, UN Doc. A/CN.4/SER.A/1963; UN Doc. A/CN.4/L.103, para. 1 (Working Paper).

72 *See* [1963] 1 Y.B. Int'l L. Comm'n 300, para. 5 (Rosenne), 302, para. 28 (Ago), 303, para. 35 (Lachs), and 305, para. 65 (Gros), UN Doc. A/CN.4/SER.A/1963.

73 *See* Rosenne, in [1963] 1 Y.B. Int'l L. Comm'n 300, para. 5, UN Doc. A/CN.4/SER.A/1963; *id.*, in 55 *Annuaire* 214, 330 (1973); *but see* Al-Baharna, in [1987] 1 Y.B. Int'l L. Comm'n 202, para. 32, UN Doc. A/CN.4/SER.A/1987. Thus, in our case Rosenne would rather focus on the immunity aspect, not on the international organization/legal status aspect, and take the phenomenon of the international organization for granted; *see also* SCHERMERS, at 1029, para. 1565 (referring to the "doctrinal debate concerning the basis of international legal personality of international organizations").

74 *See* Ago, in [1963] 1 Y.B. Int'l L. Comm'n 302, para. 28, UN Doc. A/CN.4/SER.A/1963.

First, an examination of the legal status will create a solid *foundation* upon which to build the subsequent parts of our analysis, because the legal status of an international organization is a starting-point whenever we are concerned with rights and duties of an organization, immunities and responsibility issues included.[75]

Second, a study of the notion of the legal status of international organizations before examining their immunities will reveal a *relationship* in the light of the functional necessity concept in its application to the legal position of international organizations. The concept of functional necessity provides a means for explaining and defining both the basis and the extent of an organization's legal status and immunities.[76] A closer examination of the legal status will identify the object or addressee of functional necessity. In this way, one can determine who is entitled in law, and to what extent, to the enjoyment of certain organizational immunities.

Having said this, it should be made clear that it is not the aim of the present study "to establish whether, to what extent and which intergovernmental organizations have the capacity to perform 'sovereign' or international acts and are subjects of international law, or international persons."[77] Nor does this chapter intend to recapitulate the ensemble of principles governing the legal status of international organizations in contemporary international law or to question the validity of the sources of this status that have developed in international law and legal doctrine. Instead, the purpose of the present chapter is to provide an *additional*, alternative viewpoint of legal status by focusing on certain aspects which represent the essence of the functional necessity concept. The essential point is to determine the general status of the entities studied, assessed in the light of their functions and purposes, and to establish accordingly a legal basis on which to build a system of privileges and immunities applicable generally to international organizations.[78] Thus, status is viewed here in terms of the specific purposes, functions and tools with which an organization is vested. In order to avoid getting entangled in theoretical and doctrinal controversy on the question of the legal status of intergovernmental organizations, its study will be confined to the development of a functional typology. It suffices to refer to

75 *See, e.g.*, Calero Rodrigues, in [1985] 1 Y.B. Int'l L. Comm'n 292, para. 25, UN Doc. A/CN.4/SER.A/1985.

76 As Reuter has stated, "[t]he status and work of international organisations depends on their 'functions.'" REUTER, INSTITUTIONS, at 230.

77 *See* Seyersted, Personality, at 1.

78 *See* Bartos, in [1963] 1 Y.B. Int'l L. Comm'n 306, para. 71, UN Doc. A/CN.4/SER.A/1963.

some of the aspects of legal *status* as illustrative examples of the fundamental impact of functional necessity on the broader question of the legal *position* of international organizations. To that end, the question of the legal status will be studied from the angle of functional necessity only.[79] While keeping in mind these restrictions, it will be logical to deal first with the legal status of intergovernmental organizations, as a first step, and then to move on to the question of their immunities.[80] This is the approach that was favored by a number of members within the ILC who were of the opinion that an initial study of certain aspects of legal status was best suited to a systematic and logical treatment of the subject.[81]

1.3.2 A Division into Three Elements

Before we enter into a discussion of the question of privileges and immunities, in Step Two, some brief preliminary consideration of an introductory character should be given to the separate questions of the legal personality, capacity and competence (powers) of intergovernmental organizations.

The study of the legal status of international organizations falls within three different categories of law:

(1) general international law;
(2) the domestic laws of States;
(3) the internal law of the international organization concerned.[82]

The first category deals with the questions of the international personality and international capacities of an organization. The private law personality and capacities of the organization is the subject-matter of the second

79 This approach avoids general considerations by focusing instead on more concrete points. *See* Lachs, in [1963] 1 Y.B. Int'l L. Comm'n 303, para. 35, UN Doc. A/CN.4/SER.A/1963.

80 *See, e.g.*, Jagota, in [1985] 1 Y.B. Int'l L. Comm'n 299, para. 39, UN Doc. A/CN.4/SER.A/1985. According to Koroma, to exclude the problem of the legal personality and capacity of international organizations and concentrate instead on their privileges and immunities would be an over-simplification of the issues at stake. *See* [1987] 1 Y.B. Int'l L. Comm'n 204, para. 56, UN Doc. A/CN.4/SER.A/1987; *see also* JENKS, at xxxviii.

81 *See* [1967] 2 Y.B. Int'l L. Comm'n 138, para. 28, UN Doc. A/CN.4/SER.A/1967/Add. 1, containing a summary of the ILC's discussions at its fifteenth and sixteenth sessions.

82 *See* Díaz González, in [1985] 1 Y.B. Int'l L. Comm'n 284, para. 14, UN Doc. A/CN.4/SER.A/1985, calling it the law applicable by the organization, as opposed to that applicable *to* it represented by the first two categories. It should be pointed out that the 'internal law' of the international organizations is 'international law' hierarchically on a par with the 'international law' governing the legal status of such entities, *see* Rosenne, in 55 *Annuaire* 214, 334 (1973). *See also* H.J. Hahn, *Euratom: The Conception of an International Personality*, 71 Harv. L.R. 1001, 1010–1011 (1958)[hereinafter: Hahn].

category. The fundamental importance of these two notions was described by one ILC member as follows:

> When States established an international organization, they did so for the purpose of jointly carrying out a particular activity at the international level; without legal personality and capacity, an organization would be unable to carry out the activities for which it had been set up. If it was denied legal personality, it would be stillborn.[83]

The third category concerns the competence of the organization to perform certain acts. These different categories will be discussed separately below, from which an overall status picture will emerge, as applied to the functional necessity concept. Studying an organization's legal personality, capacity and competence, at the different levels of international law, domestic law and the law of international organizations, serves to identify the beneficiary of immunities, which will prove of material importance when we address the issues of the nature and scope of these immunities in Steps Two and Three of our analysis.

1.3.2.1 *The* First *Element: Personality*

1.3.2.1.1 Introduction

The personality aspect of an organization's legal status involves two essentially distinct[84] and separate levels of international and domestic law.

(i) *Legal Personality under International Law*

The first attribute of intergovernmental organizations is international personality, or legal personality under public international law. This is a *static* notion which describes a quality[85] inherent to the entity concerned, i.e., what the entity *is*.[86] As such it entails a recognition of the fact that

83 *See* Balanda, in [1985] 1 Y.B. Int'l L. Comm'n 294, para. 47, UN Doc. A/CN.4/SER.A/1985.

84 *See* Hahn, at 1046; *contra* De Luna, in [1963] 1 Y.B. Int'l L. Comm'n 301, para. 16, UN Doc. A/CN.4/SER.A/1963.

85 This term is used in [1963] 2 Y.B. Int'l L. Comm'n 167, para. 60, UN Doc. A/CN.4/SER.A/1963.

86 In German: '*Rechtspersönlichkeit.*' *See* Beier, F.-K., Hartel, K. & Schricker, G., eds., Europäisches Patentübereinkommen. Münchner Gemeinschaftskommentar, Art. 5, at 17 (1984)[hereinafter: BEIER *et al.*]. For a general exposition of international legal personality, see SCHERMERS, at 1026–1036, paras. 1562–1571; I. Seidl-Hohenveldern, *The Legal Personality of International and Supranational Organizations*, 21 R.E.D.I. 35, 35–72 (1965)[hereinafter: Seidl-Hohenveldern, Personality]; Q. Wright, *The Jural Personality of the United Nations*, 43 AJIL 509 (1949)[hereinafter: Wright]; Yasseen, at 43; Hahn, at 1044.

intergovernmental organizations are members of the family of subjects of international law.[87]

Prior to the establishment of international organizations, States had been the only subjects of international law recognized as having full international personality. There has in the past been divergence of opinion on whether entities other than States, such as individuals and international organizations, can be regarded as possessing full personality.[88] Schermers has explained that this relates back to the archontocratic system of international law, with its emphasis on governance by the national governments in which an international organization can be no more than a representative acting on behalf of a group of States, rather than on a par with States. According to the same authority, however, this view has become obsolete and no longer corresponds with actual developments in international (institutional) law.[89] For the purposes of our study, we will therefore adhere to a more pragmatic school of thought, which reflects the inherently static character of the international personality of international organizations and which takes the *concrete exercise* of, or at least the potential ability to exercise, certain rights and the fulfilment of certain obligations as the basis for concluding that an international organization has an international personality distinct from that of its member States.[90] Or, to put it in another way,

---

87 As Sir Elihu Lauterpacht has explained, "in itself the attribution of personality to an entity means nothing. 'Personality' — the quality of being a 'person' — only possesses significance in terms of a specific system of law. ... In fact, there is no definition of personality in international law which is sufficiently comprehensive to apply in some constructive or realistic way to all the different types of entity which operate in the international field." Lauterpacht, Development, at 403. *See*, generally, J.E. Nijman, The Concept of International Legal Personality: An Inquiry into the History and Theory of International Law (2004).

88 *See* C.W. Jenks, *The Legal Personality of International Organizations*, 22 BYBIL 267, 267 (1945)[hereinafter; Jenks, Personality]; *see also* SCHERMERS, at 1026–1028, paras. 1562–1564; G. Weissberg, The International Status of the United Nations 1–9 (1961) [hereinafter: WEISSBERG]. In any event, it is important to keep in mind, as the International Court of Justice has stated, that "[t]he subjects of law in any legal system are not necessarily identical in their nature or in the extent of their rights, and their nature depends upon the needs of the community." 1949 ICJ Rep. 174, 178.

89 *See* SCHERMERS, at 1026–1027, paras. 1562–1563.

90 *See* Ago, in [1963] 1 Y.B. Int'l L. Comm'n 302, para. 28, UN Doc. A/CN.4/SER.A/1963; *see also* Bartos, *id.* at 305, para. 69, who was "more concerned with *practice* than with the prevailing theory in international law. And *practice* showed that international organizations were living entities with an influence of their own." (emphasis added); H. Lauterpacht, International Law and Human Rights 12 (1950)("[i]n each particular case the question whether ... a body is a subject of international law must be answered in a pragmatic manner by reference to actual experience and to the reason of the law as distinguished from a preconceived notion as to who can be subjects of international

as Seyersted has advocated, "it is not the provisions of the constitution or the intention of its framers which establish the international personality of a State or an intergovernmental organization, but the *objective fact* of its *existence*."(emphasis added)[91] Thus, the crucial factor is not *how* international organizations have been established, but *that they exist*.[92] The existence of a 'constitution' is not a necessary requirement: in fact, any document may constitute a constituent instrument, whether it is a treaty or a mere resolution.[93] The absence of a constituent instrument does not prevent an international organization from having international personality, if we accept as did Seyersted that the necessary and sufficient characteristics of international personality are: (1) the existence of international organs (i.e., organs established by two or more sovereign communities) which are not all subject to the authority of any other organized community (but only to that of the participating communities acting jointly through their representatives on such organs) which perform 'sovereign' and/or international acts in their own name; and (2) which are not authorized by all their acts to assume obligations (merely) on behalf of the several participating communities.[94] If these two criteria are satisfied,[95] and they can be determined from the factual existence and the operation in practice of the international organization concerned, the organization is an international person, with all the consequences which that characterization entails.[96]

---

law."). This has certain ramifications on the level of the legal capacity of international organizations, as will be demonstrated below.

91 Seyersted, Personality, at 39–40. *See also* F.L. Bordin, *The Quest for International Legal Status: On Finn Seyersted and the Challenges of Theorizing International Organizations Law*, 34(1) EJIL 169–194 (2023).

92 Seyersted, Personality, at 40.

93 *Id.*, at 43.

94 *Id.*, at 40–41, 53. Seyersted uses the word 'sovereign' as meaning "legally independent (i.e., not subject to the jurisdiction) of any other organized community except the participating physical or legal persons acting jointly through the organs of the Organization." *Id.*, at 42.

95 Notice incidentally that if these criteria are *not* met, Seyersted accepts that an international organization "can be a subject of international law only if and to the extent that States have conferred international functions upon it, and only in relation to these States and to States which have expressly or by implication recognized these functions." *Id.* at 50; *but see*, on the latter point, Koroma, in [1987] 1 Y.B. Int'l L. Comm'n 205, para. 58, UN Doc. A/CN.4/SER.A/1987, according to whom the opinion of the ICJ in the *Reparation case* "constituted the repudiation of a certain form of neo-positivism which tended to make the existence of the international personality of an international organization dependent on recognition of States."

96 Schermers can be said to be another prominent advocate of this school of thought, where he states that a subject of international law is every person who is bound by international law, covering all persons *who operate* independently in the international

However, since personality is a static notion, this general characterization does not provide any information regarding the modalities of an organization's status.[97] These modalities will emerge from an examination of the notions of legal capacity and competence, seen in the light of considerations of functional necessity. At the level of personality, functional necessity dictates that an organization should be clothed with such legal status as to enable it to exercise its functions.[98] Thus, to study the question of personality from a functional standpoint is to examine an organization's specific functions and an organization's personality is a *functional* personality.[99] As Pellet has stated, the legal personality of international organizations must necessarily be of a function order, such as to justify, wholly but exclusively, the powers they need in order to fulfill their purposes.[100] While it may be true that considerations of functional necessity limit an organization's

---

field. SCHERMERS, at 1027, para. 1563. *See also* ILC Special Rapporteur Díaz González, in [1985] 2 Y.B. Int'l L. Comm'n 107, para. 31, UN Doc. A/CN.4/SER.A/1985/Add. 1 (Part 1) ("Once an international organization has been established by the will of States, that body ... acts and operates in the international community with its own personality."). Seyersted has provided ample evidence for his proposition that it is generally accepted that intergovernmental organizations in practice perform international acts even when these have not been authorized in their constituent instruments, pointing in support to every organization's exclusive jurisdiction over their organs, capacity to conclude treaties, active and passive *jus legationis*, convocation of and participation in international conferences, membership of other organizations, active and passive responsibility, procedural capacity, and such other facts as being depositories of international conventions. Seyersted, Personality, at 6–19.

97 *See* ILC Special Rapporteur Díaz González, who has said that simply to affirm that international organizations are legal persons is not sufficient to define the legal régime governing them: [1985] 1 Y.B. Int'l L. Comm'n 286, para. 23, UN Doc. A/CN.4/SER.A/1985; Lauterpacht, Development, at 403. Or, as Reuter has pointed out, "le recours à 'la personnalité internationale' est incapable de servir utilement à définir les compétences des Organisations en matière de relations extérieurs." 55 *Annuaire* 214, 324 (1973).

98 *See* Koroma, in [1987] 1 Y.B. Int'l L. Comm'n 205, para. 58, UN Doc. A/CN.4/SER.A/1987; Hahn, at 1043.

99 *See* Illueca, in [1983] 1 Y.B. Int'l L. Comm'n 247, para. 45, UN Doc. A/CN.4/SER.A/1983; U.A. Weber & A. Reinisch, *In the Shadow of Waite and Kennedy – The Jurisdictional Immunity of International Organizations, the Individual's Right of Access to the Courts and Administrative Tribunals as Alternative Means of Dispute Settlement*, 1(1) IOLR 59, 63 (2004)(noting that "[a]s opposed to states, the international legal personality of international organizations is generally considered to be functionally limited" and "international organizations enjoy legal personality only to the extent required to perform their functions," which means that "[i]n a legal sense they are unable to act beyond their functional personality").

100 *See* [1990] 1 Y.B. Int'l L. Comm'n 215, para. 19, UN Doc. A/CN.4/SER.A/1990.

capacities or even *competence* to perform certain acts, that does not change the fact that it is a *subject* of international law.[101]

The question of the international personality of intergovernmental organizations has been authoritatively addressed by the International Court of Justice in one of its landmark advisory opinions, which in a sense has attained the status of judicial legislation, or at least the persuasive authority of judicial decision, on this particular issue.[102] The General Assembly of the United Nations, in accordance with its resolution 258(III) of 3 December 1948,[103] consulted the principal judicial organ of the UN on the question whether the UN, as an international organization, has the capacity to bring

101 It is a separate question whether the international personality of an organization is valid also *vis-à-vis non-member States ipso facto* without recognition, *i.e.*, the question of opposability or *objective* international personality. With respect to the United Nations, the ICJ has accepted its international personality to be effective also against non-member States, regardless of any recognition by them of this organization, reasoning that "fifty States, representing the vast majority of the international community, had the power, in conformity with international law, to bring into being an entity possessing objective international personality, and not merely personality recognized by them alone." 1949 ICJ Rep. 174, 185. The ICJ thus based the objective personality of the UN on the pre-eminence of the Charter and the size of its membership. For an extensive exposé on objective personality see F. Seyersted, *Is the International Personality of Intergovernmental Organizations valid vis-à-vis non-Members?*, 4 Indian J. Int'l L. 233 (1964). *See also* I. Seidl-Hohenveldern, Corporations In and Under International Law 86–88 (1987)[hereinafter: SEIDL-HOHENVELDERN, CORPORATIONS]. The advantage of Seyersted's views on legal personality, emphasizing an organization's *concrete exercise* as a prime criterion instead of that of the existence and interpretation of a constituent instrument, is that they help to avoid the problems created by the maxim *res inter alios acta* according to which a third State may disregard any treaty whereby other States have established an international organization. On the legal personality of international organizations in the law of non-member States see SCHERMERS, at 1069–1070, para. 1598.

102 It should be noted that there has been some discussion on the applicability of the views expressed by the Court in its advisory opinions on this subject to international organizations other than the United Nations: *see, e.g.*, Reuter's reservations in [1974] 2 Y.B. Int'l L. Comm'n 149, sub (17)–(18), UN Doc. A/CN.4/SER.A/1974/Add. 1 (Part 1). Díaz González, in his *Second Report, reprinted in* [1985] 2 Y.B. Int'l L. Comm'n 112, para. 70, UN Doc. A/CN.4/SER.A/1985/Add. 1 (Part 1), made the following apt remarks: "Although the Court was referring to the United Nations, the solution recommended in the case of that Organization now extends to all international (intergovernmental) organizations, subject of course to the limitations imposed by the mission and functions of each organization. This extension, accepted in a general form by doctrine, is in accordance with reality, since all international (intergovernmental) organizations are legal persons to which a specific mission is entrusted; and while that mission may differ in importance for each of them, it is identical in so far as it concerns their international character."

103 *See* UN Doc. A/810 (1948), at 172.

an international claim against a State to obtain reparation in respect of the damage caused by injury to an agent of the organization suffered in the course of the performance of his duties.[104]

The Court, in its advisory opinion on *Reparation for Injuries Suffered in the Service of the United Nations* delivered on 11 April 1949,[105] first determined that this question concerning the procedural capacity of the United Nations was tantamount to asking whether the organization has international personality, on which the actual terms of the UN Charter are silent. In a unanimous ruling, the Court answered this question in the affirmative. It ruled that, to say that an international organization possesses personality means that "it is a subject of international law and capable of possessing international rights and duties, and that it has capacity to maintain its rights by bringing international claims."[106] The Court linked the notion of personality to functional necessity, in other words to an organization's purposes and functions, by its statement that "to achieve these ends the attribution of international personality is indispensable."[107] The Court stressed that one element in its definition of personality, namely, the capability of possessing international rights and duties, depends upon the organization's purposes and functions.[108] In accepting the international personality of the United Nations, the Court reasoned:

> [the United Nations] was intended to exercise and enjoy, and is in fact exercising and enjoying, functions and rights, which can only be explained on the basis of the possession of a large measure of international personality and the capacity to operate upon an international plane. It is at present the supreme type of international organization, and it could not carry out the intentions of its founders if it was devoid of international personality.[109]

---

104 *See Repertory of United Nations Practice*, Vol. V, at 334–337, paras. 40–49, UN Sales No. 1955.V.2 (Vol. V, 1955).

105 1949 ICJ Rep. 174. For an earlier precedent, see *Interpretation of the Greco-Turkish Agreement of December 1st, 1926*, 1928 PCIJ (ser. B) No. 16, at 4 (Aug. 28), discussed in Lauterpacht, Development, at 404. *See also id.* at 406–413.

106 1949 ICJ Rep. 174, 179. The Court stated also that "if the Organization is recognized as having that [international] personality, it is an entity capable of availing itself of obligations incumbent upon its Members." *Id.*, at 178.

107 Id., at 178. *See also* WEISSBERG, at 177–178 ("Personality was thus coupled with the functional theory and placed in its proper perspective.").

108 *See* 1949 ICJ Rep. 174, 180.

109 *Id.*, at 179. The Court placed particular emphasis on the important political purposes of the United Nations, namely the maintenance of international peace and security. For an analysis of the basis, connotation and development of the international legal

In connection with its conclusion that the UN is an international person, the Court sought at the same time to avoid any appearance of the UN being a super-State.[110] It follows from the Court's definition of international personality, and in particular its suggested link to the possible possession of rights and duties which are dependent upon the organization's purposes and functions, that, by way of an example, the fact that international organizations by nature do not enjoy rights such as sovereign ownership over the territory in which their headquarters are situated, must necessarily mean that the extent to which they enjoy rights is different than that of States, who do possess full sovereign rights over their territories. The Court's general statement is recalled here: "The subjects of law in any legal system are not identical in their nature or in the extent of their rights."[111]

It is interesting to note that the Court based its conclusion that the UN is an international person in part on the immunity régime applicable to the UN, as laid down in the *Convention on the Privileges and Immunities of the United Nations* of 1946,[112] by stating that "[i]t is difficult to see how such a convention could operate except upon the international plane and as between parties possessing international personality."[113]

personality of the United Nations, see WEISSBERG, at 10–32. Some commentators have placed an emphasis on rights over functions in determining international legal personality. *See*, e.g., Fry, at 224 (positing that "the ICJ's opinion has more to do with state parties bestowing functions and *rights* on the international institution for it to have international legal personality, rather than functions alone" and that "[f]ocusing on this function-related language without its rights-related context is to pervert the doctrine of functional necessity as the basis for an international organization's powers"). According to Fry, the ICJ's qualifying reference to "a large measure of" international legal personality "reflects no more than the remains of the state-dominant theory from the Cold War (and prior), and the somewhat strange status that was then given to international organizations." *Id.*, at 234.

110 The Court stated as follows: "That is not the same thing as saying that it is a State, which it certainly is not, or that its legal personality and rights and duties are the same as those of a State. Still less is it the same thing as saying that it is a 'super-State', whatever that expression may mean." 1949 ICJ Rep. 174, 179.

111 *Id.*, at 178. On the difference between States and international organizations in particular, the Court stated as follows: "Whereas a State possesses the totality of international rights and duties recognized by international law, the rights and duties of an entity such as the Organization must depend upon its purposes and functions ...." *Id.*, at 180.

112 Adopted by the General Assembly on 13 Feb. 1946, 1 U.N.T.S. 15.

113 1949 ICJ Rep. 174, 179; *see also* Chr. Dominicé, *L'immunité de juridiction et d'exécution des organisations internationales*, 187 RdC 145, 162–164 (1984 IV)[hereinafter: Dominicé, L'immunité]; Reuter, in [1972] 2 Y.B. Int'l L. Comm'n 175, para. 14, UN Doc. A/CN.4/SER.A/1972/Add. 1 (Part 1).

International personality thus coincides with an entity being a subject in a certain field of law, in this case public international law. This fact is now beyond any doubt.[114] From this quality stem a series of rights on the international level, which will be considered below. On the other hand, international personality also entails certain duties, such as responsibility under international law (discussed elsewhere in this book). In sum, these rights and duties can be seen as an expression of the existence of legal personality under public international law.[115] The possession of international personality reflects the elements which international organizations have in common, in particular that of having an identity distinct from that of the member States[116] and the capacity to enter into legal relations on the international plane.

Explicit acknowledgement of the possession of international personality is not necessary, at least not for the organization's member States and third

---

114 *See* Schermers, Organizations, at 69, para. 10, and 74, para. 32; Seidl-Hohenveldern, Responsibility, 424; D. Hug, Die Rechtsstellung der in der Schweiz Niedergelassenen Internationalen Organisationen 62 and n.330 (giving further references)(1984)[hereinafter: HUG]; A. Reinisch, First report on the settlement of international disputes to which international organizations are parties, pp. 29–32, International Law Commission, Seventy-fourth session, UN Doc. A/CN.4/756 (2023). *See* already Sir Hersch Lauterpacht, in [1953] 2 Y.B. Int'l L. Comm'n 100, UN Doc. A/CN.4/SER.A/1953/Add. 1.

115 *See* Sucharitkul, in [1985] 1 Y.B. Int'l L. Comm'n 287, para. 31, UN Doc. A/CN.4/SER.A/1985; Hahn, at 1045, 1047. Conversely, the lack of proof of the exercise of certain rights by an entity has been held by the International Court of Justice to indicate that the entity concerned does *not* have international legal personality and capacity. *See Judgment No. 2867 of the Administrative Tribunal of the International Labour Organization upon a complaint filed against the International Fund for Agricultural Development*, Advisory Opinion, 2012 ICJ Rep. 10, at 34, para. 57 (noting that the Global Mechanism "is not given any express powers of contracting or entering into any agreement by the Convention nor by a headquarters agreement" and "the record before the Court does not include any instances of it entering into contracts or agreements") and 36, para. 61 ("the Global Mechanism had no power and has not purported to exercise any power to enter into contracts, agreements or 'arrangements', internationally and nationally"). As one commentator has pointed out, "one problem with the test articulated in *Global Mechanism* is that it is not helpful to pose the question in respect of an entity that has never concluded an agreement before," in other words, in situations where there is no available evidence from practice notwithstanding indications in the entity's constituent instrument that it has the legal capacity to enter into agreements and arrangements with other entities in principle. R.S.J. Martha, The Financial Obligation in International Law 195 (2015).

116 *See* Ushakov, in [1983] 1 Y.B. Int'l L. Comm'n 246, para. 37, UN Doc. A/CN.4/SER.A/1983.

States that have entered into relations with or have otherwise implicitly recognized the organization concerned,[117] since it is based on the concrete exercise of acts and the objective fact of its existence. In any event, it is rarely found in treaty law.[118] The Charter of the United Nations does not expressly provide for the international legal personality of that organization. This question was deliberately omitted. Committee IV/2 of the United Nations Conference on International Organization, held at San Francisco in 1945, considered it superfluous to make the international personality of the United Nations the subject of a text, because it wanted to avoid any appearance of the organization being a "super-State." It was decided instead that the international personality of the United Nations "will be determined implicitly from the provisions of the Charter taken as a whole."[119] In contrast to the United Nations, the constituent instrument of the European Union

117 *See Reparation* Opinion, 1949 ICJ Rep. 172, 178 (noting that "if the Organization is recognized as having that personality, it is an entity capable of availing itself of obligations incumbent upon its Members"). *See also* Seidl-Hohenveldern, Responsibility, at 424 n.33; Hahn, at 1048–1049; R.S.J. Martha, C. Grafton & S. Bailey, The Legal Foundations of INTERPOL ch. 3, s. 4 (2020). Fry goes one step further, positing that "objectivity of the international legal personality holds true for all states regardless of their membership in the international organization and that objectivity does not depend on non-members' consent or recognition." Fry, at 233. As regards the legal personality of the North Atlantic Treaty Organization (NATO), see D. Nauta, The International Responsibility of NATO and Its Personnel during Military Operations (2018); D. Grütters, *NATO, International Organizations and Functional Immunity*, 13(2) IOLR 211 (2016). For an example of a national court rejecting a claim of an international organization to "objective" international personality in a situation where the country of the forum was not a member of the organization, see *ECOWAS v. BCCI*, Cour d'Appèl, Paris, judgment of 13 Jan. 1993, 113 ILR 473 (1993).

118 The *Convention on the Privileges and Immunities of the United Nations* of 1946 expressly provides in Article I, Section 1, that "[t]he United Nations shall possess juridical personality," Section 3 of the *Convention on the Privileges and Immunities of the Specialized Agencies* of 1947 containing similar wording. For a compilation of treaty provisions concerning the legal status of international organizations, see Parts II of UN Docs. ST/LEG/SER.B/10 (1959)(relating to international organizations in general and the United Nations in particular) and ST/LEG.SER.B/11 (1961)(relating to the specialized agencies and certain other organizations). *See also* K. Chen, *The Legal Status, Privileges and Immunities of the Specialized Agencies*, 42 AJIL 900, 901 (1945)[hereinafter: Chen]; SCHERMERS, at 1028, para. 1565; Lauterpacht, Development, at 403; WHITEMAN, 13 DIGEST, at 2.

119 13 U.N.C.I.O. Doc. 803, IV/2/A/7 (1945), at 817; *see also* EGGER, at 114. The absence of any explicit provisions on international legal personality in the UN Charter also supports views such as the one advocated by Seyersted that personality of international organizations should follow from the objective fact of their existence.

expressly confirms that organization's legal personality through a succinct statement: "The Union shall have legal personality."[120] The international legal personality of the Association of Southeast Asian Nations (ASEAN), a political and economic union comprising 10 Southeast Asian countries and established in 1967, was not formally conferred until 2007, when the ASEAN Charter was adopted.[121]

(ii) *Legal Personality under Domestic Law*

The legal personality of intergovernmental organizations also operates at the domestic or national level.[122] This aspect of the personality of international organizations is concerned with the recognition of the status of an international organization within the legal system of the State with whom the organization maintains relations or in whose territory it operates. The possession of legal personality in domestic law enables international organizations to act as any other legal person within the domestic legal system.[123] Most important, it is "an essential attribute of the possessor of privileges and immunities."[124]

---

120 *See* Art. 47 (46A), Treaty of Lisbon amending the Treaty on European Union and the Treaty establishing the European Community, signed at Lisbon on 13 Dec. 2007, entry into force on 1 Dec. 2009, Official Journal of the European Union, 17.12.20007, No. C 306. Prior to the adoption of this instrument, the organization was not expressly acknowledged to have legal personality. *See* SCHERMERS, at 1033–1034, para. 1569; R.A. Wessel, *Immunities of the European Union*, 10 IOLR 395 (2013); J. Klabbers, *Presumptive Personality: The European Union in International Law*, in International Law Aspects of the European Union 231–253 (M. Koskenniemi ed. 1998). As Schermers has explained, "[a]lthough not specified, this provision covers both international legal personality and legal personality within the domestic legal orders of the member states" of the European Union. SCHERMERS, at 1034.

121 *See* Art. 3, Charter of the Association of Southeast Nations, done in Singapore on 20 Nov. 2007, entry into force 15 Dec. 2008 ("ASEAN, as an inter-governmental organisation, is hereby conferred legal personality"). *See also* H.D. Phan, *The Association of Southeast Asian Nations: International Legal Personality and Its Treaty-Making Power*, 13(2) IOLR 273 (2016).

122 The ICJ, in the *Reparation* case, referred to the domestic aspect of an organization's functioning, when it explained that, to say that an international organization is an international person "does not even imply that all its rights and duties must be upon the international plane, any more than all the rights and duties of a State must be upon that plane." 1949 ICJ Rep. 174, 179.

123 *See* SCHERMERS, at 1065 *et seq.*, para. 1591 *et seq.*; Seidl-Hohenveldern, Personality, at 63.

124 Arangio-Ruiz, in [1985] 1 Y.B. Int'l L. Comm'n 291, para. 17, UN Doc. A/CN.4/SER.A/1985.

Domestic legal personality is sometimes expressly provided for in the constituent instrument of international organizations, in other international agreements, or in the laws of the national legal order concerned.[125] Such provisions may be termed 'enabling'[126] or 'clarifying' clauses. But even without such explicit provisions in international agreements or in domestic legislation, legal personality under domestic law should follow by implication from the existence of the organization.[127] If such personality were not implied under domestic law this would mean that the organization would depend, for the carrying out of its activities, upon the common action of all the member States together. This would clearly impede the unhampered exercise of functions and rights, as dictated by considerations of functional necessity.[128]

National courts have accepted in practice the legal personality of international organizations even in the absence of express provisions to that effect.[129] They have derived it from the fact that the organization concerned was recognized as having *international* personality,[130] or from express provisions in the constituent instrument of the organization granting it the capacity to perform certain acts.[131] As Schermers has pointed out, legal

125 For a compilation of legislative texts of over thirty States, see Parts I of UN Docs. ST/LEG/SER.B/10 (1959) & ST/LEG/SER.B/11 (1961).

126 This word is used in *Repertory of United Nations Practice*, Vol. V, at 326, para. 5, UN Sales No. 1955.V.2 (Vol. V, 1955).

127 According to Seidl-Hohenveldern, Responsibility, at 424 n.36, "such implication appears to result almost inevitably from the *very existence* of any organization."(emphasis added); *see also* Yasseen, at 54; Dominicé, L'immunité, at 165–166. Reuter accepts as a result of the fact that international organizations have international personality that "they have the right to obtain from the national law of each State the legal status appropriate to the proper exercise of their functions inside each country." Reuter, Institutions, at 232. Seidl-Hohenveldern has suggested "to regard the treaty provisions as the national law of the organization. An international organization will thus exist in the domestic law of member and non-member States alike as a *societé sans loi nationale*."(emphasis added). Seidl-Hohenveldern, Corporations, at 108.

128 As the ICJ stated in the *Reparation* case: "The functions of the Organization are of such a character that they could not be effectively discharged if they involved the concurrent action, ..., of fifty-eight or more Foreign Offices ...." 1949 ICJ Rep. 174, 180. *See also* Seidl-Hohenveldern, Personality, at 63.

129 *See* SCHERMERS, at 1069, para. 1598; *see also* [1967] 2 Y.B. Int'l L. Comm'n 299–302, UN Doc. A/CN.4/SER.A/1967.

130 *See, e.g.*, *Branno v. Ministry of War*, Italian Court of Cassation, Decision of 14 June 1954, 1955 ILR 756, *Giurisprudenza Italiana*, 1954, I, at 904, *cited in* SCHERMERS, at 1068, para. 1595.

131 For an example of Dutch case law, see *U.N.R.R.A. v. Daan, Hoge Raad*, Decision of 19 May 1950, NJ 1951, 150, 1949 ILR 337 (case 114) *cited in* SCHERMERS, at 1068, para.

personality in the legal order of member and non-member States in practice has always been granted on one or two grounds:

(1) The State *recognizes* the international personality of the organization and legal personality under domestic law follows from personality under public international law; or
(2) The organization has been *lawfully established* by foreign States and according to the rules of *private international law* legal personality acquired abroad is accepted.[132]

1.3.2.2 *The* Second *Element: Capacity*

1.3.2.2.1 Introduction

The notion of legal capacity describes what the entity is potentially entitled to *do*.[133] This may be called the operational or dynamic aspect of legal status. The existence of legal capacity confirms that an international organization *can perform* a potential scale of international acts as an international person. As will be demonstrated below, it is a *competence* issue *which specific* acts an individual international organization can actually perform within the sphere of the potential capacities that international organizations have. In this section we are merely concerned with identifying the scale of acts which an international organization may perform at different levels of the legal order.

(i) *Legal Capacity under International Law*

Under public international law, an international organization in general has certain capacities to act at the international level. As such may be mentioned the capacity to bring international claims, or international procedural capacity,[134] treaty-making capacity, the right to establish

---

1595. For an example of the non-recognition of the legal personality of an international organization in a national legal order, *see id.* at 1068–1069, para. 1596.

132 *See* SCHERMERS, at 1069, para. 1598, referring to Art. 1 of the Hague Convention on the Recognition of the Legal Personality of Foreign Corporations, Associations and Foundations of 1 June 1956, Trb. 1956, No.131; *see also* the remarks by Sinclair, in [1985] 1 Y.B. Int'l L. Comm'n 289, para. 3, UN Doc. A/CN.4/SER.A/1985; F. Seyersted, *Is the International Personality of Intergovernmental Organizations Valid vis-à-vis Non-Members?*, 4 Indian J. Int'l L. 233 (1964).

133 In German: *Rechtsfähigkeit. See* BEIER *et al.*, Art. 5, at 17.

134 An example of this international procedural capacity is the right to request an advisory opinion of the International Court of Justice, which must, however, be explicit. In addition to the United Nations (General Assembly, Security Council, Economic and Social Council, Trusteeship Council, Interim Committee of the General Assembly,), the following UN specialized agencies are at present authorized to request advisory opinions of the Court on legal questions: ILO, FAO, UNESCO, ICAO, WHO, IBRD, IFC,

diplomatic relations, and the right to recognize other subjects of international law.[135]

With respect to the *capacity to bring international claims*, it is recalled that the International Court of Justice, in its advisory opinion of 1949, accepted that the UN had such capacity "when necessitated by the discharge of its functions," thereby directly linking this capacity to functional necessity and recognizing that the capacities of an international organization are not confined to those specified in any treaty provisions.[136] The Court reasoned that in discharging its functions in the service of the maintenance of

---

IDA, IMF, ITU, WMO, IMO, WIPO, IFAD, UNIDO, and also IAEA. Other international organizations also may be authorized to request an advisory opinion of the ICJ based on a separate instrument providing for this right. The international instruments that make provision for the advisory jurisdiction of the Court are listed in the annual volumes of the *ICJ Yearbook*.

135 For an example of the right of recognition, or rather, of non-recognition, see the membership issue over the dissolved Socialist Federal Republic of Yugoslavia in the United Nations, as expressed in UN Security Council Res. 777 (1992) of 19 Sept. 1992 and UN General Assembly Res. 47/1 of 22 Sept. 1992. *See also* UN Doc. A/47/485 of 29 Sept. 1992 and the statements by the ICJ in *Application of the Convention on the Prevention and Punishment of the Crime of Genocide* (*Bosnia and Herzegovina v. Yugoslavia* (*Serbia and Montenegro*)). 1993 ICJ Rep. 3, 12–14, paras. 15–17 (Provisional Measures, Order of 8 April 1993).

136 1949 ICJ Rep. 174, 180. For a review of the capacity of the United Nations to espouse international claims in the light of the *Reparation* case, see WEISSBERG, at 170–200. Reuter, in [1974] 2 Y.B. Int'l L. Comm'n 149, sub (18), UN Doc. A/CN.4/SER.A/1974/Add. 1 (Part 1), has argued against the general applicability to all international organizations of the Court's views on (procedural) capacity (but in 1958, he wrote that "international organisations ... have the right to 'bring international claims when necessitated by the discharge of their functions.'" Reuter, Institutions, at 232, sub (2)). Kelsen has argued against the Court's holding itself, stating that "if the constituent treaty does not contain a provision conferring expressly upon the community international juridical personality [compare the UN Charter which is silent on the point of international legal personality, PB], ..., the community has only those special capacities as conferred upon it by particular provisions." *See* H. Kelsen, The Law of the United Nations, A Critical Analysis of its Fundamental Problems 329–330 (1966)[hereinafter: KELSEN]. But another authority on international immunities, namely Ignaz Seidl-Hohenveldern, has argued in this context that it is a well-established principle that "the presence or absence of a certain clause in a number of treaties is no proof for or against the existence of a rule of customary international law identical to the content of that clause." I. Seidl-Hohenveldern, *Piercing the Corporate Veil of International Organizations: The International Tin Council Case in the English Court of Appeals,* 32 GYBIL 43, 45 (1989) [hereinafter: Seidl-Hohenveldern, Tin]. *See also* Fry, at 241 (positing that "[i]f an international organization has a separate will and rights that are either expressly conferred or implied from its constitutive instrument, then one must also acknowledge that where a right cannot be enforced, its enjoyment and exercise by a separate will in the international legal system is meaningless").

international peace and security, the United Nations may find it necessary to entrust its agents with missions to be performed in disturbed parts of the world. Only by having the capacity to exercise functional protection in respect of its agents can the organization effectively carry out its duties.[137] The Charter provisions on advisory procedures also provide an example of the role which functional necessity plays in setting limits for certain rights enjoyed by international organizations.[138] Thus, paragraph 1 of Article 96 broadly authorizes the General Assembly and the Security Council, both of which are principal organs of the most universal organization, to request the ICJ to give an advisory opinion "on any legal question," whereas paragraph 2 lays down that other UN organs and specialized agencies, having been so authorized by the General Assembly, may only request opinions "on legal questions *arising within the scope of their activities*." (emphasis added).

International organizations, enjoying international personality or being subjects of international law, may possess *treaty-making capacity*, i.e., the capacity to conclude international agreements.[139] The *extent* of the treaty-making capacity of an individual organization depends, however, on its internal rules of *competence*: international organizations, notwithstanding the fact that they may in general have treaty-making *capacity*, are only *competent* to enter into agreements in those fields that have been assigned to them, and only when and to the extent dictated by the requirements of functional necessity, i.e., so as to give effect to the purposes for which the

137 For a commentary on the Court's views in the light of the principle of functional protection see M.J. L. Hardy, *Claims by International Organizations in respect of Injuries to their Agents*, 37 BYBIL 516 (1961).

138 It must be emphasized, though, that the capacity to request advisory opinions of the ICJ cannot be derived from considerations of functional necessity alone, *i.e.*, it cannot have functional necessity as a sole basis, but requires instead an explicit authorization to that effect. This particular kind of procedural capacity is atypical compared to the other international capacities that international organizations usually enjoy, which may be derived from functional necessity.

139 *See* Hudson, in [1950] 1 Y.B. Int'l L. Comm'n 85, para. 37, 88, paras. 71–72, UN Doc. A/CN.4/SER.A/1950; El-Erian, in [1963] 2 Y.B. Int'l L. Comm'n para. 60, UN Doc. A/CN.4/SER.A/1963/Add. 1; SCHERMERS, at 1174, para. 1748 ("There can be no doubt that international organizations generally have the capacity to enter into agreements"); Yasseen, at 49; WHITEMAN, 13 DIGEST, at 28–31. For a general discussion of this capacity, see H. Chiu, The Capacity of International Organizations to Conclude Treaties, and the Special Legal Aspects of the Treaties So Concluded (1966); J. Carroz & Y. Probst, Personnalité juridique internationale et capacité de conclure des traités de l'O.N. et des institutions specialisées (1953); *see also* R.-J. Dupuy, in 55 *Annuaire* 214–415 (1973)(III. *L'application des règles du droit international général des traités aux accords conclus par les Organisations internationales*).

member States have created the organization.[140] Consequently, the extent of this capacity varies according to the peculiar character of each organization. Within these boundaries, international organizations in practice have concluded agreements with both member and non-member States, and with other international organizations,[141] even in the absence of a specific or general authorization to that effect in their constituent instruments.[142] Also, the constituent instrument may indicate the *incapacity* to conclude certain agreements. Thus, Article 71 of the 1951 Treaty establishing the European Coal and Steel Community (ECSC) states that the "competence of the governments of the member States with respect to commercial policy shall not be affected by application of the present Treaty,"[143] which in effect denies the ECSC the capacity to conclude commercial trade agreements

140 *See also* McCaffrey, in [1985] l Y.B. Int'l L. Comm'n 293, para. 37, UN Doc. A/CN.4/SER.A/1985; SCHERMERS, at 1175, para. 1748. Yasseen, at 51, 55, has spelled out the two elements of functional necessity, stating that "l'assignation à une organisation internationale de certaines fonctions d'importance sur le plan international dont l'accomplissement suppose ou nécessite la coopération avec d'autres sujets de droit international implique que lui soit reconnue la capacité de conclure des traités" (basis-element), and that it is at the same time "limitée par la spécificité de l'organisation; celle-ci ne peut pas signer des traités sur des questions qui n'ont aucun rapport avec son statut ou avec ses fonctions" (extent-element). *See also* the report of Dupuy, in 55 *Annuaire* 214, 253 and 255, respectively (1973).

141 Between 1970 and 1981, the question of 'Treaties Concluded between States and International Organizations or between Two or More International Organizations' was the subject of study by the ILC, with Paul Reuter as Special Rapporteur. This work has resulted in a convention, the *Vienna Convention on the Law of Treaties between States and International Organizations or between International Organizations,* done at Vienna on 21 March 1986, which has, however, not yet entered into force. For a background note on the ILC's study see The Work of the International Law Commission 83–89 (4th ed. 1988)(text of the Convention *reprinted in id.* at 359). For a selected bibliography on this question see UN Doc. A/CN.4/277 (*1974*) *reprinted in* (1974] 2 Y.B. Int'l L. Comm'n 3–7, UN Doc. A/CN.4/SER.A/1974/Add. 1 (Part 2).

142 For examples see Seyersted, Personality, at 8–9. An interesting example for the purpose of our study is the *Interim Arrangement on Privileges and Immunities of the United Nations concluded between the Secretary-General of the United Nations and the Swiss Federal Council,* signed at Bern on 11 June 1946 and at New York on 1 July 1946, 1 U.N.T.S. 163, since this is an agreement concluded with a *non-member* State (as Switzerland was until 2002), the legal basis for which could only be found through a flexible interpretation of Art. 105, para. 3, of the UN Charter. *See* F. Seyersted, *United Nations Forces, Some Legal Problems,* 37 BYBIL 351, 449 (1961) [hereinafter: Seyersted, UN Forces]. Without such treaty-making capacity, an international organization could not spell out in an international agreement its legal position within a host State.

143 261 U.N.T.S. 140, at 211 *reprinted in* 46 AJIL 107, 140 (Supp. 1952); *see also* Hahn, at 1051–1055.

relating to coal and steel. But this provision does not render inapplicable the strict requirements of functional necessity, according to which the organization in any event is not competent to enter into treaties or commitments outside its purposes and functions.

In general, the possession of a certain capacity does not depend upon an explicit provision that the organization has *personality*, because "[a]n international organization, regardless of any legal theory, must, *for the purpose of fulfilling its task and the aims for which it has been established, operate* even though its personality is not clearly defined" and "[h]ere lies the criterion of the functional independence that an international organization must enjoy *vis-a-vis* the States which establish it." (emphasis added)[144]

It is interesting to point to an example from the European Communities[145] to demonstrate the relationship between personality and capacity and to see how functional necessity can provide the basis for legal capacity. As the Court of Justice of the European Communities (the predecessor to the European Union) has held:

> 13. Article 210 provides that 'The Community shall have legal personality.'
>
> 14. This provision, placed at the head of Part Six of the Treaty, ..., means that in its external relations the Community enjoys the capacity

144 Díaz González, in (1985] 2 Y.B. Int'l L. Comm'n 107, para. 31, UN Doc. A/CN.4/SER.A/1985/Add. 1 (Part 1). The Special Rapporteur also stated that the determination and exercise of the international legal capacity of international organizations depends on international law alone. *Id.* at 110, para. 60. In 1953, Sir Hersch Lauterpacht observed, in his capacity as the ILC's Special Rapporteur on the Law of Treaties, that "[t]he capacity to conclude treaties is both a corollary of international personality and a condition of the effective fulfilment of their functions on the part of the international organizations." [1953] 2 Y.B. Int'l L. Comm'n 90, 100, UN Doc. A/CN.4/SER.A/1953/Add. 1. It is recalled that the ICJ in the *Reparation* case referred to the UN's treaty-making capacity as one of the *indicia* of that organization's international legal personality. 1949 ICJ Rep. 174, 179.

145 The Treaty on the Functioning of the European Union articulates the European Union's capacity to conclude treaties in broad terms. *See* Art. 216, para. 1: "The Union may conclude an agreement with one or more third countries or international organisations where the Treaties so provide or where the conclusion of an agreement is necessary in order to achieve, within the framework of the Union's policies, one of the objectives referred to in the Treaties, or is provided for in a legally binding Union act or is likely to affect common rules or alter their scope." (Consolidated Version of the) Treaty on the Functioning of the European Union, Official Journal of the European Union, 26.10.2012, No. C 326/47.

> to enter into international commitments *over the whole field of objectives* defined in Part One of the Treaty, which Part Six supplements.[146] (emphasis added)

In another case, the Luxemburg Court stated:

> 3. ... Whenever Community law has created for the institutions of the Community powers within its internal system *for the purpose of attaining a specific objective*, the Community has authority to enter into the international commitments *necessary for the attainment of that objective* even in the absence of an express provision in that connection.
>
> 4. ... the power to bind the Community vis-à-vis third countries ... flows by implication from the provisions of the Treaty creating the internal power and in so far as the participation of the Community in the international agreement is, as here, *necessary for the attainment of one of the objectives of the Community*.[147] (emphasis added)

One finds here a similar reasoning to that employed by the International Court of Justice in the *Reparation* case, where it held that certain capacities of an international organization, in this case the United Nations, may arise *by necessary intendment* out of the organization's constituent instrument.[148]

---

146 ERTA Case, *Commission of the EC v. Council of the EC,* Case 22/70, Judgment of 31 Mar. 1971, paras. 13–14, [1971] ECR 263, 274; 1971 CMLR 335. The Court thus held that the treaty-making capacity found in the EEC Treaty was not exhaustive. *See also* Pescatore, in *55 Annuaire* 214, 348 (1973); SCHERMERS, at 1179, para. 1754; Lauterpacht, Development, at 408–409, 426–427.

147 Opinion 1/76, *European Laying-Up Fund for Inland Waterway Vessels,* Decision of 26 April 1977, paras. 3–4, [1977] ECR 754; 1977 CMLR 279; *see also* Skubiszewski, at 865–867, giving further references.

148 In *Reparation for Injuries Suffered in the Service of the United Nations*, the Court used the necessary intendment criterion to accept the capacity of the United Nations to exercise functional protection over its agents. See 1949 ICJ Rep. 174, 184. In *Effect of Awards of Compensation made by the United Nations Administrative Tribunal,* it was used to construe that organization's capacity to establish a tribunal to do justice as between the organization and its staff members, despite the absence of an express provision for the establishment of judicial bodies or organs. The Court reasoned that this capacity was "essential to ensure the efficient working of the Secretariat, and to give effect to the paramount consideration of securing the highest standards of efficiency, competence and integrity." *See* 1954 ICJ Rep. 47, 56–57. For a discussion of the relevant jurisprudence of the ICJ and that of its predecessor, see Díaz González, in [1985] 2 Y.B. Int'l L. Comm'n 111, paras. 64–66, UN Doc. A/CN.4/ SER.A/1985/Add. 1 (Part 1); Lauterpacht, Development, at 420–426.

But the term 'intendment' should not be associated too strictly with the intention of the drafters[149] or even with the terms of the constituent instrument itself.[150] Instead, it may be called a functional institutional intendment. Although the term 'implied powers'[151] is sometimes used to describe this phenomenon, it is more appropriate to speak of 'inherent capacities,'[152]

---

149 *See* Lauterpacht, Development, at 438–447.

150 *See* Seyersted, Personality, at 1 and 4. Writers have placed too much emphasis on the *final* words of the Court's statement that "[u]pon examination of the character of the functions entrusted to the Organization and of the nature of the missions of its agents, it becomes clear that the capacity of the Organization to exercise a measure of functional protection of its agents arises by necessary intendment out of the Charter." 1949 ICJ Rep. 174, 184. The *opening* words are more important as they establish the true basis, namely the functions of an organization, for determining status issues.

151 The doctrine of implied *powers* lies, in any event, outside the discussion of the *capacities* of international organizations. The powers of an organization belong to the subject-matter of the *third* element of legal status, concerning the competence of international organizations. A classic definition of implied powers was given by Judge Hackworth in his dissenting opinion in the *Reparation* case. 1949 ICJ Rep. 174, 198, by describing them as those powers that "flow from a grant of expressed powers, and are limited to those that are 'necessary' to the exercise of powers expressly granted." Seidl-Hohenveldern, Personality, at 71, has defined them more broadly as "powers not enumerated in the instruments but none the less necessary to fulfil the aims stated therein." *See also* D.W. Bowett, The Law of International Institutions 337–338 (1982) [hereinafter: BOWETT]; M. Rama-Montaldo, *InternationalLegal Personality and Implied Powers of International Organizations,* 44 BYBIL 111–155 (1970); H.F. Köck, *Die 'implied powers der Europäischen Gemeinschaften als Anwendungsfall der 'implied powers' internationaler Organisationen überhaupt, in* Law of Nations, Law of International Organizations, World's Economic Law, *Liber Amicorum* Honouring Ignaz Seidl-Hohenveldern 279 (1988); SCHERMERS, at 194–202, paras. 232–236; Lauterpacht, Development, at 423. For a review of the role of the ICJ in the development of implied powers, see J. Makarczyk, *The International Court of Justice on the Implied Powers of International Organizations, in* Essays in International Law in Honour of Judge Manfred Lachs 502 (J. Makarczyk ed. 1984); Skubiszewski, at 863–865. To ILC Special Rapporteur Díaz González, in [1985] 2 Y.B. Int'l L. Comm'n 110, para. 63, UN Doc. A/CN.4/SER.A/ 1985/ Add. 1 (Part 1), the implied powers theory seemed "no more than an amplified interpretation of functionalism." The implied powers doctrine must be distinguished from yet another one, that of *delegated* powers, according to which an international organization can exercise only the powers authorized by and spelled out in its constituent instrument. *See* Seyersted, UN Forces, at 447. On the inherent power of the UN to establish and command forces, *see id.* at 460.

152 *See* Seyersted, Personality, at 19, 55. But Seidl-Hohenveldern, Personality, at 62, does not want to grant international organizations "an inherent capacity to perform all acts, *which States can perform.*"(emphasis added). It seems that Seyersted would extend an organization's inherent capacity also to the latter category. Skubiszewski, at 862, distinguishes powers which are necessary or essential in view of the purposes, functions or express competences of the organization from powers that can be said to be

in order to stress that what matters here is not an intendment from a *document*[153] but rather one arising from the nature and needs of a given *organization*.[154] In other words, it is the existence and nature of the entity and not the instrument by which the entity was created that governs the determination of whether the entity has a certain capacity. If the latter were the case the whole question would in the final analysis turn on whether something is functionally necessary in order to ensure that a certain *document* is properly executed, instead of ensuring that the *organization* performs in the way it was meant to perform. To take this approach would be to turn a blind eye to the evolving and dynamic nature of the international organization: organizations evolve, whereas documents remain established black-letter texts, subject to differing interpretations.[155] Thus, the ultimate question should not be whether a certain capacity was 'implied in the *constitution*' but rather whether it is 'inherent in the *organization*.'[156] It is even better to abolish the 'implied/inherent' rethoric altogether and to adopt a functional terminology instead, according to which international organizations are endowed with certain international capacities which they need for the successful fulfilment of their purposes. If this view is adopted, it

inherent in those purposes, functions or competences, treating inherence and implication as different factors.

153 Nor that of the parties which drafted the document, *see* Skubiszewski, at 860.

154 *Cf.* Bernhardt's views on inherent powers *quoted in* Skubiszewski, at 863.

155 Or, as eloquently put by Manfred Lachs, in *55 Annuaire* 214, 390 (1973): « La conclusion d'accords est donc devenue une manifestation de leurs fonctions et de leur objet à mesure que ceux-ci évoluent. » *See also* Pescatore, in *id.* at 392. This has been called the phenomenon of the 'living constitution,' *i.e.*, "the constitution as actually applied in practice as distinguished from the formal text of the constitution." S. Engel, *'Living' International Constitutions and the World Court (The Subsequent Practice of International Organs under their Constituent Instruments)*, 16 ICLQ 865, 865 (1967)[hereinafter: Engel].

156 *See also* Seyersted, Personality, at 40. For this reason, we cannot agree with Fiore, where he states that: "This capacity [to conclude treaties, PB] ... may be possessed by associations to which international personality has been attributed ... within the limits, nevertheless, of the purposes *for which personality was recognized.*" *See* P. Fiore, International Law Codified and Its Legal Sanction 329 (E.M. Borchard trans. 1918) *cited by* El-Erian, in [1963] 2 Y.B. Int'l L. Comm'n 174, para. 114, UN Doc. A/CN.4/SER.A/1963/Add. 1 (emphasis added). Instead, it should in our view read "of the purposes *for which the organization was established,*" which is a different matter, emphasizing the purposes and functions for which the organization was created. *Compare* the views expressed by Herbert W. Briggs, in *55 Annuaire* 214, 387 (1973), who, on the matter of *ultra vires* and validity of international agreements concluded by organizations, proposed that "[w]here the instrument is silent on the point, the test of validity might conceivably be 'in conformity with the objects and purposes *of the organization*'." (emphasis added).

becomes clear that legal capacities do not originate from, nor are they dependent upon, the organization's constituent instrument, or any other written text, but they emerge from the coming into being and subsequent operation of an international organization.[157] Spelling out the capacities of the organization in explicit provisions is not a necessary condition for the organization to enjoy these international capacities, although it may be instructive, to the effect that it may take away any doubts as to the existence of these capacities and clarify the organization's legal status in relation to other subjects of international law.[158] Dupuy has emphasized the fact that constituent instruments are not at all conclusive in this particular respect, and has called for the application of a rule of *effet utile*:

> Le principe de spécialité des Organisations oblige à se référer aux traités constitutifs *et à la pratique qui en résulte* pour déterminer le volume exact de la capacité de conclure. Mais ce nécessaire recours à la constitution de 1'Organisation ne saurait être systématiquement restrictif et *doit être compensé par l'application de la règle de l'effet utile, ce qui conduit à une interprétation fonctionnelle*[159] (emphasis added)

Thus, functional necessity may be regarded as a device by which the contents of the constituent instrument of an organization acquire effectiveness.[160]

It is functional necessity which, in the final analysis, provides the basis as well as the limits for the capacity of international organizations to undertake certain activities.[161] It provides a basis for capacity inasmuch as it endows an international organization with a certain capacity which is necessary for the exercise of the organization's functions in the fulfilment

157 *See also* SCHERMERS, at 1028–1029, para. 1565.

158 *See id.*.

159 R.-J. Dupuy, in 55 *Annuaire* 214, 254 (1973). *See also* Seidl-Hohenveldern, Corporations, at 83, according to whom "*effet utile* requires use of the interpretation which is more favorable for the realization of the aims of the organization." For an elaborate survey of the principle of effectiveness as applied by international tribunals in the development of the law of international organization, see Lauterpacht, Development, at 420–465.

160 *Cf.* Skubiszewski's characterization of the doctrine of implied powers. Skubiszewski, at 860.

161 *See* Dupuy, in 55 *Annuaire* 214, 255 (1973). *But see* Reuter, in *id.* at 396–397, who was hesitant to accept treaty-making capacity for international organizations *in general* purely on the basis of an organization's purposes and functions, and who insisted instead that reference be made at least to their practice, or to the relevant rules of individual organizations.

of its purposes.[162] By its limitative aspect, an international organization cannot, from a legal point of view, have any capacity that is not connected to its functions and purposes, which means that capacities do not come with a *carte blanche* once it is determined that an organization is equipped with them: functional necessity requirements are attached. It follows that international organizations do not all have the same capacities, but rather they differ according to their specific mandate in terms of the functions and purposes for which they were created.[163]

(ii) *Legal Capacity under Domestic Law*

The possession of personality in domestic law entails the capacity to perform the full scale of acts which legal persons may normally perform in the domestic legal order.[164] In this sense, the notion of capacity is closely linked to that of personality. International organizations, being international persons or subjects of international law, have certain capacities, and accordingly, an individual organization has them too, in the absence of any contrary indication. In other words, unless explicit restrictions have been laid down, an individual organization can profit from the full range of international *and* domestic capacities that any international organization has, subject to its specific functions and purposes.[165]

The activities of an international organization within the State on whose territory it operates inevitably bring it into contact with the domestic laws of that State. The practical importance of the possession of capacity in domestic law has thus been explained as follows:

162 *See, e.g.*, WEISSBERG, at 37; Dominicé, L'immunité, at 164.

163 *See* Reuter, *Third Report,* UN Doc. A/CN.4/279 (1974) *reprinted in* (1974) 2 Y.B. Int'l L. Comm'n 146, sub (5)–(6), UN Doc. A/CN.4/SER.A/1974/Add. 1 (Part I); Mahiou, in [1983] I Y.B. Int'l L. Comm'n 245, para. 32, UN Doc. A/CN.4/SER.A/1983.

164 *See*, e.g., Art. 335 of the Treaty on the Functioning of the European Union: "In each of the Member States, the Union shall enjoy the most extensive legal capacity accorded to legal persons under their laws; it may, in particular, acquire or dispose of movable and immovable property and may be a party to legal proceedings. … ." (Consolidated Version of the) Treaty on the Functioning of the European Union, Official Journal of the European Union, 16.10.2012, No. C 326/47..

165 *See* Seyersted, Personality, at 19, according to whom this is a well-established principle of the customary law of intergovernmental organizations. *See id.*, UN Forces, at 453. Díaz González, in [1985] 2 Y.B. Int'l L. Comm'n 109, para. 46, UN Doc. A/CN.4/SER.A/1985/Add. 1 (Part 1), speaks of "capacity, to which … organizations are *deemed to be entitled.*" (emphasis added).

> … public international organizations of a permanent character which have responsibilities of any substantial importance will almost always be called upon, in the discharge of their responsibilities, to enter into a wide variety of legal relations with individuals and corporate bodies in connection with banking transactions, real property, contracts for supplies, public utility services, transportation and insurance, printing contracts, copyright and other matters.[166]

Within the framework of domestic law, international organizations can sue in domestic courts, acquire and dispose of movable and immovable property, register patents, open and operate a bank account, enter into contracts for the purchase of office equipment, the lease or renting of premises, printing, hiring of personnel, etc. These capacities are necessary to service the unhampered performance of an organization's functions and purposes. To deprive the organization of these capacities would seriously affect its daily operations in the territory of the State concerned.[167]

Most important, an international organization enjoys these capacities without the national authorities being able to dispute their legal basis. But even though a domestic legal framework may provide the opportunity to exercise certain capacities, no organization can carry out any activity outside its competence, as measured by the criterion of whether or not it is necessary for the fulfilment of its functions in accomplishing the purposes for which the organization was created. This is where the limitative element of function comes in, which operates in combination with the elements of authorization and obligation. The scope of the organization's functions and purposes limits its potential capacity to act in certain fields including the domestic arena.[168] As a matter of fact, as will be explained below, the potential *capacities* which an international organization may enjoy, whether under international or domestic law, may be meaningless if

---

166 Jenks, Personality, at 272.

167 As Fry has posited, "[t]he same logic applies to both members and non-members of an international organization" and where a non-member State "has entered into some form of interface with the organization, for example by injuring the organization's personnel or damaging the property of the organization, a legal relationship must have arisen implicitly" and "the right to claim against that state … would become even more important, as without it an international organization would be susceptible to all forms of external interference without any recourse to a remedy." Fry, at 242.

168 *See also* Reuter, in [1987] 1 Y.B. Int'l L. Comm'n 190. para. 7, UN Doc. A/CN.4/SER.A/1987.

the organization does not have the *competence*, by way of certain *powers*, to perform the legal acts by which a certain capacity is exercised in practice. In other words, the (limited) powers of the organization may prevent the organization from using a potential, and seemingly broad, capacity.[169]

The most prominent example of an international legal instrument linking the question of capacity to functional necessity is Article 104 of the UN Charter, which provides that the United Nations shall enjoy in the territory of each of its member States such capacity as may be necessary for the exercise of its functions and the fulfilment of its purposes.[170] Article 104 thus imposes upon the member States of the United Nations the treaty obligation to attribute a certain measure of legal capacity to that organization so as to enable it to freely exercise its functions and fulfil its purposes, leaving to the governments of the member States the task of implementing this legal capacity through national legislation.[171] In this regard the Report of the Rapporteur of Committee IV/2 of the San Francisco Conference states:

> It is to be noted that this provision is conceived in very general terms. It is confined to a statement of the obligation incumbent upon each

169 This has been summarized by Seidl-Hohenveldern, Personality, at 63, as follows: "In its private law capacity an organization can perform any act, which may be performed by any other person enjoying a private law personality. However, any activity of the organization, ..., must be in a reasonably close connection with the aims for which it was founded."

170 The full text of Article 104 reads as follows: "The Organization shall enjoy in the territory of each of its Members such legal capacity as may be necessary for the exercise of its functions and the fulfilment of its purposes." *See* The Charter of the United Nations: A Commentary 2138–2157 (B. Simma et al., eds., 2012). Art. 1, S.1, of the 1946 General Convention implements Art. 104, *see Repertory of United Nations Practice,* Vol. V, at 332–334, paras. 28–38, UN Sales No. 1955.V.2 (Vol. V, 1955). For more examples see Parts II of UN Docs. ST/LEG/SER.B/10 (1959) & ST/LEG/SER.B/11 (1961). Another prominent example is Art. 211 of the Treaty of Rome of 25 March 1957 establishing the European Economic Community, which reads: "In each of the Member States, the Community shall enjoy the most extensive legal capacity accorded to legal persons under their laws." (*See Treaties Establishing the European Communities,* Luxembourg, 1973, at 327). Similarly, Art. 6 ECSC Treaty, 261 U.N.T.S. 140 *reprinted in* 46 AJIL 107 (Supp. 1952) ("in its international relations, the Community shall enjoy the juridical capacity necessary to the exercise of its functions and the attainment of its ends. In each of the member States, the Community shall enjoy the most extensive juridical capacity which is recognized for legal persons of the nationality of the country in question").

171 *See also* L. Goodrich and E. Hambro, Charter of the United Nations, Commentary and Documents 281 (1946)[hereinafter: GOODRICH & HAMBRO]; EGGER, at 114.

> member State to act in such a way that the Organization enjoys in its territory *a juridical status permitting it to exercise its functions. The Organization should be capable, in effect, as regards internal law, of performing the juridical acts required to put its capacities into operation.* The Organization must be able, in its own name, to contract, to hold movable and immovable property, to appear in court. These are only examples. The Committee has preferred to express no opinion on the procedures of internal law necessary to assure this result. These procedures may differ according to the legislation of each member State. It is possible that among the majority of them it may be indispensable that the Organization be recognized as a juridical personality.[172] (emphasis added)

A prominent example of national legislation which explicitly recognizes the legal capacity of an international organization, thereby implementing treaty obligations such as that under Article 104 UN Charter, is the United States' *International Organizations Immunities Act* of 29 December 1945.[173] In Title I, Section 2(a) of this Act, the United States expressly recognizes that international organizations covered by the Act, to the extent consistent with the instrument creating them,[174] have the capacity: (i) to contract; (ii) to acquire and dispose of real and personal property; and (iii) to institute legal proceedings. But this does not mean that international organizations do not have certain other capacities. It means only that these three capacities have been explicitly recognized, leaving no misunderstanding about their application on the domestic plane. From the *Report to the President on the*

172 13 U.N.C.I.O. Doc. 803, IV/2/A/7 (1945), at 817. According to KELSEN, at 337, it would have been advisable to insert a provision which gave more substance to the very general wording of Article 104, by specifying that the legal capacity granted by this article only authorizes the UN to carry out such legal activities as are necessary to achieve its purposes, so as to make sure that it does not authorize the UN to perform any legal transaction whatever. Seyersted, Personality, at 26, 38, holds the opposite view according to which an organization has an inherent capacity to perform any legal transaction, provided it has not been explicitly *excluded.* According to him, not even a *general* provision is necessary. *Id.,* UN Forces, at 450, n.5.

173 U.S. Public Law 291, 79th Congress, 59 Stat. 669 (1945), 22 U.S.C. §288;. Legislative texts from numerous other States may be found in Parts I of UN Docs. ST/LEG/SER.B/10 (1959) & ST/LEG/SER.B/11 (1961).

174 *Compare* this formula with the one used in the ILC's Draft on "Relations between States and International Organizations (second part)," in which the possession of capacity is reserved "to the extent compatible with the instrument establishing them." (text in [1985] 2 Y.B. Int'l L. Comm'n 113, UN Doc. A/CN.4/SER.A/1985/Add. 1 (Part 1)).

Results of the San Francisco Conference by the Chairman of the United States delegation it becomes clear that the United States subscribed to the test of the necessity of the independent exercise of the functions of an organization.[175]

With respect to the relationship between domestic law and the capacity of an international organization under international law, there is a clash between the view that the function of domestic law is only declaratory and another which supports the constitutive argument, meaning that domestic laws have to create legal capacity for it to exist at the national level. According to the former view, member States can enact domestic legislation to the extent that such legislation is not contrary to the organization's constituent instrument and does not restrict its parameters.[176] Former ILC Chairman Jagota has argued in this regard that, while provision may be made for the legal status to be *exercised* in conformity with local law, such laws would be relevant but would not be a direct source of personality or capacity.[177] This view is opposed by, *inter alia*, Ushakov[178] and Kelsen.[179]

The courts of sovereign States have accepted in practice the capacity under domestic law of international organizations, without imposing upon them the requirement of an explicit provision in the national legal order to this effect.[180]

---

175 *See* U.S. Dep't State Publication 2349, Conference Series 71, at 159–160 *quoted in* C.W. Jenks, *Some Constitutional Problems of International Organizations,* 22 BYBIL 11, 59 n.1 (1945).

176 *See also* Yasseen, at 54; JENKS, at 270; Dominicé, L'immunité, at 165.

177 [1985] 1 Y.B. Int'l L. Comm'n 300, para. 46, UN Doc. A/CN.4/SER.A/1985. *See also* Díaz González, in [1985] 2 Y.B. lnt'I L. Comm'n 110, para. 59, UN Doc. A/CN.4/SER.A/ 1985/ Add. 1 (Part 1); EI-Erian, in [1978] 2 Y.B. lnt'l L. Comm'n 280, para. 110, UN Doc. A/ CN.4/SER.A/1978/Add.1 (Part 1); Seidl-Hohenveldern, Personality, at 63; Dominicé, L'immunité, at 163; F. Wolf, Le Droit aux Privilèges et Immunités des Intstitutions Specialisées reliées aux Nations Unies 11 (1948).

178 [1985] 1 Y.B. Int'l L. Comm'n 295, para. 2, UN Doc. A/CN.4/SER.A/1985.

179 KELSEN, at 336. An intermediate position is espoused by K. Ahluwalia, The Legal Status, Privileges and Immunities of the Specialized Agencies of the United Nations and Certain Other International Organizations 60 (1964)[hereinafter: AHLUWALIA], who has stated that "[w]hereas juridical personality of an international organization is neither derived from nor limited by the laws of any one State, it is the national laws of each State which determine the *extent* to which such an organization shall enjoy legal capacity."(emphasis added).

180 An instructive example is found in *Branno v. Ministry of War* (*cited in* SCHERMERS, at 1068, para. 1595, where the Italian Court of Cassation held: "Subjects of international law and public bodies alike, *in order to achieve the purposes for which they were*

1.3.2.3 *The* Third *Element: Competence*

The notion of *competence* lies at the heart of an organization's legal status. Competence describes what a given international organization, being a subject of law endowed with the potential capacity to act, is specifically empowered to do.[181] It is the competence to make use of the capacities conferred upon an international organization by international and/or domestic law. *Competence* designates the object itself of function, namely, the field or range of activities which the international organization is entitled to undertake, and the conditions attached thereto, in the pursuit of its purposes.[182] Thus, in exercising its *function* of purchasing and selling tin for the *purpose* of stabilizing tin prices, the International Tin Council (ITC) had the *competence* to enter into purchasing and selling agreements with respect to tin, but not with respect to any other types of commodities. To use the proper terminology, although the ITC, being endowed with *personality*, may have the general *capacity* to contract, it is only *competent* to contract with respect to tin. The rules governing competence are to be found not in domestic law but in the *internal law* of the international organization concerned and, to a certain extent, in general international (institutional) law.

As the International Court of Justice has held with regard to the United Nations in its advisory opinion on *Reparation for Injuries Suffered in the Service of the United Nations*, there is a direct relationship between functions and competence. The Court stated: "It must be acknowledged that its Members, *by entrusting certain functions to it*, with the attendant duties and responsibilities, have clothed it with the *competence* required to *enable those functions to be effectively discharged.*"(emphasis added)[183]

---

established ... may perform acts of a private law nature, including entering into contracts which are regulated by rules of private law." Italy's highest court thus based its recognition of the domestic capacity of international organizations on considerations of functional necessity rather than on domestic law.

181 On the relationship between the notion of international personality and competence, Reuter has stated: "'la personnalité internationale' n'est que la somme des compétences reconnues dans les relations internationales à un sujet de droit déterminé. On peut remonter des compétences à la personnalité juridique, on ne peut descendre de 'la personnalité internationale' à des competences non établies par ailleurs." *55 Annuaire* 214, 324 (1973). *See also* Hahn, at 1046, according to whom "even when *international personality* is expressly conferred upon an entity, the *competence* to conduct foreign relations of its own makes sense only when the substantive provisions of its charter call for a display of such *functions.*"(emphasis added).

182 *See* Virally, Fonction, at 294.

183 1949 ICJ Rep. 174, 179.

As far as their competence is concerned, international organizations differ fundamentally from States in one important respect, although both are subjects of international law. Whereas States may perform *all* activities unless their incompetence can be demonstrated, international organizations may *not* perform any activities *unless* their competence can be demonstrated to come within the realm of the framework of their purposes and functions.[184] In the final analysis, this means that international organizations may perform any act which is necessary in the exercise of their functions to achieve the goals for which they were created. At the same time, it means that international organizations may not perform any act which is beyond the direct or indirect fulfilment of their purposes.[185] This is the *standard* or *limitation* element which the notion of function represents.

When we use the word 'framework,' we refer to something that is broader than explicit rules laid down in a written document. In order to make use of its capacity to act or to perform, an organization's competence must be clear.[186] To say that competence must be clear means that it must have as its basis any of the following sources:

(1) the competence may be spelled out *explicitly* and conclusively in the organization's constituent instrument,[187] in any subsequent agreements, or in any relevant rules of the organization;[188]

---

184 Addressed here is the external validity of an act performed rather than the validity of the internal procedure by which the decision to perform the act was adopted, in respect of which the organization's constituent instrument may prescribe certain binding procedures. *See 55 Annuaire* 214, 263–277 (1973); *see also* Seyersted, Personality, at 23–24; Lauterpacht, Development, at 407, 409. In this respect there exists a difference between internal and external validity of certain decisions, *see* Seyersted, Personality, at 27–40.

185 *See* Seyersted, Personality, at 29, according to whom this is the view held by "all writers, even the most liberal."

186 Yasseen, at 51, has likewise accepted that the capacity to conclude treaties may follow by implication "si cette aptitude se dégage *clairement* de l'ensemble des règles qui la régissent."(emphasis added).

187 This element refers to the following emphasized part in the ICJ's statement in the *Reparation* case, 1949 ICJ Rep. 174, 180: "… the rights and duties of an entity such as the Organization must depend upon its purposes and functions *as specified* or implied *in its constituent documents* and developed in practice."

188 *See* 1986 Vienna Convention, Art. 2, para. 10: "'rules of the organization' means, in particular, the constituent instruments, decisions and resolutions adopted in accordance with them, and established practice of the organization." *See also* Draft articles on the responsibility of international organizations. adopted by the International Law Commission at its sixty-third session, and submitted to the UN General Assembly as part of the ILC's report covering the work of that session, UN Doc. A/66/10

(2) the competence may be '*implied*' from explicit provisions contained in the constituent instrument,[189] in any subsequent agreements, or in any relevant rules of the organization;[190]
(3) the competence may be '*inherent*' to the exercise of functions necessary for the achievement of the organization's purposes;[191] or
(4) the competence may have been developed in *practice*[192] according to functional needs:

(a) by the decisions and rules of the competent organs of the organization, as developed in the light of, and in pursuance of the organization's purposes (inside the organization);[193]

(b) by the development of international institutional law, i.e., the law of international organizations in general (outside the organization).

[hereinafter: ARIO], Art. 2(b): "'rules of the organization' means, in particular, the constituent instruments, decisions, resolutions and other acts of the international organization adopted in accordance with those instruments, and established practice of the organization."

189 This part corresponds to the use of the word 'implied' in the Court's statement in the *Reparation* case. 1949 ICJ Rep. 174, 180.

190 *See Legality of the Use by a State of Nuclear Weapons in Armed Conflict*, Advisory Opinion, 1996 ICJ Rep. 66, at 78–79, para. 25 ("The powers conferred on international organizations are normally the subject of an express statement in their constituent instruments. Nevertheless, the necessities of international life may point to the need for organizations, in order to achieve their objectives, to possess subsidiary powers which are not expressly provided for in the basic instruments which govern their activities. It is generally accepted that international organizations can exercise such powers, known as 'implied' powers"). *See also* Seyersted, in 55 *Annuaire* 214, 404 (1973) ("... the reference must not be confined to the constitution, but must comprise the entire internal law of the Organisation (as does the reference in Art. 46 of the [1986] Vienna Convention).").

191 *See* Seyersted, UN Forces, at 447.

192 These words correspond to the final three words used by the Court in the *Reparation* case. 1949 ICJ Rep. 174, 180. The relevance of practice is also demonstrated by the reference to it in Art. 31, para. 3(b), of the 1969 Vienna Convention on the Law of Treaties, which is made applicable to international organizations through Art. 5.

193 The International Law Commission used a similar formula. *See* Commentary (4) to Draft article 3(1) on the Law of Treaties, where it was pointed out that capacity "does not depend exclusively on the terms of the constituent instrument of the organization but also on the decisions and rules of its competent organs," *Report of the International Law Commission Covering the Work of its Fourteenth Session,* UN Doc. A/5209 *reprinted in* [1962] 2 Y.B. Int'l L. Comm'n 157, 164, UN Doc. A/CN.4/SER.A/1962/Add. 1. *See also* Seyersted, Personality, at 56–57; Lachs, in 55 *Annuaire* 214, 390 (1973).

It is this framework which reflects the institutional structure of an international organization. As has been demonstrated, this structure goes beyond the constituent instrument of the organization, but it remains within the realm and the spirit of the purposes and functions which the organization is meant to pursue.[194]

To say that the notion of competence describes what a given international organization is empowered to do is to look, in other words, to the *powers* with which international organizations are vested. Skubiszewski has explained that powers relate to "measures that the organization can or must take and which produce legal effects for the organization and/or its Members" and that, given that the purposes and functions of an international organization are usually defined in a broad way, powers are the key to making them real and effective.[195]

The powers of international organizations vary according to the functions which they exercise in pursuing certain objectives. In international institutional law terms, a power is an instrumental tool, available within a given sphere of competence, by which a function is carried out in pursuance of an organization's purposes. A former dean of Harvard Law School has stated in the context of the law of corporations that to attribute powers to a fictional legal person is "simple mechanical efficiency in the carrying out of legal acts,"[196] providing as an example the ability of a corporation to own real estate in its own name. Similarly, most international organizations have the capacity to own buildings used for their operations, and are accordingly equipped with the power to enter into legal contracts to effectuate ownership.

The *extent* of these powers that are indicative of what activities an international organization is authorized to carry out and what their legal consequences are within its field of competence, is determined by the standard of functional necessity: in general, an international organization only has those powers which are necessary to accomplish the purposes for which it

---

194 *See also* Pescatore, in 55 *Annuaire* 214, 347 (1973); Zourek, *id.* at 340. The ICJ referred to a similar competence framework in its *Namibia* Opinion. 1971 ICJ Rep. 16, 50, para. 105. *See also Legality of the Use by a State of Nuclear Weapons in Armed Conflict*, Advisory Opinion, 1996 ICJ Rep. 66, at 78–79, para. 25 ("the necessities of international life may point to the need for organizations, *in order to achieve their objectives*, to possess subsidiary powers which are not expressly provided for in the basic instruments which govern their activities")(emphasis added).

195 Skubiszewski, at 858.

196 R.C. Clark, Corporate Law 19 (1986).

was created.[197] An illustrative example of the close link between the powers and the functions and purposes of an international organization is found in Article 24 of the UN Charter under the heading 'Functions and Powers.' Paragraph 2 of this article stipulates that when the Security Council exercises a power granted to it under Chapters VI, VII, VIII and XII of the Charter, it must, for the discharge of its duties, "act in accordance with the Purposes and Principles of the United Nations" laid down in Articles 1 and 2 of Chapter I of the Charter.[198]

In its advisory opinion rendered in the *Reparation* Case in 1949, the International Court of Justice recognized that the powers of the United Nations are not confined to those specified in the organization's constituent instrument and stated that it is a principle of law that "the Organization must be deemed to have those powers which, though not expressly provided in the Charter, are conferred upon it by necessary implication as being essential to the performance of its duties."[199] The Court's statement indicates that powers of an international organization are dictated by necessity in carrying out its functions and purposes, these powers being at the same time restricted to that end.[200] As ILC member Al-Baharna has noted, the Court's formulation has both positive and negative implications: positive inasmuch as it states that the powers of the United Nations, and of any international

197 *See* Seidl-Hohenveldern, Corporations, at 81, referring, in note 381, to Art. 6(2) of the ECSC Treaty. For an early example of the interpretation of the (extent of) powers in the light of an entity's purposes, see *Jurisdiction of the European Commission of the Danube between Galatz and Braila,* Advisory Opinion, 1927 PCIJ (ser. B) No. 14 (8 Dec.). ILC Special Rapporteur Díaz González, in (1985] 2 Y.B. Int'l L. Comm'n 110, para. 63, UN Doc. A/CN.4/SER.A/1985/Add. 1 (Part 1), aptly summarized the basis- and extent-elements of functional necessity in its application to powers as follows: "Although international organizations can be given only functions and powers which are related to their purposes, they must be given all the powers necessary for the realization of those purposes. This goes beyond the limits set by the texts;" *see also id.,* in [1989] 1 Y.B. Int'l L. Comm'n 282, para. 7, UN Doc. A/CN.4/SER.A/1989.

198 On the link between function and power, see Skubiszewski, at 858.

199 1949 ICJ Rep. 174, 182, referring to an earlier holding by the Permanent Court of International Justice in *Competence of the International Labour Organization to Regulate, Incidentally, the Personal Work of the Employer,* Advisory Opinion, 1926 PCIJ (ser. B) No. 13, at 18 (23 July).

200 *See* Wright, at 515; *but see* H. McKinnon Wood, *Legal Relations between Individuals and a World Organization of States,* 30 Transactions of the Grotius Society 154 (1944, 1962) [hereinafter: McKinnon Wood], who considered it "uncertain and embarrassing ... [to leave] necessary powers ... to be inferred from general considerations regarding the functions of the organization."

organization, transcend its constituent instrument, and negative inasmuch as these powers are limited by considerations of functional necessity.[201] As has been pointed out in the course of the ILC's study of the topic:

> Legal doctrine and jurisprudence show a marked tendency to recognize that, although international organizations enjoy international legal competence, that enjoyment is neither general nor complete. It has certain limitations, since, unlike States, international organizations are not sovereign entities. These limitations are *defined by the purposes* for which the organization was established. The legal régime of the limitations is *determined by the special function* of the organization. The organization is a medium for carrying out the purposes of general interest of its creators. ....[202] (emphasis added)

It is worthwhile to compare the Court's statement on *powers*, which it said were being conferred upon the organization by necessary implication "as being essential to the performance of its duties,"[203] and that on an organization's *capacities* where, in connection with the capacity to exercise functional protection, the Court stated that it "arises by necessary intendment *out of the Charter*," (emphasis added)[204] in other words out of the organization's constituent instrument. The latter might seem to be more strict, but it must be read in conjunction with the Court's general statement regarding *personality*, of which it said that "the rights and duties of an entity such as the Organization must depend upon its purposes and functions as specified or implied in its constituent documents *and developed in practice*."(emphasis added)[205] The addition by the Court of the latter words are the more remarkable if one realizes that the subject-matter of the advisory opinion of 1949 was the United Nations, an organization which had only been created in 1945, when the Charter came into force on 24 October of that year. They provide proof of considerable vision by the 1949 Court, in making provision for the practical developments that would undoubtedly ensue in the United Nations, without however being able to assess the force of them, as we know it today. The *Reparation* case

201 Al-Baharna, in [1987] 1 Y.B. Int'l L. Comm'n 202, para. 33, UN Doc. A/CN.4/SER.A/1987.

202 Díaz González, *Second Report,* UN Doc. A/CN.4/391 and Add. 1 (1985) *reprinted in* [1985] 2 Y.B. Int'l L. Comm'n 110, para. 61, UN Doc. A/CN.4/SER.A/1985/Add. 1 (Part 1).

203 1949 ICJ Rep. 174, 182.

204 *Id.*, at 184.

205 *Id.*, at 180; *see also* Skubiszewski, at 858–859.

is thus proof of the Court's broad approach to the bases of an organization's legal status.[206] The limits of this approach were highlighted in the Court's advisory opinion rendered in a case involving the Global Mechanism of the United Nations Convention to Combat Desertification in Those Countries Experiencing Serious Drought and/or Desertification, particularly in Africa.[207] In that case, the ICJ observed that the Global Mechanism "had no power and has not purported to exercise any power to enter into contracts, agreements or 'arrangements', internationally or nationally."[208] As a result, the Court concluded that, in the absence of a separate legal personality, the Global Mechanism had to "identify an organization to house it and to make appropriate arrangements with such an organization for its administrative operations." This arrangement included acting on behalf of IFAD, the hosting organization, in employing staff members, including the staff member who filed a complaint with the ILO Administrative Tribunal that led IFAD to initiate advisory proceedings before the International Court of Justice.

Functional necessity thus sets the limits for the exercise of the powers of an organization and as we have seen these powers have as their ultimate bases the "purposes and functions as specified or implied in its constituent document and developed in practice."[209] In other words, an international organization possesses functional legal status, which in effect means functional competence.[210] As aptly summarized by ILC Special Rapporteur

---

206 *See also* Skubiszewski, at 864, 866.

207 *Judgment No. 2867 of the Administrative Tribunal of the International Labour Organization upon a complaint filed against the International Fund for Agricultural Development*, Advisory Opinion, 2012 ICJ Rep. 10. The author served as counsel to IFAD in the ICJ proceeding.

208 *Id.*, at 36, para. 61.

209 1949 ICJ Rep. 174, 180. *See also* BOWETT, at 337: "... the test is a functional one; reference to the functions and powers of the organization exercised on the international plane, and not the abstract and variable notion of personality, will alone give guidance on what powers may properly be implied." As Lauterpacht, Development, at 407, has pointed out, the important distinction made by the ICJ in the *Reparation* case "acknowledges that the mere possession of personality does not dispense with the need to determine whether in the particular case the person possesses the appropriate power."

210 *See* Díaz González, in (1985] 2 Y.B. Int'l L. Comm'n 110, para. 62, and 112, para. 71, UN Doc. A/CN.4/SER.A/1985/Add. 1 (Part 1). According to Reuter, "international organisations have no right to use their powers arbitrarily in relation to their functions. If the terms 'power,' 'sovereignty' and so on imply a right to act without any need to justify the purpose, they cannot be used in connection with international organisations," and "[i]f there are individual powers, then they must be intimately connected with the

Díaz González: "International organizations, according to their speciality, exercise the powers attributed to them within the framework of their functions, which depend on the purposes assigned to them by their creators. Thus ... their powers are functional."[211]

What then is the precise role of the constituent instruments of international organizations? If their powers to perform acts are governed, in both their bases and their limitations, by functional necessity, one might think that the treaty establishing an international organization can only play a residual role.

In our view, the proper approach is to take the constituent instrument of an international organization, if one exists, as a starting-point. It has been the consistent jurisprudence of the International Court of Justice, when called upon to give its views on the legality of acts carried out by an organization, to begin by enquiring whether the act was covered, in one way or another, by the purposes[212] and functions[213] of the organization. In other words, one has to begin by examining the roots of functional necessity, which are the purposes and functions of any given organization. It is the purposes/functions framework described above which determines an organization's constitutional structure, a term which is much broader than 'constituent instrument.'

According to Seyersted, the provisions of constituent instruments have legal significance only in a negative sense, i.e., only insofar as they contain

functions of the Organisation." Reuter, Institutions, at 230. *See also id.*, in [1974] 2 Y.B. lnt'l L. Comm'n 147, paras. 9–10, UN Doc. A/CN.4/SER.A/1974/Add. 1 (Part 1), and in [1987] 1 Y.B. lnt'l L. Comm'n 190, para. 7, UN Doc. A/CN.4/SER.A/1987; Ago, in *55 Annuaire* 214, 320, para. 4 (1973).

211 Díaz González, in [1985] 2 Y.B. lnt'l L. Comm'n 110, para. 62, UN Doc. A/CN.4/ SER.A/ 1985/Add. 1 (Part 1); similarly Pellet, according to whom international organizations have "all the powers necessary to achieve [their] aims, but no others." *See* [1990] 1 Y.B. Int'l L. Comm'n 215, para. 17, UN Doc. A/CN.4/SER.A/1990. *See also* Sucharitkul, in [1983] 1 Y.B. Int'l L. Comm'n 239, para. 16, UN Doc. A/CN.4/SER.A/1983; ILC Chairman Shi, in [1990] 1 Y.B. Int'l L. Comm'n 205, para. 36, UN Doc. A/CN.4/SER.A/1990.

212 *See Certain Expenses of the United Nations (Article 17, paragraph 2, of the Charter)*, Advisory Opinion, 1962 ICJ Rep. 151, 167 (third paragraph). *See also* Hahn, at 1046, according to whom "[o]ne must turn to the language and meaning of the substantive provisions of the constitutive documents for an examination of the prospective role an entity may play internationally in view of its purposes. This consideration seems to have been so forceful that in the majority of cases the basic instruments have abstained from expressly conferring international personality on the respective entities."

213 *See Reparation for Injuries Suffered in the Service of the United Nations,* 1949 ICJ Rep. 174, 182 (fifth paragraph).

limitations upon an organization's power to perform acts.[214] In his view, no act in general may be performed by an organization in order to further purposes other than those authorized[215] and no particular acts may be performed which are precluded by any explicit provision of its constituent instrument. But apart from these restrictions, every international organization has inherent powers to perform such acts as may be necessary for the exercise of its functions and the fulfilment of its purposes. Any contrary agreement notwithstanding, no international organization has an inherent authority to perform any acts which do not satisfy the functional necessity criterion. Seyersted admits that these are necessary limitations as the constituent instruments of most organizations contain provisions which define, and thereby limit, their purposes.[216] We disagree with him where he concludes that, as long as the organization's constituent instrument does not explicitly exclude the performance of certain acts and the organization is in a practical position to perform them, the organization is legally entitled to perform any act. In our view, to imply the validity of an act from the fact that "neither the Organization, nor the other contracting party is ever known to have challenged the validity of a treaty, or to have declared themselves not bound by it, because it did not fall within the scope of the stated purposes of the Organization,"[217] is problematical in that it might prevent such acts from being *contra legem* where they clearly are, when judged by the functional necessity test. In this respect, we regard Seyersted's view as too liberal, because he rejects a strict functional necessity criterion as the final test for determining whether a certain act can be validly performed. We find it difficult to accept that an act the legality of

---

214 Seyersted, Personality, at 26. *See also* the statement of the PCIJ in *Jurisdiction of the European Commission of the Danube between Galatz and Braila,* Advisory Opinion, 1927 PCIJ (ser. B) No. 14, at 64 (8 Dec.): "As the European Commission is not a State, but an international institution with a special purpose, it only has the functions bestowed upon it by the Definitive Statute with a view to the fulfilment of that purpose, but it has power to exercise these functions to their full extent, *in so far as the Statute does not impose restrictions upon it."*(emphasis added).

215 According to Seyersted, Personality, at 62, "the constitutional limitation of the purposes of intergovernmental organizations may be viewed as an internal limitation upon their freedom of action."

216 *Id.*, at 27.

217 *Id.*, at 32, referring to the League of Nations as an example for demonstrating that practice supports his thesis that, in the absence of explicit limitations in constituent instruments, nothing prevents international organizations from performing any act of whatever nature.

which is not challenged thereby becomes valid. Quite to the contrary, while such an act may be accepted by States in practice, from a legal point of view it is a 'limbering' act which may be demonstrated to be illegal, subject of course to certain general principles of law such as acquiescence, estoppel and good faith. The act's illegality may be established by demonstrating that its performance was not strictly necessary or essential for the exercise of the organization's functions in fulfilment of its purposes.[218] Contrary to Seyersted,[219] we accept that acts may be challenged which have been performed in order to attain aims covered in the constituent instrument on the basis that such acts were not strictly necessary or essential to achieve these aims. Contrary also to Seyersted,[220] we believe that the conditions contained in the statement of the International Court of Justice in the *Reparation* Case should be applied literally, i.e., in accordance with the normal meaning of the terms 'necessary' or 'essential' used by the Court, and should apply as a real limitation upon the powers of an intergovernmental organization.[221]

218 As Seidl-Hohenveldern, Tin, at 53, has pointed out, "any ... activity of an organization will have to be necessary to enable the organization to achieve its purposes and to exercise its functions. As the organization enjoys legal capacity only within these limits any act outside these limits would be *ultra vires." See also* E. Osieke, *Ultra Vires Acts in International Organizations – the Experience of the ILO,* 48 BYBIL 259 (1976–77); *id., The Legal Validity of Ultra Vires Decisions of International Organizations,* 77 AJIL 239 (1983). Reference should be made in this respect to *Certain Expenses of the United Nations (Article 17, paragraph 2, of the Charter)*, Advisory Opinion, 1962 ICJ Rep. 151, 168, where the ICJ stated: "... when the Organization takes action which warrants the assertion that it was *appropriate for the fulfilment of one of the stated purposes* of the United Nations, the presumption is that such action is not *ultra vires* the Organization." (emphasis added). For the different implications on the internal and external validity of acts see *id.,* and Seyersted, Personality, at 19–40; in an *ultra vires* situation it remains to be determined whether the act concerned is void *ab initio* or *ex nunc, i.e.,* merely after having been successfully challenged. *See also* Seidl-Hohenveldern, Corporations, at 84; Lauterpacht, Development, at 409–410. On the question who can determine this, see R.-J. Dupuy, in 55 *Annuaire* 214, 256–259 (1973), according to whom: "[d]ès lors que l'Organisation s'écarte de la poursuite de son objet, elle perd sa qualité même d'entité indépendante et il lui devient impossible de s'engager valablement. Les accords qu'elle peut être amenée à conclure dans cette situation sont donc *nuls." See also* P. Guggenheim, *La validité et la nullité des actes juridiques internationaux,* 74 RdC 191 (1949 I).

219 Seyersted, Personality, at 22.

220 *Id.,* UN Forces, at 455.

221 Contrary to Seyersted, *id.* at 456, we believe that the ICJ used these terms not *ex abundante cautela,* but precisely because it wanted to lay down a fairly strict criterion that should be applied literally in practice. From our personal experience both in the

It follows that in our view even the absence of explicit restrictive constitutional provisions may not safeguard the activities carried out by international organizations if the requirements of functional necessity are not strictly complied with. The investigation does not end where a constituent instrument is found to contain no limitations and practice does not provide proof of opposition to the performance of a certain act. The investigation would end there in the case of actions by sovereign States. But international organizations lack sovereignty and depend, as concerns their legal status, on the purposes for which they were created, in contrast to States which are subjects of international law with an inherent power to perform any act whatsoever, subject of course to any political constraints and applicable rules of international law. Explicit competence-supplying rules, whether embodied in a constituent instrument or in some other document, always operate in close co-operation with the requirements of functional necessity. Compliance with these explicit rules may be a necessary but not a sufficient condition for an act to be considered legal.[222] For this reason, we cannot accept Seyersted's view that "the constitutional limitations of the *purposes* of the Organization are not usually relevant to the question of the *competence* of the Organization *to perform any types of international acts*, but concern only the question of *for what purposes it may perform such acts*." (emphasis added)[223] To the contrary, these purposes assert their influence through the functional necessity criterion, according to which an organization is *not competent* to perform any act which goes beyond the functions and purposes of the organization. Functional necessity applies in every situation where international organizations act,

---

Registry of the International Court of Justice (as a staff lawyer) and in the Secretariat of the United Nations (as an intern/researcher) we cannot subscribe to Seyersted's contention, *id.* at 455, that neither the Court nor the United Nations has pursued a policy of applying these terms literally. Unfortunately, the Court, in its advisory opinion of 15 December 1989 on the *Applicability of Article VI, Section 22, of the Convention on the Privileges and Immunities of the United Nations*, 1989 ICJ Rep. 177, was only requested by ECOSOC to give its views on the *applicability* of that provision, and had therefore no opportunity to address the question of the *application* of it, which might have triggered an interpretation of the term 'necessary,' to which it referred several times (starting at paragraph 41).

222 In cases in which explicit rules provide for incompetence, reference to these rules of course suffices. In such cases, functional necessity operates as an additional tool to demonstrate incompetence.

223 Seyersted, Personality, at 35.

operating as an invisible 'referee' in adjudging the legality of acts performed by such organizations. Since the functional necessity criterion relies, in the final analysis, upon the statutory purposes of an organization, the organization's founding documents remain of importance.[224] But they are not sacrosanct or set in stone, as purposes may have been developed or even added by subsequent agreements, relevant rules, or by practice. It is worth recalling Michalek's astute observation that "the successes or failures of international organizations *stem not so much from their formal-legal covenants* as from changing configurations and distributions of power, systematic issues and forces, and the attitudes and resources of member states."(emphasis added)[225]

An emphasis on functional necessity rather than strict reliance on the constituent instrument of an organization may have an important additional advantage, which is a shift away from controversies with respect to the proper *interpretation*[226] of the constituent instrument that may arise both between the organization and its member States and between or among the member States themselves.[227] This aspect provides further proof for the competence framework as set out above. As the International Court of Justice has declared in its advisory opinion on *Namibia*, "an international instrument has to be interpreted and applied within the framework of the entire legal system prevailing at the time of the interpretation."[228] For an

224 As Rosenne has stated, "I would agree that the constituent instrument is dominant, but subject thereto, I accept the 'functional necessity' approach." 55 *Annuaire* 214, 330 (1973). *See also* Monaco, 153–172.

225 S.J. Michalek, *The League of Nations and the United Nations in world politics: a plea for comparative research and universal international organizations,* 15 International Studies Quarterly 387, 387 (1971) *quoted in* ARCHER, at 27.

226 As Lauterpacht, Development, at 414, has stated, "the process of interpretation lies at the core of the law of international organization," and cannot, therefore, be avoided.

227 In this respect, Seyersted, Personality, at 72, has rightly voiced the warning that "the inclusion [in the constituent instrument, PB] of provisions designed to empower the Organization to perform specific types of 'sovereign' or international acts is not only useless, but may even be misleading, inasmuch as it may invite false *a contrario* conclusions that the Organization does not have the capacity to perform other acts, or that it cannot perform the acts which have been specified in cases (contexts) other than those provided for." For a survey of the interpretation of the constituent instruments of the main international (financial) organizations, see Lauterpacht, Development, at 414–465; E.P. Hexner, *Interpretation by Public International Organizations of their Basic Instruments,* 53 AHL 341 (1959); F.A. Mann, *The 'Interpretation' of the Constitutions of the International Financial Organizations,* 43 BYBIL 1 (1968–69); BOS, METHODOLOGY, at 159–165.

228 *Legal Consequences for States of the Continued Presence of South Africa in Namibia (South West Africa) notwithstanding Security Council Resolution 276 (1970)*, Advisory Opinion, 1971 ICJ Rep. 16, 31, para. 53. The rules of interpretation set forth in Art. 31 of

international organization, this framework is provided not only by its constituent instrument, but also by any subsequent agreements, relevant rules, practice and functional necessity considerations relating to the organization concerned and reflecting the individual character peculiar to it. In other words, the unavoidable issues of interpretation evoked by a stricter reliance on the functional necessity concept cover a much wider and more relevant ambit than a constituent instrument. Although this approach might not dispose entirely of interpretative issues, it is salutory as it does justice to the broader framework within which international organizations operate.

1.4 *Draft Articles on Legal Status by the International Law Commission*

The question of the *treaty-making capacity* of international organizations in particular was hotly debated within both the International law Commission and the *Institut de Droit International*.[229] Within the ILC, it was considered under no fewer than three different agenda items: the 'Law of Treaties,' 'Relations between States and International Organizations,' and 'Question of Treaties Concluded between States and International Organizations or between Two or More International Organizations.'[230] From the discussions on the Law of Treaties, it appears that no unanimity or uniformity emerged, with the ILC finally deciding to definitively drop the question from its draft and debates. Even after this decision, the question, and in particular its proper legal sources, remained controversial among members of the ILC. Special Rapporteur Reuter, in his Second Report on the 'Question of Treaties Concluded between States and International Organizations or between Two or More International Organizations,'[231] proposed not to have any provision on the capacity of international organizations at all, citing in support an alleged lack of any rule of general international law on the subject.[232] But this

---

the 1969 Vienna Convention on the Law of Treaties are made applicable also to the constituent instruments of international organizations through Art. 5. *See* Reuter, in [1974] 2 Y.B. Int'l L. Comm'n 147, sub (12), 148, sub (13), UN Doc. A/CN.4/SER.A/1974/Add. 1 (Part I); Lauterpacht, Development, at 417–419.

229 For the latter see 55 *Annuaire* 214–415 (1973)(III. *L'application des règles du droit international général des traités aux accords conclus par les Organisations internationales*).

230 The *First Report* of Special Rapporteur Reuter on the 'Question of Treaties Concluded between States and International Organizations or between Two or More International Organizations' contains a review of the ILC's discussions on the subject during its consideration of the Law of Treaties, see [1972] 2 Y.B. Int'l L. Comm'n 178–182, paras. 25–36, UN Doc. A/CN.4/ SER.A/1972/Add. 1.

231 *See* [1973] 2 Y.B. Int'l L. Comm'n 81–83, paras. 38–52, UN Doc. A/CN.4/SER.A/1973/Add. 1.

232 *See* [1973] 2 Y.B. Int'l L. Comm'n 82, para. 40, UN Doc. A/CN.4/SER.A/1973/Add. 1.

proposal was rejected by a number of ILC members,[233] who believed that the capacity to conclude treaties should be explicitly recognized for international organizations as had been affirmed for States in Article 6 of the 1969 Vienna Convention on the Law of Treaties.[234] Pursuant to the ILC's wishes, Reuter's Third Report, submitted in 1974, contained a draft article 6, with a commentary.[235] The draft article read as follows:

> In the case of international organizations, capacity to conclude treaties is determined by the relevant rules of each organization.

In his commentary, the Special Rapporteur mentioned the draft article's silence on the role of general international law in the establishment of the capacity of international organizations to conclude treaties.[236] He explained that if it is the law peculiar to each organization which determines such capacity, it exists by virtue of a general rule of international law authorizing it.[237] Accordingly, he proposed the following alternative text for draft article 6:

> The extent of the capacity of international organizations to conclude treaties, a capacity acknowledged in principle by international law, is determined by the relevant rules of each organization.[238]

The Special Rapporteur, in his comments on the expression "the relevant rules of each organization," argued that this formula is "as neutral as possible: it imposes nothing but excludes nothing, and leaves the question of determining the solution chosen for a given organization to the principles

233 *See, e.g.,* [1973] 1 Y.B. Int'l L. Comm'n 204, para. 14 (Martinez Moreno), 207, para. 46 (Sir Francis Vallat), 207, para. 54 (Yasseen), UN Doc. A/CN.4/SER.A/1973. For the discussions within the ILC on Reuter's Second Report, see [1973] 1 Y.B. Int'l L. Comm'n 187–189, 198–210, 1238th, 124lst-1243rd mtgs., UN Doc. A/CN.4/SER.A/1973.

234 Art. 6 of the 1969 Vienna Convention on the Law of Treaties reads as follows: "Every State possesses capacity to conclude treaties." *See also* M.E. Villiger, Commentary on the 1969 Vienna Convention on the Law of Treaties 125–131 (2009).

235 *See* [1974] 2 Y.B. Int'l L. Comm'n 135, 145–152, UN Doc. A/CN.4/SER.A/1973/Add. 1 (Part 1).

236 *See* [1974] 2 Y.B. Int'l L. Comm'n 150, para.20, UN Doc. A/CN.4/SER.A/1974/Add. 1 (Part 1).

237 *Id.*

238 At the conclusion of the discussions within the ILC, Mr. Reuter stated that, personally, he was inclined to prefer the alternative version, but that, as Special Rapporteur, he preferred the first version. *See* [1974] 1 Y.B. Int'l L. Comm'n 164, para. 69, UN Doc. A/CN.4/SER.A/1974.

and procedures of each organization."[239] The broad terms of the formula, which had never been questioned within the ILC, did not necessarily derive from the same sources in the case of each organization. Most importantly, he pointed out that the formula covered, or did not exclude, both practices which are established and those which are liable to become so.[240] The latter position is different from the one taken by Díaz González in his Second Report on 'Relations between States and International Organizations,' in which he defended the proposition that 'practice' must refer to an established one, not contested by the member States.[241] Although it is true that the 1975 and 1986 Vienna Conventions use the expression 'established practice,'[242] one can safely assume that these texts were not intended to hamper or even rule out any subsequent developments within international organizations.[243] In this respect, the use of the reference to a 'developed practice' by the International Court of Justice in *Reparation for Injuries Suffered in the Service of the United Nations*,[244] may provide a salutory medium ground formula, one which stands between an established and a non-established practice and which allows a certain practice to mature by stressing the 'development' element, ensuring at the same time its early consideration as a factor in interpreting an organization's potential treaty-making capacity.[245]

---

239 *See* [1974] 2 Y.B. Int'l L. Comm'n 151, para. 26, UN Doc. A/CN.4/SER.A/1974/Add. 1 (Part 1).

240 *See* [1974] 2 Y.B. Int'l L. Comm'n 151–152, paras. 27–28, UN Doc. A/CN.4/SER.A/1974/ Add. 1 (Part 1); *see also* his comments in [1974] 1 Y.B. Int'l L. Comm'n 134–135, para. 38, UN Doc. A/CN.4/SER.A/1974.

241 *See* Díaz González, in [1985] 2 Y.B. Int'l L. Comm'n 111, para. 68, UN Doc. A/CN.4/ SER.A/1985/ Add. 1 (Part 1).

242 Art. 1, para. 1(34), of the 1975 Vienna Convention reads as follows: "'rules of the organization' means, in particular, the constituent instruments, relevant decisions and resolutions, and established practice of the Organization." Art. 2, para. 1(j), of the 1986 Vienna Convention, contains similar wording, with the words "adopted in accordance with them" added after "resolutions."

243 In fact, the ILC, in reporting on the work of its thirty-third session, explained that by referring to 'established' practice, it sought only to rule out uncertain or disputed practice, emphasizing that it did not wish to freeze practice at a particular moment in an organization's history. *See* [1981] 2 Y.B. Int'l L. Comm'n 124, sub (24), UN Doc. A/CN.4/ SER.A/1981/Add. 1 (Part 2); Al-Baharna, in [1987] 1 Y.B. Int'l L. Comm'n 203, paras. 38–39, UN Doc. A/CN.4/ SER.A/1987. Ago, in 55 *Annuaire* 214, 321 (1973), also made a plea for flexibility in this respect.

244 1949 ICJ Rep. 174, 180.

245 In the end, practice was not mentioned in Article 6. The ILC explained its absence by pointing out that practice finds its place in the development of each organization in and through the 'rules of the organization,' which varies from one organization to another. *See* [1981] 2 Y.B. Int'l L. Comm'n 127, sub (5), UN Doc. A/CN.4/SER.A/1981/Add. 1

The ILC considered draft article 6 on the treaty-making capacity of international organizations during its twenty-sixth session held in 1974.[246] Several members argued that the issue was not so much the *establishment* of treaty-making capacity, which could be assumed on the basis of general international law, but rather the *exercise* or *extent* of it, involving certain limitations dictated by the proper law of each organization.[247] The exercise of this capacity is necessarily determined by the nature of the activities of each organization, which it carries out in pursuance of the purposes for which it was created. Notwithstanding the fear expressed by Dutch ILC-member Arnold Tammes that the ILC "might once again be entering the treacherous field of semantics by attempting to deal, in one and the same article, with the two problems of capacity and competence,"[248] this was precisely the course that the ILC should have followed. By not distinguishing between these two separate notions, a text emerged which may not only lead to uncertainty in practice as to its proper application but also to theoretical incorrectness. Most important, the absence in the discussions of any explicit reference to the criterion of functional necessity was striking. While some members mentioned that in their treaty-making capacity international organizations were limited to their purposes,[249] there was no general trend within the ILC favoring the adoption of a more functional terminology, with the sole exception of Turkish ILC-member Ali Suat Bilge. He pointed out that States, in setting up an international organization, gave it capacity to carry out the functions enabling it to achieve an aim which

---

(Part 2). For a chronological survey of international decisions which evidence the massive amount of judicial support for recourse to the practice of international organizations as an independent legal basis, see Lauterpacht, Development, at 447–465. For a concise survey of the jurisprudence of the PCIJ and the ICJ concerning the subsequent practice of international organs under their constituent instruments, and the role such practice has played in their judgments and advisory opinions, see Engel, at 869–910.

246 *See* (1974) 1 Y.B. Int'l L. Comm'n 133–137, 144–151, 162–164, 1275th, 1277th, 1279th mtgs., UN Doc. A/CN.4/SER.A/1974.

247 *See, e.g.,* (1974) 1 Y.B. Int'l L. Comm'n 136, para. 51 (Ushakov), 136, para. 54 (Tammes), 137, paras. 58–59 (Calle Y Calle), 145, para. 3 (Hambro), 145, para. 8 (Martinez Moreno), 149, para. 45 (Bilge), UN Doc. A/CN.4/SER.A/1974.

248 *See* (1974) 1 Y.B. Int'l L. Comm'n 136–137, para. 56, UN Doc. A/CN.4/SER.A/1974. For another reference to the two notions of capacity and competence, see *id.* at 148, para. 38 (Kearney), and at 150, para. 49 (Quentin-Baxter). Even the Special Rapporteur took account of this difference, evidence of which is provided by the fact that he proposed an alternative text and acknowledged that the *content* of the capacity of an international organization depends essentially on the law peculiar to each organization. *See* [1974] 2 Y.B. Int'l L. Comm'n 146, sub (6), UN Doc. A/CN.4/SER.A/1974/Add. 1 (Part 1).

249 *See, e.g.,* (1974) 1 Y.B. Int'l L. Comm'n 136, para. 51 (Ushakov), 137, para. 59 (Calle Y Calle), 149, para. 47 (Quentin-Baxter), UN Doc. A/CN.4/SER.A/1974.

the founding States could not attain by themselves. He made a plea for the criterion of *functional* capacity, as identified by the International Court of Justice in the *Reparation* case, and which limits the capacity of an organization to conclude treaties to what is strictly necessary for the performance of its functions in the achievement of its purposes.[250] It appears, however, that the Special Rapporteur was of the view that a more functional terminology than was used in his original proposal would complicate the article unnecessarily.[251]

At the end of the discussions on the draft articles submitted by Special Rapporteur Reuter, the ILC agreed to refer draft article 6, in the form as originally proposed by Mr. Reuter, to the Drafting Committee.[252] Further to the ILC's discussions, the Special Rapporteur submitted an amended version of the draft article at the ILC's thirty-third session held in 1981,[253] which was adopted by the ILC after having been left unchanged by the Drafting Committee.[254] It became Article 6 of the *Vienna Convention on the Law of Treaties between States and International Organizations or between International Organizations*, done at Vienna on 21 March 1986, and it simply reads as follows:

> The capacity of an international organization to conclude treaties is governed by the rules of that organization.[255]

This text does not contain a clear distinction between the basis of treaty-making capacity, which is international law, and the extent of it, which is the law of the organization concerned, in particular the rules of the

250 *See* [1974] 1 Y.B. Int'l L. Comm'n 149, para. 45, UN Doc. A/CN.4/SER.A/1974.

251 *See* [1974) 2 Y.B. Int'l L. Comm'n 150, sub (21), UN Doc. A/CN.4/SER.A/1974/Add. 1 (Part 1).

252 *See* [1974] 1 Y.B. Int'l L. Comm'n 164, para. 72, UN Doc. A/CN.4/SER.A/1974.

253 *See* (1981] 1 Y.B. Int'l L. Comm'n 16, para. 36, UN Doc. A/CN.4/SER.A/1981; *see also* [1981] 2 Y.B. Int'l L. Comm'n 52–53, para. 36, UN Doc. A/CN.4/SER.A/1981/Add. 1 (Part 1).

254 *See* [1981] 1 Y.B. Int'l L. Comm'n 199, para. 20, 1681st mtg., UN Doc. A/CN.4/SER.A/ 1981. Notice incidentally that the Chairman of the Drafting Committee was Mr. Leonardo Díaz González, who would later become Special Rapporteur on 'Relations between States and International Organizations (second part).'

255 The adjective 'relevant' with the word 'rules' was dropped in order to ensure uniformity of language of the 1969, 1975, and 1986 Vienna Conventions, notwithstanding the commentary by the Special Rapporteur in [1981] 2 Y.B. Int'l L. Comm'n 51, para. 27, 52–53, para. 36, UN Doc. A/CN.4/SER.A/1981/Add. 1 (Part 1), and in [1981] 2 Y.B. Int'l L. Comm'n 127, sub (3), UN Doc. A/CN.4/SER.A/1981/Add. 1 (Part 2).

organization regarding competence to conclude treaties in connection with the organization's functions and purposes.[256] If it was deemed important to capture this capacity in one single sentence, it would have been preferable to follow more closely the text of Article 6 of the 1969 *Vienna Convention on the Law of Treaties* concerning the capacity of States to conclude treaties and to adapt its text to the functional necessity requirements that apply in the case of international organizations, resulting in the following formula:

> An international organization possesses capacity to conclude treaties in accordance with its relevant [competence] rules.[257]

With a view to placing the wording of article 6 of the 1969 Vienna Convention in its proper perspective, it is useful to quote from the following passage on the article in the report of the ILC on the work of its thirty-third session:

> The wording eventually adopted by the Commission for article 6 is the result of a compromise based essentially on the finding that this article *should in no way be regarded as having the purpose or effect of deciding the question of the status of international organizations in international law. That question remains open* .... The purpose of article 6 is merely to lay down a rule relating to the law of treaties; the article indicates, for the sole purposes of the régime of treaties to which international organizations are parties, by what rules the capacity to conclude treaties should be assessed.[258] (emphasis added)

256 Oddly enough, the latter words correspond to the formula employed in Article 46 of the 1986 Vienna Convention, the use of which in Article 6 was, however, not supported by the Special Rapporteur, who thought there would be nothing, save a tautological effect, to be gained by using it there. *See* [1981] 2 Y.B. Int'l L. Comm'n 52–53, para. 36, UN Doc. A/CN.4/SER.A/1981/Add. 1 (Part 1).

257 From this text, it follows clearly that, contrary to its State counterpart, the treaty-making capacity of international organizations is not unrestricted, while it avoids at the same time the use of the words "is governed by," which do not take away the confusion over the precise source of this capacity, namely, international law or the law of the organization concerned. Instead, the words "in accordance with" suggest that the *exercise of* treaty-making capacity, *established* otherwise, i.e., under international law, is dependent upon the *competence* of each organization to make use of a potential capacity. *See* [1974] 1 Y.B. Int'l L. Comm'n 148, para. 38 (Kearney), UN Doc. A/CN.4/SER.A/1974.

258 *See* [1981] 2 Y.B. Int'l L. Comm'n 127, sub (2), UN Doc. A/CN.4/SER.A/1981/Add. 1 (Part 2).

The broader *status* question of the legal personality and capacity of international organizations under both international and domestic law was dealt with extensively by ILC Special Rapporteur Díaz González in his *Second Report* on 'Relations between States and International Organizations (second part of the topic),' which was submitted in 1985.[259] It contained a draft article entitled 'Legal Personality,' which was presented to the plenary of the ILC in two alternatives. The text of Alternative A read as follows:

> Article 1
>
> 1. International organizations shall enjoy legal personality under international law and under the internal law of their member States. They shall have the capacity, to the extent compatible with the instrument establishing them, to:
> (a) contract;
> (b) acquire and dispose of movable and immovable property; and
> (c) institute legal proceedings.
>
> 2. The capacity of an international organization to conclude treaties is governed by the relevant rules of that organization.[260]

In Alternative B, the two paragraphs were separated into two articles containing the same words as are used in Alternative A.

The ILC briefly discussed this draft article at its thirty-seventh session held in 1985[261] and it resumed its consideration at the thirty-ninth session in 1987.[262] Subsequent to these plenary discussions, the Special Rapporteur, on the occasion of the submission of his *Fourth Report* in 1988, introduced two separate provisions, draft articles 5 and 6, which slightly amended the 1985 version.[263] These articles were the subject of discussion at the ILC's

---

259 UN Doc. A/CN.4/391 and Add. 1 *reprinted in* [1985] 2 Y.B. Int'l L. Comm'n 103–113, UN Doc. A/CN.4/SER.A/1985/Add. 1 (Part 1).

260 Paragraph 2 closely resembles Article 6 of the 1986 Vienna Convention, with the addition of the word "relevant."

261 *See* [1985] 1 Y.B. Int'l L. Comm'n 283, 1925th-1927th, and 1929th mtgs., UN Doc. A/CN.4/SER.A/1985.

262 *See* [1987] 1 Y.B. Int'l L. Comm'n 187, 2023rd-2027th, 2029th mtgs., UN Doc. A/CN.4/SER.A/1987.

263 Article 6, as amended, reads: "The capacity of an international organization to conclude treaties is governed by the relevant rules of that organization *and by international law.*"(emphasis added). *See* [1989] 2 Y.B. Int'l L. Comm'n 157, paras. 22–23, UN Doc. A/CN.4/SER.A/ 1989/Add. 1 (Part 1).

forty-second plenary session held in 1990.[264] The various discussions revealed broad support for the draft, subject to some reservations about the wording of the text. Some members felt that to say that an international organization "shall" enjoy legal personality was too categoric a statement, which would recognize an 'objective' personality for all international organizations, i.e., one opposable to member and non-member States alike. Instead, they favored substitution of "shall" with the word "may."[265] The limitation of the legal capacity of international organization "to the extent compatible with the instrument establishing them" and the specific mentioning of the categories under (a)–(c) were criticized by Al-Baharna, who stated that these provisions were couched in unduly narrow terms, giving the impression that international organizations had no attributes other than those expressly specified.[266] This concern was also voiced during the discussions on the revised version of the draft article at the ILC's forty-second session. It was suggested that the words "in particular" be added after the words "shall have the capacity."[267] There was also some discussion on the reference in article 6 to "the relevant rules of that organization." During the 1985 discussions, Arangio-Ruiz argued that this formula had nothing to do with the capacity to conclude treaties with non-member States since that right depends on general international law.[268] But Calero Rodrigues agreed with the Special Rapporteur and explained that the formula simply meant that an international organization could conclude treaties only if it was authorized to do so by its internal rules.[269] In addition,

---

264 *See Report of the International Law Commission on the work of its forty-second session,* 45 GAOR Supp. (No. 10) at 233–235, paras. 441–446, UN Doc. A/45/10 (1990).

265 *See* [1985] 1 Y.B. Int'l L. Comm'n 292, para. 27 (Calero Rodrigues), 293, para. 39 (McCaffrey), 298, para. 26 (Tomuschat), UN Doc. A/CN.4/SER.A/1985. It must, however, be pointed out that the draft article would eventually become part of a multilateral convention, to which only those States which ratified it would become Members, leaving untouched the matter of recognition by other States.

266 [1987] I Y.B. Int'l L. Comm'n 203, para. 39, UN Doc. A/CN.4/SER.A/1987.

267 *See Report of the International Law Commission on the work of its forty-second session,* 45 GAOR Supp. (No.10) at 234, para. 444, UN Doc. A/45/10 (1990).

268 *See* [1985] I Y.B. Int'l L. Comm'n 291, para. 20, UN Doc. A/CN.4/SER.A/1985.

269 *See id.*, at 292, para. 28. *But see* Pellet, in [1990] I Y.B. Int'l L. Comm'n 215, para. 17, UN Doc. A/CN.4/SER.A/1990, according to whom the functional theory dictates that the capacity of an international organization to conclude treaties is governed not by the "relevant rules" of the organization, but by its aims from which it derives all necessary powers. Notice that in our competence framework set out above, any relevant rules are closely linked to the functions and purposes of an organization.

Tomuschat favored a wider application of the formula by way of a general limitation applicable to all activities of an international organization, not only its treaty-making activity.[270] By contrast to the 1974 discussions, in 1990, during the ILC's forty-second session at which the Fourth Report was discussed, the views expressed by many members on draft articles 5 and 6 contained explicit references to the functional criterion.[271] Several members argued that a clear distinction, by way of separate articles, should be made between legal personality and capacity under international law and under domestic law.[272]

However, similar to the ILC's consideration, in 1974, of draft article 6 in connection with the 'Question of Treaties Concluded between States and International Organizations or between Two or More International Organizations,' the discussion on this point reveals a confusion between the two separate notions of capacity and competence (powers) of an international organization. The Draft should have made a clear distinction between the basis-element and the extent-element. The basis for legal capacity is provided by international law and by domestic law. The extent to which an international organization can use such capacity depends upon its competence to do so, which is determined by the framework described above. It would have been sufficient to employ the wording of Article 104 of the UN Charter, with some additions. In order to reconcile the positions taken within the ILC, it might therefore have been advisable to replace draft articles 5 and 6 with something along the following lines:

Article 5

1. Subject to their functions and purposes, international organizations shall enjoy legal personality under international law and under the domestic law of their member States.

2. They shall have such legal capacity under international law and under the domestic law of their member States as may be necessary

270 *See* [1985] 1 Y.B. Int'l L. Comm'n 298, para. 28, UN Doc. A/CN.4/SER.A/1985.

271 *See* [1990] 1 Y.B. Int'l L. Comm'n 201, paras. 6–7, 202, paras. 12–13 (Hayes), 204, paras. 32–33 and 205, paras. 36–38 (Shi), 212, para. 60 (Graefrath), 215, paras. 17–19 (Pellet), 217, paras. 34, 36, 38 and 218, paras. 39–41 (McCaffrey), 221, para. 7 and 222, paras. 8–9 (Beesley), 223, paras. 19 and 24 (Eiriksson), UN Doc. A/CN.4/SER.A/1990.

272 *See, e.g.*, [1990] 1 Y.B. Int'l L. Comm'n 203, para. 21 (Tomuschat), 205, para. 40 (Koroma), 212, para. 59 (Graefrath), 216, para. 19 (Pellet), 218, para. 47 (Barsegov), UN Doc. A/CN.4/ SER.A/1990.

for the exercise of their functions in the fulfilment of their purposes, in particular the capacity to
(a) conclude treaties;
(b) contract;
(c) acquire and dispose of movable and immovable property; and
(d) institute legal proceedings.
3. The extent to which international organizations shall enjoy legal capacity is dictated by the relevant competence rules of each organization and their developed practice in accordance with the functional needs of the organization.[273]

2 Step Two: Selection

2.1 *Introduction*

In the previous section of Chapter 2, introducing Step One of our functional necessity analysis, the legal status of intergovernmental organizations was examined through an identification process of their legal personality, capacity and competence in the light of the functions and purposes of these entities. As Fedder observed in 1960:

> [t]he reliance on the functional principle in determining the extent of protection for international organizations since World War II did not stop at *legal status*. The change from previous practice is also evident in the *privileges and immunities* accorded to the organizations.[274] (emphasis added)

Before we enter into a closer examination of the influence of functional necessity on the privileges and immunities of international organizations, the preliminary question of the relationship between the legal status and the privileges and immunities of international organizations needs to be addressed. Several authors have given consideration to this fundamental question and from their works divergent views have emerged.

---

273 Compare the alternative wording for article 5 proposed by Eiriksson, in *id.*, at 224, para. 25: "International organizations shall have legal personality and shall enjoy in the territories of their member States and in their relations with other international organizations such legal capacity as may be necessary to perform their functions and achieve their ends."

274 Fedder, at 63.

According to Lalive,[275] the privileges and immunities which are necessary for the performance of the functions of an international organization, are an attribute of the organization's legal personality. This view seems to be supported by Ahluwalia, according to whom "these privileges and immunities are granted as a result of the recognition of their international personality ...."[276] Moreover, Bowett has pointed out that "[p]ossession of such international personality will normally involve, as a consequence, the attribution ... of privileges and immunities ...."[277] Support for this view may be found in treaty-law. For instance, Article 1, Section 1, of the *Interim Arrangement on Privileges and Immunities of the United Nations concluded between the Secretary-General of the United Nations and the Swiss Federal Council* provides:

> The Swiss Federal Council recognizes the international personality and legal capacity of the United Nations. *Consequently*, according to the rules of international law, the Organization cannot be sued before the Swiss Courts without its express consent.[278] (emphasis added)

The view just referred to has, however, been rejected by Dominicé,[279] who has argued that immunities, instead of being a necessary attribute of the legal personality of an international organization, derive from the specific rules prescribing them.[280] According to Dominicé, the relationship between

275 J.-F. Lalive, *L'immunité de juridiction des états et des organisations internationales,* 84 RdC 205, 304, 314 (1953 III)[hereinafter: Lalive].

276 AHLUWALIA, at 208.

277 BOWETT, at 339 and 341; *see also* Calero Rodrigues, in [1985] 1 Y.B. Int'l L. Comm'n 292, para. 25, UN Doc. A/CN.4/SER.A/1985, who stated that international organizations have to be granted privileges and immunities because they enjoy legal personality and have the capacity to perform certain acts. *But see* A. Cassese, *L'immunité de juridiction civile des organisations internationales dans la jurisprudence italienne,* 30 AFDI 556, 566 (1984)[hereinafter: Cassese].

278 1 U.N.T.S. 163.

279 Dominicé, L'immunité, at 164 *et seq. See also* N.Q. Dinh, *Les privilèges et immunités des organismes internationaux d'après les jurisprudences nationales depuis 1945,* 3 AFDI 262, 275 (1957)[hereinafter: Dinh].

280 *See also* Chr. Dominicé, *La nature et l'étendue de l'immunité de juridiction des organisations internationales, in* Law of Nations, Law of International Organizations, World's Economic Law, *Liber Amicorum* Honouring Ignaz Seidl-Hohenveldern 77, 92 (1988) [hereinafter: Dominicé, LIBER SEIDL]. For a general survey of these rules see the third section of this Part of our study concerning the legal sources of organizational immunities.

an organization's legal status and its immunities is merely constituted by the fact that:

> ... le bénéfice des immunités est accordé aux organisations internationales, par les conventions, éventuellement par la coutume, en leur qualité de personnes juridiques internationales et au plan du droit international. Elles en sont titulaires et peuvent s'en réclamer á 1'encontre des Etats.[281]

This means, therefore, that international organizations enjoy privileges and immunities, granted to them in certain legal instruments, as subjects of international law. The relationship between the two notions of the personality and the immunities of international organizations is of a logical, practical nature, since, as Dominicé argues, "accorder des immunités á une organisation qui n'aurait pas, en droit interne, la personnalité juridique, n'aurait pas grand sens, car ce ne serait pas 1'organisation qui, par example, devrait être assignée en justice."[282] According to Dominicé, the relevance of the question of an organization's legal personality is primarily constituted by the fact that it helps to solve the question of its capacity to appear in court, which strictly speaking is independent from that of its immunity from jurisdiction.

The solution proposed by Dominicé would appear to correspond to the conclusion that the International Court of Justice reached in the *Reparation* case. There, the Court stated that the Charter of the United Nations, by conferring privileges and immunities and other rights on the organization, defines the position of the member States in relation to the organization, which led the Court to conclude that the United Nations "occupies a position in certain respects in detachment from its Members."[283] The Court thus held that the privileges and immunities provided for in Article 105 of the UN Charter can be regarded as *indicia* of the legal personality of the United Nations.[284]

281 Dominicé, L'immunité, at 164.

282 *Id.*, at 166.

283 1949 ICJ Rep. 174, 179.

284 For a general review of these *indicia* see Yasseen, at 48 *et seq.* According to M. Wenckstern, Die Immunität Internationaler Organisationen 33 (1991)[hereinafter: Wenckstern], however, the fact that an international organization may be a subject of international law can be evidence in support of the immunity of the organization. This view seems to be based upon a reverse reading of the *Reparation* case of the ICJ.

From a theoretical point of view, this approach, which takes as a starting-point the privileges and immunities *giving evidence of* personality, would seem more logical than to conclude from the notion of personality that an organization, *by consequence of* this personality, enjoys certain privileges and immunities. As will be demonstrated below, the granting of privileges and immunities to international organizations can only be explained on the basis of, and be justified by, certain basic considerations and principles, in particular that of functional necessity, which are reflected in a variety of legal instruments. To say that organizational immunities find their origin in specific rules of international law appears to be a better approach than attempting to base them, directly or indirectly, on an organization's personality. While the possession of personality may be of relevance to the question of the right to immunity, in that it helps to identify the grantee or beneficiary of the right conferred,[285] the extent or degree of such personality really is of secondary importance. In the end, all organizational immunities depend, not on an automatic assimilation with an organization having personality, but on the functions and purposes of the organization concerned, to which the immunities are subsidiary.[286] It is not by consequence of an organization's personality but by consequence of the needs arising from its purposes and functions that an international organization enjoys or is entitled to enjoy certain privileges and immunities. This is the essence of the *functional* approach outlined in this study.[287] As Jenks has pointed out in his important work on *International Immunities*, "[i]t is these functional needs which constitute both the justification for and the measure of international immunities."[288]

Before we enter into a closer examination of the privileges and immunities granted to international organizations, a few remarks must be made with regard to the meaning of the generic term 'privileges and immunities.'

'Privileges and immunities' is usually employed as a general formula. There have been writers who have tried to distinguish between 'privileges' and 'immunities,' but no such distinction has gained general acceptance.

---

285 *See* Dominicé, LIBER SEIDL, at 92.

286 *See* Pawlak, in [1987] 1 Y.B. Int'l L. Comm'n 190, para. 12, UN Doc. A/CN.4/SER.A/1987; Sucharitkul, in (1977) 1 Y.B. Int'l L. Comm'n 207, para. 52, UN Doc. A/CN.4/SER.A/1977 ("The privileges and immunities of an international organization, of whatever type, were necessarily qualified or limited by the functions of the organization"); Hayes, in [1990] 1 Y.B. Int'l L. Comm'n 201, paras. 6–7, UN Doc. A/CN.4/SER.A/1990.

287 *See also* Tsuruoka, in [1978] I Y.B. Int'l L. Comm'n 267, para. 26, UN Doc. A/CN.4/SER.A/1978.

288 JENKS, at xxxviii; *see also* Kunz, at 847.

Hammerskjöld proposed to identify 'privileges' with 'honour' and 'prestige,' while reserving the notion of 'immunities' to 'guarantee.'[289] According to Kunz, "[t]he accent obviously will have to be on the 'immunities' necessary for independent functioning, rather than on 'privileges,' which deal more with questions of honor, courtesy, and protocol."[290]

Van Vollenhoven has argued that the term 'immunities' should be reserved to "guarantees of inviolability," while 'privileges' point to 'Ehrenrechte' or rights of honor.[291]

According to Akehurst, the meaning of the words 'privilege' and 'immunity' overlap so much that it is impracticable to distinguish between them.[292]

According to one national court, "[i]mmunity is the sum of the privileges that a State grants to another State or to an international organization to help it achieve its goals."[293]

Whatever the validity of these views, the term 'privileges and immunities' will henceforth be used as a general formula.

Furthermore, we shall, as a matter of convenience, employ the term 'organizational immunities' where we mean the body of law pertaining to the privileges and immunities of international organizations as such,[294] which, for the purposes of the present study, would seem a more appropriate term than 'international immunities.' The latter is usually reserved to indicate the privileges and immunities granted to the officials and other functionaries of international organizations,[295] which are outside the scope of this study.

---

289 Ake Hammerskjöld, *Les Immunités des personnes investies de fonctions internationales*, 56 RdC 107, 137 (1936 II).

290 Kunz, at 847.

291 C. van Vollenhoven, *Diplomatic Prerogatives of Non-Diplomats*, 19 AJIL 469, 474 (1925).

292 M. Akehurst, A Modern Introduction to International Law 117 {6th. ed. 1987). *See also* Restatement (Third) § 467, Comment (a), at 494; SCHERMERS, at 267, para. 323 ("There is no sharp distinction between privileges and immunities").

293 *Gérald René Trempe v. ICAO Staff Association et al. and Gérald René Trempe v. Dirk Jan Goossen et al.*, High Court, Province of Quebec, District of Montreal, judgment of 20 Nov. 2003, at para. 58, English text reproduced in 2003 UN Jurid. Y.B 585, at 596, UN Doc. ST/LEG/SER.C/41 (2003).

294 The term 'organizational immunities' has been used by G.H. Glenn, M.M. Kearney & D.J. Padilla, *Immunities of International Organizations*, 22 Va. J. Int'l L. 247, 266 (1982) [hereinafter: Glenn *et al.*].

295 *See* D.B. Michaels, International Privileges and Immunities. A Case for a Universal Statute XII, XV (1971)[hereinafter: Michaels]; C. McCormick Croswell, Protection of International Personnel Abroad – Law and Practice Affecting the Privileges and Immunities of International Organization v-vi (1952)[hereinafter: CROSWELL]; WHITEMAN, 13 DIGEST, at 142–188.

Having made these preliminary remarks, it must next be explained that the purpose of this section is not to describe in detail the privileges and immunities of all international organizations or of any one in particular. Following Jenks,[296] a leading authority in the field of international immunities, it will be more useful to try to select from the mass of detail which still threatens to encumber discussion of the subject some of the general principles involved with a view to indicating the basic reasons for granting various privileges and immunities to international organizations and some of the problems which may arise in connection with their application, as well as a structural survey of the *legal sources* underlying privileges and immunities to international organizations. To put it in another way, the scope of this section is restricted to the questions of *why*, *what* and *where*: *why* are international organizations granted *what* privileges and immunities and *where* can these privileges and immunities be found? Little consideration will be given to the material aspects of privileges and immunities, i.e., to defining their exact meaning, since this particular aspect has been given extensive consideration in legal doctrine.

2.2 Why: *Basic Considerations in Granting Organizational Immunities*

2.2.1 Introduction

A specialist on the law of the immunities of international organizations wrote in 1964 that "there is a dire need for a better understanding of the purposes and scope of ... privileges and immunities."[297] A report published in the late 1960s under the aegis of the Council of Europe noted that "there has been a failure to observe any coherent body of principles and insufficient regard has been paid to the rule embodied in the General Assembly Resolution of 1946 ... that 'no privileges and immunities which are not really necessary should be asked for.'"[298] The Committee of Ministers of the Council of Europe had instructed the European Committee on Legal Co-operation (CCJ) to study the privileges and immunities of international organizations with a view to promoting and, if possible, agreeing on a

296 JENKS, at 12.

297 AHLUWALIA, at 208; *see also* S.C. Ivrakis, Privileges and Immunities of the United Nations – Precedents and Present-Day Developments 659 (1954)[hereinafter: IVRAKIS].

298 *See* Resolution (69)29, adopted by the Committee of Ministers of the Council of Europe on 26 September 1969 and Explanatory Report prepared by the sub-committee of the European Committee on Legal Co-operation, *Memorandum by the Government of the United Kingdom (Foreign Office, 10 March 1965)*, at 79, para. 17 [hereinafter: Council of Europe Report 1969).

common policy between member States with respect to the granting of privileges and immunities to international organizations in general. The CCJ report starts by setting out various principles[299] justifying the grant of privileges and immunities to international organizations. This report is one of the few documents which deal explicitly with the *rationale* that lies behind the granting of privileges and immunities as provided in several legal sources, which will be discussed below. The report can, however, only serve as a modest starting-point for examining the *raison d'être* of organizational immunities, since it deals with this matter in a rather limited number of pages and was published in the 1960s. Within the scope of the present study the general reasons for granting privileges and immunities to international organizations as such are given more detailed consideration. It is one of the main purposes of this study to contribute to a better understanding of the *rationale* behind granting privileges and immunities to international organizations, in the form of a compact review of the basic considerations involved, with the understanding that they are closely interrelated and that each should be construed in the context of the other considerations. It also should be borne in mind that the functional necessity concept should not be regarded in isolation. Functional necessity interacts with, and is closely related to, a whole range of basic considerations, which together militate in favor of granting those immunities necessary to an organization's functions and purposes.[300]

2.2.2 (i) Political Independence of the Organization

As we have seen above, intergovernmental organizations are subjects of international law created by States in order to fulfil purposes which their member States have in common. As ILC Special Rapporteur Díaz González has pointed out, States set up independent and permanent institutions with a view to carrying out functions, in order to regulate, channel and engage in co-operation in resolving and coping with political, social, economic, humanitarian and technological problems that are too difficult and complex

299 R. Zacklin, *Diplomatic Relations: Status, Privileges and Immunities, in* A Handbook on International Organizations 179, 182–183 (R.-J. Dupuy ed. 1988)[hereinafter: Zacklin, DUPUY], also employs the term 'principles.' *But see* the EMBL Award of 29 June 1990, at 49, and discussed below in Step Three, where the Arbitration Tribunal states that it seems questionable that a general legal principle exists under which the headquarters State must not derive any financial advantages from the activities of the organization on its territory.

300 *See also* IVRAKIS, at 653; SCHERMERS, at 268–269, para. 324.

for any one Member of the international community to deal with individually, or which an international organization can perform more efficiently.[301]

An international organization can only truly operate in the *common* interest of all member States participating in it if it is not subject to the control or jurisdiction of any of the individual member States. In its application to organizational immunities the functional concept is, therefore, based on the idea of independence of international organizations from any one of its member States or any one bloc of its member States:[302] for the fulfilment of its international purposes an international organization has a need for *independence* in relation to its member States. This independence is, therefore, a functional independence, which can be ensured by the granting of such privileges and immunities as may be necessary to enable the organization to exercise its functions in the fulfilment of its purposes.[303] As Jenks has noted, "[f]or international institutions the right to meet and decide freely is the right to life itself."[304] This need of an international organization to be independent from its member States, which follows from the fact that it is required to perform *international* tasks as a multilateral institution,[305] is recognized to be the essential reason for according international organizations a legal position resembling in a way that of sovereign States, which enjoyed privileges and immunities long before international organizations were granted similar rights.[306] The report of the CCJ of the Council of Europe referred to this special position by stating:

---

301 *See* Díaz González, *Second Report,* UN Doc. A/CN.4/391 and Add. 1 *reprinted in* [1985] 2 Y.B. Int'l L. Comm'n 103, 105, paras. 17–18, UN Doc. A/CN.4/SER.A/1985/Add. 1 (Part 1); *see also id.* at 108, paras. 36–37; [1986] 2 Y.B. Int'l L. Comm'n 167, para. 30, UN Doc. A/CN.4/SER.A/1986/Add. 1 (Part 1).

302 *See* MICHAELS, at 50.

303 *See* Council of Europe Report 1969, at 21, para. 27, third sentence. An example of the materialization of this freedom from interference can be found in Section 3 of the 1946 General Convention. *See also* [1967] 2 Y.B. Int'l L. Comm'n 224, para. 76, 228, para. 96, UN Doc. A/CN.4/SER.A/1967/Add. 1.

304 C. W. Jenks, The Headquarters of International Institutions. A Study of Their Location and Status 36 (1945).

305 *See also Jam v. International Finance Corp.*, 139 S. CT. 759 (2019), Diss. Op. Breyer, J. ("multilateralism is threatened if one nation alone, through application of its own liability rules (by nonexpert judges), can shape the policy choices or actions that an international organization believes it must take or refrain from taking").

306 *See also* BEIER *et al.*, at 3; I. Seidl-Hohenveldern, Die Immunität internationaler organisationen in dienstrechtsstreitfällen, Rechtsgutachten für Eurocontrol (Schriften zum Völkerrecht 71), at 31 (1981)[hereinafter: SEIDL-HOHENVELDERN, EUROCONTROL]; Lalive, at 299; Kunz, at 836.

> [s]ince an international organisation is brought into being by sovereign and independent states and is an association of states, it must be given a special status in relation to the exercise of jurisdictional and administrative authority by individual states.[[307]] Its independence which is an essential element of this status must be ensured by the grant of such privileges and immunities as may be necessary to enable it to achieve, without being subjected to undue interference, the aims for which it has been set up.[308]

According to a 1945 Memorandum by the ILO, "international institutions should have a status which protects them against control or interference by any one government in the performance of functions for the effective discharge of which they are responsible to democratically constituted international bodies in which all the nations concerned are represented."[309] The attribution of privileges and immunities to international organizations can, therefore, be regarded as an essential device for protecting these organizations from unilateral interference by individual governments of member States as well as non-member States, since an international organization may be sited in a State which is not a member of it.[310] As Jenks has explained, the granting of privileges and immunities to international organizations is neither merely a housekeeping problem of these international organizations nor an insidious encroachment on the equal application of the rule of law, but is rather an essential device for protecting these organizations from unilateral and sometimes irresponsible interference by individual governments.[311]

An international organization may, however, not only have a need for protection from interference by the individual *governments* of individual States, but from prejudice and divergent judgments by the national independent *courts* as well. In this respect, several reasons have been given why international organizations should enjoy immunity from legal process.

(1) There is the danger of prejudice against international organizations in national courts.[312] Although such prejudice would not necessarily be in bad

---

307 Another reference to this special status was made by Ushakov, in [1977] 1 Y.B. Int'l L. Comm'n 212, para. 34, UN Doc. A/CN.4/SER.A/1977.

308 Council of Europe Report 1969, at 12, para. 9 sub (a).

309 *International Labour Office, Official Bulletin,* 10 Dec. 1945, Vol. XXVII, No. 2, at 199.

310 *E.g.,* Switzerland and the United Nations until 2002.

311 JENKS, at xiii.

312 McKinnon Wood, at 143–144; AHLUWALIA, at 200; BOWETT, at 349; A. Ehrenfeld, *United Nations Immunity Distinguished From Sovereign Immunity,* 52 Proc. Am. Soc'y Int'l L. 88, 90 (1958)[hereinafter: Ehrenfeld].

faith, the risk is apparent in times of strain. Lalive has referred to this risk through the following remarks:

> ... en période de tension internationale, à un moment où 1'organisation souffre, à tort ou à raison, d'un certain discrédit auprès de 1'opinion publique et où elle peut avoir à exercer une activité, à prendre des décisions qui seraient impopulaires dans le pays d'accueil, on discerne les inconvénients de lui appliquer le droit commun et de la soumettre à un contrôle juridictionnel exercé par des juges ou jurés qui, eux, ne seraient pas toujours á l'abri de pressions gouvernementales ou privées. Certains gouvernements pourraient même, selon le cas, être tantés, par la menace d'actions devant les tribunaux, d'influencer 1'activité ou la politique de 1'Organisation. Il faut tenir compte également de la réaction psychologique des *juges nationaux*, occupés, surchargés souvent par des affaires de pur droit privé, peu aptes à saisir les besoins et problèmes particuliers des services public internationaux.[313] (emphasis added)

The threat may, therefore, come from either the *governments*, putting the national courts under pressure to adjudicate upon the affairs of international bodies, or from the *courts* themselves, since national judges may be not well equipped to handle such cases or may even be politically motivated because their re-election depends upon it. Moreover, "[t]heir experience and participation in a particular legal order will have impressed legal notions upon judges which will differ from the climate of judicial opinion elsewhere."[314]

(2) International organizations must be protected against "baseless actions brought from improper motives or by the numerous cranks, fanatics or cantankerous persons who may conceive that they have a duty to compel the organization to take some particular step or that they have suffered wrong at its hands."[315] Here the threat originates not from the national government or the courts but from *individuals*, constituting a third group of potential wrongdoers against an international organization. An example of the protection of an international organization against the actions of individuals may be found in Article 16(a) of the Headquarters Agreement between the United Nations and the United States, which provides for a due diligence obligation on the part of the host State to prevent any disturbances in the

313 Lalive, at 299.

314 SCHERMERS, at 1079, para. 1611.

315 McKinnon Wood, at 144; *see also* Lalive, at 299.

immediate vicinity of the UN headquarters district. Such disturbance may, e.g., be caused by picketing activities near entrances to the organization's premises.[316]

(3) It would be undesirable to allow the national courts of particular States, quite possibly in various ways, to determine the legal effects of acts performed by international organizations, since various courts would likely render inconsistent judgments and no mechanism exists to reconcile them.[317] As we have seen above, when we introduced the principle of independence, an intergovernmental organization must act in the *common* interest of its member States in order to maintain its credibility. The organization must, therefore, speak with *one* voice and can only regulate its legal relations through one *uniform* body of law.[318] The uniformity of the organization, which is essential to the performance by the organization of its designated purposes, would be endangered were it forced to defend its actions in the municipal courts of various States.

2.2.3 (ii) Impartiality of the Organization

Closely related to the fundamental consideration of the independence of an international organization, yet more concerned with a psychological element on the part of the member States, is the principle of *impartiality* of an international organization. As Michaels has pointed out, to confer neutrality on international organizations, by way of immunities, is to grant independence from the influence and control of a single contracting party.[319] An international organization can only perform its tasks towards its member States, if *all* member States are convinced of the impartiality of the organization. A member State will only then be prepared to implement the decisions taken by an organization which go against this State's interests, if it

316 *See People v. Carcel,* 2 Misc.2d 827, 833, 150 N.Y.S.2d 436, 441–42 (City Magist. Ct. 1956), *rev'd,* 3 N.Y.S.2d 327, 330, 165 N.Y.S.2d 113, 115, 144 N.E.2d 81, 83 (1957) *quoted in* Restatement (Third), § 468, Reporters' Note 3, at 507. Although the individual may sometimes not be held liable because the activity is not covered by local criminal laws, the host State certainly may, on the basis of its international due diligence obligation. *See also Boos v. Barry,* 485 U.S. 312 (1988), where the U.S. Supreme Court upheld a statute that made it unlawful "to congregate" within a certain distance of an embassy "and refuse to disperse after having been ordered to do so by the police."

317 *See* McKinnon Wood, at 144; SCHERMERS, at 1080, para. 1611; AHLUWALIA, at 200; BOWETT, at 349.

318 *See* Seidl-Hohenveldern, Eurocontrol, at 13; Lalive, at 299; Ehrenfeld, at 90 ("a Member State ought not to be able to exercise power, through its national courts, over the execution of the Organization's functions or the disposition of its funds, which have, in the first instance, been determined and contributed collectively.").

319 MICHAELS, at 37, calling this "a grant of inviolability."

can depend on the fact that the organization genuinely acts in the *common* interest of *all* its member States and not in the sole interest of one particular member State or influential bloc of member States within the organization. In this respect reference may again be made to Jenks, who has stated:

> [t]he basic function of international immunities is to bridle the sovereignty of States in their treatment of international organisations. This bridling of sovereignty is as much in the interest of States as in that of international organisations. While it debars each State from illicit interference, it also protects it from such interference by other States. It represents, indeed, an indispensable guarantee to each member State that the organisation will not become, by means of pressure and constraint which are not fully apparent and over which there is therefore no possibility of control, an instrument of the policy of other States directed against its own policy and interests, but will serve legally the common interest as determined by the recognized constitutional processes of the organisation.[320]

An organization can only act in a convincing manner towards all its member States if it treats them on an *equal* basis,[321] i.e., when it does not discriminate among individual Members. This is an important principle, since there is always the danger that an unsatisfied member State will hinder the decision-making process of an international organization, thereby threatening to disturb its efficiency and unity.[322] Without impartiality no organization can act in the pure interest of the entirety of its creators, i.e., its member States. Granting privileges and immunities to international organizations can play a contributory role in safeguarding the essential principle of impartiality.

2.2.4 (iii) Equality of the Member States

Justification for the granting of privileges and immunities to international organizations can also be found in the principle of the *equality of the member States* of the organization. As international organizations are created by sovereign States which in principle are equal among themselves, these

320 JENKS, at 166.

321 *See also* I. Seidl-Hohenveldern, Das Recht der Internationalen Organisationen einschliesslich der Supranationalen Gemeinschaften 281, para. 1901 (4th ed. 1984)[hereinafter: SEIDL-HOHENVELDERN, RECHT]; similarly, Díaz González, *Second Report reprinted in* [1985] 2 Y.B. Int'l L. Comm'n 108, para. 37, UN Doc. A/CN.4/SER.A/1985/Add. 1 (Part 1).

322 *See* Seidl-Hohenveldern, Eurocontrol, at 13.

States should all be on an equal footing *vis-a-vis* the organization of which they become Members.[323] By granting the necessary privileges and immunities to the organization to which they belong, States contribute to the creation of a situation in which such equality is guaranteed in an institutional manner. This will stimulate co-operation between or among the member States within the organization, emphasizing the duty of affirmative good faith of the member States in their mutual dealings with each other, which duty is essential to the smooth functioning of every international organization.[324] In this way, the loyal execution of decisions taken by the organization, which is a consequence of the duty of good faith just referred to, will enhance the efficiency by which the organization exercises its functions and fulfills its purposes.

The United Nations, as an international organization, actively contributes to upholding an atmosphere of equality in the immunity régime applicable to it, by its efforts to develop a uniform set of provisions contained in the various bilateral agreements it concludes with States. As was stated in the *United Nations Juridical Yearbook* of 1974, the organization considers it:

> essential that no substantive difference should exist among the provisions on privileges and immunities contained in the agreements concluded with various host countries; the provisions of the draft agreement are therefore of a standard nature and they are, as a consequence, usually included unchanged in the final agreements.[325]

This approach ensures adherence to the fundamental principle of the sovereign equality of all UN member States,[326] and thus encourages the development of at least a psychology of equality. Moreover, the approach is beneficial for both the organization and the individual States. The United Nations benefits because the privileges and immunities provided by a series of bilateral agreements contribute to developing an independent body of organizational immunities, through which the organization can claim certain immunities that are of a wider scale than those laid down in

---

323 *See* Council of Europe Report 1969, at 12, para. 9 sub (c); Díaz González, in [1983] 1 Y.B. Int'l L. Comm'n, 238, para. 4, UN Doc. A/CN.4/SER.A/1983; Kunz, at 847; Ehrenfeld, at 90.

324 *See* Glenn *et al.*, at 268.

325 1974 UN Jurid. Y.B, p. 144, UN Doc. ST/LEG/SER.C/12 (1976).

326 *See* UN Charter, Art. 2, para. 1.

existing general multilateral agreements. At the same time, this practice ensures that individual States are accorded a position in the negotiating process that is not less favorable than that accorded by the United Nations to any other State.

2.2.5 (iv) Avoidance of Undue National Financial Advantage: Financial Independence

The relationship of confidence the member States have towards the international organization and towards each other would be endangered if one particular member State could take undue *financial advantage* of the organization or if it was in a position to put the organization under financial pressure by means not intended at the time of the organization's creation.[327] To avoid such undesired effects special fiscal and financial privileges and immunities, such as those from direct taxes and customs duties, have been created.[328]

No State, in particular the host State, should derive any undue fiscal advantage of the common international funds of an organization present or operating within its territory.[329] In a memorandum of law of 1953, the Office of Legal Affairs of the UN Secretariat set forth the necessity for the organization's immunity from taxation. Were the United Nations devoid of this immunity, the memorandum indicated, the independent functioning of the organization would be compromised by the ability of member States to impose taxes on the essential assets of the organization. This would constitute enrichment of one member State at the expense of all others.[330] As Ahluwalia has stated:

> [i]mmunity from taxation is aimed at preventing the host States from securing a financial advantage at the expense of the common budget.

---

327 *See* Seidl-Hohenveldern, Recht, at 282, para. 1901.

328 *See also* [1967] Y.B. Int'l L. Comm'n 241–250, UN Doc. A/CN.4/SER.A/1967/Add. 1; Council of Europe Report 1969, at 30–33.

329 *See* Council of Europe Report 1969, at 12, para. 9, sub (c); *Memorandum of the International Labour Office, ILO Official Bulletin,* 10 Dec. 1945, Vol. XXVII, No.2, at 199; Satow's Diplomatic Practice 301, para. 21.24 (Sir Ivor Roberts ed., 6th ed. 2009)[hereinafter: SATOW); SCHERMERS, at 393, para. 530; *but see* Köck, at 63 n.64, referring to a statement at the 1975 Vienna Conference by Professor Zemanek of the Austrian delegation, who argued that in general host States had to defray more expenses than they would gain by the money spent by diplomatic missions.

330 *See* [1967) 2 Y.B. Int'l L. Comm'n 245, para. 167, UN Doc. A/CN.4/SER.A/1967.

> That is, various sovereign States contribute to the funds of international organizations and that fund is meant to be used for furthering common international purposes. Therefore, it would be inequitable if the host State obtains some financial gain at the international expense by levying such taxes.[331]

In addition to the danger of unwarranted financial enrichment, a legal situation in which the organization enjoys no protection from the taxation laws of its member States would provide the taxing authority concerned with a measure of indirect control over the activities of the organization sited or operating within its territory. This has a direct bearing upon the principle of independence and, more particularly, that of equality between member States. The principle of equality between member States can thus also be seen as another justification for granting exemption from taxation to international organizations, which once again demonstrates the close relationship between the basic considerations behind the granting of privileges and immunities to international organizations.[332]

2.2.6 (v) Precedent and Equality of Status with Other Organizations

It has become general practice for newly created international organizations to be granted more or less the same privileges and immunities accorded to already existing organizations.[333] Established immunity régimes provide a precedent from which new régimes are crafted. The Council of Europe Report of 1969 sounded a note of caution, however, against the wholesale adoption of existing immunity régimes to new organizations:

> [f]or practical purposes, the privileges and immunities accorded to similar organisations in the past afforded a useful guide when considering the privileges and immunities of a new organisation. Nevertheless, it would be advisable to take precedents into account only when dealing with organisations which were comparable. The subcommittee was of the opinion that precedent had played too important a part until now.[334]

---

331 AHLUWALIA, at 89–90.

332 *See also* Council of Europe Report 1969, at 30, para. 58.

333 Examples in the practice of international organizations can be traced back as early as 1946. In that year, the representative of Switzerland, Mr. Perréard, assured the UN representative, Mr. Moderow, that the Swiss authorities would endow the UN with the same privileges and immunities as they had accorded other international organizations in the past. *See* EGGER, at 138.

334 Council of Europe Report 1969, at 13, para. 9 sub (d).

We agree with this critical note to the extent that one organization cannot necessarily be compared with the other in light of the principle of the speciality of international organizations and that an organization of more limited membership with narrower and less controversial functions and purposes than a universal, political organization such as the United Nations cannot be regarded as having comparable needs in the matter of privileges and immunities.

The Government of the United Kingdom has stated in this regard that "*in practice*, precedent and equality of status with other organisations are the *dominant* principles. A relatively consistent series of precedents having been established, it comes to be thought that a new organisation must be put in the same position as its predecessors if it is to have the requisite international standing."(emphasis added)[335]

It can, therefore, be said that, for practical reasons, the organizational immunities granted in the past to a variety of similar organizations may form a usual reference point in considering the question of what privileges and immunities may be granted to a new organization.[336]

2.2.7 (vi) Prestige and Authority of the Organization

Although closely related to the previous considerations, the *prestige* and *authority* of the organization have been accorded a separate place on the list of reasons justifying the granting of privileges and immunities.[337] Some degree of immunity seems essential to ensure that an international organization enjoys the international status and authority with which similar organizations are already vested.[338] Jenks has called the concept of international immunities "an essential element in the ... authority of international organisations."[339] The Council of Europe Report, however, took the opposite view, by stating the following:

> The sub-committee was of the opinion that, in general, prestige was not a factor to be taken into account in determining the privileges and immunities of international organisations and persons connected with

---

335 *Memorandum by the Government of the United Kingdom on the privileges and immunities of international organisations and persons connected with them (Foreign Office, 10 March 1965)*, Appendix to Council of Europe Report 1969, 73–79, at 75, para. 8.

336 *See also Report of the International Law Commission on the work of its forty-first session*, 44 GAOR Supp. (No. 10) at 377, para. 721, UN Doc. A/44/10 (1989).

337 *See, inter alia*, MICHAELS, at 26; Kunz, at 847; Seidl-Hohenveldern, Responsibility, at 426; Council of Europe Report 1969, at 13.

338 *See* BEIER *et al.*, Art. 8, at 4; Lalive, at 300; Kunz, at 847.

339 JENKS, at 18.

> them, though prestige might be considered to be one of the justifications for according the full scale of diplomatic privileges and immunities to some high officers and some representatives of states to international organisations.[340]

Whatever the validity of the view expressed in this report, it does not seem to be widely supported by legal doctrine and practice. It cannot be denied that, for practical purposes, prestige has been used as a consideration in determining the privileges and immunities to be accorded to international organizations and it is for this reason that it merits reference here.

2.2.8 (vii) The Need for Special Protection in Initial Stages

Another justification for granting privileges and immunities to international organizations is constituted by the vulnerable position in which newly created organizations often find themselves, especially in the initial stages of their development, and which requires a certain measure of special protection.[341] As Lalive has stated, "institutions nouvelles, elles sont en plein essor, traversant ici et là des crises de jeunesse et de croissance."[342] Whatever value must be attached to this consideration, which originated in the period after the Second World War when international co-operation on a large scale was only just beginning, it entails some serious risks. It will be difficult to deprive an international organization of certain privileges and immunities granted to it in its initial stages once it has finally reached a state of maturity.[343] Moreover, one may ask which factors must be taken into account in order to determine whether such special protection continued to be needed and to what extent, as it will be difficult to identify the point at which the organization becomes mature. Having regard to these problems, we are of the opinion that, whenever it is decided to accord a 'young' international organization special protection by way of certain privileges and immunities, it should be laid down explicitly in the agreement granting these privileges and immunities when such special initial protective régime will end. Since, as was stated above, this will be difficult to determine, it is questionable whether such practice can be meaningfully established.

---

340 Council of Europe Report 1969, at 13, para. 9 sub (f).

341 *See* JENKS, at 18.

342 Lalive, at 300.

343 As is stated in SATOW, at 304, para. 21.28, it has not "proved feasible to re-negotiate any existing international agreement on privileges and immunities in a downward direction."

2.2.9 Conclusion

In the preceding paragraphs an effort was made to present a compact overview of each of the underlying, and partly overlapping considerations which justify the granting of privileges and immunities to international organizations as separate legal entities. The principles of the political and financial independence are of a particularly pre-eminent nature, being rooted in a more conceptual framework formed by the international functions performed by international organizations. As was shown, this independence is of a functional nature, necessary to enable an organization to exercise its functions in the fulfilment of the purposes for which it was created. International organizations are accorded special protection out of a functional need for the independent performance of the tasks member States assign to them.

In the final section of this chapter, we will examine the *legal sources* of the privileges and immunities of international organizations as they reflect the fundamental considerations outlined above.

2.3 What: *Functional Necessity as a Basis for Selecting Organizational Immunities*

2.3.1 Introduction

According to the *basis*-element of the functional necessity concept, an international organization is *entitled* to those privileges and immunities it *needs* for *the exercise of its functions in the fulfilment of its purposes.* Thus, unless a particular privilege or immunity is necessary for the exercise of the organization's functions in the achievement of its purposes, there is no reason for deviating from the normal duty of compliance with local rules of judicial competence.[344] It has been pointed out that "[m]ost rules of national law are applicable to international organizations in the same way as to other subjects within the national jurisdiction,"[345] and, as a general rule, laws will apply to them when not excluded by express provision.[346] Immunity from

344 *See* T.J. O'Toole, *Sovereign Immunity Redivivus: Suits against International Organizations,* 4 Suff. Transnat'l L.J. 1, 3 (1980)[hereinafter: O'Toole]; Sucharitkul, in [1978] 1 Y.B. Int'l L. Comm'n 266, para. 15, UN Doc. A/CN.4/SER.A/1978. This duty of compliance is one of the duties referred to in the qualification of international organizations as subjects of international law by the ICJ in the *Reparation* case. 1949 ICJ Rep. 174, 179.

345 SCHERMERS, at 1076, para. 1610.

346 *See Jurisdictional Immunities of the State (Germany v. Italy; Greece intervening),* Judgment, 2012 ICJ Rep. 99, at 124, para. 58 (observing that the law of immunity "regulates the exercise of jurisdiction in respect of particular conduct and is thus entirely distinct from the substantive law which determines whether that conduct is lawful or unlawful"). *See also* Sucharitkul, in [1977] 1 Y.8. Int'I L. Comm'n 207, para. 52, UN Doc. A/

legal process prevents, however, their *adjudication* in domestic courts.[347] In other words, domestic law is *unenforcable* against the organization[348] and "the law of immunity is essentially procedural in nature."[349] Similar to the position regarding domestic law, "the fact that immunity may bar the exercise of jurisdiction in a particular case does not alter the applicability of the substantive rules of international law."[350] Since immunity is a derogation from the normal exercise of jurisdiction by the courts, it should only be accorded in clear cases.[351] At the same time, it must be noted that "the rules governing the jurisdiction of national courts must be carefully distinguished from those governing jurisdictional immunities: jurisdiction does not imply absence of immunity, while absence of immunity does not imply

CN.4/SER.A/ 1977; the first preambular paragraph contained in the 1957 resolution on judicial redress against the decisions of international organs, adopted, by 39 votes in favor, with none against and 2 abstentions, by the *Institut de Droit International,* 47 *Annuaire,* Vol. II, at 274 (1957). Schermers has gone as far as to state that there is "a general rule of international institutional law to the effect that national laws should not be applied to international organizations if they could affect the proper functioning of the organization." SCHERMERS, at 1075, para. 1608. At the same time, Schermers posits that organizational privileges and immunities "must be interpreted restrictively" and that international organizations "should waive them when they are not really necessary." *Id.*

347 *See* SCHERMERS, at 1076, para. 260; AHLUWALIA, at 66; Kunz, at 838; F.W. Henderson, *How Much Immunity for International Organizations?: Mendaro v. World Bank,* 10 N.C.J. INT'L L. COMM. REG. 487,491 (1985)[hereinafter: Henderson]; KELSEN, at 339; JENKS, at 42; Sucharitkul, in [1977] 1 Y.B. Int'I L. Comm'n 207, paras. 51–52, UN Doc. A/CN.4/ SER.A/1977.

348 *See, e.g., Firma Baumeister Ing. Richard L v. O...,* Supreme Court of Austria, judgment of 14 Dec. 2004, English translated text in 2004 UN Jurid. Y.B 394, at 397, UN Doc. ST/LEG/SER.C/42 (2004) ("Immunity constitutes merely a procedural barrier to the enforcement of the law; it does not, however, alter the validity of substantive law"). *See also* M. Akehurst, A Modern Introduction to International Law 121 n.12 (6th ed. 1987).

349 *Jurisdictional Immunities of the State (Germany v. Italy; Greece intervening),* Judgment, 2012 ICJ Rep. 99, at 124, para. 58 (citing *Arrest Warrant of 11 April 2000 (Democratic Republic of the Congo v. Belgium),* Judgment, 2002 ICJ Rep. 3, at 25, para. 60) and 140, para. 93 (observing that the rules of immunity "do not bear upon the question whether or not the conduct in respect of which the proceedings are brought was lawful or unlawful").

350 *Id.,* at 143, para. 100 (citing *Arrest Warrant of 11 April 2000 (Democratic Republic of the Congo v. Belgium),* Judgment, 2002 ICJ Rep. 3, at 25, para. 60).

351 *See Victory Transport Inc. v. Comisaria General de Abastecientos y Transportes,* 336 F.2d 354 (2d Cir. 1964) *quoted in* H.J. Steiner, D.F. Vagts & H.H. Koh, Transnational Legal Problems. Materials and Text 765 (4th ed. 1994).

jurisdiction."[352] While it has been observed that organizational "immunity from jurisdiction is a matter to be judged not by reference to domestic law, but to public international law,"[353] courts in dualist-type jurisdictions such as the United States decide organizational immunity questions first and foremost by reference to domestic law, including domestic law giving effect to the constituent instrument of a given international organization.

As to the origin of the functional necessity concept of immunities, it has been stated:

> [t]he functional immunities of international organizations, which are those necessary for the accomplishment of common purposes and goals, evolved relatively quickly from the recognition of interested nations that the common benefits to be achieved from organized co-operation would not be attainable if individual members were permitted to apply their own laws at will to the functions and activities of international organizations.[354]

This concept can be traced back to the establishment of such organizations as the United Nations and the Organization of American States in the 1940s, when international co-operation through intergovernmental organizations was still a relatively new idea. The test of simple necessity provided a useful practical basis for granting privileges and immunities to these organizations. Its association with practicalities is one of the main advantages of the functional necessity concept.

That functional necessity justifies the granting of privileges and immunities to international organizations now seems to be universally accepted. This criterion is emphasized in Articles 104 and 105 of the UN Charter,[355] thereby giving "[t]he indispensability of jurisdictional immunity to the

---

352 *Arrest Warrant of 11 April 2000* (*Democratic Republic of the Congo v. Belgium*), Judgment, 2002 ICJ Rep. 3, at 24, para. 59.

353 Schermers, at 1076, para. 1610.

354 Glenn *et al.*, at 266; this passage evidences also the close relationship of this concept with the other considerations justifying the granting of privileges and immunities to international organizations; *see also* O'Toole, at 11, according to whom "the functional analysis hinges upon the need to preserve the operational independence and integrity of the organizations."

355 According to UN Charter, Art. 105, para. 1:

"The Organization shall enjoy in the territory of each of its Members such privileges and immunities *as are necessary for the fulfilment of its purposes.*" (emphasis added).

effective functioning of international organizations ... wide acceptance as a principle of international law."[356] As the Rapporteur of Committee IV/2 stated in his Report at the San Francisco Conference:

> [t]he draft article ... does not specify the privileges and immunities respect for which it imposes on the member states. This has been thought superfluous. The terms *privileges* and *immunities* indicate in a general way all that could be considered *necessary to the realization of the purposes of the organization* ...: exemption from tax, immunity from jurisdiction, facilities for communication, inviolability of buildings, properties, and archives, etc.[357] (emphasis added)

The Committee thus chose a "standard, based, for the purposes of the Organization, on the necessity of realizing its purposes ...."[358] The legal instruments of most other international organizations contain similar provisions basing the grant of privileges and immunities on the criterion of functional necessity.[359]

The concept of functional necessity has been underlined by the jurisprudence of the International Court of Justice. On the basis of the Court's advisory opinion on *Reparation for Injuries Suffered in the Service of the United Nations*[360] it can be concluded that organizational immunities are based on

356 Glenn *et al.*, at 276.

357 *See* 13 U.N.C.I.O. Doc. 933, IV/2/42(2), at 705 (1945).

358 *See id.*, at 704.

359 *See, e.g.*, Art. 103 Charter of the Organization of American States, 119 U.N.T.S. 3; *see also* the Preamble of the *Protocol on the Privileges and Immunities of the European Communities* of 1965, according to which the Communities "enjoy in the territories of the Member States such privileges and immunities as are necessary for the performance of their tasks." *See* Sweet & Maxwell's European Community Treaties – Including the European Communities Act 1972 228 (K.R. Simmonds adv. ed. 1972); R.A. Wessel, *Immunities of the European Union*, 10 IOLR 395 (2013). For the relevant constitutional texts of the specialized agencies, see UN Doc. ST/LEG/SER.B/11 (1961), at 101.

360 1949 ICJ Rep. 174; more recently, the Court reiterated the importance of the functional criterion in *Applicability of Article VI, Section 22, of the Convention on the Privileges and Immunities of the United Nations*, Advisory Opinion, 1989 ICJ Rep. 177, 194–195, paras. 47, 50, 52. For a commentary, see T.D. Gill, *International Decisions*, 84 AJIL 742 (1990); R. Ostrihansky, *The 'Mazilu Opinion' of the International Court of Justice and its Contribution to the Clarification of International Law*, 18 Pol. Y.B. Int'l L. 1989–1990 (1992). For a decision by another international tribunal, namely, the Court of Justice of the European Communities, see its decision in the *Zwartveld* case, Judgment of 13 July 1990, Nr.

the criterion of functional necessity. A similar conclusion can be derived from the decisions of a variety of national courts.[361]

International legal theory[362] and practice[363] accept that international organizations should be granted whatever privileges and immunities may be

---

C-2/88, *reprinted in* Comm. Mkt. L. Rep. 457 (1990)(3), at Para. 19, where the Court points out that the privileges and immunities of the EC "are only functional in the sense that they aim to prevent any obstacle in the functioning and the independence of the Communities."

361 For a recognition by courts of the applicability of functional necessity in defining the privileges and immunities of international organizations, see the rulings of several U.S. courts *quoted in* Glenn *et al.*, at 277; for decisions of the courts of other countries, see *id.* at 275 n.144. *See also* Dinh, at 262 *et seq.;* Cassese, at 556; Dominicé, LIBER SEIDL, at 77. For a decision by an Austrian court, see 47 OJZ 661, item 161 (1992). The Supreme Court (*Hoge Raad*) of The Netherlands adopted the functional necessity concept of organizational immunities in *Spaans v. Iran-United States Claims Tribunal,* 438 NJ 1691–1702 (1985)(this judgment will be discussed in greater detail below when we deal with Step Three).

362 *See, e.g.,* Fedder, at 60; REUTER, INSTITUTIONS, at 230; BOWETT, at 346; Kunz, at 838, 841, 847 (giving further references, including Vattel; *see also* Glenn *et al.,* at 267, referring to early American Federalist writings); Henderson, at 492; M. Brandon, *The Legal Status of the Premises of the United Nations,* 28 BYBIL 90, 94 (1951)[hereinafter: Brandon]; AHLUWALIA, at *199 et seq.;* Council of Europe Report 1969, at 39; O'Toole, at 3; *Boimah v. United Nations General Assembly: International Organizations Immunity is Absolutely Not Restrictive,* 15 BROOKLYN J. INT'L L. 497, 502, 513, 519 (1989)(authored by A.A. Farrugia) [hereinafter: Farrugia]; MICHAELS, at 50; Schwebel, in [1977] 1 Y.B. Int'l L. Comm'n 210, para. 19, UN Doc. A/CN.4/SER.A/1977 ("Everybody agreed that international organizations must have the functional privileges and immunities necessary for the performance of their tasks"); Sir Francis Vallat, in *id.* at 212, para. 37; Sucharitkul, in [1978] 1 Y.B. Int'l L. Comm'n 265, para. 15, UN Doc. A/CN.4/SER.A/1978; *id.,* in [1983] Y.B. Int'l L. Comm'n 240, para. 20, and 253, para. 48, UN Doc. A/CN.4/SER.A/1983; Yankov, in [1987] 1 Y.B. Int'l L. Comm'n 192, para. 27, UN Doc. A/CN.4/SER.A/1987; Sinclair, in [1983] 1 Y.B. Int'l L. Comm'n 242, para. 4, UN Doc. A/CN.4/SER.A/1983; Koroma, in *id.,* at 244, para. 20; Mahiou, in *id.,* at 245, para. 32; Njenga, in *id.,* at 250, para. 23; Zacklin, DUPUY, at 181, 190; EGGER, at 119; Restatement (Third), at 492.

363 *See, e.g.,* the statements made by a variety of States in Council of Europe Report 1969, Appendix, at 73 *et seq.,* in particular the *Comments by the United Kingdom on replies received up to 1 November 1965* (*Foreign Office, 1 November 1965*), at 90: "Almost all the governments which have replied have stated that they agree with the view expressed in the memorandum that the grant of privileges and immunities to international organisations should be related in future to the concept of *functional need. No criticism of this view was expressed.*" (emphasis added); OAS Guide, Guideline 2, 'Objective of jurisdictional immunities' ("Jurisdictional immunities are granted to international organizations to enable them to accomplish their object and purpose").

necessary in order to carry out the tasks entrusted to them. It has been remarked that:

> [n]o scholar appears to contradict this principle. Some say that no rule of law exists, that IGOs possess only the immunities specified in their constitutive agreements; but even they immediately go on to refer to functional immunity as important in international practice .... And international practice appears to be based on functional necessity.[364]

Before concluding that functional necessity can serve as a basis for justifying the granting of privileges and immunities to international organizations, the question should be addressed as to whether this criterion is sufficiently *precise*. According to Lalive,[365] the functional necessity test has the disadvantage of being vague, for it does not say anything about the material contents of the privileges and immunities. It may be doubted whether this view is entirely valid, since functional necessity, in its *basis*-element, operates as a means of selecting privileges and immunities. In this phase it is above all a *justifying principle*, i.e., a tool for deciding whether an identified organization is one having a need for certain privileges and immunities that are necessary to fulfil its purposes. At this stage, functional necessity operates without going into details regarding the exact scope of the privileges and immunities concerned. This is the role played by the scope-element of functional necessity, which is Step Three of the functional analysis discussed below. A sharp distinction should therefore be made between the different *phases* of granting privileges and immunities to international organizations.

The uncertainty is reduced by entering into an examination of the functions and purposes of the organization, as required by the functional concept. As we have seen in Step One, every international organization will, by definition, have its own functions and purposes. It is necessary in order to engage in a functional necessity analysis to have recourse to the instrument containing the functions and purposes of the organization in question. It is from a survey of these instruments and from the organization's operation in practice that one is able to conclude what the exact functions

364 Note, *Jurisdictional Immunities of Intergovernmental Organizations*, 91 Yale L.J. 1167, 1181, n.126 and references therein (1982)(authored by Kathleen Cully); *see also* A. Bianchi, Book Review, 88 AJIL 212 (1994)(reviewing S. de Bellis, L'Immunità delle Organizzazioni Internazionali dalla Giurisdizione (1992)[hereinafter: Bianchi].

365 Lalive, at 304, 348.

and purposes of an international organization are and to what extent the fulfilment of these functions and purposes may need to be protected by way of certain privileges and immunities. This is not tantamount to saying that a review of the organization's functions and purposes will put an end to all uncertainty. What it does say is that the functional necessity criterion can only operate in close co-operation with the instrument embodying the organization's 'necessary functions:' this instrument, whether constitutional or of any other nature, and the experience of its application in practice will specify the criterion, making it a useful guideline for deciding which privileges and immunities, if any, are needed. This construction has the advantage of staying closely within the constitutional framework of the organization, agreed upon by the member States. It must, however, be admitted that the constitutional framework often describes these functions and purposes in very general terms, thereby leaving considerable scope for extension in practice. This problem will recur in our discussion of Step Three.

In sum, the criterion of functional necessity may be regarded as an essential *basis* for justifying with sufficient precision the granting of privileges and immunities to international organizations. The practicability of the functional necessity criterion is enhanced by the fact that it has a general application whatever the nature and size of the international organization concerned, thereby furnishing a criterion which is generally applicable to all types of intergovernmental organizations.[366] This is the case despite the fact that there is a large variety of international organizations, each having its own characteristics and needs. Consequently, their requirements in terms of privileges and immunities are not identical.[367] Thus, the United Nations is at the top of the pyramid of privileges and immunities to be accorded to international organizations.[368] The privileges and immunities which have

366 *See* Njenga, in [1983] 1 Y.B. Int'l L. Comm'n 250, para. 24, UN Doc. A/CN.4/SER.A/1983.

367 *See* Sucharitkul, in [1983] 1 Y.B. Int'l L. Comm'n 239, para. 16,UN Doc. A/CN.4/SER.A/1983.

368 *See* Castrén, in [1963] 1 Y.B. Int'l L. Comm'n 301, para. 11, UN Doc. A/CN.4/SER.A/1963; Sucharitkul, in [1983] 1 Y.B. Int'l L. Comm'n 239, para. 16, UN Doc. A/CN.4/SER.A/1983; Rao, in [1987] 1 Y.B. Int'l L. Comm'n 203, para. 43, UN Doc. A/CN.4/SER.A/1987; UN Doc. A/CN.4/SR.2234 (8 July 1991), at 8 (Njenga); *see also* ILC Special Rapporteur Díaz González, in [1985] 1 Y.B. Int'l L. Comm'n 283, para. 5, UN Doc. A/CN.4/SER.A/1985, pointing out that the United Nations holds first place among international organizations by reason of the importance of its functions, its universality and the magnitude of its work. *See also* A.J. Miller, *The Privileges and Immunities of the United Nations*, 6 IOLR 7 (2009).

been granted to the United Nations may, therefore, be used as a maximum standard in determining whether a given organization has a similar need for protection. The other extreme is an organization which performs purely commercial functions, entering the marketplace seeking customers for its industrial-type goods and services. The latter type of organization probably has no justified need for any privileges and immunities at all,[369] provided that the exclusion from certain privileges and immunities does not prevent such organization from effectively exercising its functions. The latter condition forms the minimum requirement of the functional necessity concept.[370] In short, the general considerations inherent in Step Two of the functional necessity concept, while they are generally applicable, may not apply to every international organization to the same degree. As an excerpt from a Memorandum by the Government of the United Kingdom of 1965 indicates:

> 11. In practice it is difficult to apply these considerations to particular immunities and privileges and to particular organisations. What is appropriate in one case may not be so in another. Thus the United

---

369 *See Memorandum by the Government of the United Kingdom on the privileges and immunities of international organisations and persons connected with them* (*Foreign Office, 10 March 1965*), Appendix to Council of Europe Report 1969, at 76, para. 11. The United Nations has traditionally exercised restraint in the commercial field. *See, e.g.*, 1990 UN Jurid. Y.B, pp. 257–258, UN Doc. ST/LEG/SER.C/28 (1993), reproducing an Internal Memorandum of 23 July 1990 from the UN Office of Legal Affairs to the Executive Officer of the UN Department of Public Information (DPI). In this Memorandum, DPI is advised not to enter into a profit making joint venture with a private publishing firm which would manage and market the UN publication 'Development Business.' The proposed commercial UN activity – participation in an independent commercial venture directed to producing revenue – would not be within the scope of the principles and objectives set forth in the UN Charter, and could put the status and character of the UN in question.

370 *Memorandum by the Government of the United Kingdom on the privileges and immunities of international organisations and persons connected with them* (*Foreign Office, 10 March 1965*), Appendix to Council of Europe Report 1969, at 77, paras. 14–16 on the immunities of the European Space Research Organization (ESRO) and the European Launcher Development Organization (ELDO), which were involved in commercial activities; *see also* the reply from the Federal Republic of Germany (German Federal Foreign Office, 25 June 1965) to the British Embassy's Note Verbale No. 20(1921) of 10 March 1965, *in* Council of Europe Report 1969, at 83, para. 2; *see also* Art. IV of the Convention for the Establishment of a European Space Agency, *reprinted in* N.M. Matte, Aerospace Law. From Scientific Exploration to Commercial Utilization 23 (1977); [1967] 2 Y.B. Int'l L. Comm'n 210, para. 11, UN Doc. A/CN.4/SER.A/1967/Add. 1.

> Nations Organisation may be called upon to act in emergencies in all parts of the world in difficult situations. Its functions are largely political in character and therefore liable to attract a large measure of unfavourable criticism. For these and other reasons it has need of an exalted status for itself and its staff members to enhance its authority. Its privileges and immunities should, and do, reflect these considerations. An organisation of more limited membership with narrower and less controversial functions cannot be regarded as having comparable needs in the matter of privileges and immunities, while an organisation operating commercially in competition with non-governmental bodies probably does not require any immunities at all.
>
> 12. No doubt some considerations apply equally to all international organisations. Their members are sovereign states and their funds are provided by sovereign states. But such organisations differ considerably among themselves in terms of the 'political' context of their functions and thus the pressures to which they may be subjected, the range of their membership, the degree to which they may become involved in every-day legal situations arising out of contracts and the like, and the extent to which they may be in competition with non-governmental organisations.[371]

These distinctions had already been observed by the Preparatory Commission of the United Nations:

> ... it must be recognized that not all specialized agencies require all the privileges and immunities which may be needed by others. No specialized agency would, however, require greater privileges than the United Nations itself. The privileges and immunities, therefore, of the United Nations might be regarded as a maximum within which the various specialized agencies should enjoy just such privileges and immunities *as the proper fulfilment of their respective functions may require*. It should be a principle that *no immunities and privileges, which are not really necessary, should be asked for*.[372] (emphasis added)

---

371 *Memorandum by the Government of the United Kingdom on the privileges and immunities of international organisations and persons connected with them (Foreign Office, 10 March 1965)*, Appendix to Council of Europe Report 1969, at 76.

372 *Report of the Preparatory Commission of the United Nations*, UN Doc. PC/20 (1945), at 61–62.

Generally speaking, it can be said that the more controversial or political the functions and purposes of an international organization, the stronger will be its need for protective privileges and immunities. Thus, a small organization, which lacks a permanent diplomatic conference center similar to that enjoyed by the United Nations General Assembly, probably has no justifiable need for exemption from customs duties with respect to wines, spirits and food, imported for consumption in delegates' cafeterias and restaurants. In contrast, in the case of the United Nations, where important consultations continue in the Delegates' Lounge just outside the General Assembly Hall, it will be more "justifiable to regard some official entertainment as within the official activities of an international organisation and ... the organisation ought to be accorded exemption from custom duties with respect to *reasonable* quantities of these commodities required for that purpose." (emphasis added)[373] The inapplicability of New York State liquor laws in the United Nations headquarters district, has, for instance, been explained by noting that the alternative would interfere with the "enjoyment by the United Nations within the headquarters district of any privilege or immunity necessary for the unhampered exercise of its functions or fulfillment of its purposes."[374]

Also, non-political organizations may have less need for publication facilities, if it is not necessary for the exercise of their functions to publish documents on a regular basis, as is the practice of the United Nations. But even if an organization is granted certain publication facilities, it may not use them outside the realm of its functions and purposes, as will be demonstrated below in Step Three.[375]

---

373 Council of Europe Report 1969, at 33, para. 68. One should be alert to the danger of overusing a term such as "reasonable" since it is open to wide interpretation. *See also* Díaz González, *Sixth Report*, UN Doc. A/CN.4/439 (1991), at 8, para. 29. The question of quantity is, strictly speaking, the area of Step Three of our three-step approach, which is concerned with the extent to which a certain privilege or immunity should be granted. The issue as to whether an organization needs such a privilege or immunity in the first place is, however, a typical combined Step One-Step Two question.

374 *See* 'Opinion of 26 October 1951 addressed by Attorney General Nathaniel L. Goldstein to the New York State Liquor Authority concerning Applicability of State Alcoholic Beverage Control Law to the United Nations and its Headquarters District,' *reprinted in* UN Doc. ST/LEG/SER.B/10 (1959), 165–168, at 168; Restatement (Third) § 468, Reporters' Note 5, at 507–508.

375 *E.g.*, an organization such as the European Union may publish and even sell to the general public the printed reports of its (economic) activities and books concerning economic problems, but it may not use its publications facilities to sell novels. *See* Seidl-Hohenveldern, Personality, at 51.

2.3.2 A List of Organizational Immunities

Subject to the comments made above, a list of privileges and immunities of international organizations may be drawn up, from which a selection may be made in the case of a given organization.[376] However, the words contained in the Council of Europe report of 1969 should be noted here:

> ... the sub-committee decided that it was not necessary or desirable to lay down a scale of privileges and immunities which would be applicable to international organisations generally; nor was it easy to lay down general rules or criteria by which any individual organisation could automatically be accorded a scale of privileges and immunities.[377]

It should, therefore, be made clear that the list presented below does not in any way represent an exhaustive enumeration of the privileges and immunities to which any given international organization is generally entitled. It is a list from which those privileges and immunities may be selected that pass the first two steps of the functional necessity test for the organization concerned. Consequently, as Sir Ian Sinclair has pointed out, functional necessity can dictate a higher scale of privileges and immunities for one organization, and a lower one for another.[378] Schermers has explained that "[b]ecause of their special tasks, some international organizations may need

---

376 As was announced above, little or no consideration will be given in this study to the material aspects of organizational immunities, *i.e.*, to defining what their exact contents are, since this particular aspect has been given sufficient consideration in legal doctrine. The interested reader is advised to consult, *e.g.*, *'The Practice of the United Nations, the Specialized Agencies and the International Atomic Energy Agency concerning their Status, Privileges and Immunities,'* UN Doc. A/CN.4/L.118 and Ad. 1–2 *reprinted in* (1967] 2 Y.B. Int'l L. Comm'n 207 *et seq.;* UN Doc. A/CN.4/L.383 and Add. 1–3 *reprinted in* (1985] 2 Y.B. Int'l L. Comm'n 145, UN Doc. A/CN.4/SER.A/1985/Add. 1 (Part 1/ Add. 1); the sections relating to UN Charter Art. 105(1) in *Repertory of United Nations Practice,* UN Sales No. 1955.V.2 (1955) and *Supplements 1–5;* Council of Europe Report 1969, at 23–37; Restatement (Third), §§ 467–648; WHITEMAN, 13 DIGEST, at 47–111; JENKS, at 37 *et seq.;* AHLUWALIA, at 81 *et seq.;* HUG, at 83 *et seq.;* Zacklin, DUPUY, at 184–190; Wenckstern; J. Duffar, Contribution à l'étude des privilèges et immunités des organisations internationales (1982)[hereinafter: DUFFAR].

377 Council of Europe Report 1969, at 15, para. 14. Similarly, the comments made by the Rapporteur of San Francisco Conference Committee IV/2 in 13 U.N.C.I.O. Doc. 933, IV/ 2/42(2), at 705 (1945).

378 *See* Sinclair, in [1983] 1 Y.B. Int'l L. Comm'n 242, para. 4, UN Doc. A/CN.4/SER.A/1983.

more privileges than others, but the basic privileges guaranteeing their independent functioning are needed by all."[379] Privileges and immunities, once selected through Step Two, are then fine-tuned to the specific characteristics (functions and purposes) of a given organization through the analysis dictated by Step Three. In this manner, the basis-element represented by Step Two of the functional necessity concept, with its inquiry into the necessity of a privilege or immunity to the functions and purposes of a given organization, performs a 'filter function.'

The tentative outline submitted by ILC Special Rapporteur Díaz González at the thirty-eighth session of the ILC held in 1986, contains a distinction between non-fiscal and financial-fiscal privileges and immunities.[380] The Special Rapporteur had submitted draft articles relating to these privileges and immunities in his Fourth, Fifth and Sixth Reports which appeared between 1989 and 1991. Draft articles 1–11 were referred to the Drafting Committee in 1990, followed by articles 12–22 a year later.[381] These privileges and immunities constitute Parts III and IV of the Draft, entitled 'Property, Funds and Assets' and 'Communications,' respectively.

Non-fiscal privileges and immunities of international organizations include:

- Immunity from legal process (or jurisdiction);[382]
- Inviolability of premises and exercise of control by the organization over those premises;[383]

379 SCHERMERS, at 1076, para. 1609. For a basic description of organizational immunities, see, e.g., C.F. Amerasinghe, Principles of the Institutional Law of International Organizations 320–343 (2005)[hereinafter: AMERASINGHE].

380 *See* Díaz González, *Third Report,* UN Doc. A/CN.4/401 (1986) *reprinted in* [1986] 2 Y.B. Int'l L. Comm'n 163, 167, para. 31, UN Doc. A/CN.4/SER.A/1986/Add. 1 (Part 1).

381 *See Report of the International Law Commission on the work of its forty-second session,* 45 GAOR Supp. (No. 10) at 241, para. 464, UN Doc. A/45/10 (1990) and [1991] 1 Y.B. Int'l L. Comm'n 186, para. 7, UN Doc. A/CN.4/SER.A/1991.

382 Draft article 7 of Part III entitled "Property, Funds and Assets" reads as follows:

International organizations, their property, funds and assets, wherever located and by whomsoever held, shall enjoy immunity from every form of legal process except in so far as in any particular case they have expressly waived their immunity. It is, however, understood that no waiver of immunity shall extend to any measure of execution or coercion.

For a summary of the discussions held within the ILC with regard to draft article 7, see *Report of the International Law Commission on the work of its forty-second session,* GAOR Supp. (No. 10) at 235–237, paras. 448–452, UN Doc. A/45/10 (1990).

383 ILC Draft articles 8 and 9 relate to the premises of an international organization and are drafted in the following terms:

- Immunity of its property and assets from search and from any other form of interference;[384]
- Inviolability of its archives and documents;[385]
- Privileges and immunities in respect of communication facilities (including the right to use codes or ciphers, to receive and dispatch correspondence by diplomatic courier or in sealed bags having the status of

---

Article 8

1. The premises of international organizations used solely for the performance of their official functions shall be inviolable. The property, funds and assets of international organizations, wherever located and by whomsoever held, shall be immune from search, requisition, confiscation, expropriation and any other form of interference or coercion, whether by executive, administrative, judicial or legislative action.
2. International organizations shall notify the host State of the location and description of the premises and the date on which occupation begins. They shall also notify the host State of the vacation of premises and the date of such vacation.
3. The dates of the notification provided for in paragraph 2 of this article, except where otherwise agreed by the parties concerned, shall determine when the enjoyment of the inviolability of the premises, as provided for in paragraph 1 of this article, begins and ends.

Article 9

Without prejudice to the provisions of the present draft articles (convention), international organizations shall not allow their headquarters to serve as a refuge for persons trying to evade arrest under the legal provisions of the host country, or sought by the authorities of that country with a view to the execution of a judicial decision, or wanted on account of *flagrans crimen,* or against whom a court order or deportation order has been issued by the authorities of the host country.

For a summary of the discussions held within the ILC with regard to draft articles 8–9, see *Report of the International Law Commission on the work of its forty-second session,* GAOR Supp. (No. 10) at 237–239, paras. 453–458, UN Doc. A/45/10 (1990).

384 This aspect is covered by the terms of draft article 7 set forth above.

385 Part IV of the ILC Draft entitled "Communications" contains an article on the archives of international organizations and is drafted in the following terms:

Article 12

1. The archives of international organizations and, in general, all documents belonging to or held by them shall be inviolable wherever they are located.
2. Archives of international organizations shall be understood to mean all papers, documents, correspondence, books, films, tape recordings, files and registers of the international organization, together with ciphers, codes, and the filing cabinets and furniture intended to protect and conserve them.

For a summary of the discussions held within the ILC with regard to draft article 12, see *Report of the International Law Commission on the work of its forty-third session,* GAOR Supp. (No. 10) at 312–313, paras. 286–287, UN Doc. A/46/10 (1991).

diplomatic bags, immunity from censorship[386] and the right to operate telecommunication equipment);[387]

- The privilege of unrestricted and uncensored distribution of publications.[388]

---

386 A new heading entitled "Immunity from censorship of United Nations public information material" was introduced in *Supplement No. 4 to the Repertory of United Nations Practice* in 1982. *See* UN Sales No. E.82.V.7 (1982), at 374, 378, para. 33, Sec. II B, 2(a) (vi); *see also Supplement No. 5*, UN Sales No. E.86.V.7 (1986), at 180, para. 39.

387 This matter is regulated by draft articles 14–16:

Article 14

International organizations shall enjoy, in the territory of each State party (to this Convention) in respect of such organizations, for their official communications, treatment not less favourable than that accorded by the Government of such State to any other Government, including the latter's diplomatic missions, in the mater of priorities, rates and taxes on mails, cables, telegrams, radiograms, telephotos, telephone, telefax and other communications, and press rates for information to the press, cinema, radio and television. However, the international organization may install and use a wireless transmitter only with the consent of the host State.

For a summary of the discussions held within the ILC with regard to draft article 14, see *Report of the International Law Commission on the work of its forty-third session*, GAOR Supp. (No. 10) at 314–315, para. 290, UN Doc. A/46/10 (1991).

Article 15

The official correspondence and other official communications of an international organization shall be inviolable.

Official correspondence and official communications mean all correspondence and communications relating to an organization and its functions.

For a summary of the discussions within the ILC with regard to draft article 15, see *Report of the International Law Commission on the work of its forty-third session*, GAOR Supp. (No. 10) at 315, para. 291, UN Doc. A/46/10 (1991).

Article 16

International organizations shall have the right to use codes and to dispatch and receive their official communications by courier or in sealed bags, which shall have the same immunities and privileges as diplomatic couriers and bags under the provisions of the multilateral conventions in force governing matters relating to the diplomatic courier and the diplomatic bag not accompanied by diplomatic courier.

For a summary of the discussions held within the ILC with regard to draft article 16, see *Report of the International Law Commission on the work of its forty-third session*, GAOR Supp. (No. 10) at 316, para. 292, UN Doc. A/46/10 (1991).

388 This is the subject-matter of draft article 13, which reads:

International organizations shall enjoy in the territory of each State party (to this Convention) the free circulation and distribution of their publications and public information material necessary for their activities, including films, photographs, printed matter and recordings prepared as part of the public information programme of an organization and exported or imported for display or re-transmission, as well as books, periodicals and other printed matter.

Financial and *fiscal* privileges and immunities of international organizations include:

- Exemption from taxes;[389]
- Exemption from customs duties, including exemption from prohibitions and restrictions on imports and exports;[390]

For a summary of the discussions held within the ILC with regard to draft article 13, see *Report of the International Law Commission on the work of its forty-third session*, GAOR Supp. (No. 10) at 313–314, paras. 288–289, UN Doc. A/46/10 (1991).

389 The matter of taxes is regulated by draft articles 18–19 and 21, which read as follows:

Article 18

International organizations, their assets, income and other property intended for their official activities shall be exempt from all direct taxes; it is understood, however, that international organizations will not claim exemptions from taxes which are, in fact, no more than payment for public utility services.

See Report of the International Law Commission on the work its forty-third session, GAOR Supp. (No. 10) at 317–318, para. 295, UN Doc. A/46/10 (1991).

Article 19

1. International organizations shall be exempt from all national, regional or municipal dues and taxes on the premises of the organization, whether owned or leased, other than such as represent payment for specific services rendered.
2. The exemption from taxation referred to in this article shall not apply to such dues and taxes payable under the law of the host State by persons contracting with the international organization.

See Report of the International Law Commission on the work of its forty-third session, GAOR Supp. (No. 10) at 318, para. 296, UN Doc. A/46/10 (1991).

Draft article 21 imposes the following restrictions:

1. International organizations shall not, in principle, claim exemption from consumer taxes or sales taxes on movable and immovable property that are incorporated in the price to be paid.
2. Notwithstanding the provisions of the foregoing paragraph, when international organizations make, for their official use, large purchases of goods on which such duties and taxes have been, or may be, imposed. States parties (to the present Convention) shall, wherever possible, adopt the necessary administrative provisions for the remission or refund of the amount corresponding to such duties or taxes.

See Report of the International Law Commission on the work of its forty-third session, GAOR Supp. (No. 10) at 320, para. 298, UN Doc. A/46/10 (1991).

390 According to draft article 20:

International organizations, their assets, income and other property shall, in accordance with the laws and regulations promulgated by the host State, be exempt from:

(a) All kinds of Customs duties, taxes and related charges, other than charges for storage, cartage and similar services, as well as from import and export prohibitions and restrictions with respect to articles imported or exported by international organizations for their official use; it is understood, however, that articles imported under such exemption may not be disposed of, whether or not in

- Exemption from currency controls and restrictions, including the right to hold and transfer funds and immunity from bank deposits.[391]

2.4 Where: *Legal Bases of Organizational Immunities*

2.4.1 Introduction

After the question of *why* international organizations should be endowed with certain privileges and immunities, the question of *where* these privileges and immunities can be found may next be addressed. The section that follows constitutes an examination of the *legal bases* of the privileges and immunities of international organizations as they reflect the considerations behind the granting of organizational immunities elaborated upon in the previous section of this chapter. These legal bases are mainly conventional sources, domestic legislation and customary international law.

As the ILC's second Special Rapporteur on 'Relations between States and International Organizations,' Díaz González, has explained, privileges and immunities of international organizations are no longer granted as a courtesy, as may have been the case in the past, since, as will be demonstrated below, they are based on solid conventional sources, setting forth *rights* which are unrelated to any consideration of comity or favor.[392]

---

return for payment, in the country into which they have been imported, except under conditions agreed with the Government of that country;

(b) Customs duties and prohibitions and restrictions with respect to the import and export of their publications intended for official use.

For a summary of the discussions held within the ILC with regard to draft article 20, see *Report of the International Law Commission on the work of its forty-third session*, GAOR Supp. (No. 10) at 319, para. 297, UN Doc. A/46/10 (1991).

391 The ILC draft contains an article on funds and currency which reads as follows:

Article 10

Without being restricted by controls, inspections, regulations or moratoria of any kind,

(a) International organizations may hold funds, gold or currency of any kind and operate bank accounts in any currency,

(b) International organizations may freely transfer their funds, gold or currency from one country to another or within any country and convert any currency held by them into any other currency,

(c) International organizations shall, in exercising their rights under (a) and (b) of this article, pay due regard to any representations made by the Government of any member State party to these draft articles (Convention) in so far as it is considered that effect can be given to such representations without detriment to their own interests.

For a summary of the discussions held within the ILC with regard to draft article 10, see *Report of the International Law Commission on the work of its forty-second session*, GAOR Supp. (No. 10) at 239–240, paras. 459–461, UN Doc. A/45/10 (1990).

392 *Report of the International Law Commission on the work of its forty-first session*, GAOR Supp. (No. 10) at 378, para. 725, UN Doc. A/44/10 (1989).

International organizations enjoy privileges and immunities *proprio motu*, being granted them in multilateral conventions, headquarters agreements or by custom, in their capacity as international legal persons, as subjects of international law. They are entitled to certain privileges and immunities and can require them of States.[393]

Treaty law constitutes the great bulk of the law of organizational immunities. The conventional sources of the law of organizational immunities may be divided into three main categories.

The first category consists of the *constituent instruments* of international organizations. These basic agreements, which establish an organization, set forth the organization's functions and purposes, and express the political will of the member States to co-operate within a defined framework.[394]

The basic nature of an organization's constituent instrument justifies a primary examination of this particular kind of agreement before turning to a second category of treaty law, constituted by a variety of *general multilateral conventions*, defining in greater detail an organization's immunities régime.

The third category of treaty law consists of a large number of *bilateral agreements*, concluded between an international organization and an individual State, in cases where an additional agreement is necessary, tailored to the specific requirements of an organization's activities in a particular State.

A *State's laws and judicial decisions* provide an additional source of organizational immunities.

Finally, we will address the role of *customary international law* as a possible source of privileges and immunities of international organizations.

2.4.2 Treaties

2.4.2.1 *Constituent Instruments of International Organizations*

2.4.2.1.1 Introduction

When dealing with *treaties* as legal bases of the privileges and immunities of international organizations, the first texts that may provide information on the subject are the *constituent instruments* of international organizations.

A 'constituent instrument' has been described as "a treaty between states and, at the same time, the constitution of a new international

---

393 Díaz González, *Fourth Report*, UN Doc. A/CN.4/424 (1989) *reprinted in* [1989] 2 Y.B. Int'l L. Comm'n 153, 158, para. 32, UN Doc. A/CN. 4/SER. A/1989/Add. 1 (Part 1); *see also id.*, in [1983] 1 Y.B. Int'l L. Comm'n 238, paras. 5–6, UN Doc. A/CN.4/SER.A/1983; Malek, in *id.*, at 252, para. 36.

394 *See* SCHERMERS, at 14, para. 13F.

entity."[395] The primary aim of a constitution is to determine the structure, and to regulate the functions, of the newly created organization.[396] Constituent instruments are ratified by all the member States of an organization and hence occupy a special place in the hierarchy of international instruments. The basic, creative function of a constituent instrument sets it apart from ordinary treaties. For this reason we shall examine these particular instruments first, before reviewing other instruments granting privileges and immunities to international organizations.

It must, however, be noted that, since clauses concerning privileges and immunities can be found in the constituent instruments of most intergovernmental organizations, a complete review is impossible for practical reasons. We shall, therefore, confine ourselves to giving examples from the United Nations Family and major regional organizations only.

The constituent instruments of most international organizations now existing provide for at least the basic privileges and immunities of the organization established thereby. This practice has the advantage of creating identical and binding international obligations upon all the member States and thus uniformizing the régime of privileges and immunities in all member States, because by definition all member States will have ratified the constituent instrument, being a condition for membership. This advantage does not always apply in cases where an ordinary multilateral, or even a bilateral, treaty has been concluded, as will be demonstrated below.

Being the founding document of the organization, in which a wide variety of subjects are regulated, constituent instruments most frequently contain provisions of a general character only and thus may contain somewhat vague wording. In accordance with the functional necessity concept for granting privileges and immunities to international organizations, it has become the usual practice for the constituent instruments of organizations to provide in the broadest possible terms that the organization will enjoy such privileges and immunities as may be necessary for the exercise of its functions and the fulfilment of its purposes.

Provisions of this kind can be found, varying somewhat in form, *inter alia*, in the Charter of the United Nations and in the constituent instruments of the UN Specialized Agencies,[397] for example in the Constitution of

---

395 *Id.*, at 753, para. 1142.

396 *Id.*, at 14–16, paras. 13F–13G.

397 For the texts of these instruments, see *Legislative Texts and Treaty Provisions concerning the Legal Status, Privileges and Immunities of International Organizations*, Vol. II, UN Doc. ST/LEG/SER.B/11 (1961); *see also* MICHAELS, at 60 *et seq.*

the International Labour Organization,[398] the Constitution of the World Health Organization,[399] the Convention of the World Meteorological Organization,[400] as well as in the Statute of the International Atomic Energy Agency.[401]

General immunity provisions drafted in functional terms also can be found in the constituent instruments of *regional* organizations[402] or in special protocols established pursuant to such instruments.[403] Examples of this kind are Article 40 of the Statute of the Council of Europe,[404] Article 103 of the Charter of the Organization of American States,[405] and Article XIII of the Charter of the Council for Mutual Economic Assistance.[406]

---

398 Art. 40, 15 U.N.T.S. 40.

399 Art. 67, 14 U.N.T.S. 186.

400 Art. 27(b)(i), 77 U.N.T.S. 144.

401 Art. XV(A), 276 U.N.T.S. 4.

402 For example, Art. 17, para. 1, ASEAN Charter ("ASEAN shall enjoy in the territories of the Member States such immunities and privileges as are necessary for the fulfilment of its purposes").

403 For example, Protocol on the Privileges and Immunities of the European Union, Official Journal of the European Union, No. C 310/261 (2004). It provides in its first preambular paragraph: "CONSIDERING that, in accordance with Article III–434 of the [Treaty establishing a] Constitution [for Europe], the [European] Union shall enjoy in the territories of the Member States such privileges and immunities as are necessary for the performance of its tasks." Art. III–434 of the Treaty establishing a Constitution for Europe reads: "The Union shall enjoy in the territories of the Member States such privileges and immunities as are necessary for the performance of its tasks, under the conditions laid down in the Protocol on the privileges and immunities of the European Union." Treaty establishing a Constitution for Europe, signed in Rome on 29 Oct. 2004, Official Journal of the European Union, 16.12.2004, No. C 310 (did not enter into force). See, generally, R.A. Wessel, *Immunities of the European Union*, 10(2) IOLR 395 (2013).

404 87 U.N.T.S. 103.

405 119 U.N.T.S. 3, 48.

406 368 U.N.T.S. 253. In the case of some organizations, such as the European Free Trade Association, the privileges and immunities of the organization have been further defined in a *protocol* annexed to or accompanying the organization's constituent instrument (see Convention establishing the European Free Trade Association, Art. 35(1), 370 U.N.T.S. 3). Another example is the *Protocol on the Privileges and Immunities of the European Communities, reprinted in* Sweet & Maxwell's European Community Treaties – Including the European Communities Act 1972, at 228 (K.R. Simmonds adv.ed. 1972). On the immunity of the EC, see I. Seidl-Hohenveldern, *L'immunité de juridiction des Communautés Européennes*, 338 REVUE DU MARCHÉ COMMUN 475–479 (1990)[hereinafter: Seidl-Hohenveldern, Communautés]. On the immunities of the European Union (EU), see R.A. Wessel, *Immunities of the European Union*, 10 IOLR 395 (2013).

Usually these provisions are brief and general, following the format of Article 105, paragraph 1, of the UN Charter.

2.4.2.1.2 Article 105 UN Charter

At the United Nations Conference on International Organization held at San Francisco in 1945, the task of studying all aspects of the organization of the United Nations was entrusted to *Commission IV*. In order to facilitate its work. Commission IV was sub-divided into two committees, one of which, the second committee (hereinafter referred to as *Committee IV/2*), was charged with preparing the provisions relating to the functioning of the Organization which had not been included in the original Dumbarton Oaks Proposals and which were to be inserted in the Charter. Among these were the provisions relating to the privileges and immunities to be granted to the organization, the drafting of which was entrusted to Subcommittee A of Committee IV/2.[407]

The Rapporteur of Committee IV/2 stated in his report that paragraph 1(1) of the draft article relating to privileges and immunities referred to the Organization as a distinct entity and covered all its agencies, i.e., those established by the Charter as well as other bodies or organs which may subsequently be established by virtue of the powers conferred by the Charter.[408]

Of the utmost importance is the fact that, in order to determine the nature of the privileges and immunities, the Committee avoided the term 'diplomatic' as used in Article 7, paragraph 4, of the Covenant of the League of Nations and "preferred to substitute a more appropriate standard, based, for the purpose of the Organization, on the necessity of realizing its purposes."[409] In this respect there is a clear departure from the provisions of the Covenant of the League of Nations. Article 7 of the Covenant provided in paragraph 5 that:

> The buildings and other property occupied by the League or its officials or by Representatives attending its meetings shall be inviolable.

Thus, whereas the Covenant of the League required only *inviolability* of the buildings and other property occupied by the League, the Charter of the

---

407 *See* 13 U.N.C.I.O. Doc. 228, IV/2/10, at 578–579 (1945); *see also Handbook on the legal status, privileges and immunities of the United Nations*, at 16, UN Doc. ST/LEG/2 (1952); El-Erian, *First Report*, UN Doc. A/CN.4/161 and Add. 1 (1963) *reprinted in* [1963] 2 Y.B. Int'l L. Comm'n 159, 171–172, paras. 100–102, UN Doc. A/CN.4/SER.A/1963/Add. 1; EGGER, at 118 *et seq.*

408 *See* 13 U.N.C.I.O. Doc. 933, IV/2/42(2), at 704 (1945).

409 *Id.*

United Nations provides that the *necessary* privileges and immunities shall be granted to the Organization, covering a wider ambit of privileges and immunities.[410]

According to the report of the Rapporteur of Committee IV/2, as approved by the Committee,[411] paragraph 1 laid down a rule binding all member States from the date the Charter would enter into effect. The Committee further opined that the rule set forth in paragraph 1 should apply in any circumstances, its authority being in no way subordinate to the exercise by the General Assembly of its power, under paragraph 3 of draft article 105, to make recommendations or propose conventions to the member States for determining the details of the application of paragraphs 1 and 2.[412] The following observation was made in the report:

> [T]he draft article proposed by the Committee does not specify the privileges and immunities respect for which it imposes on the member states. This has been thought superfluous. The terms *privileges* and *immunities* indicate in a general way all that could be considered necessary to the realization of the purposes of the Organization, to the full functioning of its organs, and to the independent exercise of the functions and duties of their officials.

The report stated furthermore:

> It would moreover have been impossible to establish a list valid for all the member states and taking account of the special situation in which some of them might find themselves by reason of the activities of the Organization or of its organs in their territory. But if there is one certain principle it is that no member state may hinder in any way the working of the Organization or take any measures the effect of which might be to increase its burdens, financial or other.[413]

---

410 On this difference see KELSEN, at 338 *et seq.* It must, however, be noted that the principle of *functional* independence already played a role under the League of Nations practice. Thus, it was emphasized in the Secretary-General's Circular No. 316 dated 28 October 1922, which clarified the rights conferred and the obligations imposed upon members of the League's Secretariat by Article 7 of the Covenant. *See* Tarassenko & Zacklin, at 4. *See also Statement by the Legal Counsel at the 1016th meeting of the Sixth Committee on 6 December 1967*, UN Doc. A/C.6/385 *reprinted in* 22 GAOR, Annexes, (Agenda Item 98)(1967), at 4, 5, paras. 10–12.

411 13 U.N.C.I.O. Doc. 933, IV/2/42(2), at 703, 704 (1945).

412 *Id.*, at 704–705.

413 *Id.*, at 705.

The report of Committee IV/2 was approved by the Coordination Committee and by Commission IV[414] and the recommended draft provision contained therein, after its approval by the Conference at its ninth Plenary Session held on 25 June 1945, became Article 105 of the United Nations Charter, which reads in full:[415]

> 1. The Organization shall enjoy in the territory of each of its Members such privileges and immunities as are necessary for the fulfilment of its purposes.
>
> 2. Representatives of the Members of the United Nations and officials of the Organization shall similarly enjoy such privileges and immunities as are necessary for the independent exercise of their functions in connexion with the Organization.
>
> 3. The General Assembly may make recommendations with a view to determining the details of the application of paragraphs 1 and 2 of this Article or may propose conventions to the Members of the United Nations for this purpose.

This provision has ever since served as a model for similar provisions contained in the legal instruments of a wide variety of other international organizations.

2.4.2.1.3 A Special Case: International Financial Institutions

When we observed above that constitutional provisions relating to privileges and immunities as a rule are drafted in a brief and general manner, we did not mention the international financial institutions, sometimes called operational or managing organizations,[416] among the examples given. This was done on purpose, because the constituent instruments of these organizations constitute an important exception to the general practice of constituent instruments granting privileges and immunities in a brief and general manner only. The constituent instruments of the International Bank for

---

414 *See* 13 U.N.C.I.O. Doc. 450, IV/2/20, at 607 (1945); *id.*, Doc. 886, IV/2/38, at 665 (1945); *id.*, Doc. 1153, IV/12(1), at 103; 17 U.N.C.I.O. Doc. WD 32, CO/16, at 21 (1945).

415 *See* The Charter of the United Nations: A Commentary 2158–2178 (B. Simma et al., eds., 2012).

416 *See* El-Erian, *First Report*, UN Doc. A/CN.4/161 and Add. 1 (1963) *reprinted in* [1963] 2 Y.B. Int'l L. Comm'n 159, 163, para. 76, UN Doc. A/CN.4/SER.A/1963/Add. 1. For a summary of the organizational structure of the international financial organizations, see [1967] 2 Y.B. Int'l L. Comm'n 204–205, UN Doc. A/CN.4/SER.A/1967/Add. 1.

Reconstruction and Development,[417] the International Finance Corporation,[418] the International Development Association,[419] the Multilateral Investment Guarantee Agency,[420] and, to a lesser extent, the International Monetary Fund,[421] contain more *detailed* provisions with regard to the extent of immunity from judicial process, immunity of assets from seizure and restrictions, immunity of archives and communications facilities and immunity from taxation.

Moreover, international financial institutions are exceptional in that their jurisdictional immunities are often specifically limited. Thus, Article VI, Section 3, of the Articles of Agreement of the International Finance Corporation (IFC), which is run as an enterprise, provides that legal proceedings may be instituted against the IFC in the courts of the member States where it "has an office, has appointed an agent for the purpose of accepting service or notice of process, or has issued or guaranteed securities."[422]

---

417 Art. VII, Articles of Agreement of the International Bank for Reconstruction and Development, 2 U.N.T.S. 134.

418 Art. VI, Articles of Agreement of the International Finance Corporation, 264 U.N. T.S. 117.

419 Art. VIII, Articles of Agreement of the International Development Association, 439 U.N.T.S. 249.

420 Arts. 43–46 of the Convention Establishing the Multilateral Investment Guarantee Agency (MIGA), done at Seoul on 11 October 1985, entered into force on 12 April 1988. *See* 24 ILM 692, 1598, 1622 (1985), 27 ILM 1227 (1988). MIGA, an affiliate of the World Bank, was established to ensure private investments in developing countries against non-commercial risks such as armed conflict, government repudiation of contract, nationalization, currency conversion and repatriation restrictions. For the text of the Operational Regulations of the Agency, adopted by the MIGA Board of Directors on 22 June 1988, see 27 ILM 1228 (1988).

421 Art. IX, Articles of Agreement of the International Monetary Fund, 2 U.N.T.S. 39. *See also* H. Aufricht, *The Expansion of the Concept of Sovereign Immunity: With Special Reference to International Organizations*, 46 Proc. Am. Soc'y Int'l L. 85, 91 (1952)[hereinafter: Aufricht].

422 The constituent instruments of the other monetary organizations, with the exception of the IMF, contain similar provisions as the IFC. Art. IX § 3 of the IMF's Articles of Agreement provides that the Fund, "its property, and its assets ... shall enjoy immunity from every form of judicial process except to the extent that [the Fund] expressly waives its immunity for the purpose of any proceedings or by the terms of any contract." *See also* 22 U.S.C. § 286h (incorporating relevant articles into U.S. law). *See also* Art. XI § 3, Agreement Establishing the Inter-American Development Bank, adopted on 8 Apr. 1959, 10 U.S.T. 3068, 3095 ("Actions may be brought against the Bank only in a court of competent jurisdiction in the territories of a member in which the Bank has an office, has appointed an agent for the purpose of accepting service or notice of process, or has issued or guaranteed securities."). U.S. courts have construed this provision as not merely a "venue provision for actions resulting from individual waivers; rather it

Consequently, monetary organizations such as the IFC, the IBRD, the IDA and MIGA, by contrast to the majority of international organizations, often enjoy only limited immunity from jurisdiction,[423] in that, as a rule, they can be sued by third parties. An exception is, however, made for actions brought by member States or persons acting for or deriving claims from member States, against which these organizations are protected by immunity.[424]

The reason behind this special practice is "to avoid giving those organizations an unfair advantage in the various financial and commercial transactions in which they engage daily with private persons, such as the sale of bonds and the purchase of goods and services,"[425] and thus to secure public confidence. The commercial operations of monetary organizations hence make it desirable to allow suit by creditors and bondholders.[426] From this special practice it may be concluded that, within the context of international financial institutions, the concept of restrictive immunity, which, as will be explained below, draws a distinction between State activities proper and commercial activities, has had a certain impact upon the law of organizational immunities.[427]

2.4.2.1.4 Constituent Instruments *Not* Containing any Provisions on the Subject

There are also international organizations whose constituent instruments do not contain any provisions relating to privileges and immunities. Examples of this kind are the constitutions of the International Telecommunication Union[428] and the Universal Postal Union.[429] A possible explanation for

---

is a provision waiving immunity and laying venue for the suits permitted." *Atkinson v. Inter-Am. Dev. Bank et al.*, 156 F.3d 1335 (D.C. Cir. 1998)(citing *Lutcher S.A. Celulose e Papel v. Inter-Am. Dev. Bank*, 382 F.2d 454, 457 (D.C. Cir. 1967).

423 *See* AHLUWALIA, at 67–68; Aufricht, at 99; Restatement (Third) § 467, Reporters' Note 3, at 499.

424 *See*, e.g., Art. VII § 3, IBRD Articles of Agreement. *See also* 22 U.S.C. § 286h (incorporating the IBRD's Articles of Agreement into U.S. law); Art. XI, Section 3, paragraph 1, ("Actions may be brought against the Bank only in a court of competent jurisdiction in the territories of a member in which the Bank has an office, has appointed an agent for the purpose of accepting service or notice of process, or has issued or guaranteed securities").

425 Tsuruoka, in [1978] 1 Y.B. Int'l L. Comm'n, at 267, para. 25, UN Doc. A/CN.4/SER.A/1978; *see also* Dominicé, L'immunité, at 196.

426 *See* BOWETT, at 349–350.

427 *See also* JENKS, at 45.

428 L.N.T.S. 1365, 1905, 3479; U.K. Treaty Series No. 76, (1950), Cmnd. 8124.

429 611 U.N.T.S. 7.

this phenomenon is that these organizations came into existence during the second half of the 19th century, when a practice of explicitly granting privileges and immunities had not yet been established.[430] Moreover, the organizations just referred to were originally administered by the Swiss authorities, and they enjoyed all the necessary privileges and immunities in practice. It should be remembered that the subject-matter of the present study did not become a significant one until the proliferation of public international organizations after the Second World War. The omission of an immunity clause usually is only found in small organizations with purely administrative functions. As will be discussed directly below, in such cases one has to turn to other documents or sources in order to determine what régime applies to such organizations.[431]

2.4.2.2 *General Multilateral Agreements*

2.4.2.2.1 Introduction

Having observed that the constitutional provisions relating to privileges and immunities are usually drafted in a general, often insufficiently specific manner, it is not surprising that it has become the common practice for the constituent instruments of international organizations to provide that the necessary privileges and immunities may be defined in greater detail by subsequent agreements.[432] Such agreements are concluded between the member States of an international organization with a view to defining the latter's legal position and investing it with specific privileges and immunities. These agreements have as their principal goal the implementation of the brief and general provisions of the constituent instrument of the organization, so as to create a uniform position in all the member States after ratification by them.[433]

Before we enter into a closer examination of several of these agreements, it is necessary to make some remarks with regard to their form. These agreements are multilateral instruments concluded among some or all member

---

430 *See also* AHLUWALIA, at 51–52; Kunz, at 828 et *seq.*

431 For the situation with regard to the UPU, see "Echange de Lettres concernant le statut juridique de l'Union Postale Universelle (UPU), du 5 février et 22 avril 1948," *Recueil officiel des lois et ordonnances de la Confèderation suisse* 1194 (1956) *reprinted in* UN Doc. ST/LEG/SER.B/11 (1961), at 321–323.

432 *See* UN Charter, Art. 105, para. 3; *see also* Dinh, at 264.

433 On the relationship between the various UN instruments relating to immunities, see *Statement by the Legal Counsel at the 1016th meeting of the Sixth Committee on 6 December 1967*, UN Doc. A/C.6/385 *reprinted in* 22 GAOR, Annexes (Agenda Item 98) (1967), at 4, 5–6, paras. 9–15; *see also* the statement of the representative of Venezuela, in explanation of his State's vote on Res. 2328 (XXII), 22 GAOR, Verbatim records of meetings, Vol. Ill, UN Doc. A/PV. 1627–1673 (1971), at 9, para. 90 (Agenda Item 98).

States of an international organization.[434] The organization itself, which is the object of such a multilateral agreement, is not formally speaking a party to it, even if the agreement is formulated by one of its organs. According to Dominicé,[435] it is, however, obvious that the organization enjoys the rights which the agreement creates, for that is precisely the goal of the agreement. Support for this view can be found in the opinion of the International Court of Justice in the *Reparation* Case, where the Court stated that "the 'Convention on the privileges and immunities of the United Nations' of 1946 creates rights and duties between each of the signatories *and the Organization*." (emphasis added)[436]

According to another authority, it is "the prevailing view that the UN itself should be considered to be a party to the General Convention. Thus, in a sense this is not only a multilateral inter-State agreement, but also a series of bilateral agreements between the UN and each State party to the Convention, defining rights and obligations for both parties."[437] This view is supported by Kunz, according to whom:

> [t]he 'UN General Convention' is … a genuine international treaty, which has to be ratified by each member; the vote of approval by the General Assembly was equivalent to ratification by the UN. The Contracting Parties are, on the one hand, each Member State and, on the other, the UN as such. Thus, identical norms are created for all Member States, the coming into force of which as well as amendments are controlled by the UN.[438]

---

434 Such general agreements, in principle, bind all Members which accept them. *See* SCHERMERS, at 270, para. 325; Dinh, at 264.

435 Dominicé, L'immunité, at 170.

436 1949 ICJ Rep. 174, 179.

437 P.C. Szasz, *International Organizations, Privileges and Immunities, in* [Installment] 5 Encyclopedia of Public International Law 152–159, 154 (1983)[hereinafter: Szasz, Immunities].

438 Kunz, at 848; *see also* EGGER, at 128. Moreover, as BOWETT, at 344, has argued, the UN Secretariat clearly took the view that the UN is a party to the Convention in registering the instrument *ex officio*. From Section 35 of the General Convention it may be inferred that the UN is a party to this convention, since it provides: "*This Convention shall continue in force as between the United Nations and every Member* which has deposited an instrument of accession for so long as that Member remains a Member of the United Nations, or until a revised general convention has been approved by the General Assembly and that Member has become a party to this revised convention," (emphasis added). Section 35 thus makes clear that the obligations run from the UN member States to the United Nations. *See Statement by the Legal Counsel at the 1016th meeting of the Sixth Committee on 6 December 1967*, UN Doc. A/C.6/385 *reprinted in* 22

In any case, as was observed in the 'Written Statement submitted on behalf of the Secretary-General of the United Nations to the International Court of Justice' in the *Mazilu* Case before the ICJ in 1989:

> [E]ven if the Organization should not be considered as a 'party' *stricto sensu* to the General Convention, it is clearly a 'third organization' that can derive obligations and rights under that instrument pursuant to the principles codified in Articles 35 and 36 of the 1986 Vienna Convention on the Law of Treaties between States and International Organizations or between International Organizations. The acceptance or assent of the Organization to such obligations and rights is evidently that given by the General Assembly in adopting the Convention and proposing it to Member States, an action taken pursuant to the explicit authorization of paragraph 3 of Article 105 of the Charter.[439]

2.4.2.2.2 A Model: The United Nations Family

At this point it is useful to examine two multilateral agreements of a general character, which have served, subject to appropriate modifications in individual cases, as a model for later agreements made by various other international organizations.[440]

The UN General Assembly at its very first session, by resolution 22 D(I) of 13 February 1946,[441] and on the basis of a draft formulated by the UN Preparatory Commission, adopted the *Convention on the Privileges and Immunities of the United Nations*.[442]

GAOR, Annexes (Agenda Item 98) (1967), at 4–5, paras. 5–8. *But see* Zacklin, DUPUY, at 183, who argues that the organizations *in general* are not themselves parties to the general multilateral conventions but rather the chief beneficiaries and guardians of these instruments.

439 *'Written Statement submitted on behalf of the Secretary-General of the United Nations to the International Court of Justice,'* at 26, para. 53, *reprinted in ICJ Pleadings, Applicability of Article VI, Section 22, of the Convention on the Privileges and Immunities of the United Nations*, at 185 (1992). *See also* Reuter, in [1973] 2 Y.B. Int'l L. Comm'n 80, paras. 31–32, UN Doc. A/CN.4/SER.A/1973/Add. 1 (Part 1).

440 For examples of general conventions implementing the constitutional provisions of regional organizations, see El-Erian, *First Report*, UN Doc. A/CN.4/161 and Add. 1 *reprinted in* [1963] 2 Y.B. Int'l L. Comm'n 159, 173 n.97, UN Doc. A/CN.4/SER.A/1963/Add. 1.

441 *See Resolutions Adopted by the General Assembly During the First Part of its First Session*, UN Doc. A/64 (1946), at 33.

442 For the *text* of the Convention, *see* 1 U.N.T.S. 15 and 90 U.N.T.S. 327 (corr.); *see also* UN Doc. ST/LEG/SER.B/10 (1959), at 184 *et. seq.* [hereinafter: General Convention]. For a list of States parties to the General Convention, see *Multilateral Treaties Deposited*

In accordance with the provisions of the General Convention, the United Nations shall possess juridical personality and legal capacity (Article I, Section 1), and its property and assets shall enjoy immunity from every form of legal process (Article II, Section 2), its premises are inviolable (Section 3), and the property and assets of the organization are immune from search, requisition, confiscation, expropriation or any other form of interference, whether by executive, administrative, judicial or legislative action (Section 3). The United Nations is also exempt from all direct taxes (Section 7 (a)) and customs duties (Section 7(b)) and its publications are exempt from prohibitions and restrictions on imports and exports (Section 7(c)).[443] Moreover, the General Convention grants the UN facilities in respect of communications through Article III, Sections 9–10.

Since the General Convention is in force for 162 States as of 1 December 2024, it may be regarded as practically universal.[444]

In pursuance of the resolution on the co-ordination of the privileges and immunities of the United Nations and the Specialized Agencies,[445] a separate *Convention on the Privileges and Immunities of the Specialized Agencies* was approved by the UN General Assembly on 21 November 1947.[446] This Convention consists of two distinct parts:

(1) a general part defining the *standard* privileges and immunities which are applicable to all the specialized agencies, and;

(2) a number of *annexes* setting out those divergences from the standard privileges and immunities in the case of each specialized agency which does not require the whole set of standard privileges and

---

with the Secretary-General, available on the website http://treaties.un.org. For materials relating to the General Convention, *see ICJ Pleadings, Applicability of Article VI, Section 22, of the Convention on the Privileges and Immunities of the United Nations*, at 105–106 (1992).

443 For a summary of the provisions of this Convention *see Repertory of United Nations Practice* (Article 105, paragraph 1), UN Sales No. 1955.V.2 (Vol. V, 1955) and *Supplements* 1–5; Kunz, at 850.

444 *See also* R.R. Baxter, *Multilateral Treaties as Evidence of Customary International Law*, 41 BYBIL 275, 277–78 (1965–66).

445 *See* GA Res. 22 D(I), *Resolutions Adopted by the General Assembly During the First Part of its First Session*, UN Doc. A/64 (1946), at 33.

446 Res. 179(II), *Official Records of the Second Session of the General Assembly*, UN Doc. A/519 (1948), at 112; entered into force on 2 Dec. 1948; 33 U.N.T.S. 261, *reprinted in* UN Doc. ST/LEG/SER.B/11 (1961), at 101 [hereinafter: Specialized Agencies Convention]; *see also* EGGER, at 139–143; WHITEMAN, DIGEST, at 42–44.

> immunities or which, on account of the special nature of its functions and purposes, requires certain special privileges and immunities.

The *standard clauses* of the Specialized Agencies Convention, apart from only slight modifications, contain similar provisions as the General Convention and they were in fact drafted on the basis of the latter.

The second part of the Specialized Agencies Convention contains several *Annexes*, the purpose of which has been described as being "to adapt the standard clauses to each specialized agency (on the basis of the nature of the functions performed by it) and to define the extent to which they apply to the agency concerned. Thus, privileges and immunities of each specialized agency are defined by the standard clauses as modified by the annex relating to that agency."[447] Through this arrangement, the special requirements of each specialized agency can be taken into account.

The Specialized Agencies Convention incorporates the functional necessity criterion laid down in Articles 104 and 105 of the UN Charter. The Convention is applicable, subject to variations set forth in the annexes for each agency, which are subject to approval by the respective specialized agencies in accordance with their constitutional procedures,[448] to all 17 specialized agencies, namely the International Labour Organization (Annex I), the Food and Agriculture Organization of the United Nations (Annex II), the International Civil Aviation Organization (Annex III), the United Nations Educational, Scientific and Cultural Organization (Annex IV), the International Monetary Fund (Annex V), the International Bank for Reconstruction and Development (Annex VI), the World Health Organization (Annex VII), the Universal Postal Union (Annex VIII), the International Telecommunication Union (Annex IX), the World Meteorological Organization (Annex XI), the International Maritime Organization (Annex XII), the International Finance Corporation (Annex XIII), the International Development Association (Annex XIV), the World Intellectual Property Organization (Annex XV), the International Fund for Agricultural Development (Annex XVI), the United Nations Industrial Development Organization (Annex XVII) and the World Tourism Organization (Annex XVIII), as well as to any other agency subsequently brought into relationship with the United Nations in accordance with Articles 57 and 63 of the Charter.[449]

---

447 AHLUWALIA, at 57.

448 *See* Specialized Agencies Convention, Art. X.

449 *Id.*, Art. I, S. 1 sub (ii)(j). As to Annex X concerning the International Refugee Organization, Resolution 108, adopted by the General Council of the IRO at its 101st meeting

This Convention follows closely the provisions of the General Convention, with only a limited number of variations.[450]

As of 1 December 2024, 131 States were parties to the Specialized Agencies Convention.[451] The United States of America, which serves as the host country for multiple specialized agencies, is not a party to this multilateral treaty.

2.4.2.2.3 Regional Multilateral Agreements

Within the context of *regional* organization, general multilateral conventions addressing organizational immunities have also been concluded, for which the General Convention and the Specialized Agencies Convention have served as prototypes.

In this regard reference may be made to the Agreement on Privileges and Immunities of the Organization of American States,[452] the General Agreement on privileges and immunities of the Council of Europe,[453] the Convention on the Privileges and Immunities of the League of Arab States[454] and the Convention concerning the juridical personality, privileges and immunities of the Council for Mutual Economic Assistance.[455] These general immunities agreements specify the privileges and immunities régimes laid down in the constituent instruments of the regional organizations concerned.[456]

2.4.2.3 *Bilateral Agreements*

2.4.2.3.1 Introduction

The third category of international instruments granting privileges and immunities to international organizations consists of a great variety of *bilateral*

---

held on 15 February 1952, provided for the liquidation of the organization. For references to the three relevant texts see UN Doc. ST/LEG/SER.E/11 (1993), at 40–51.

450 For more examples of multilateral agreements granting privileges and immunities to international organizations, see, *e.g.*, JENKS, at 6. *See also* the annual volumes of the United Nations Juridical Yearbook.

451 *See* the online database of treaties accessible through the website of the United Nations. A third general multilateral convention is the Agreement on the privileges and immunities of the International Atomic Energy Agency of 1 July 1959, 374 U.N.T.S. 147.

452 *See* Pan American Union, *Law and Treaty Series*, No. 31 *reprinted in* UN Doc. ST/LEG/SER.B/11 (1961), at 377.

453 250 U.N.T.S. 14.

454 Approved by the Council of the League of Arab States on 10 May 1953. Text *reprinted in* UN Doc. ST/LEG/SER.B/11 (1961), at 414.

455 Signed at Sofia on 14 December 1959.

456 For the *text* of various general multilateral conventions, see UN Docs. ST/LEG/SER.B/10 and 11, and the online database of treaties accessible through the website of the United Nations.

agreements defining the privileges and immunities of various international organizations in relation to individual States.

These bilateral agreements are necessary, since the majority of the general privileges and immunities agreements only cover most routine contacts between international organizations and their member States. Whenever more intensive or sustained relations are foreseen, the general agreements are supplemented or even replaced by special bilateral treaties relating to that specific relationship, so as to cover whatever situation that might occur. It has become the usual practice for these kinds of treaties to specify precisely how the general immunities agreement is to apply to this relationship.

Under the heading of bilateral agreements may be listed, *inter alia*:[457]

- Headquarters and Host Agreements;[458]
- Conference Agreements (Agreements concerning Particular Meetings);
- Technical Assistance and Supply Agreements;[459]
- Loan and Guarantee Agreements;[460]
- Postal Agreements;[461]
- Agreements relating to Special Political Tasks;[462]
- Status-of-Forces Agreements (SOFAS);[463]

---

457 For a synoptic survey of special agreements on privileges and immunities of the United Nations Family, *see Repertory of United Nations Practice*, UN Sales No. 1955.V.2 (Vol. v, 1955), and *Supplements 1–5*. For examples see 1990 UN Jurid. Y.B, pp. 6–56, UN Doc. ST/LEG/SER.C/28 (1993).

458 For examples see JENKS, at 7–8; El-Erian, *First Report*, UN Doc. A/CN.4/161 and Add. 1 (1963) *reprinted in* [1963] 2 Y.B. Int'l L. Comm'n 159, 172, para. 105, UN Doc. A/CN.4/SER.A/1963/Add. 1; Zacklin, DUPUY, at 182. There is a difference between Headquarters and Host Agreements in the sense that not every State which is a host to an international organization necessarily is the State in which that organization has its established headquarters. For example, a State could be a host merely with regard to a meeting convened and arranged by the organization's secretariat away from an established headquarters. Host agreements are, consequently, of a more temporary and *ad hoc* nature. See in this regard also section 2.4.2.3.4 below on Conference Agreements.

459 With regard to Standard Basic Assistance Agreements between the recipient government and the United Nations Development Programme, see 1990 UN Jurid. Y.B, p. 42, UN Doc. ST/LEG/SER.C/28 (1993).

460 *See* JENKS, at 11.

461 For examples see *id.*, at 11; Zacklin, DUPUY, at 182 n.11.

462 For examples see JENKS, at 9.

463 This concerns agreements under which international forces may be stationed in a country for peacekeeping or other purposes. For examples see Seyersted, UN Forces; Zacklin, DUPUY, at 182 n.12. *See also* SATOW, 309–315, paras. 21.38–21.48; A. Sari, *Status of Forces and Status of Mission Agreements under the ESDP: the EU's Evolving Practice*,

– Status-of-Mission Agreements (SOMAs).[464]

In the subsequent paragraphs we shall take a closer look at some of these bilateral agreements, in particular the headquarters agreements, which constitute the great majority of existing bilateral agreements.[465]

2.4.2.3.2 Headquarters Agreements

In almost all cases, international organizations have concluded agreements with the States in whose territory their headquarters or seats are located, describing their legal status, privileges and immunities in the host State. Such agreements are generally called 'headquarters agreement' or '*accord de siège*.'[466]

The expression 'headquarters' of an international organization has been explained to include "the buildings or parts of buildings used for the purposes of the organization, irrespective of whether they are owned by the organization or are leased or rented. It also comprises the surrounding land and other appurtenances, including a garden or a car park."[467]

Article 1, paragraph 1 sub (15), of the 1975 *Vienna Convention on the Representation of States in their Relations with International Organizations of a Universal Character*, defines a 'host State' as the State in whose territory (i) the organization has its seat or an office, or (ii) a meeting of one of its organs or a conference convened by it is held.[468]

As has been rightly observed by Hug,[469] the conclusion of a headquarters agreement is independent of the existence of a general agreement on

---

19 EJIL 67 (2008); A. Sari, *The Conclusion of International Agreements by the European Union in the context of the ESDP*, 57 ICLQ 53 (2008).

464 These agreements are concluded in support of special political missions. An example is the United Nations Verification Mission in Colombia, which was established in support of that country's peace process. *See also* SATOW, 312, paras. 21.43–21.44, and 314, paras. 21.46–21.47.

465 For other examples of the above-mentioned categories we refer to the literature mentioned in the pertinent footnotes.

466 For a general study of headquarters agreements see P. Cahier, Etudes des accords de sièges conclus entre les organisations internationales et les états où elles résident (1959); *see also* EGGER, at 143–146; R. Wolfrum, *International Organizations Headquarters, in* [Installment] 5 Encyclopedia of Public International Law 140 (1983); A.S. Muller, International Organizations and their Host States—Aspects of their Legal Relationship (1995).

467 AHLUWALIA, at 49.

468 *See also* Part I, Art. I, para. 1(e) of the draft articles submitted by the Special Rapporteur on 'Relations between States and international organizations,' *reprinted in Report of the International Law Commission on the work of its forty-first session*, 44 GAOR Supp. (No. 10) at 368–369, UN Doc. A/44/10 (1989).

469 HUG, at 53.

privileges and immunities: the international organization enters into such a close relationship, *de facto* and *de jure*, because the other legal sources for granting the necessary privileges and immunities, i.e., constituent instruments, general agreements, domestic legislation or customary international law, are not sufficiently specific for the regulation of this kind of relationship. In relation to the host State the organization often has a need for privileges and immunities of a wider scope and diversity than those provided for in general multilateral agreements. Moreover, only by means of a headquarters agreement can this special relationship be tailored to the particular circumstances which characterize a host State.[470]

Jenks has described the importance of headquarters agreements as follows:

> [T]he inclusion of such provisions in a headquarters agreement can be of great value to both the international organisation and the government concerned. They formulate a clear principle on which the international organisation can rely in relation to the host State and that State can rely in relation to other States in respect of all matters relating to the international organisation.[471]

The first headquarters agreement to be negotiated subsequent to the Second World War was the Agreement of 11 March 1946 between the Swiss Federal Council and the International Labour Organization concerning the legal status of the ILO in Switzerland subsequent to the dissolution of the League of Nations.[472]

One of the most important headquarters agreements, which still has a major impact on today's conditions, is the *Agreement between the United Nations and the United States of America regarding the Headquarters of the United Nations*.[473]

---

470 As is explained in SATOW, at 306, para. 21.31, a headquarters agreement may be *in addition to* the multilateral agreement which specifies the privileges and immunities to be accorded by all member States, it may be *in substitution for* the multilateral agreement if the host State is not a party to that agreement, or it may be required because the multilateral agreement may contain *no detailed provisions* in regard to privileges and immunities of the international organization.

471 JENKS, at 20.

472 15 U.N.T.S. 377 *reprinted in* UN Doc. ST/LEG/SER.B/11 (1961), at 138; *see also* EGGER, at 143–144.

473 Signed at Lake Success, on 26 June 1947; brought into effect on 21 November 1947 by an Exchange of Notes between UN Secretary-General Trygve Lie and Warren R. Austin, the U.S. Representative to the UN, in accordance with Section 28; GA Res. 169(11), UN Doc. A/519, at 91 (1948); 11 U.N.T.S. 11; supplemented, 554 U.N.T.S. 308,

Bilateral agreements referring to privileges and immunities have as an advantage that they may be concluded between an international organization and a *non-member* State. Consequently, the conclusion of a headquarters agreement is independent of the question of the membership of an international organization. In these circumstances a bilateral treaty is required, because the constituent instruments and general multilateral immunity agreements of international organizations are *res inter alios acta* for the non-Member host.[474] A prime example of such an instrument is the *Interim Arrangement on Privileges and Immunities of the United Nations concluded between the Secretary-General of the United Nations and the Swiss Federal Council* of 1946.[475] The provisions of this agreement are identical, apart from their express application to Switzerland, a non-Member at the time of the conclusion of the agreement, with those of the General Convention, with the exception of minor deviations in Article 1, dealing with international personality, and in Sections 5 and 27, concerning exemption from taxation and settlement of disputes, respectively.[476]

---

687 U.N.T.S. 408; text *reprinted in* UN Doc. ST/LEG/SER.B/10 (1959), at 204. For an extensive survey of this Agreement see IVRAKIS, at 372 *et seq.*; EGGER, at 133–135; KELSEN, at 350–356; Lalive, at 324 *et seq. See also* Note, *International Agreements: United Nations Headquarters Agreement —Dispute over the United States' Denial of a Visa to Yasir Arafat*, 30 Harv. Int'l L.J. 536, 536 n.1 (1989) (authored by S. Sadiq Reza). For further examples we refer to Brandon, at 90–113; *see also* UN Docs. ST/LEG/SER.B/10 & 11.

474 *See also* HUG, at 51.

475 Signed at Bern on 11 June 1946, and at New York on 1 July 1946; came into force on 1 July 1946; subsequent approval by the UN General Assembly was given on 14 December 1946; 1 U.N.T.S. 163; text *reprinted in* UN Doc. ST/LEG/SER.B/10 (1959), at 196; this arrangement was of importance to GATT until its replacement by the World Trade Organization in January 1995, since the privileges and immunities of GATT, which had its seat in Switzerland, depended upon a grant by the Swiss Government that extended the privileges and immunities generally extended to the UN to the "Interim Commission for the International Trade Organization" (ICITO), GATT's secretariat and, technically speaking, a sub-body of the UN. By letter dated 31 May 1948 from the Swiss Federal Department of Politics, the Swiss Government informed the Executive-Secretary of ICITO that the Swiss Council had decided "d'appliquer, par analogie, à la Commission intérimaire de l'Organisation internationale du commerce, l'Arrangement provisoire sur les privilèges et immunités de l'Organisation des Nations Unies ...." *See* J.H. Jackson, World Trade and the Law of GATT 140 n.5 (1969); EGGER, at 135–139. For Swiss domestic law, *see* Federal Act on the Privileges, Immunities and Facilities and the Financial Subsidies granted by Switzerland as a Host State of 22 June 2007, English translation in 2008 UN Jurid. Y.B, p. 3, UN Doc. ST/LEG/SER.C/46 (2008).

476 For the main points of difference between the General Convention and the Interim Agreement, both concluded in 1946, see IVRAKIS, at 362.

2.4.2.3.3 Relationship between General Agreements and Headquarters Agreements

Given that a headquarters agreement, at least in the case of member States, complements a general agreement on the privileges and immunities of an international organization, it becomes interesting to examine the relationship between these two instruments. The sub-committee of the European Committee on Legal Co-operation of the Council of Europe undertook such an examination in its study of 1969. The sub-committee considered the following:

> ... whether or not the host state was a party to the general agreement, the headquarters agreement should in principle only constitute an adaptation of the terms of the general agreement to the legal system, and take into account the particular circumstances deriving from the location of the organisation, in the host state. While it was recognised that there are some privileges and immunities which concern only the host state, the headquarters agreement should not extend the privileges and immunities set out in the general agreement, unless there are special reasons of a local character to justify so doing and the other member states give their approval through the competent representative organ of the organisation.[477]

Although at first blush this might seem a somewhat strict view, it actually is not, because the sub-committee at the same time noted a series of special cases in which a derogation from the general rule should be possible. Since the sub-committee referred to adjustments which might be necessary for local reasons, we find no difficulty in supporting its view. We agree that the régime which applies to the privileges and immunities of an international organization should be as uniform as can be, in order that it will be interpreted and applied in an equal manner in all those States with which the organization has some kind of relationship. If this search for uniformity at the same time takes into account the particular circumstances deriving from the location of the organization, then this situation is to be preferred over one in which a great variety of separate bilateral agreements exist. The very purpose of the present study, as was that of the sub-committee, is to make clear that there is a *common* standard with respect to the granting of privileges and immunities to international organizations, a *separate* body of

477 Council of Europe Report 1969, at 17, para. 18; *see also* EGGER, at 137–138, 144.

law, with its own rules and principles, which lies at the heart of every organizational immunity granted.

2.4.2.3.4 Conference Agreements

When meetings[478] are convened away from the established headquarters of an international organization, *ad hoc* agreements must be concluded by the organization with the State on whose territory the meeting is held, in order to cover situations in which the existing legal arrangements are deemed to be insufficient. In such cases the host relationship is only a *temporary* one, which makes the conference agreement in effect a simplified headquarters agreement, being limited in time.

Early examples of this kind are the Exchange of Letters of 17 August 1951 constituting an Agreement between the United Nations and France relating to the holding of the Sixth Session of the General Assembly in Paris[479] and the Agreement between Kenya and the United Nations Educational, Scientific and Cultural Organization concerning the 19th Session of the General Congress of UNESCO in 1976.[480]

As regards the relationship between the United Nations and its member States, the legal basis for concluding agreements of this kind can be found in Section 36 of the General Convention, which reads:

> The Secretary-General may conclude with any Member or Members supplementary agreements adjusting the provisions of the convention so far as that Member or those Members are concerned. These supplementary agreements shall in each case be subject to the approval of the General Assembly.[481]

With regard to conferences, the United Nations and the government of the State upon whose invitation the conference is organized, normally conclude an agreement in the form of a treaty, whereas an exchange of letters, or possibly a Memorandum of Understanding, is used for seminars, symposia, workshops and other meetings.

Based on longstanding practice, the United Nations has developed both a 'Model conference agreement' and a model Agreement in the form of an

---

478 In most cases this concerns conferences, which are only of an *ad hoc*, temporary character.

479 122 U.N.T.S. 191 *reprinted in* UN Doc. ST/LEG/SER.B/10 (1959), at 347–360; see EGGER, at 127.

480 1976 UN Jurid. Y.B 55–61, UN Doc. ST/LEG/SER.C/14 (1978).

481 The latter provision follows, of course, from UN Charter, Art. 105, para. 3.

exchange of letters, containing standard clauses to be included in *ad hoc* agreements for seminars, symposia, workshops and other meetings convened and arranged by the UN Secretariat away from UN headquarters.[482] These model agreements, which have in most cases been subject to minor deviations only, regulate such matters as status of premises, equipment, utilities and supplies, accommodation, medical facilities, transport, police protection, locally recruited personnel, financial arrangements, liability, privileges and immunities and the settlement of disputes.

2.4.3 Domestic Legislation

In many cases international organizations are granted privileges and immunities by *national* law, i.e., internal legislation of individual States and judicial decisions.

Szasz has summarized the principal reasons for this practice as follows:

> Usually such legislation is designed to implement domestically the international obligations that are defined by treaty instruments ... In some States, the legislation is meant to supplement these treaties. Finally, in a few States unwilling to enter into such treaties, the national legislation largely takes the place of treaty provisions.[483]

The legislation of the United States of America, discussed below, the United Kingdom[484] and Switzerland[485] can be regarded as the most interesting and representative of all domestic legislation existing today. The United States and the United Kingdom legislation are among the earliest of the current national instruments, whereas Swiss municipal law is of particular interest because of the Swiss' host relationship as a non-member State with the United Nations until 2002. Since a comparative review of the current legislation would go far beyond the scope of the present study, we shall confine

---

482 *See* Annex to UN Doc. ST/AI/342.

483 Szasz, Immunities, at 155. It should be kept in mind that several of the existing national laws, notably those of the U.K. and the U.S., were already in force when no general multilateral agreements had been concluded.

484 The legislation currently in force in the United Kingdom is the International Organisations (Privileges and Immunities) Act 1968, *Halsbury's Statutes of England,* Vol. 6, at 1051 (3rd ed. 1969); *see* House of Lords Judgment of 26 October 1989 *in Maclaine Watson & Co. Ltd. v. Department of Trade and Industry and related appeals; Maclaine Watson & Co. Ltd. v. International Tin Council,* [1990] 2 App.Cas. 418, [1989] 3 All E.R. 523, [1989] 3 W.L.R. 969, *reprinted in* 29 ILM 670, 688–690 (1990), discussed in Chapter 3 of this book; *see also* Dominicé, L'immunité, at 172–173; EGGER, at 146–148.

485 *See* Council of Europe Report 1969, at 88–89; HUG, at 53 *et seq.*.

ourselves to a general discussion of United States law, the United States being the host State of major organizations such as the UN, with its headquarters in New York City, and the World Bank Group and the Organization of American States, which are both headquartered in Washington, D.C.[486]

The main source of U.S. domestic legislation on organizational immunities is the *International Organizations Immunities Act* (IOIA) of 29 December 1945.[487] The IOIA provides in Section 1 that the term 'international organization' is limited to public international organizations in which the United States participates either by treaty or by authorization of the U.S. Congress, and which have been designated by Presidential Executive Order as being entitled to enjoy the (statutory) privileges and immunities provided by the IOIA.[488] With respect to the topic of organizational immunities, the most interesting provisions of the IOIA are Section 2(b), granting international organizations, their property and their assets immunity from suit and every form of judicial process, Section 2(c), which deals with immunity from search and confiscation and inviolability of archives, Section 2 (d) concerning, *inter alia*, customs duties and communications, and Section 6 granting exemption from all property taxes.[489]

As regards judicial decisions,[490] it may be said that the judicial authorities of the United States have more or less consistently given effect to the

486 For a comprehensive collection of domestic legislative texts, see *Handbook on the Legal Status, Privileges and Immunities of the United Nations*, UN Doc. ST/LEG/2 (1952); UN Docs. ST/LEG/SER.B/10 & 11, as well as annual volumes of the UN Jurid. Y.B.

487 International Organizations Immunities Act (IOIA) of 29 December 1945, U.S. Public Law 291, 79th Congress, P.L. 79–291, 59 Stat. 669 (1945), 22 U.S.C. 288–288h. The IOIA was enacted in the U.S. in pursuance of its obligation under UN Charter Art. 105; *see* 1980 UN Jurid. Y.B 224,232, UN Doc. ST/LEG/SER.C/18 (1983). EGGER, at 148 *et seq.*, provides a critical approach; *see also* L. Preuss, *The International Organizations Immunities Act,* 40 AJIL 332 (1946)[hereinafter: Preuss]; IVRAKIS, at 586; Henderson, at 487–497; Glenn *et al.*, at 247–290; AHLUWALIA, at 53; Dinh, at 265. *See also* Restatement (Third), § 467, Comment (t), at 496; WHITEMAN, 13 DIGEST, at 4–5; Farrugia, at 503–507.

488 The United Nations has been the object of Executive Order No. 9.698 of 19 February 1946. In addition, some international organizations of which the U.S. is not a member State have also been designated pursuant to authorization by special statute. *See* Restatement (Third), § 467, Comment (f), at 496. Other international organizations will have to rely for their immunities on customary law. *See also* Dinh, at 267 n.9.

489 For the text of the IOIA, *see* UN Doc. ST/LEG/SER.B/10 (1959), at 128–133; for a review of this Act *see* Preuss, at 332–345; Henderson, at 487–497; Dominicé, L'immunité, at 173- 174; Glenn *et al.*, at 247–290; AHLUWALIA, at 53.

490 For the decisions of various *international* tribunals, reference is made to Step Three of our analysis.

immunities flowing from the treaty obligations of the United States, in particular Article 105 of the Charter of the United Nations.[491] For example, in *Curran v. City of New York*,[492] in which a taxpayer challenged the exemption of the United Nations from taxation, the New York State court held, *inter alia*, that the provisions of Article 105 UN Charter:

> ... in a Treaty made under the Authority of the United Nations, are the law of the land[[493]] ... Also that without further action by Congress or the State, the immunities 'necessary for the fulfilment of its purposes', conferred upon the United Nations by Article 105, includes immunity from taxation.

In *Balfour, Guthrie and Co, Ltd. v. United States*,[494] an American federal court held that Article 104 UN Charter, conferring legal capacity on the United Nations, was also self-executing and that therefore "[n]o implemental legislation would appear to be necessary ...." In *Brzak v. United Nations et al.*,[495] the U.S. Court of Appeals for the Second Circuit, New York's highest federal court, confirmed that the General Convention of 1946 "unequivocally grants the United Nations absolute immunity without exception" and that this treaty instrument is a self-executing treaty for U.S. law purposes, i.e., it is binding in U.S. courts. In *Sacks v. International Monetary Fund*, the U.S. Court of Appeals for the District of Columbia Circuit (covering Washington, D.C.), found that the IMF had not expressly waived the immunity from every form of judicial process to which it is entitled under Article IX of the Fund's Articles of Agreement, as incorporated into U.S. law.[496]

In the United States, an international organization's immunity may be treaty-based in the event the United States is a member of the international organization concerned and the organization's constituent/immunity instrument is self-executing and hence is binding U.S. law,[497] and/or it may have

491 *See* Restatement (Third) § 467, Reporters' Note 3, at 498–499; Dinh, at 265 *et seq.*; WHITEMAN, 13 DIGEST, at 4 *et seq.*

492 191 Misc. 229, 77 N.Y.S.2d 206,212 (1947), *aff'd*, 275 App. Div. 784, 88 N.Y.S.2d 924 (2d Dep't 1949); *see also* Dinh, at 266, 269; IVRAKIS, at 591 n.9.

493 *See* U.S. Const. art. 6, cl. 2 ("all Treaties ... shall be the supreme Law of the Land").

494 90 F.Supp. 831 U.S.D.C., ND, Cal. 1950; IVRAKIS, at 592 n.10; WHITEMAN, 13 DIGEST, at 4–6.

495 *Cynthia Brzak, Nasr Ishak v. United Nations, Kofi Annan, Ruud Lubbers, Wendy Chamberlin*, 597 F.3d 114 (2d Cir. 2010).

496 *Sacks v. International Monetary Fund*, 26 F.4th 470, 471 (D.C. Cir. 2022).

497 In addition to treaties having been confirmed by the U.S. Senate pursuant to Article 2, section 2, clause 2, of the U.S. Constitution, *ex post* congressional-executive agreements

a statutory basis, namely, through the International Organizations Immunities Act.[498]

As regards the situation in The Netherlands, another prominent host country for international institutions, reference may be made to a statement made in 1959 by the Permanent Representative of The Netherlands to the United Nations, which reads:

---

have been referred to as possibly providing a basis for making a treaty self-executing and hence binding U.S. law. *Cf. Kling et al. v. World Health Organization*, 532 F.Supp. 3d 141 (S.D.N.Y. 2021)(upholding the WHO's claim of immunity in a lawsuit seeking damages for the WHO's alleged negligence in responding to the COVID-19 pandemic based on the IOIA, after acknowledging literature endorsing congressional-executive agreements as being presumed self-executing but without ruling on the issue); *with Rodriguez v. Pan American Health Organization*, 29 F.4th 706 (D.C. Cir. 2022)(rejecting the immunity of PAHO, the WHO's Regional Office for the Americas, under the IOIA and the WHO's constituent instrument after finding that the immunity provisions of the WHO Constitution are not self-executing and hence are not part of U.S. law). In *Medellín v. Texas*, the U.S. Supreme Court recognized the "distinction between treaties that automatically have effect as domestic law, and those that—while they constitute international law commitments—do not by themselves function as binding federal law" and noted that "not all international law obligations automatically constitute binding federal law enforceable in United States courts." 552 U.S. 491, 504 (2008). The Supreme Court explained that a self-executing treaty "operates of itself without the aid of any legislative provision (*id.* at 505 (citing *Foster v. Neilson*, 27 U.S. 253, 314 (1829)), while non-self-executing treaties "can only be enforced pursuant to legislation to carry them into effect" (*id.* (citing *Whitney v. Robertson*, 124 U.S. 190, 194 (1888)). For examples of U.S. court decisions based solely on treaty-based immunity considerations, see *Georges v United Nations*, No. 15–455-cv, judgment of 18 Aug. 2016 (2d Cir. 2016)(basing immunity analysis on the General Convention of 1946); *International Bank for Reconstruction and Development v. District of Columbia*, 171 F.3d 687 (D.C. Cir. 1999), 38 ILM 818 (1999)(rejecting claim that a private contactor, retained by the World Bank to provide food and beverage services to individuals on the Bank's premises, has derivative immunity from District of Columbia taxes on the contractor's sales of food and beverages based on the Articles of Agreement of the IBRD, as incorporated into U.S. law).

498 This includes the Bretton Woods Agreements Act. *See* 22 U.S.C. §§ 286–286m, § 286h (providing for the participation of the United States in the IMF and the IBRD and incorporating relevant provisions from the Articles of Agreement of the IMF and of the IBRD into U.S. law). *See also Sacks v. International Monetary Fund*, 26 F.4th 470, 471 (D.C. Cir. 2022). For international organizations falling within the scope of the Bretton Woods Agreements Act, their immunity, which reflects the immunity provided in the constituent instruments of those organizations, is at a different level, and in certain respects is more protective, than the immunity afforded by the IOIA. *Id.*, at 474. For examples of U.S. court decisions considering both treaty grounds and statutory grounds for organizational immunity, see *Rodriguez v. Pan American Health Organization*, 29 F.4th 706 (D.C. Cir. 2022); *Kling et al. v. World Health Organization*, 532 F. Supp. 3d 141 (S.D.N.Y. 2021).

> The Acting Permanent Representative has been instructed to inform the Secretary-General that there is no special law or regulation in force in the Netherlands relating to privileges and immunities of the United Nations, its Specialized Agencies and other Inter-governmental Organizations. The reason for this is that international agreements, also those containing provisions regarding privileges and immunities, acquire force of law as soon as they have been ratified or otherwise accepted by the Netherlands.[499]

In general, it may be concluded that international organizations can rely directly on the privileges and immunities granted to them by way of an international agreement, if it contains self-executing provisions,[500] used here as meaning provisions which, by their nature, do not require subsequent domestic legislation implementing them. As was stated in a memorandum of law prepared by the Office of Legal Affairs of the UN Secretariat in 1953,[501] domestic legislation must to this extent be considered to be declaratory. Such legislation may, however, be desirable for reasons of clarity or to provide administrative certainty. National legislation concerned with the privileges and immunities of international organizations is, therefore, primarily a legal source of a supplementary nature. The U.S. Supreme Court has noted that "the privileges and immunities accorded by the [International Organizations Immunities Act of 1945] are only default rules" and that "the organization's charter can always specify a different level of immunity."[502]

---

499 Note of 20 August 1959 received from the Acting Permanent Representative of The Netherlands to the United Nations *reprinted in* UN Doc. ST/LEG/SER.B/10 (1959), at 55. For the situation under German law, see H.P. Kunz-Hallstein, *Privilegien und Immunitäten internationaler Organisationen im Bereich nicht-hoheitlicher Privatrechtsgeschäfte,*48 NJW 3069, 3071 (1992)[hereinafter: Kunz-Hallstein, Privilegien].

500 *See* R. Wallace, International Law 43 (1986)[hereinafter: WALLACE]. As regards UN Charter Art. 105, Ehrenfeld, at 88, has argued that the U.N.C.I.O. report made it clear that Article 105 was intended to be self-executing and that the power of the General Assembly to propose conventions should not derogate from the obligatory character of the article itself. *See* 13 U.N.C.I.O. Docs., at 778–780. According to Restatement (Third), § 467, Comment (f), at 496, the provisions contained in the several international agreements to which the U.S. is a Party are "probably self-executing and to be given effect even without legislative implementation."

501 *Reprinted in* [1961] 2 Y.B. Int'l L. Comm'n 245–246, UN Doc. A/CN.4/SER.A/1967/Add. 1.

502 *Jam v. International Finance Corp.*, 139 S. CT. 759, 771 (2019). *See also Polak v. International Monetary Fund*, 657 F.Supp. 2d 116, 120 (D.D.C. 2009)("The IOIA serves as a separate and independent source of immunity for international organizations such as the defendant [IMF]."); *Kling et al. v. World Health Organization*, 532

However, the constituent instruments of many intergovernmental organizations do not have the force of law in the United States (because the United States is not a member of the international organization and/or the constituent instrument is not a self-executing treaty under U.S. law), meaning such organizations remain reliant on the IOIA.[503]

As has been explained by Szasz,[504] "although IGOs rely on national legislative provisions applicable to them, particularly when it is convenient to do so *vis-à-vis* national authorities, such provisions *can in no way alter or diminish* the rights that they are entitled to by reason of treaties (especially their constitutional instruments, to which all members are parties) ...." (emphasis added). According to Henderson,[505] "international organizations owe their primary allegiance to the principles and policies established by their organic documents, and not to the legislation of any one member." Bowett is in no doubt about this point, observing that "[w]hatever view the municipal courts take, such legislation is not the source of the State's international obligations; that source remains the constituent texts and such supplementary agreements as may exist."[506] Finally, we agree with Kunz that "the granting of immunities merely by municipal statute, whether to a particular organization, or by an Act of a more general nature, a voluntary granting, is certainly no adequate method, as such law may at any time be changed or repealed by the state in question. It would also make impossible the uniformity of the law of immunities."[507]

We referred to the above discussion, because of the confusion caused by the different theories which have evolved on the relationship of domestic law to international law. These theories can be divided into two principal schools, namely, the *monistic* school, which, in the event of a conflict between international law and domestic legislation, contends that international law should prevail, and the *dualistic* school, which holds that, if

---

F.Supp. 3d 141 (S.D.N.Y. 2021)("Immunity under the IOIA is concurrent with and separate from any treaty-based immunity the WHO may have.").

503 *See, e.g., Rodriguez v. Pan American Health Organization*, 29 F.4th 706 (2022)(rejecting the immunity of PAHO, the WHO's Regional Office for the Americas, under both the IOIA and under the WHO's constituent instrument, in the latter case after finding that the immunity provisions of the WHO Constitution are not self-executing and hence are not part of U.S. law that is binding in U.S. courts).

504 Szasz, Immunities, at 155.

505 Henderson, at 490, referring to a decision by the Court of Appeals for the District of Columbia Circuit in *Mendaro v. World Bank*, 717 F.2d 610, 619 (D.C. Cir. 1983).

506 BOWETT, at 347–348.

507 Kunz, at 847–848; *see also* AHLUWALIA, at 52 and n.15.

international law is applied within a State it is only because it has been expressly incorporated into domestic legislation.[508] The problems entailed by these conflicting theories are, however, mitigated by the fact that even the courts of States which would seem to apply a more dualistic system, such as the United States, have held that self-executing treaty obligations do not depend for force and effect on implementing domestic legislation.[509] The fact that the great majority of treaty provisions concerning organizational immunities can be considered as self-executing justifies the conclusion that domestic legislation concerning organizational immunities is primarily of a *supplementary* nature.

A review of the existing domestic legislation, which consists of Acts or (executive) Orders of usually limited length, reveals an international consensus on functional organizational immunities, being in conformity with the international agreements referred to in the previous sections of this part of our study.[510]

2.4.4 Customary International Law

Although, as we have seen, it has become the usual practice for the constituent instruments of international organizations, multilateral and bilateral agreements, as well as the domestic law of States to provide for the necessary privileges and immunities, the question remains whether in the absence or inapplicability of the above-mentioned written legal sources a State is under any duty to grant certain privileges and immunities to an international organization.

Recourse to customary international law may be necessary for several reasons. For a concise summary of these reasons we refer to Szasz,[511] from whom the following excerpt may be cited:

> While, for obvious reasons, both the organizations and their members generally prefer to rely on specific treaties or on applicable national legislation to define their respective rights and obligations, there are

508 *See* R. Jennings & A. Watts, Oppenheim's International Law 52–86 (9th ed. 1996); WALLACE, at 31 *et seq.* Thus, The Netherlands is an example of a country taking a 'monistic' approach, whereas the United States belongs to the 'dualistic' category.

509 *See also* Ehrenfeld, at 88. It should be noted with WALLACE, at 32, that in practice the differences between international law and a particular domestic system are minimized and that every effort is made to achieve a harmonization between the two systems.

510 *See* the national laws of a number of States listed in UN Docs. ST/LEG/SER.B/10 & 11.

511 Szasz, Immunities, at 155.

> certain instances when such reliance is not possible or sufficient. Such circumstances may arise when no applicable treaty relationship exists at all between or relating to an IGO and a State – for example, if the State is not a member of the organization. However, as the International Court of Justice recognized in Reparation for Injuries Suffered in Service of UN (Advisory Opinion), even non-member States may not be able to avoid all responsibilities towards an international organization. In some cases, although certain relevant treaty obligations exist, a State concerned may not be a party to any agreement that regulates a particular question in detail. In such instances an IGO may contend that a particular provision (...) of such agreements actually expresses a generally applicable principle that is in any event binding on States.

The International Court of Justice has held that evidence of customary law can be found in the uniformity of State practice and *opinio juris sive necessitatis*, i.e., the conviction by States that, in following a certain practice, they are conforming to what amounts to a legal obligation.[512]

The growing influence of customary international law as a legal basis for according privileges and immunities has been evidenced by legal practice.[513] The elements just referred to are, for instance, reflected in the views of the majority of the delegations that discussed the general problems relating to the diplomatic law of international organizations in the Sixth Committee of the UN General Assembly in 1967.[514] These discussions revealed broad support for the granting of appropriate privileges and immunities for the effective functioning of international organizations. The Report of the Assembly's Sixth Committee, in providing a summary of the debate on the draft resolution, referred to the widespread view among delegations according to which the United Nations should enjoy a special status so as to

---

512 *See, e.g., North Sea Continental Shelf* (FRG/Den.; FRG/Neth.), 1969 ICJ Rep. 3, 28, para. 37, 44, para. 77; for a summary of the concept of customary international law see R. Bernhardt, *Customary International Law, in* [Installment] 7 Encyclopedia of Public International Law 61–66 (1984), and further references therein.

513 For a survey of practice see El-Erian, *Preliminary Report* on the topic of 'Relations between States and International Organizations (Second Part),' UN Doc. A/CN.4/304 (1977) *reprinted in* [1977] 2 Y.B. Int'l L. Comm'n 139, 151–152, paras. 59–62, UN Doc. A/CN.4/SER.A/1977/Add. 1 (Part 1); for decisions by national courts in which international organizations have been accorded immunity from jurisdiction, despite the absence of treaty provisions, see. *e.g.*, SEIDL-HOHENVELDERN, EUROCONTROL, at 42 n.34.

514 *See* 22 GAOR, Annexes (Agenda Item 98), UN Doc. A/6965 (1967).

secure the free and successful performance of its functions. Most important, the rules governing privileges and immunities were stated to have acquired the status of norms of international law, there being no difficulty with regard to the content of the law, which from a juridical standpoint was considered clear and well-developed.[515] It was concluded with regard to the 1946 General Convention that its contents now form part of general international law between the United Nations and its member States and they are accordingly binding on States even in the absence of an express act of accession.[516]

In his statement at the 1016th meeting of the Sixth Committee held in 1967,[517] the UN Legal Counsel expressed his organization's views as follows:

> It should be noted that there are now ninety-six States which have acceded to the [General] Convention. Moreover, in most of the remaining Member States as well as in many non-member States, the provisions of the Convention have been applied by special agreement. While it may be true that in 1946 many of the provisions of the Convention had the character of *lege ferenda*, in the nearly twenty-two years since the adoption of the Convention by the Assembly its provisions have become the standard and norm for governing relations between States and the United Nations throughout the world. I doubt that I am being over-bold in suggesting that the standards and principles of the Convention have been so widely accepted that they have now become a part of the general international law governing the relations of States and the United Nations.[518]

This statement rings even more true today, with more than 160 States having become parties to the General Convention.

---

515 *See Report of the Sixth Committee,* UN Doc. A/6965 *reprinted in* 22 GAOR, Annexes (Agenda Item 98)(1967) at 6, 9.

516 *See* 22 GAOR, Verbatim records of meetings, Vol. III, UN Doc. A/PV.1627–1673 (1971), at 5–9 (Agenda Item 98); *Report of the Sixth Committee,* UN Doc. A/6965 *reprinted in* 22 GAOR, Annexes (Agenda Item 98)(1967), at 6, 8–10, paras. 10–19; El-Erian, *Third Report,* UN Doc. A/CN.4/203 and Add. 1–5 *reprinted in* [1968] 2 Y.B. Int'l L. Comm'n 119, at 121, para. 6, and 122, para. 8, UN Doc. A/CN.4/SER.A/1968/Add. 1.

517 *See* 22 GAOR, Annexes (Agenda Item 98), UN Doc. A/C.6/385 (1967).

518 *See* UN Doc. A/C.6/385 *reprinted in* 22 GAOR, Annexes (Agenda Item 98)(1967), at 4, 6, para. 13. *See also* El-Erian, *Third Report,* UN Doc. A/CN.4/203 and Add. 1–5 *reprinted in* [1968] 2 Y.B. Int'l L. Comm'n 119, 123, para. 13, UN Doc. A/CN.4/SER.A/1968/Add. 1.

It has always been the position of the United Nations that its immunity from suit forms part of general international law, even in the absence of any implementing international or domestic legislation and, moreover, that the Organization's immunity from legal process is derived from Articles 104 and 105 of the UN Charter, a treaty forming part of the legal systems of the more than 190 member States.[519] Consequently, the United States, as a UN member State, is obliged to grant the United Nations immunity from legal process, even though immunity from legal process is not provided for under the Headquarters Agreement between the United Nations and the United States.

Among the material sources which may be indicative of rules of customary international law are resolutions of the General Assembly of the United Nations relating to legal questions. However, only General Assembly resolutions whose voting figures indicate overwhelming generality of practice may be evidence of customary international law. One such resolution is Resolution 2328 (XXII) on the 'Question of diplomatic privileges and immunities,'[520] adopted by the General Assembly at its 1637th plenary meeting held on 18 December 1967, by a vote of 101 to none, with one abstention (Colombia), operative paragraph 3 of which reads:

> *Urges* States Members of the United Nations, whether or not they have acceded to the Convention on the Privileges and Immunities of the United Nations, to take every measure necessary to secure the implementation of the privileges and immunities accorded under Article 105 of the Charter of the Organization ….[521]

519 *See* [1967] 2 Y.B. Int'l L. Comm'n 223 n.49, UN Doc. A/CN.4/SER.A/1967/Add. 1.

520 *See* 22 GAOR Supp. (No. 16) at 83, UN Doc. A/6716 (1968). The full title of Agenda Item 98 is: 'Question of diplomatic privileges and immunities: (a) Measures tending to implement the privileges and immunities of representatives of Member States to the principal and subsidiary organs of the United Nations and to conferences convened by the United Nations and *the privileges and immunities* of the staff and *of the Organization itself,* as well as the obligations of States concerning the protection of diplomatic personnel and property; (b) Reaffirmation of an important immunity of representatives of Member States to the principal and subsidiary organs of the United Nations and to conferences convened by the United Nations.' *See* 22 GAOR, Verbatim records of meetings, Vol. III, at 5–6, UN Doc. A/PV.1627–1673 (1971)(emphasis added).

521 It may, of course, be argued that the use of the word *'urges'* in Res. 2328 is not sufficient enough to constitute conclusive evidence of a rule of (customary) law and that, in any event, General Assembly resolutions are not binding by nature. But 'binding' is different from 'being of legal significance.' As the ICJ held in *Legal Consequences for*

The above survey focused primarily on the position of one particular organization only, namely, the United Nations, and not on international organizations in general. The diverse practice and often more limited membership of international organizations in this respect dictates a rather cautious attitude toward custom as a legal source of organizational immunities applicable to international organizations generally.[522] The point is not an entirely academic one, since conventional rules conferring immunities upon international organizations are not opposable to States non-parties to these conventions unless they form part of customary international law.

The *courts* of some jurisdictions have recognized that an international organization may be entitled to immunity in the absence of a treaty instrument conferring immunity as a matter of conventional law, finding a basis in customary international law. For example, the Supreme Court (*Hoge Raad*) of The Netherlands, which serves as the host country for a number of international organizations, has ruled that, in the absence of a treaty conferring privileges and immunities on an international organization, an organization may be similarly entitled to such privileges and immunities based on customary international law, at least in the State on whose territory the organization is located with the approval of the government of that State.[523] The Dutch Supreme Court also has recognized that there may

---

States of the Continued Presence of South Africa in Namibia (South West Africa) notwithstanding Security Council Resolution 276 (1970), Advisory Opinion, 1971 ICJ Rep. 16, 50, para. 105: "it would not be correct to assume, because the General Assembly is in principle vested with recommendatory powers, it is debarred from adopting, in specific cases within the framework of its competence, resolutions which make determinations or have operative design." Also, the further contents of the resolution, as well as the number of States voting for it, should be taken into account in interpreting the legal value of its pronouncements. *See* R. Higgins, *The Role of Resolutions of International Organizations in the Process of Creating Norms in the International System, in* International Law and the International System 21, 24 (W.E. Butler ed. 1987). Res. 2328 thus belongs to the category of "provisions stating the existence of a right on which the generality of the States has expressed agreement" and which confirm or reaffirm a customary rule recognized by the community of States: *see Texaco Overseas Petroleum et al. v. Libyan Arab Republic,* Arbitral Award of 19 Jan. 1977, para. 87, *reprinted in* 17 ILM 1 (1978).

522 *See also* Council of Europe Report 1969, at 14, para. 11; AKEHURST, at 120; Dinh, at 274–275.

523 *Supreme Site Services GmbH et al v. Supreme Headquarters Allied Powers Europe and Allied Joint Force Command Headquarters Brunssum,* Supreme Court of The Netherlands, case no. 20/00937, judgment of 24 Dec. 2021, para. 3.1.2 (with reference to *X v. Iran-United States Claims Tribunal,* Supreme Court of The Netherlands, judgment of

be circumstances justifying the invocation of custom-based immunity by an international organization that is not based or located in The Netherlands, including in situations where such an organization is affiliated with an international organization that is based in The Netherlands and granting immunity to the non-local organization is necessary to prevent the custom-based immunity of the international organization that is based in The Netherlands from being rendered meaningless.[524]

The influence of customary international law as a possible legal basis for granting privileges and immunities to international organizations has been widely recognized in *legal doctrine*.[525]

---

20 Dec. 1985). For a different view, see *Amaratunga v. Northwest Atlantic Fisheries Organization*, Supreme Court of Canada, judgment of 29 Nov. 2013, 2013 SCC 66, [2013]3 SCR 866, at para. 29 ("In the case of international organizations, unlike that of states, the prevailing view at present is that no rule of customary international law confers immunity on them. International organizations derive their existence from treaties, and the same holds true for their rights to immunities.").

524 *Id. See also* OKEKE, at 277 (noting that "[w]here a host State is a member of the international organization, even in the absence of a treaty, some courts have upheld the immunity of the international organization as a matter of customary international law," citing decisions from Dutch and Italian courts); SCHERMERS, at 1079, para. 1611. *But see X v. Organization of the Petroleum Exporting Countries*, No. SV 1/2021–23, Austrian Constitutional Court (*Verfassungsgerichtshof*), judgment of 29 Sept. 2022, Margin Number 42 (rejecting the argument that Austria is obligated, under customary international law, to accord immunity to an international organization of which Austria is not a member "even if no reasonable alternative remedy for settling employment disputes is available").

525 *See, e.g.*, HUG, at 59; Seyersted, Personality, at 20, n.71 and 49, n.164; WEISSBERG, at 143–146, 208; AHLUWALIA, at 207; Lalive, at 304–305, 331; SEIDL-HOHENVELDERN, RECHT, at 283; *id.*, EUROCONTROL, at 14–15, 49; *id.*, L'immunité, at 160; *id.*, *Dienstrechtliche Klagen gegen Internationalen Organisationen, in* Festschrift für Hans-Jörgen Schlochauer 615 (I. von Münch ed. 1981); *id.*, Personality, at 51; Kunz-Hallstein, Privilegien, at 3070; Aufricht, at 92; P. Guggenheim, Traité de Droit International Public 51–52 (Vol. I, 1953)[hereinafter: GUGGENHEIM]; BEIER *et al.*, at 4; Francis, in [1977] 1 Y.B. Int'l L. Comm'n 210, para. 15, UN Doc. A/CN.4/SER.A/1977; Quintin-Baxter, in *id.*, at 211, para. 24; Yankov, in [1983] 1 Y.B. Int'l L. Comm'n 241, para. 28, UN Doc. A/CN.4/SER.A/1983; (1967] 2 Y.B. Int'l L. Comm'n 140–141; *but see* FOX-WEBB, at 580 ("In the absence of a grant of privileges and immunities to international organizations by a State, it would seem that a third State is under no obligation in customary international law to confer them"); I. Brownlie, Principles of Public International Law 683 (5th ed. 1998)(acknowledging that "the requisite privileges and immunities in respect of the territorial jurisdiction of host states are recognized in the customary law," while noting that "there is as yet no general agreement on the precise content of customary law concerning the immunities of international organizations")[hereinafter: BROWNLIE]; BOWETT, at 348; AMERASINGHE, at 344–348; M. Wood, *Do International*

Seidl-Hohenveldern has argued that the existence of customary international law in this matter may be based on the fact that all international agreements contain very similar provisions.[526] Consequently, such agreements might be seen as merely declaratory statements of already existing rules of customary international law. According to Seidl-Hohenveldern:

> [l]e bon fonctionnement de toute organisation internaționale n'est assuré que si, par des privilèges et immunités, celle-ci est mise à l'abri d'ingérences non autorisées des Etats membres. Ce besoin de toute organisation internaționale est si fondamental que les diverses codifications qui l'aient exprimé sont presque identiques. Puisqu'on ne peut guère concevoir 1'existence d'une organisation sans ces immunités, on peut considérer que ces codifications sont *déclaratoires* d'un droit coutumier que, le cas échéant, les Etats membres ont respectés même avant 1'adoption d'un accord.[527]

Articles 11 and 12 sub(c) of the 1965 *Protocol on the Privileges and Immunities of the European Communities*, according to which the "customary" privileges and immunities[528] must be granted may be referred to as supporting this view.[529]

Organizations Enjoy Immunity under Customary International Law?, 10 IOLR 287 (2013). *See also* Restatement (Third), § 467(i). For a survey of the immunity of international organizations as a rule of customary international law, see F. Schroer, *De l'application de l'immunité juridictionnelle des états étrangers aux organisations internationales,* 75 R.G.D.I.P. 712 (1971).

526 SEIDL-HOHENVELDERN, RECHT, at 283, para. 1905; *id.,* L'immunité, at 160; *see also* BEIER *et al.,* at 4; Dominicé, L'immunité, at 175–176; *id.,* LIBER SEIDL, at 93; Bianchi, at 213.

527 Seidl-Hohenveldern, L'immunité, at 160; *but see* Dominicé, L'immunité, at 175–177.

528 *See Protocol on the Privileges and Immunities of the European Communities,* 8 April 1965, 1B Handbook on the European Communities (Fusian Treaty) – Suppl.36 (Oct. 1967), at 19. It must, however, be noted, that Articles 11 and 12 concern the immunities of the representatives of member States and of EC officials, and that the term 'customary' does not appear in Chapters I and II of the Protocol dealing with the organization as such.

529 The 1965 Protocol has been replaced by the Protocol on the privileges and immunities of the European Union, see OJ 2010, C 83/266. *See also* the final words of Section 21 of the Specialized Agencies Convention; *Spaans v. Iran-United States Claims Tribunal,* Supreme Court (*Hoge Raad*) of The Netherlands, Judgment nr.12627 of 20 Dec. 1985, NJ 438, 1691–1702, s. 3.3.4. *But see* Reuter, in [1977] 1 Y.B. Int'l L. Comm'n 209, para. 12, UN Doc. A/CN.4/SER.A/1977, expressing his serious reservations as to so-called customary

Guggenheim, on the contrary, has stated in this regard that "[l]e fait que certaines conventions internationales ont des contenus identiques, ce qui est particulièrement caractéristiques pour les traités d'établissement, de consulat et d'extradition, n'entraine pas en soi la formation d'une règle coutumière."[530]

It has also been suggested that, besides basing the obligation of the member States to grant the organization the necessary privileges and immunities on the principle that these privileges and immunities exist under general international law and independently of international agreements, this obligation may be deemed implicit in the express obligations of membership spelled out in the constituent instrument of the organization.[531] Schermers[532] speaks in this regard of a general rule of international institutional law, according to which privileges and immunities must be accorded which have not been expressly mentioned in any agreement, without, however, indicating what particular privilege or immunity is prescribed by this general rule.[533] Yet another construction has been suggested by the same scholar, who has argued that "[e]ven without ... express provision, national courts may grant immunity on the ground that international organizations are composed of sovereign states, each of which is immune from local jurisdiction ...."[534] In other words, an international organization should *as a*

rules, arguing that it is not unusual for agreements relating to organizations, particularly those operating in the economic field, to be signed in haste and to contain a general reference to "the customary privileges and immunities" which those bodies will enjoy. But it is not unusual for it to be stipulated that this question will be the subject of an additional agreement, so that not much is really gained, according to Reuter. In such cases, it could indeed be said that the term 'customary' is merely a synonym for 'traditional,' indicating that the implementing agreement defining the privileges and immunities should incorporate those organizational immunities which have been laid down in other treaty instruments.

530 GUGGENHEIM, at 52. On this issue in general, see M.E. Villiger, Customary International Law and Treaties: A Study of Their Interactions and Interrelations with Special Consideration of the 1969 Vienna Convention on the Law of Treaties (1985); R.R. Baxter, *Multilateral Treaties as Evidence of Customary International Law,* 41 BYBIL 275 (1965–66); *see also* Bianchi, at 213.

531 *See* AHLUWALIA, at 208, referring to a study by the American Law Institute.

532 SCHERMERS, at 1075, para. 1608; *see also* Szasz, Immunities, at 155.

533 *See also* FOX-WEBB, at 580 (noting that, "as a Member State of the organization, it is under a general negative obligation not to hamper the accomplishment of the organization's purposes"). On the institutional function of international immunities, see JENKS, at 166.

534 SCHERMERS, at 1079, para. 1611. *See also* the judgment of the Municipal Court of the District of Columbia of 27 November 1925, which seems to be based on this reasoning, 20 AJIL 255–262 (1926), *cited in* SCHERMERS, at 1079 n.276. For a more recent example of U.S. case law, see *Internat'l Ass'n of Machinists and Aerospace Workers* (*IAM*)

collectivity of member States be accorded the immunities which its individual member States grant to each other.[535] This view may be supported subject to the following important condition. It must be stressed that the law of organizational immunities, concerning immunities granted to international organizations as such, is a separate body of law, quite distinct from the law of sovereign and diplomatic immunity by reason of the special nature of international organizations. Organizational immunities are *not* derivative immunities. In legal terms, the privileges and immunities of an international organization cannot be considered as aggregate of those enjoyed by its member States, which are sovereign entities. There has been a misunderstanding on this point for quite some time. Studies like the present one try to take away the uncertainty that seems to exist (and persist) in this respect, so as to give the law of organizational immunities its own deserved identity. As long as this is taken into consideration the views advanced by Schermers and others have the support of the present author.

2.4.5 Conclusion

From the above discussion no clear and absolute propositions can be formulated with regard to the precise extent to which customary international law confers particular privileges and immunities on international organizations generally.[536] The situation concerning the United Nations can be regarded as the most developed one, providing proof of the existence of at least some customary law in this field. Thus, although the probability of the existence of a rule of customary international law granting privileges and immunities to international organizations has been widely accepted, its precise *scope* remains uncertain. The uncertainty seems to stem in large part

---

v. Organization of the Petroleum Exporting Countries, 477 F.Supp. 553, 569 (C.D. Cal. 1979)(dismissing case brought against OPEC and its member countries by an American labor association alleging that the price-setting activities of OPEC and its member countries violated U.S. antitrust laws, on the basis of (the collective) sovereign immunity of the OPEC member countries, while observing that "[t]he action of sovereign nations coming together to agree on how each will perform certain sovereign acts [pertaining to natural resources located within their territory] can only, itself, be a sovereign act"), *aff'd* on other grounds, 649 F.2d 1354 (9th Cir. 1981)(affirming lower court's dismissal based on the alternate ground of 'Act of State' doctrine). *See also* Restatement (Third), § 467, Comment (a), at 494 and Reporters' Note 4, at 501.

535 *See* Restatement (Third), § 223, Reporters' Note 4, at 143. *But see* Seidl-Hohenveldern, Corporations, at 70–71.

536 AMERASINGHE, at 346 ("It is difficult to identify exactly what these [custom-based] privileges and immunities [arising from a functional need] might be. The inviolability of archives and the freedom of communication are perhaps two of them.").

from the fact that in practice the privileges and immunities necessary for the proper functioning of an international organization derive directly from treaty law and thus recourse to customary law is unnecessary. In this respect, scope-related issues concern the question of what particular immunities from the list set out above a given international organization is entitled to, whether these apply equally to universal and to regional organizations, and whether customary law obliges both member and non-member States to extend privileges and immunities to an organization. On the latter point, a survey of legal doctrine dictates one assumption: if a rule of customary international law granting privileges and immunities to international organizations does exist, this rule applies to the *member States* of the organization only,[537] which are obliged to vest the organization concerned with certain privileges and immunities, in general all those which are necessary to the exercise of the organization's functions in the the fulfilment of its purposes, and immunity from jurisdiction for official activities in particular.[538] A possible special rule applies again to the United Nations, which in the *Reparation* Case could also rely on certain rights against a *non-member* State. With Hug[539] it may be observed that the uncertainty about the lack of its precise scope and content decreases somewhat the utility of customary international law as a solid legal basis for granting privileges and immunities to international organizations in general.[540] It has, however, been rightly explained by the same author that the existence of such a rule of customary international law, which may not as yet have reached full specificity, can be useful for filling gaps left by the other legal bases, and it can serve as a controlling device for determining whether international organizations are accorded the privileges and immunities they need in order to fulfil their functions and purposes. All theoretical and legal bases available should be used in order to construe a consistent body of law pertaining to organizational immunities. In this respect the role of customary international law is still an evolving one. A survey of the existing legislative texts, treaty provisions, practice and doctrine concerning the privileges and immunities of

537 *See, e.g.*, Seidl-Hohenveldern, Communautés, at 475–476; *id.*, L'immunité, at 160.

538 In other words, which particular privileges and immunities international organizations are generally entitled to and which not, and to what extent, still seems unsettled.

539 Hug, at 61.

540 At the same time, it must be emphasized as did Bianchi, at 213, that "the lack of general agreement on the precise content of customary law concerning international organization immunity is not conclusive evidence of the nonexistence of at least a minimum customary principle."

international organizations teaches that *functional necessity* is generally accepted as their basis. Hence the proposition that from the existing instruments and practice a *general rule or principle of international institutional law* has emerged, in the form of the maxim *ne impediatur officia*,[541] which may be said to indicate that international organizations are entitled to such privileges and immunities as are necessary for the unhampered exercise of functions in the fulfilment of the purposes for which they were created, seems not only accurate, but also salutory. One should not overrate the importance of custom. From a practical point of view, having regard to the fact that the law of organizational immunities is almost entirely conventional or statutory in nature, it is only rarely necessary to invoke customary international law.[542] Given the uncertain position which customary international occupies in this field, this source of law is not likely to provide any clear-cut answers to gaps left by conventional law.

3 Step Three: Extent – Scope *Ratione Materiae*. The Role of Functional Necessity as a Yardstick for Determining the *Extent* of Organizational Immunities

3.1 *Introduction*

This part, which constitutes Step Three of our analysis, examines the role of the functional necessity concept as a yardstick to determine the standard of the *extent* or *scope* of privileges and immunities of international organizations, dictating a higher scale of privileges and immunities for one organization, and a lower one for another.[543] In this regard the functional necessity

541 *See* SCHERMERS, at 1075, para. 1608; Szasz, Immunities, at 155; *Report of the International Law Commission on the work of its forty-first session*, GAOR Supp. (No. 10) at 377, para. 722, UN Doc. A/44/10 (1989); EGGER, at 149; IVRAKIS, at 653.

542 *See, e.g.*, *Supreme Site Services GmbH et al v. Supreme Headquarters Allied Powers Europe and Allied Joint Force Command Headquarters Brunssum*, Supreme Court of The Netherlands, case no. 20/00937, judgment of 24 Dec. 2021, at para. 3.1.2. *See also* Zacklin, DUPUY, at 181; Yankov, in [1987] 1 Y.B. Int'l L. Comm'n 191, para. 25, UN Doc. A/CN.4/SER.A/1987; El-Erian, *First Report,* UN Doc. A/CN.4/161 and Add. 1 (1963) *reprinted in* [1963] 2 Y.B. Int'l L. Comm'n 159, 183, para. 169, UN Doc. A/CN.4/SER.A/1963/Add. 1.

543 *See* Sinclair, in [1983] 1 Y.B. Int'l L. Comm'n 242, para.4, UN Doc. A/CN.4/SER.A/1983. *See also* AMERASINGHE, at 346–347 ("The functional basis of international privileges and immunities in customary law could have the result not only that some organizations may have privileges and immunities that others do not but that an organization

concept can be said to dictate that the scope of the privileges and immunities of international organizations shall be *limited* to only those *necessary* for the exercise of the organization's functions in the fulfilment of its purposes.[544] After the selection process of Step Two, Step Three determines the exact scope of selected privileges and immunities, taking into account the particular characteristics of the entity concerned, as identified in Step One.

The principles developed in sovereign and diplomatic immunity law have provided the initial guidelines or guideposts in establishing organizational immunities but have at the same time introduced an element of confusion in the understanding of the role of functional necessity in granting privileges and immunities to international organizations. Already in 1947, Kunz stated with regard to this confusion that it "has hampered and even still hampers the building up of an adequate law of privileges and immunities for international organizations."[545] Thus, a distinction must first be made between the law of sovereign and diplomatic immunity and the law of organizational immunities to clear the way for developing a sound theory appropriate to the law of organizational immunities.

3.2 *Organizational Immunities versus Other Types of Immunities*

At present three categories of evolving systems of privileges and immunities are recognized. Besides the law of State or (foreign) *sovereign* immunity, which deals with the immunities of sovereign States, and the law of diplomatic immunity, which concerns the privileges and immunities of the representatives (agents or envoys) of States to other States, a new body of legal norms has developed, defining the privileges and immunities of international organizations. For the latter body of law we have reserved the term *organizational* immunities, which is part of the law commonly described as international immunities, including also the immunities which attach to the members of Permanent Missions of member States to an international organization, and to the employees, or staff members, of the organization, its officials, experts on mission and other persons who may perform functions on the organization's behalf.[546]

---

may not have in one state the privileges and immunities it enjoys in another, for instance, because the former state is not a member of the organization but also for other reasons").

544 The meaning of these terms will be discussed in Section 3.4 below.

545 Kunz, at 841.

546 *See* Satow, 294–297 (summarizing the immunities of these various categories); A.J. Miller, *Privileges and Immunities of United Nations Officials*, 4(2) IOLR 169 (2008);

Although it goes beyond the scope of the present study to engage in a detailed review of the *differences* which exist between the immunities of States[547] and the immunities granted to international organizations, it should be given some attention here, for the purpose of our analysis.[548]

The brief for the United Nations as *Amicus Curiae* in the U.S. court case of *Broadbent v. Organization of American States* summarizes the dissimilarities between the conceptual bases of the immunity of States and of intergovernmental organizations that militate against a wholesale application of the principles of State or sovereign immunity to international organizations. The summary is worth quoting in full, because it lists exhaustively the key differences between the two regimes of immunity:

> (a) States have sovereignty, but international organizations do not;
>
> (b) States have territory, international organizations do not, but function within the territory of States;
>
> (c) States have citizens, but international organizations merely have officials who are generally citizens of their member States, though freed of certain responsibilities towards such States;
>
> (d) States are considerably protected from undue intrusion of other States by their ability to invoke the principle of reciprocity, or can protect themselves by their ability to retaliate; international organizations, not standing on a parity with States, cannot depend on reciprocity, nor are they in a position to retaliate against any violation of their integrity;

A.J. Miller, *United Nations Experts on Mission and their Privileges and Immunities*, 4(1) IOLR 11 (2007).

547 Including diplomats, *i.e.*, the diplomatic personnel of an embassy, who can be classified as agents of States, representing their State abroad.

548 *See* H. Damian, Staatenimmunität und Gerichtszwang 84–86 (1985)[hereinafter: DAMIAN]; AHLUWALIA, at 199; BEIER *et al.*, at 6; SEIDL-HOHENVELDERN, RECHT, at 284, para. 1907; ILC Chairman Sir Francis Vallat, in [1977] 1 Y.B. lnt'l L. Comm'n 213, para. 43, UN Doc. A/CN.4/SER.A/1977; El-Erian, *Preliminary Report* (Second Part of the topic), UN Doc. A/CN.4/304 *reprinted in* [1977) 2 Y.B. Int'l L. Comm'n 139, 152, paras. 63–64, UN Doc. A/CN.4/SER.A/1977/Add. 1 (Part 1); [1990) 1 Y.B. Int'l L. Comm'n 219, paras. 48- 49 (Barsegov) and 220, para. 58 (Solari Tudela), UN Doc. A/CN.4/SER.A/1990; Lalive, at 296. Even though international organizations differ in privileges and immunities granted to them from those of States, some similarities exist as well, *see* AHLUWALIA, at 48; Aufricht, at 86; Restatement (Third), § 467, at 492–493. *See also* A. Orakhelashvili, *Responsibility and Immunities: Similarities and Differences between International Organizations and States*, 11(1) IOLR 114 (2014).

(e) More particularly, States can grant to or withhold immunity from each other, and generally do so on the basis of agreements or principles of comity embodied in international law; international organizations normally do not exercise jurisdiction over anyone except, and only to a limited extent, their own officials, and thus are not in a position to grant to or withhold immunity from States;

(f) States are protected from interference by international organizations in their affairs by provisions in the constitutions of these organizations (for example, United Nations Charter, Article 2(7)) and by the fact that representatives of States constitute the political organs and control the administrative organs of these organizations; international organizations are protected from interference by States principally by the immunities provided for by international law;

(g) Consequently the immunities of States are those attributable to sovereigns and thus reflect those that States reserve to themselves, whether absolute or relative; those of international organizations are functional and thus reflect their needs, which require complete protection from national jurisdiction.[549]

Of fundamental importance is the distinction in theoretical basis. The age-old principles of *par in parem non habet iurisdictionem* and *ne impediatur legatio* have justified the privileges and immunities granted to States and their representatives.[550] The International Law Commission stated in its general comments on the draft articles on diplomatic relations and immunities, that the theories of 'exterritoriality,'[551] and 'representative character,'[552] had in modern times been supplemented by the functional necessity theory.[553] The theories of exterritoriality, personal representation

549 1980 UN Jurid. Y.B 224, 229–30, UN Doc. ST/LEG/SER.C/18 (1983); *see also* Glenn *et al.*, at 266; Dominicé, LIBER SEIDL, at 84–85; Fox-WEBB, at 578 (noting that "[t]he immunities and privileges accorded to international organizations are shaped by conditions that differentiate them from those enjoyed by States").

550 *See, e.g.*, FOX-WEBB, at 27.

551 According to this theory, the premises of a diplomatic mission represent an extension of the territory of the sending State.

552 This theory bases diplomatic immunities on the idea that the diplomatic mission personifies the sending State.

553 *See* [1958] 2 Y.B. Int'l L. Comm'n 95, UN Doc. A/CN.4/SER.A/1958/Add. 1; *see also* Zacklin, DUPUY, at 181.

and functional necessity hence can be regarded as the three most important doctrines in the development of the law of diplomatic immunity.[554] Sovereign or State immunity is based primarily on the principle of the sovereign equality of States,[555] the respect for the territorial boundaries of other sovereigns and the recognition of the strict *quid pro quo* of reciprocity.[556] An international organization possesses neither sovereignty nor territoriality, which renders the corresponding doctrines inapplicable to them: only sovereigns can perform sovereign acts.[557] In the case of international organizations, their immunities hence can be based on functional necessity only, which has been called the principle of *ne impediatur officia*, designed to enable international organizations to perform the functions entrusted to them without interruption or hindrance.[558] As the Dutch

---

554 *See also* Kunz, at 837; MICHAELS, at 47.

555 *See*, generally, R. Jennings & A. Watts, Oppenheim's International Law 339–379 (9th ed. 1996); FOX-WEBB, at 25–49.

556 *See Jurisdictional Immunities of the State* (*Germany v. Italy; Greece intervening*), Judgment, 2012 ICJ Rep. 99, at 123, para. 57 (observing that "the principle of sovereign equality of States ... has to be viewed together with the principle that each State possesses sovereignty over its own territory" and that immunity "may represent a departure from the principle of territorial sovereignty and the jurisdiction which flows from it"). *See also* Glenn *et al.*, at 267. The reciprocity element has in its usual sense no meaning insofar as the immunities of international organizations are concerned, because the different nature of the parties does not permit organizations to offer equivalent advantages in return for privileges and immunities granted to them. *See* FOX-WEBB, at 578 ("The principle of reciprocity, which is critical to State immunity, finds no place with respect to international organizations"); Council of Europe Report 1969, at 13, para. 9 sub (e); Ehrenfeld, at 92–93; MICHAELS, at 27; Yankov, in [1983] 1 Y.B Int'l L. Comm'n 240, para. 26, UN Doc. A/CN.4/SER.A/1983; Sucharitkul, in *id.*, at 240, para. 20.

557 *See also* FOX-WEBB, at 578 ("No such principle of equality exists between States and international organizations; it also does not exist between organizations"), 586 ("the principle of sovereign equality (a principle that is admittedly more theoretical than real) does not apply to international organizations").

558 *See Report of the International Law Commission on the work of its forty-first session*, GAOR Supp. (No. 10) at 377, para. 722, UN Doc. A/44/10 (1989). An earlier reference to the principle of *ne impediatur officia* may be found at EGGER, at 149; *see also* IVRAKIS, at 653; N.M. Blokker, *Jurisdictional Immunities of International Organisations – Origins, Fundamentals and Challenges*, *in* The Cambridge Handbook of Immunities and International Law (T. Ruys, N. Angelet and L. Ferro eds. 2019). For examples of court decisions, see, e.g., *Supreme Site Services GmbH et al v. Supreme Headquarters Allied Powers Europe and Allied Joint Force Command Headquarters Brunssum*, Supreme Court (*Hoge Raad*) of The Netherlands, case no. 20/00937, judgment of 24 Dec. 2021, at para. 3.1.2 ("The foundation-stone for these privileges and immunities [of international organizations] is that they are necessary for the independent functioning of the international organization, without unilateral interference by individual states" [translation from the original Dutch text by the present author]); *Amaratunga v. Northwest Atlantic*

Supreme Court (*Hoge Raad*) observed in a case involving the immunity of the United Nations in relation to a peacekeeping operation carried out in the former Yugoslavia, both the basis and the extent of the immunity of international organizations, which has as its aim to guarantee the independent functioning of the organization and hence serves a legitimate purpose, are different from the immunity to which States are entitled: the latter is based on general international law (*par in parem non habet imperium*) and is restricted to acts of a foreign State in the performance of its governmental task (*acta jure imperii*).[559]

Another fundamental dissimilarity arises from the fact that the immunities enjoyed by international organizations and their personnel are essentially immunities *ratione materiae*, whereas those enjoyed by diplomats representing States are both *ratione materiae* and *ratione personae* inasmuch as they extend to protection of the diplomat by reason of his representative function, i.e., of representing a sovereign State. There is, however, one important exception to this general rule, to the effect that the high-ranking officials of international organizations are usually accorded complete immunity, i.e., *ratione materiae* as well as *ratione personae*. In the case of the United Nations, the Secretary-General and the Under-Secretaries-General and Assistant-Secretaries-General enjoy diplomatic immunity.[560]

At present modern international law follows the doctrine of *restrictive* or qualified sovereign immunity.[561] In the so-called Tate Letter of 1952,[562] the United States abandoned the rather rigid doctrine of absolute immunity, by

---

Fisheries Organization, Supreme Court of Canada, judgment of 29 Nov. 2013, 2013 SCC 66, [2013] 3 SCR 866, at paras. 29 (referring to organizational immunity as being "essential to the efficient and independent functioning of international organizations") and 45 ("Without immunity, an international organization would be vulnerable to intrusions into its operations and agenda by the host state and that state's courts").

559 *Stichting Mothers of Srebrenica et al. v. State of The Netherlands and United Nations*, Supreme Court (*Hoge Raad*) of The Netherlands, case no. 10/04437, judgment of 13 April 2012, at para. 4.2.

560 *See* 1946 General Convention, S. 19.

561 *See*, e.g., Art. 10 (exempting commercial transactions), United Nations Convention on Jurisdictional Immunities of States and Their Property, done at New York, 2 Dec. 2004, not yet in force, UN Doc. A/59/508 (2004).

562 The inequities produced by the doctrine of absolute immunity to commercial activities of States provided the impetus for the United States Department of State's adoption of the restrictive doctrine of sovereign immunity. *See* Letter from Jack B. Tate, Acting Legal Adviser of the Department of State, to Philip B. Perlman, Acting Attorney General, repr. in 26 U.S. Dep't St. Bull. 984 (1952); for a commentary on this Letter see DAMIAN, at 135.

which foreign States enjoyed blanket immunity in respect of all their activities, and instead officially acknowledged the restrictive doctrine. The restrictive doctrine draws a distinction between acts performed by a State in its sovereign or governmental capacity – *acta jure imperii* – and commercial-type acts – *acta jure gestionis* – and restricts immunity to acts *jure imperii*.[563] Higgins has pointed out that it is not correct to suggest that this distinction has any relevance to international organizations, because they cannot be assimilated to States and the basis of immunity of these subjects of international law is different.[564] It bears reminding that the Tate Letter is silent on international organizations.

A ruling addressing the jurisdictional immunities of States issued by the International Court of Justice in 2012 included the following reminder:

> [T]he terms '*jure imperii*' and '*jure gestionis*' do not imply that the acts in question are lawful but refer rather to whether the acts in question fall to be assessed by reference to the law governing the exercise of

---

563 *See*, e.g., Art. 7, European Convention on State Immunity, done at Basle on 16 May 1972, entry into force 11 June 1976, Eur. Treaty Series No. 074; Art. 10, United Nations Convention on Jurisdictional Immunities of States and Their Property, adopted by UN General Assembly res. A/59/38 of 2 Dec. 2004, not yet in force. For an analysis of the restrictive theory of sovereign immunity, see I. Sinclair, *The Law of Sovereign Immunity*, 167 RdC 113, 197 (1980 II); S. Sucharitkul, State Immunities and Trading Activities in International Law (1959); *id.*, *Immunities of Foreign States before National Authorities*, 149 RdC 87 (1976 I); H. Lauterpacht, *The Problem of Jurisdictional Immunities of Foreign States*, 28 BYBIL 220 (1951); L.J. Bouchez, *The Nature and Scope of State Immunity from Jurisdiction and Execution*, 10 N.Y.I.L. 3 (1979); C.C.A. Voskuil, *The International Law of State Immunity, As Reflected in the Dutch Law of Execution*, 10 N.Y.I.L. 245 (1979). A pronouncement by the Supreme Court (*Hoge Raad*) of The Netherlands on the restrictive sovereign immunity doctrine can be found in *Russian Federation v. Pied-Rich B.V.*, judgment of 28 May 1993, Nr. 15162, RvdW 1993 Nr. 116–117, at 625.

564 R. Higgins, Problems and Process – International Law and How We Use It 93 (1994). *See also* AMERASINGHE, at 328 (noting, based on a survey of national court cases, that "the distinction [between acts *jure gestionis* and acts *jure imperii*] is irrelevant to the immunities of international organizations"). *See also* FOX-WEBB, at 467 ("The scope of the immunities of international organizations is determined by their functions, not the *jure imperii/gestionis* framework used in the restrictive doctrine of State immunity"), 581–582 ("The distinction between public and private acts, or between acts *jure imperii* and *jure gestionis*, has little direct relevance in determining the scope of the immunities of an organization"), 582 ("The distinction between commercial and sovereign activity, which is applied by the restrictive doctrine to States to remove immunity from judicial review of commercial acts, cannot readily be applied to international organizations ..."), 586 ("immunities [of international organizations] are based on *function* not the commercial or private law character of the act").

> sovereign power (*jus imperii*) or the law concerning non-sovereign activities of a State, especially private and commercial activities (*jus gestionis*). To the extent that this distinction is significant for determining whether or not a State is entitled to immunity from the jurisdiction of another State's courts in respect of a particular act, it has to be applied before that jurisdiction can be exercised, whereas the legality or illegality of the act is something which can be determined only in the exercise of that jurisdiction.[565]

The restrictive doctrine of *sovereign* immunity should not apply to the law of *organizational* immunities in the same manner as it does to the law of sovereign immunity. On the other hand, the development of the law of organizational immunities was clearly influenced by, and grew out of, the already established law of sovereign immunity when international organizations of a universal character emerged in the period after the First World War. It must be remembered, though, that "[i]nternational law regarding the privileges and immunities of international organizations is an entirely modern development."[566] As Kunz has pointed out:

> ... the problem of privileges and immunities of international organizations started historically, by analogy, as an extension of diplomatic privileges to non-diplomats. Now the development has reached a point, however, where the different nature of the new problem is realized and where a new law, independent and emancipated from that of the privileges of diplomatic agents, has to be created.[567]

The law of organizational immunities was thus inspired by the existing immunity law but soon set out to sail its own course, tailored to the special functional requirements of the relatively new concept of the international organization.[568] It is in this respect interesting to point again to the

565 *Jurisdictional Immunities of the State* (*Germany v. Italy; Greece intervening*), Judgment, 2012 ICJ Rep. 99, at 124, para. 60.

566 Satow, at 292, para. 21.11.

567 Kunz, at 842; *see also Report of the International Law Commission on the work of its forty-first session,* GAOR Supp. (No. 10) at 377, para. 722, UN Doc. A/44/10 (1989).

568 *See also* Jenks, at xxxv ("The law governing international immunities no longer consists primarily of a general principle resting on the *questionable analogy of diplomatic immunities;* it has become a complex body of rules set forth in detail in conventions, agreements, statutes and regulations."(emphasis added)).

statement in the preparatory documents of the United Nations of 1945, which noted:

> In order to determine the nature of the privileges and immunities, the Committee has seen fit to avoid the term 'diplomatic' and has preferred to substitute a more appropriate standard, based, for the purposes of the Organization, on the necessity of realizing its purposes ....[569]

3.3 *Organizational Immunities Are Neither 'Absolute' Nor 'Restrictive'*

From these fundamental dissimilarities stems a basic difference in the extent to which international organizations enjoy privileges and immunities. Due to these dissimilarities the distinction drawn by the law of sovereign immunity between sovereign and commercial activities cannot, in principle, be applied to international organizations—because they lack sovereignty, international organization do not, indeed cannot, perform sovereign acts by reason of their legal status.[570] To understand this point, we must revisit Step One of our analysis. As Ahluwalia has stated:

---

569 13 U.N.C.I.O. Doc. 933, IV/2/42(2), at 704 (1945).

570 *See* AHLUWALIA, at 67 n.61 and 199. *See also* FOX-WEBB, at 586 (noting that "the restrictive doctrine of State immunity is not applicable to international organizations"). According to Ahluwalia, the new United States policy of restrictive sovereign immunity as enunciated in the Tate Letter cannot, therefore, be said to apply to international organizations. According to Schwebel, the 1976 U.S. Foreign Sovereign Immunities Act's limitation of State immunities to the sphere of non-commercial activities had not been intended to affect organizational immunities: *see* [1978] 1 Y.B. Int'l L. Comm'n 268, para. 34, UN Doc. A/CN.4/SER.A/1978; *see also* WEISSBERG, at 208 n.5 ("Note that the traditional distinction between *jure imperii* and *jure gestionis* does not exist in the case of the United Nations."); Restatement (Third), § 467, Comment 9d, at 495, Comment (f), at 497, top, Reporters' Note 4, at 501, top. This view appears to be supported by a decision of the U.S. Court of Appeals for the District of Columbia in *Broadbent v. OAS*, 628 F.2d 27 (D.C. Cir. 1980) *reprinted in* 19 ILM 208, 214 (1980), where the court refused to recognize that the restrictive immunity concept is applicable to international organizations; *see also* Glenn *et al.*, at 266 n.94, and O'Toole, at 2; Council of Europe Report 1969, at 23, para. 31; BEIER *et al.*, at 7; C.T. Ebenroth, *Shareholders' Liability in International Organizations – The Settlement of the International Tin Council Case*, 4 LJIL 171, 183 (1991)[hereinafter: Ebenroth]; SEIDL-HOHENVELDERN, EUROCONTROL, at 52; *id.*, Tin, at 53 n.62; *id.*, CORPORATIONS, at 81; JENKS, at 45; IVRAKIS, at 660; Ehrenfeld, at 89, 92 ("... none of the criteria adopted or suggested for limiting foreign governments' procedural immunity are feasible for a public international organization."). In view of the above, one must agree with JENKS, at xxxvii, that the functional requirements of international organizations need to be

> [t]here is ... one distinction of paramount importance in that whereas a State possesses the totality of international rights and duties recognized by international law, the rights and duties of an international organization are conditioned by the purposes and functions it is required to perform by its constitutional instrument.[571]

This is the constitutional framework we referred to in Step One and which was stressed by the International Court of Justice in the *Reparation* Case.[572] As the legal personality, capacity and powers of an international organization are of a *functional* character, every act of an international organization must be in close relationship with its functions and purposes, the fulfillment of which constitutes the *raison d'être* of every organization.

The legal position of international organizations is governed by the fact that their competence in every field is *restricted* by their *purposes*. Whereas States can act *jure gestionis* in the same way as any private individual, all activities of an international organization must relate as closely as possible to the functions and purposes of the organization. In other words, every act performed by an international organization must be compatible with the purposes which the organization is meant to pursue. These purposes have been entrusted to the organization by the member States in their sovereign capacities, usually because the member States cannot perform these functions themselves or because an international organization can perform them more efficiently.[573] The departure from the terminology developed in sovereign immunity law is, therefore, "a necessary consequence of the restriction of the powers of any organization to those necessary for it to fulfil its purposes."[574] As one national court has observed, "[f]unctional immunity can be described as relative, that is to say, it applies only to the extent that the action in question has been committed by the person in the performance of their duties."[575]

---

considered on their own merits and not on the basis of automatic assimilation to diplomatic and sovereign immunity concepts.

571 AHLUWALIA, at 48–49.

572 1949 ICJ Rep. 174, 179–180.

573 *See, e.g.*, Díaz González, in [1985] 2 Y.B. Int'l L. Comm'n 105, paras. 17–18, UN Doc. A/CN.4/ SER.A/1985/Add. 1 (Part 1); K.W. Abbott and D. Snidal, *Why States Act through Formal International Organizations*, 42 J. CONFLICT RESOL. 3 (1998).

574 SEIDL-HOHENVELDERN, CORPORATIONS, at 82.

575 *Gérald René Trempe v. ICAO Staff Association et al. and Gérald René Trempe v. Dirk Jan Goossen et al.*, High Court, Province of Quebec, District of Montreal, judgment of 20

Several writers and courts have attempted to apply the so-called commercial activity exception, as developed in the law of sovereign immunity, to the activities of international organizations.[576] But using the language of sovereign immunity is not appropriate. In the law of sovereign immunity a historically justifiable distinction is drawn between sovereign acts and commercial acts. But one must remember that:

> [m]any activities of an international organization are not governmental in the traditional sense of the term and the performance of its functions may well involve activities which if undertaken by a State would be dubbed commercial. Therefore, while deciding the question of immunity from legal process of an international organization it has to be determined *whether a particular activity undertaken by it is required by its functions.*[577] (emphasis added)

The functions and purposes of an international organization may very well require the performance of commercial activities, while still remaining within the organization's official framework, and, therefore, within the legitimate incidence of immunity. The fact that an international organization carries out activities that do not qualify as 'public' acts and which would be considered commercial had a State engaged in them, does not change their necessity to the organization's functions and purposes.[578] As was pointed out by ILC-member Balanda:

> ... whenever States established an international organization in order to engage in an activity at the international level, they did so in the general interest, which might of course be of a commercial nature. The fact that an international organization engaged in commercial activities did not, however, mean that it was not performing an

---

Nov. 2003, at para. 60, English text reproduced in 2003 UN Jurid. Y.B, p. 585, at 597, UN Doc. ST/LEG/SER.C/41 (2003).

576 28 U.S.C. § 1603(d) defines 'commercial activity' as follows: "A 'commercial activity' means either a regular course of commercial conduct or a particular commercial transaction or act. The commercial character of an activity shall be determined by reference to the nature of the course of conduct or particular transaction or act rather than by reference to its purpose." For a commentary on this section see G.B. Born & D. Westin, International Civil Litigation in United States Courts – Commentary & Materials 361–382 (1989).

577 AHLUWALIA, at 66.

578 *See also* Farrugia, at 519–20; Kunz-Hallstein, Privilegien, at 3072–3073; Dominicé, LIBER SEIDL, at 93.

> international public service, and it was precisely because it performed such a service that it required protection.[579]

The relevance of these excerpts may be demonstrated by reference to a practical example. The external lending activities of the International Bank for Reconstruction and Development (IBRD) are, to a certain extent, protected by immunity, whereas an indebtedness incurred by a State which negotiates or executes a loan agreement, or borrows money, would be considered 'commercial' activity under the restrictive concept of sovereign immunity.[580] Due to its special activities, however, the IBRD has been granted (specifically limited) immunities. Article VII, Section 3, of the Articles of Agreement of the IBRD, provides that the IBRD may be sued in the courts of the member States where it "has an office, has appointed an agent for the purpose of accepting service or notice of process, or has issued or guaranteed securities."[581] Its immunity from legal process is limited to actions brought by member States or persons acting for or deriving claims from Members of the Bank. The commercial operations of monetary organizations such as the IBRD make it desirable to allow suit by creditors and bondholders,[582] an opening which is provided by the organization's constituent instrument itself. Even in this case, however, the organization's property and assets are protected by complete immunity from seizure or execution, so as not to disturb the IBRD's ability to perform its functions, in particular in attracting responsible borrowers.[583] Hereby the interplay is demonstrated between the extent to which the organization has been granted the necessary privileges and immunities, and its functions and purposes, as defined in its constituent instrument.

579 [1985] 1 Y.B. Int'l L. Comm'n 294, para. 44, UN Doc. A/CN.4/SER.A/1985. *See also* Seidl Hohenveldern, Personality, at 50–51 ("The immunity of organizations for their *acta jure gestionis* will appear justified, if we accept the view, that there are certain functional limitations to their activities. Thus, even their *acta jure gestionis* will be linked to their official functions. ... This link is the social justification for the right of international organizations to full immunity.").

580 *See also* H.R. Rep. No. 94–1487, 94th Cong., 2nd Sess. 16 (1976), *reprinted in* 1976 U.S. Code Cong. & Admin. News 6614–6615.

581 Art. VII, Ss. 1–10, Articles of Agreement of the International Bank for Reconstruction and Development, 2 U.N.T.S. 134, at 180–184. For the reasons behind this practice, see Tsuruoka, in [1978] 1 Y.B. Int'l L. Comm'n 267, para.25, UN Doc. A/CN.4/SER.A/1978; Dominicé, L'immunité, at 196–198.

582 *See* BOWETT, at 349–50.

583 *See also Mendaro v. World Bank*, 717 F.2d. 610 (D.C. Cir. 1983).

3.4 *'Official Activity' versus 'Commercial Activity'*

The legitimate incidence of *sovereign* immunity turns to a large degree on the commercial activity concept in the restrictive immunity doctrine.[584] According to the United States' Foreign Sovereign Immunities Act (FSIA) of 1976,[585] foreign States shall not be immune from the jurisdiction of U.S. courts in any case based upon their commercial activity, a key exception to immunity under the FSIA. Section 1603(d) of the same Act provides that the commercial character of an activity shall be determined by reference to the nature of the activity, rather than by reference to its purpose. Courts and commentators have struggled with this commercial activity concept, without being able to put an end to the puzzling ambiguities caused by applying this concept of sovereign immunity law to international organizations. In the United States, this ambiguity is mainly caused by Section 288a(b) of the International Organizations Immunities Act (IOIA) of 1945,[586] which provides that international organizations "shall enjoy the same immunity from suit and every form of judicial process as is enjoyed by foreign governments."[587] This clause had led U.S. courts into extensive examinations of the applicability of sovereign immunity restrictions to international organizations, without, however, explicitly deciding whether international organizations are subject to absolute or restrictive immunity,[588] until the U.S. Supreme Court ruled (7–1) that "[t]he IOIA 'same as'

584 *See also Broadbent v. OAS*, 628 F.2d 27 (D.C. Cir. 1980).

585 S. 1605, Foreign Sovereign Immunities Act of 1976, P.L. 94–583, 90 Stal. 2891, 28 U.S.C. Ss. 1330, 1332, 1391(f), 1441(d), 1602–1611.

586 S. 2(b), International Organizations Immunities Act of 1945, P.L. 79–291, 59 Stal. 669, 22 U.S.C. §§ 288–288f.

587 *See* 22. U.S.C. 288a(b). The *Broadbent* court held, however, that "international organizations ... stand in a different position with respect to the issue of immunity than sovereign nations." *See* 19 ILM 208, 210 (1980).

588 *See* Farrugia, at 497 n.1, referring to *Broadbent v. OAS*, 628 F.2d 27 (D.C. Cir. 1980); *Mendaro v. World Bank*, 717 F.2d 610 (D.C. Cir. 1983); *Boimah v. United Nations General Assembly*, 664 F.Supp. 69 (E.D.N.Y. 1987). In these cases the courts held that an international organization's relationship with its internal staff is non-commercial. Writers like Farrugia and Glenn *et al.* have tried to demonstrate that such factors as statutory interpretation, congressional intent, legislative history and conceptual bases all point in the direction of absolute immunity of international organizations. We will restrict our subsequent discussion of this controversy to the case of contracts, leaving employment relationships aside, for which we refer to Farrugia and Glenn *et al.*; *see also* I. Seidl-Hohenveldern, Jurisdiction over Employment Disputes in International Organizations, in Liber Amicorum: Coleccion de Estudios Juridicos en Homenaje al Prof.Dr.D. José Perez Montero 359 (Vol. III, 1988).

formulation is best understood as making international organization immunity and foreign sovereign immunity continuously equivalent" in 2019.[589] The Supreme Court found that this reading is confirmed by the 'reference canon' of statutory interpretation, noting that the IOIA's reference to the immunity enjoyed by foreign governments is a general rather than specific reference. Whatever one may think of the reasoning of America's highest court in this case, its ultimate conclusion that "the Foreign Sovereign Immunities Act governs the immunity of international organizations"[590] is difficult to square with the fundamental difference between sovereign States and intergovernmental organizations and it ignores the foundational "speciality" principle referenced above.[591] The Supreme Court's ruling is devoid of references to international law sources, with the exception of the General Convention and the Articles of Agreement of the IFC and the IMF. The ruling does not employ 'functional' language, even though the IOIA's

589 *Jam et al. v. International Finance Corp.*, 139 S. CT. 759 (2019). In *Jam*, a group of Indian villagers had sued the IFC in U.S. federal court, alleging that the IFC's loan agreement with Coastal Gujarat Power Limited, an Indian company, to assist in the financing of the construction of a coal-fired power plant in the state of Gujarat, India, had resulted in pollution from the plant harming the surrounding air, land and water. The lower federal courts both upheld the IFC's plea of immunity from suit. *See also* C. Treichl and A. Reinisch, *Domestic Jurisdiction over International Financial Institutions for Injuries to Project-Affected Individuals: The Case of* Jam v International Finance Corporation, 16 IOLR 105 (2019).

590 *Id.*, at 772.

591 What is especially troubling about the *Jam* ruling is that the U.S. Supreme Court expressly ignored the ultimate purpose of organizational immunities in favor of a strict constructionist approach ("Whatever the ultimate purpose of international organization immunity may be, the immediate purpose of the IOIA immunity provision is expressed in language that Congress typically uses to make one thing [here, the IOIA] continuously equivalent to another [here, the FSIA]." *Id.*, at 760. *Post-Jam* rulings by lower courts have highlighted the absurdity to which the *Jam* ruling can lead. For example, in a lawsuit targeting the World Health Organization during the COVID-19 pandemic, a lower federal court in New York, after citing to the *Jam* ruling (specifically that the Foreign Sovereign Immunities Act governs the immunity of international organizations), noted that "[t]he defendant [WHO] must first 'present [] a prima facie case that it is a foreign sovereign' (citing *Cargill Int'l S.A. v. M/T Pavel Dybenko*, 991 F.2d 1012 (2nd Cir. 1993)). This is in stark contrast with the ICJ's *Reparation* ruling, in which the ICJ observed that to say that an international organization is an international person "is not the same thing as saying that it is a State, which it certainly is not, or that its legal personality and rights and duties are the same as those of a State ...." 1949 ICJ Rep. 174, 179. Therefore, conflating the immunities that these different subjects of international law enjoy is inherently flawed.

legislative record states that the purpose of the IOIA was to "facilitate fully the functioning of international organizations" in the United States.[592] The U.S. Supreme Court did point out, however, that "it is not clear that the lending activity of all development banks qualifies as commercial activity within the meaning of the FSIA" and that the FSIA includes other requirements that also must be satisfied before an intergovernmental organization can be subject to suit in the United States.[593] Moreover, the U.S. Supreme Court observed that the immunities accorded by the IOIA are only default rules[594] and that an organization's constituent instrument can always specify a different level of immunity, as is the case with the United Nations and the IMF.[595] As a consequence of the *Jam* ruling, intergovernmental

592 U.S. Senate Report No. 861, 79th Congress, 1st Sess., 3 (1945).

593 *Jam et al. v. International Finance Corp.*, 139 S. CT. 759, 772 (2019). Under the FSIA, the commercial activity must have a sufficient nexus to the United States and a lawsuit must be "based upon" either the commercial activity itself or acts performed in connection with the commercial activity. *See* 28 U.S.C. §§ 1603, 1605(a)(2). Indeed, on remand, the lower federal court in the D.C. Circuit concluded that the IFC's immunity "remains intact" after finding that the mere fact that the IFC had approved the financing of the Indian power plant in the United States, at the IFC's headquarters in Washington, D.C., and had disbursed funds from the U.S., was not sufficient to satisfy the U.S. nexus requirement. *Jam v. Int'l Fin. Corp.*, 442 F.Supp. 3d 162, 177–180 (D.D.C. 2020).

594 According to the default rule set forth in the IOIA, designated international organizations are immune "from suit and every form of judicial process" in the United States, subject to the U.S. President's authority to depart from that default rule by withholding or withdrawing organizational immunity when he considers it appropriate "in light of the functions performed" by a given organization. 22 U.S.C. § 288. Organizational immunity also may be expanded or restricted by a given organization's constituent instrument. Following the U.S. Supreme Court's *Jam* ruling, U.S. courts are in a position to deny immunity to an international organization based on one or more of the exceptions contained in the FSIA. The Supreme Court's construction of the IOIA unquestionably places decisions regarding organizational immunity in the hands of the judicial branch, which arguably undermines the U.S. President's authority under the IOIA. In the view of the Supreme Court, "the fact that the President has power to modify otherwise applicable [organizational] immunity rules is perfectly compatible with the notion that those rules might themselves change over time in light of developments in the law governing foreign sovereign immunity."

595 *Jam et al. v. International Finance Corp.*, 139 S. CT. 759, 771 (2019). For recent examples of a U.S. federal court upholding the IMF's entitlement to absolute immunity from suit, *see*, e.g., *Leonard A. Sacks & Associates, P.C. v. International Monetary Fund*, 26 F.4th 470 (D.C. Cir. 2022) (holding that an arbitration clause in IMF's contract for legal services did not waive its immunity from suit in a post-award proceeding); *John Does 1–7 v. Taliban, et al.; International Monetary Fund; International Bank for Reconstruction*

organizations based, or conducting activities, in the United States may wish to amend their constituent instrument where feasible and to seek self-executing status of applicable instruments, lest their activities be subject to U.S.-law defined statutory exceptions.[596]

A post-*Jam* amendment of the central immunity provision of the IOIA to adapt it to the present circumstances would resolve the unsatisfactory situation left by the *Jam* ruling,[597] and would do justice to the singular identity of international organizations and the international law principle of speciality. The best solution would be simply to replace the words "shall enjoy the same immunity from suit and every form of judicial process as is enjoyed by foreign governments" with "shall enjoy immunity from suit and every form of judicial process [as is enjoyed by intergovernmental organizations under international law]." This language would 'de-link' the law of international organization immunity from the law of foreign sovereign immunity (as codified in the FSIA), thereby recognizing that the one does not develop in tandem with the other.

Reasons of statutory ambiguity could not have caused both the court of first instance (*Kantongerecht*) and the district court (*Rechtbank*) of The Hague, in a case involving the Iran-United States Claims Tribunal,[598] to

---

and Development, U.S. Court of Appeals, D.C. Circuit, judgment of 26 Apr. 2024 (dismissing action against international organizations as third-party garnishees based on their immunity from suit). It must be pointed out, however, that many treaties providing for organizational immunities are not self-executing in the United States, in the sense that they are not binding in U.S. courts until the U.S Congress enacts legislation to implement them.

596 Note that the IMF's immunity in all cases, absent express waiver, is provided for in U.S. law. *See* 22 U.S.C. § 286h.

597 Even without an explicit redrafting, reference should be made to the Brief for the United Nations as *Amicus Curiae* in the *Broadbent* case, *reprinted in* 1980 UN Jurid. Y.B, p. 224, at 228, UN Doc. ST/LEG/SER.C/18 (1983), where it was pointed out that the IOIA "is merely a legislative device to facilitate the carrying out of the international obligations of the United States towards the intergovernmental organizations designated under the Act and cannot alter these international obligations. In enacting the Foreign Sovereign Immunities Act (FSIA) ... Congress indicated no intention of modifying the immunities of intergovernmental organizations provided for in the IOIA and in the treaties relating to each organization."

598 *See A.S. v. the Iran-United States Claims Tribunal,* Local Court (*Kantongerecht*) of The Hague, 8 June 1983, *De Praktijkgids* (1983) No.2022, *English summary in* 15 N.Y.I.L. 429–432 (1984); *The Iran-United States Claims Tribunal v. A.S.*, District Court (*Rechtbank*) of The Hague, 9 July 1984, *De Praktijkgids* (1984) No. 2206, *English summary in* 16 N.Y.I.L. 471–472 (1985). The Tribunal was established by the Claims Settlement Agreement between the Islamic Republic of Iran and the United States of America, which is embodied in the Declaration of the Algerian Government of 19 January 1981 concerning the

have recourse to the sovereign immunity terminology of acts *jure imperii* and acts *jure gestionis*, because The Netherlands does not have a statute similar to the American IOIA.[599] Although the *Rechtbank* overturned the specific decision of the *Kantongerecht* that the Tribunal's dismissal from employment of the plaintiff, a Dutch national who had served as an interpreter and translator under an oral private agreement with the Tribunal, was an act *jure gestionis* for which the Tribunal was not entitled to immunity from jurisdiction,[600] it too used sovereign immunity terminology to justify its holding that the translating and interpreting services provided by the Dutch employee did fall within the category of acts *jure imperii*. Most important, the *Rechtbank* did so on the ground that these services are essential for the Tribunal to duly perform its tasks, thereby recognizing at the same time the functional basis of organizational immunity. It would have been better if the court had relied solely on this functional basis, rather than blurring it with the ambiguous terminology of sovereign immunity law. The Supreme Court (*Hoge Raad*) of The Netherlands, in *Spaans v. Iran-United States Claims Tribunal*,[601] affirmed the decision of the *Rechtbank*, in a ruling which appears to be based on the functional necessity concept of organizational immunities, without at the same time determining whether such immunities should be absolute or restrictive, which is salutory. Although it explicitly

---

settlement of claims by the Government of Iran and the Government of the United States. *See* 20 ILM 224 (1981). The Tribunal is a joint institution of the two States concerned and is subject to public international law. *See* C.N. Brower and J.D. Brueschke, The Iran-United States Claims Tribunal 16 (1998).

599 *See* 'Note of 20 August 1959 received from the Acting Permanent Representative of the Netherlands to the United Nations,' *reprinted in* UN Doc. ST/LEG/SER.8/10 (1959), at 55.

600 The *Kantongerecht* relied on the fact that, in cases concerning questions of *State* immunity, the Dutch courts have developed the rule that a distinction should be made between governmental acts (*acta jure imperii*) and commercial acts (*acta jure gestionis*) and that international organizations such as the Tribunal, which have been constituted by States, enjoy in principle the same immunity that is accorded to States. For the latter conclusion, which we believe is incorrect, it relied on H.G. Schermers, Internationaal Publiekrecht Voor De Rechtspraktijk § 499 (3rd ed. 1985). Consequently, the *Kantongerecht* reasoned, the same distinction between *acta jure imperii* and *acta jure gestionis* should also be made in the case of international organizations such as the Tribunal. *See* 15 N.Y.I.L. 429,431 (1984). Besides making the typical error of confusing two different branches of immunity law, the *Kantongerecht* denied the special, strictly internal nature of employment contracts between international organizations and their staff. *See also* Seidl-Hohenveldern, L'immunité, at 165.

601 Judgment nr. 12627 of 20 Dec. 1985, NJ 438, 1691–1702, English transl. in 94 ILR 321 (1994).

distinguished the immunity case of international organizations from that of sovereign States, it would have placed the law of organizational immunities on a sounder footing if the Dutch Supreme Court had unequivocally repudiated the contention of the *Kantongerecht* that international organizations such as the Tribunal enjoy in principle the same immunity that is accorded to States and that the same distinction between *acta jure imperii* and *acta jure gestionis* should be applied in the case of international organizations.[602]

In a more recent case arising from a dispute between the Supreme group of entities (private parties) and the North Atlantic Treaty Organization (NATO), the Dutch Supreme Court rejected Supreme's appeal from an appellate court's ruling upholding the immunity of two NATO-affiliated entities, finding that the appellate court's conclusions in respect of the immunity of the NATO entities were well founded.[603] Supreme had initiated proceedings before the Dutch courts alleging non-payment under certain contracts concluded between the parties for the supply of fuel. The targeted NATO entities were the Supreme Headquarters of the Allied Powers in Europe (SHAPE), headquartered in Belgium, and the Allied Joint Force Command Brunssum (JFCB), located in The Netherlands. JFCB had acted on behalf of SHAPE in concluding contracts with Supreme regarding the supply of fuel to SHAPE in support of the NATO mission in Afghanistan, which was carried out for the International Security Assistance Force (ISAF). In its December 2021 ruling, the Dutch Supreme Court declined to overturn the appellate court's finding that, while there is no treaty basis for the immunity from jurisdiction of SHAPE and JFCB, these entities are entitled to immunity from jurisdiction before the Dutch courts on the basis of customary international law. The Dutch Supreme Court noted that there may be circumstances justifying the invocation of custom-based immunity by an international organization that is not based in The Netherlands, including in situations where such an organization is affiliated with an international organization that is based in The Netherlands and granting immunity to the non-local organization is necessary to prevent the thwarting of the custom-based

602 *See also* Conclusion of Advocate-General Gulmann (para. 7) in *Société générale d'entreprise électro-mécaniques (SGEEM) and R. Etroy v. European Investment Bank*, Court of Justice of the European Communities, Case C-370/89, Jur. 1992–10, I-6233, ECR 1992 I-06211.

603 *Supreme Site Services GmbH et al v. Supreme Headquarters Allied Powers Europe and Allied Joint Force Command Headquarters Brunssum*, Supreme Court of The Netherlands, case no. 20/00937, judgment of 24 Dec. 2021.

immunity of the international organization that is based in The Netherlands.[604] Most important, the Dutch Supreme Court let stand the appellate court's finding that, in the event SHAPE and JFCB invoke immunity in respect of their official activities, such immunity must be conferred upon them and in an absolute manner.[605] The Dutch Supreme Court considered that the foundation for the privileges and immunities of intergovernmental organizations is that such privileges and immunities are necessary for the independent functioning of an intergovernmental organization, without interference by individual States, thereby suggesting that the Supreme Court views organizational immunity as functional, and not absolute.[606] Indeed, the Dutch Supreme Court has recognized the immunity of the United Nations as being absolute—not in the sense of the absolute/restrictive distinction made in the law of State immunity, but as being the most far-reaching of the immunities of international organizations.[607]

Some writers have called for a substantial limitation of the immunities of international organizations.[608] The classification of activities of such organizations would be critical to this effort. O'Toole has stated in this respect that in determining what is a 'commercial activity' the courts should limit the category as narrowly as possible. A sounder approach, however, would begin by consistently avoiding the use of the absolute/restrictive terminology of sovereign immunity, so that the conflict which the courts had to deal with in the aforementioned cases does not even arise in the first place.[609] This alternative approach, as set forth below, would avoid an

604 *Id.*, para. 3.1.2 (with reference to *X v. Iran-United States Claims Tribunal*, Supreme Court of The Netherlands, judgment of 20 Dec. 1985).

605 *Id.*, para. 2.4.

606 *Id.*, para. 3.1.2. *See also In re* Euratom, Supreme Court (*Hoge Raad*) of The Netherlands, case no. S 01984/07 CW, judgment of 13 Nov. 2007, NJ 2008, 147, at paras. 6.2 and 6.4 (referring to "functional immunity" in relation to Euratom).

607 *Stichting Mothers of Srebrenica et al. v. State of The Netherlands and United Nations*, Supreme Court (*Hoge Raad*) of The Netherlands, case no. 10/04437, judgment of 13 Apr. 2012, at paras. 4.2 and 4.3.6 ("That [UN] immunity is absolute").

608 *See, e.g.*, Note, *Jurisdictional Immunities of Intergovernmental Organizations*, 91 Yale L.J. 1167, 1184 n.149 (1982); O'Toole, at 16.

609 *But see*, for authors who employ absolute terminology, Dominicé, LIBER SEIDL, at 88–91; Seidl-Hohenveldern, Communautés, at 475–476; *id.*, L'immunité, at 162, 165–166; Ehrenfeld, at 92. It should be noted that the vast majority of basic instruments of international organizations do not use the term 'absolute,' although the terms 'complete' and 'every' do occur.

explicit resolution of whether or not international organizations are subject to sovereign immunity restrictions, such as the commercial activity concept, the wholesale application of which runs contrary to the functional basis of organizational immunities.[610] Most important, recourse to these restrictions is unnecessary, because the same result can be achieved through terminology that is more consistent with the nature and basic documents of international organizations.

In order to avoid any future misunderstanding on this point, and for the purpose of developing a true *organizational* immunity theory, it is best not to apply the 'commercial activity' exception of sovereign immunity, but instead to look for another criterion, which is capable of fulfilling a similar need – providing a means for measuring the legitimate incidence of privileges and immunities of international organizations. A restrictive approach should be adopted, not by copying the terms or concepts developed in sovereign immunity law, but instead by looking, similar to the case of sovereign States, at the nature of the activity performed by an international organization,[611] which can be either *official* or *non-official*. A clear and strict definition of an organization's 'official activities' should be included in its

610 *See also* Farrugia, at 506, 519. The Council of Europe Report of 1969, at 24–25, paras. 34–35, stated that commercial activities in the context of international organizations do not include such transactions as the purchase of goods (*e.g.*, office equipment) or services required for administrative purposes. The Report abstained from defining the commercial field more precisely, but agreed that the definition should *not* depend on the classification of particular activities (*i.e.*, as commercial or non-commercial) for domestic purposes. Instead, it was recommended that this should be decided in relation to the scope and nature of the activities of each individual organization. *But see Jam et al. v. International Finance Corp.*, 139 S. CT. 759, 772 (2019) (holding that "the Foreign Sovereign Immunities Act [and its commercial activity exception] governs the immunity of international organizations" under U.S. law and rejecting the IFC's claim that it is entitled to "virtually absolute" immunity). The U.S. Supreme Court has stated that US. courts should look to "the gravamen" (i.e., the crux) of the action when determining whether an action is "based upon" a commercial activity in the United States. *OBB Personenverkehr AG v. Sachs*, 577 U.S. 27, 35 (2015).

611 *Cf. Sayag a.o. v. Leduc a.o.*, Court of Justice of the European Communities, Judgment of 11 July 1968, Case C-5/68 (holding that "[t]he immunity from legal proceedings ... applies exclusively to acts which, by their nature, represent a participation of the person claiming immunity in the performance of the tasks of the institution to which he belongs"). *See also Atkinson v. Inter-American Development Bank, et al.*, 156 F.3d 1335 (D.C. Cir. 1998)(citing *Jungquist v. Sheikh Sultan Bin Khalifa Al Nahyan*, 115 F.3d 1020, 1028 (D.C. Cir. 1997)("[T]he relevant inquiry in determining whether an individual was acting in an official capacity focuses on the nature of the individual's alleged actions.")).

basic instruments and should be made subject to narrow interpretation, including by specifying what kind of activity is *not* included within the scope of 'official activity.' For example, an Executive Order issued by the U.S. President in 1997, whereby he designated the World Trade Organization an international organization for the purpose of the International Organizations Immunities Act, specified that "[t]he leasing or renting by the World Trade Organization of its property to another entity or person to generate revenue shall not be considered a use for the purposes of the World Trade Organization."[612] Legislative authority such as that enshrined in the IOIA demonstrates that it is possible to provide tailor-made solutions for individual organizations as opposed to a 'one-size-fits-all' approach. Tailor-made solutions would provide an incentive for the international organization concerned to engage only in activity in furtherance of the functions and purposes for which it was established and would represent built-in checks on abuse of privileges and immunities within the organization. There is no reason why specific, limitative language of the kind expressed in executive orders or judicial pronouncements regarding the nature and scope of organizational immunity[613] could not be included in relevant international instruments. The development of 'new-generation' bilateral and multilateral investment protection treaties, which incorporate more detailed language on key rights and obligations than the treaties they replace and that are meant to reflect established arbitral case law, is a salutary one and could inspire similar revisions to international instruments addressing organizational immunities.

'Official activities' generally can be said to include "those relating to the achievement of the aims of the organisation."[614] This formula has, for instance, been applied in the *Protocol on Privileges and Immunities of the European Patent Organisation* (EPO).[615] Article 3, paragraph 4, of this Protocol states: "The official activities of the Organisation shall, for the purposes of

612 Exec. Order No. 13,042, 62 Federal Register 18,017, 14 Apr. 1997.

613 *See Sayag*, n.611. (holding specifically that "[t]he immunity from legal proceedings ... applies exclusively to acts which, by their nature, represent a participation of the person claiming immunity in the performance of the tasks of the institution to which he belongs" and "driving a motor vehicle is not in the nature of an act performed in an official capacity save in the exceptional cases in which this activity could not be accomplished otherwise than under the authority of the Community and by its own servants").

614 Council of Europe Report 1969, at 31, para. 61; *see also* BEIER *et al.*, Art. 8, at 7 *et seq.;* Díaz González, *Sixth Report,* UN Doc. A/CN.4/439 (1991), at 8, paras. 30–31.

615 *See* BEIER *et al.*, Art. 3, at 15.

this Protocol, be such as are strictly necessary for its administrative and technical operation, as set out in the Convention."[616] Another way of limiting the potential sphere of official activities is to define them as covering any activity that is carried out in order to perform the 'core' functions of the international organization in question.[617] Such a definition has the advantage of avoiding the distinction between public/governmental activities and commercial/private activities lying at the heart of the law of State immunity and it could give an international organization protective immunity even if the nature of the activity concerned is commercial, as is the case with certain international financial institutions.

The EPO definition demonstrates the close relationship which exists between the different elements in the three-step approach, with an explicit reference in its closing words to Step One, which involves an examination of that part of the constituent instrument of the organization containing its basic functions and purposes. It also demonstrates that organizational immunity involves an inherently contextual interpretation as meant in Article 31, paragraph 1, of the Vienna Convention on the Law of Treaties[618] – the context being formed by the functions and purposes set out in an international organization's constituent instrument and related instruments.

The comment[619] points out that the EPO's immunity does not hinge upon the fact that the organization has carried out an activity which, if undertaken by a State, might be considered commercial. As regards the EPO, a variety of private contracts are necessary to enable the organization to perform its administrative and technical tasks and grant European patents.[620]

616 *Id.*, at 15 and 19–21. *See also* Art. VII, para. 1, of Annex I ('Privileges and Immunities') to the Convention for the Establishment of a European Space Agency ("For the purposes of Articles V [immunity from direct taxes] and VI [immunity from import/export duties], the official activities of the Agency shall include its administrative activities, including its operations in connection with the social security scheme, and activities undertaken in the field of space research and technology and their space applications in pursuance of the purpose of the Agency as defined in the Convention").

617 *See* Y. Okada, *The immunity of international organizations before and after* Jam v IFC*: Is the functional necessity rationale still relevant?,* Questions of International Law online, 5 July 2020, available at https://www.qil-qdi.org/the-immunity-of-international-organizations-before-and-after-jam-v-ifc-is-the-functional-necessity-rationale-still-relevant/ (last visited 1 December 2024).

618 Art. 31(1) reads: "A treaty shall be interpreted in good faith in accordance with the ordinary meaning to be given to the terms of the treaty in their context and in the light of its object and purpose."

619 BEIER *et al.,* Art. 3, at 20, top.

620 Among such transactions can be named, *inter alia,* employment contracts, contracts for the purchase of office equipment, lease of premises, and printing. *See id.* at 20 sub 15.

There might, however, in some instances be difficulties in deciding what is to be considered an official activity of a given international organization, or indeed what belongs to the 'core' of an organization's functions. There will be borderline cases in which it will be difficult to determine what constitutes an official activity as opposed to a non-essential, non-official activity.[621] Such might be the case when the constitutional framework of the organization describes the organization's functions and purposes in general terms only, thereby leaving considerable scope for extending its boundaries in practice. In general, we believe that the operative realm of an organization should be defined as clearly and extensively as possible, a practice from which both the organization and those with whom it interacts can be expected to benefit. This will enhance their mutual legitimate expectations with regard to the proper operation of the organization. Operative rules should be formulated refining the basic guidelines laid down in the organization's constituent instrument. Without these operative rules, no manager, whether we are dealing with a CEO (chief executive officer) of a private company, or with a CAO (chief administrative officer) of an organization, can effectively operate an entity or make an informed decision regarding the classification of a certain activity as 'official activity' qualifying for immunity protection. One must remember that problems of interpretation are inherent to using general formulae, whether one adopts 'commercial activity' or 'official activity' as a criterion. But to start with the wrong assumptions, through mistaken analogies taken from sovereignty concepts that silence or vagueness on the issue invites, will only increase such problems.

A way out of this controversy relating to the proper boundaries of the suggested criterion might be to use as a *test* whether the organization concerned not only participates in the market by concluding agreements with private contractors, but enters the marketplace seeking customers as a supplier and trader of goods or services for profit, thereby exposing itself to the

621 It might be better to speak of non-essential, as opposed to official, activities, than of commercial activities, for, as was demonstrated above by reference to comments made by several writers, commercial activities might well be included in an organization's functions. *See also* Council of Europe Report 1969, at 31, para. 61, according to which operating restaurants, bars and shops or renting premises to private individuals or businesses would qualify as non-essential activities. We therefore adopt a negative definition for 'non-essential activity,' *i.e.*, every activity which cannot be classified as official activity, as set out in the organization's basic documents. This could be a commercial activity, but, applying this definition, commercial activity might as well be official activity, if strictly necessary to the organization's functions and purposes. For a review of the jurisprudence of the ICJ with regard to the meaning of 'essential,' see Lauterpacht, Development, at 430–432.

ordinary forces of market competition.[622] A practical example will illustrate this point. The European Launcher Development Organization (ELDO), which had as it aim to develop and construct space vehicle launchers and practical equipment for supply to eventual users, can be regarded as a technical organization with possible commercial functions that may compete with non-governmental parties.[623] Under the terms of Article 4 of the Protocol on the Privileges and Immunities of the ELDO of 1965, the organization's official activities were defined as to include its administrative activities and the design, development and construction of prototype space vehicle launchers.[624] This mission would exclude the commercial production of launchers. In case the ELDO in the future would have decided to move into the field of commercial production of launchers, it could no longer, under the Protocol, have relied on its immunity.[625]

The construction of satellites entrusted to the European Space Agency (ESA), which now incorporates the ELDO, constitutes another example. In order to carry out its purpose, the ESA is authorized to enter into a variety of commercial contracts with private contractors for the supply of technical instruments. The ESA has been granted immunity with respect to these contracts, because these kinds of activities come within the realm of its official activities as set out in the ESA's constituent instrument.[626] Most important,

---

622 *See*, e.g., OAS Guide, Guideline 4, 'Limits to jurisdictional immunities' ("International organizations lack jurisdictional immunities for acts in which they participate as actors in the marketplace, including employment disputes that do not compromise the autonomy of the organization, or when the organization waives that immunity"). BEIER *et al.*, Art. 8, at 11. Ebenroth, at 177, 179, has suggested that one should use as a test whether the activity concerned could also be implemented by a legal entity under private law such as a private commercial company. If so, he suggests to qualify the activity concerned as an activity under civil law for which the organization cannot claim immunity. But apart from the fact that, in our view, the purposes and functions of an organization may very well require the performance of 'commercial' activities, the disadvantage of Ebenroth's view is that it takes sovereign immunity and Act of State concepts as a basis.

623 *See* Council of Europe Report 1969, at 15, para. 12(d), and 78, para. 15. The ELDO (or European Organisation for the Development and Construction of Space Vehicle Launchers) and the European Space Research Organization (ESRO) merged to form the European Space Agency, headquartered in Paris, in 1975.

624 *Id.*

625 *Id.*, at 78, para.16. *See also* SATOW, at 302, para. 21.26.

626 *See* Convention for the establishment of a European Space Agency (as amended), Annex I—'Privileges and Immunities,' entered into force 30 Oct. 1980. *See also* BEIER *et al.*, Art. 8, at 8–9. As has been pointed out by Farrugia, at 519–520, such contracts

the contractual activities of the ESA are within the bounds of the test as defined above: it merely enters the marketplace in demand of goods or services from private contractors, without seeking customers in offering its own products for profit.

The immunities enjoyed by an international organization are thus confined to their 'official activities' which are strictly necessary for the exercise of functions in fulfilment of the organization's purposes.[627] As to its ordinary meaning, the Concise Oxford Dictionary describes the word 'necessary' as "indispensable, requisite, ..., inevitably resulting from ..., needed for a purpose."[628] According to Black's Law Dictionary, the term 'need' is a relative one and means "to have an urgent or essential use for."[629] As Skubiszewski has explained, "[e]ssentiality and necessity are factors which ... are, obviously, subjective: varying estimates may be given of what is necessary or essential for the accomplishment of a task or function;"[630] "(...) they are not precise criteria and may thus lead to divergent interpretations."[631] That being the case, the same author has also stated that "the definition of what is essential or necessary must remain within certain bounds; these depend on the law of the specific organization."[632] Thus, "the matter is always one of interpretation or application of law. To that extent, necessity and essentiality are subject to legal scrutiny."[633] Indeed, in a case involving the Northwest Atlantic Fisheries Organization, an international organization headquartered in the Canadian province of Nova Scotia whose mandate is

---

between international organizations and private citizens for goods and services necessary to the functioning of the organization would probably be considered commercial in nature for the purpose of *sovereign* immunity law.

627 *See also* OAS Guide, Guideline 3, 'Scope of jurisdictional immunities,' Rapporteur's Notes ("Immunity for international organizations tends to be functional, based on the presumption that it is only admissible to recognize such immunity for the activities of those organizations that are essential and necessary to accomplish its object and purpose").

628 In contrast to this definition of the term's ordinary meaning, Sir Elihu Lauterpacht has concluded from a review of the case law of the ICJ that it means something more than 'important,' but less than 'indispensably requisite,' or 'absolutely essential.' Lauterpacht, Development, at 430–432; *see also* Skubiszewski, at 861–862. Probably mere usefulness or effectiveness is insufficient, *see* the EMBL Award discussed in Section 3.4.1 below.

629 Black's Law Dictionary 715 (abr. 6th ed. 1991).

630 Skubiszewski, at 861.

631 *Id.*, at 868.

632 *Id.*

633 *Id.*, at 862.

to manage and preserve fishing resources in the Northwest Atlantic Ocean, the Supreme Court of Canada observed as follows in a ruling issued in 2013: "What is necessary for the performance of NAFO's functions, or what constitutes undue interference, must be determined on a case-by-case basis."[634] Section 3, paragraph 1, of the NAFO Privileges and Immunities Order, a Canadian legislative instrument, specifies the purpose and scope of NAFO's immunities. It grants NAFO immunities "to such extent as may be required for the performance of its functions." In the view of Canada's Supreme Court, the words "for the performance of NAFO's functions" indicate that NAFO has been granted "a broad functional immunity" and they call for a broader interpretation of the word 'required' than 'necessary' in the strictest sense.[635]

In a U.S. case involving the World Bank, the appellate court observed that the answer to the question of whether the provision of food and beverage services for staff members and guests at the organization's headquarters is part of the "operations" of the Bank, as such term is employed in the Bank's Articles of Agreement, "depends not so much on how essential the

634 *Amaratunga v. Northwest Atlantic Fisheries Organization*, Supreme Court of Canada, judgment of 29 Nov. 2013, 2013 SCC 66, [2013] 3 SCR 866, at para. 53. *See also* OAS Guide, Guideline 1, Rapporteur's Notes ("The immunities of international organizations and, specifically, jurisdictional immunities, are ... dealt with on a case-by-case basis."). In another judgment, issued in 2016, the Supreme Court of Canada clarified that in a situation where immunities are accorded "[t]o enable the [organization] to fulfil the functions with which [it is] entrusted," as is the case with the IBRD in Art. VII, section 1, of its Articles of Agreement, "[t]o import an added condition of functional necessity would undermine what appears to be a conscious choice to enumerate the specific immunities rather than to rely on one broad, functional grant of immunity," the grant of inviolability of the organization's archives in Article VII, section 5, of the IBRD's Articles of Agreement ("The archives of the Bank shall be inviolable") being an example of specific immunity. In the court's view, section 1 "does not impose a condition of functional necessity that must be satisfied whenever any immunity is asserted," even though "the scope of these immunities should nevertheless be interpreted purposively, taking into consideration their object outlined in" section 1. *World Bank Group v. Wallace*, Supreme Court of Canada, judgment of 29 Apr. 2016, 2016 SCC 15, at paras. 63–64, text *repr. in* 2016 UN Jurid. Y.B, pp. 430–451, UN Doc. ST/LEG/SER.C/54. *See also Scimet v. African Development Bank*, Court of First Instance of Brussels, 1997, 128 ILR 582, at 584 (1997)(holding that purposive immunity clause is not meant to require an international organization to justify the application of the asserted immunity).

635 *Id.*, paras. 40–41 and 44 ("To limit the immunity granted in s. 3(1) [of the NAFO Privileges and Immunities Order] as narrowly as the appellant proposes would run counter to Parliament's objectives of modernization, flexibility and respect for the independence of international organizations hosted by Canada").

Bank believes the activity to be, but on the arrangements the Bank has made to carry it out."[636]

It may be said that the 'official activities' of an international organization, in order to meet the 'strictly necessary' test, must be activities carried out by the organization *in the course of the actual exercise* of its functions in the fulfilment of its purposes. In other words, these activities should be a *natural consequence* of the organization's functions and purposes to such an extent that they could be said to *logically arise from*[637] its functions and purposes. In any event, as Pellet has argued within the ILC with regard to the classification of the activities of an organization, "il ne suffit pas qu'elles *concernent* l'organisation, elles doivent être *nécessaires* á la réalisation de ses objectifs ou du moins qu'elles s'y rapportent ....'" (emphasis added)[638]

At a minimum, in light of the functional foundation of organizational immunities, the impugned acts of an international organization must be *directly* related to the fulfilment of the purposes entrusted to the organization before its immunity can be upheld in a court of law, i.e., there must be a *direct causal relationship* in a given case.[639] Immunity applies only to acts or activities which, by their nature, represent a participation of the entity claiming immunity in the performance of the tasks of the institution to which the entity belongs.[640]

---

636 *International Bank for Reconstruction and Development v. District of Columbia*, 171 F.3d 687 (D.C. Cir. 1999), 38 ILM 818 (1999)(rejecting claim that a private contactor, retained by the World Bank to provide food and beverage services to individuals on the Bank's premises, has derivative immunity from District of Columbia taxes on the contractor's sales of food and beverages).

637 *Cf.* the views expressed with regard to implied powers by Judge Gros in his Dissenting Opinion in the *Namibia* Case, 1971 ICJ Rep. 323, at 339, para. 32, *quoted in* Skubiszewski, at 862.

638 [1991] 1 Y.B. Int'l L. Comm'n 178, para. 6, UN Doc. A/CN.4/SER.A/1991 (for the original French text, see UN Doc. A/CN.4/SR.2235 (12 July 1991), at 5). "Elles" refers to communications activities carried out by an organization of which Pellet was speaking, but may be replaced by any organizational activity.

639 *See, e.g., In re* Euratom, Supreme Court (*Hoge Raad*) of The Netherlands, case no. S 01984/07 CW, judgment of 13 Nov. 2007, NJ 2008, 147. *See also Sayag a.o. v. Leduc a.o.*, Court of Justice of the European Communities, Judgment of 11 July 1968, Case C-5/68 ("the act in question serves directly for the accomplishment of a Community task").

640 *Cf. Sayag a.o. v. Leduc a.o.*, Court of Justice of the European Communities, Judgment of 11 July 1968, Case C-5/68 (holding, with respect to an official of an international organization, that "[t]he immunity from legal proceedings ... applies exclusively to acts which, by their nature, represent a participation of the person claiming immunity in

In the course of the ILC's study of the second part of the topic 'Relations between States and international organizations Special Rapporteur Díaz González introduced two draft articles which are typical representatives of Step Three of the functional necessity analysis.

First, draft article 11, which is the closing article of Part III of the Draft entitled 'Property, funds and assets,' reads as follows:

> Notwithstanding the provisions of article 10, paragraphs (a) and (b), *the scope of the rights accorded may be limited, in the light of the functional requirements of the organization in question*, by mutual agreement of the parties concerned.(emphasis added)[641]

Functional necessity hence was chosen as the criterion to determine the extent of privileges and immunities, albeit subject to an explicit agreement of the parties and not, as we propose, as an 'invisible hand' that is inherent to the subject-matter.[642]

Second, draft article 22, which is the final article of the ILC Draft and concludes Part IV on 'Communications,' provides as follows:

> For the purposes of the foregoing articles, the terms 'official activity' or 'official use' shall mean those relating to the accomplishment of the purposes of the international organizations.[643]

The reception of these draft articles within the ILC was somewhat mixed. Several members felt that draft article 11 was unnecessary and superfluous since it dealt with a matter already covered by other articles, in particular draft article 4.[644] Al-Baharna warned his ILC colleagues that the effect of

---

the performance of the tasks of the institution to which he belongs" and that "driving a motor vehicle is not in the nature of an act performed in an official capacity save in the exceptional cases in which this activity could not be accomplished otherwise than under the authority of the Community and by its own servants").

641 *See Report of the International Law Commission on the work of its forty-second session*, GAOR Supp. (No. 10) at 240 n.295, and paras. 462–463, UN Doc. A/45/10 (1990).

642 *See also* FOX-WEBB, at 578 ("This functional criterion consequently determines the extent of an organization's immunities").

643 *See Report of the International Law Commission on the work of its forty-third session*, GAOR Supp. (No. 10) at 321 n.372, and para. 299, UN Doc. A/46/10 (1991).

644 Draft article 4 deals with the relationship between the proposed draft articles (Convention) and other international agreements, and provides that the former are without prejudice to, and shall not preclude the conclusion of, other international agreements regarding the privileges and immunities of international organizations of a universal character. *See Report of the International Law Commission on the work of its forty-*

the article would be to introduce an element of uncertainty as to the scope of draft article 10 conferring freedom of funds and currency, and would make it difficult in some cases to determine which 'functional requirements' should be taken into consideration for the purpose of limiting the provisions of draft article 10 (a) and (b).[645] Pawlak argued that the words used in draft article 11 gave the impression that the proposed common régime had not been based *solely* on the criterion that privileges and immunities should reflect the functional requirements of international organizations.[646] Similarly, Njenga suggested that these functional requirements must be the only criterion for determining the extent of the privileges and immunities accorded to international organizations.[647] According to Pellet, the restriction contained in the article is a purely voluntary one, which does not tally with the functional theory.[648]

As for draft article 22, its contents were accepted by the majority of ILC members as being in accord with the functional criterion on which the draft is based. However, they recommended that the criterion introduced by the article should be expressed in a more general provision, in another place in the draft, so as to cover all of the provisions of Parts II, III, IV and V.[649] Indeed, draft articles 11 and 22, which have general application, should have been combined and included in Part I of the draft, thereby stressing the generally applicable criterion of functional necessity.

3.4.1 The 'Official Activity' Criterion Applied: The EMBL Award

An important German arbitration under the presidency of former ICJ Judge Hermann Mosler dealt with the question of the definition and delimitation

second session, GAOR Supp. (No. 10), at 232 n.289, UN Doc. A/45/10 (1990). For the comments made within the ILC, see [1990] 1 Y.B. Int'l L. Comm'n 204, para. 31 (Al-Baharna), 209, para. 27 (Rao), 210, para. 44 (Sepulveda Gutierrez), 212, para. 63 (Graefrath), 218, para. 42 (McCaffrey), 220, para. 62 (Bennouna), 224, para. 26 (Eiriksson), UN Doc. A/CN.4/SER.A/1990; *but see id.* at 210, para. 38 (Pawlak) and 220, para. 61 (Solari Tudela), for support for the proposed draft articles.

645 *See* [1990] 1 Y.B. Int'l L. Comm'n 204, para. 31, UN Doc. A/CN.4/SER.A/1990.

646 *See id.*, at 210, para. 38. Pawlak's comment was probably triggered by the use of the words "in the light of" in draft article 11, which could be interpreted to mean that the functional criterion was not intended as the sole source.

647 *See* (1991) 1 Y.B. Int'l L. Comm'n 175, para. 12, UN Doc. A/CN.4/SER.A/1991.

648 *See* [1990] 1 Y.B. Int'l L. Comm'n 215, para. 18, UN Doc. A/CN.4/SER.A/1990.

649 *See Report of the International Law Commission on the work of its forty-third session*, GAOR Supp. (No. 10) at 321, para. 299, UN Doc. A/46/10 (1991); Pellet, in [1991] 1 Y.B. Int'l L. Comm'n 178, para. 6, UN Doc. A/CN.4/SER.A/1991; Pawlak, in *id.*, at 179, para. 16. The ILC Draft contains explicit functional terminology only in articles 8, 11, 13, 14, 15, 16, 18, 20, 21, and 22.

of the official activities of an international organization based in Germany, namely, the *European Molecular Biology Laboratory* (EMBL).[650]

After having first addressed the Step One question of the legal status of the EMBL in Germany,[651] the Award of 29 June 1990 examined (the extent of) the privileges and immunities enjoyed by the EMBL. In particular, the question was addressed whether the exploitation of the organization's guest-house, the canteen and the cafetaria, as well as the maintenance of the official residence of the EMBL Director-General were exempt from taxation because they could qualify as 'official activities' of the organization within the meaning of Article 9 of the Headquarters Agreement between the EMBL and Germany, as the host State.[652]

This provision reads as follows: "For the purposes of Articles 7 and 8 of this Agreement, the official activities of the Laboratory shall include its administrative activities and those undertaken in pursuance of the purposes of the Laboratory as defined in the Laboratory Agreement."[653]

---

650 *European Molecular Biology Laboratory v. Germany,* Arbitration Award of 29 June 1990, 105 ILR 1 (1997) (Prof.Dr. Hermann Mosler, President; Prof.Dr. Luzius Wildhaber, appointed by the EMBL; Prof.Dr. Michael Schweitzer, appointed by the German Government)[hereinafter: EMBL Award]. The information on this arbitration case set forth in the original edition of this book was taken from the English text provided to the present author by the Chairman of the Arbitration Tribunal. The German text is the authoritative one. For an early German commentary, see Kunz-Hallstein, Privilegien.

651 *See* EMBL Award, Question No. I, at 15–18, in particular at 18, para. 4: "So, the international status of the EMBL is the starting point of the assessment: on the level of public international law, the EMBL and the Federal Republic of Germany are in a position of formal equality."

652 *Id.,* Question No. III, at 31–50.

653 Articles 7 and 8 read as follows:

Article 7

Exemption from taxation

(1) Within the scope of its official activities, the Laboratory and its property and income shall be exempt from all direct taxes.

(2) When the Laboratory makes substantial purchases or uses substantial services, strictly necessary for the exercise of its official activities, in the price of which taxes or duties are included, appropriate measures shall be taken by the Federal Republic of Germany, whenever possible, to remit or reimburse the amount of such taxes or duties.

(3) Exemption shall not be accorded in respect of duties and taxes which are in fact no more than charges for public utility services.

Article 8

Exemption from customs duties

Goods imported or exported by the Laboratory and strictly necessary for the exercise of its official activities shall be exempt from all customs duties and other charges other than such as represent payments for specific services rendered, and from all prohibitions and restrictions on import or export.

First, as regards the operation of *the guest-house, the canteen and the cafeteria*, the EMBL maintained that Article II of the 1973 Agreement Establishing the EMBL,[654] which expressly mentions as part of the EMBL's functions the provision of working accommodation and research facilities for visiting scientists or advanced training and teaching, grants the right to operate the facilities necessary for its program. These facilities should include not only the necessary buildings to contain the equipment and for the administration of the organization, but also such buildings as are necessary for the discharge of its other functions. Thus, in the EMBL's view, the activities of the guest-house and the cafeteria were inseparably linked to the area of functions of the EMBL and were indispensable for the execution of its scientific programs.[655] It was argued that this included also the supplying of visiting scientists with accommodation and meals, because only in this manner could their often short-term stays, typical for the method of operation of the EMBL, be made possible in light of the difficult housing market situation in Heidelberg, where the EMBL has its seat.[656] Most important, the EMBL stressed that, instead of the distinction between 'official activities' and 'economic activities,' the decisive criterion for delimitation was the immediate connection with the effective discharge of the functions conferred upon the EMBL. Thus, the guest-house and canteen activities were said to be immediately related to the discharge of the scientific functions of the EMBL and could not be regarded as 'ordinary' activities of a business enterprise.[657] The EMBL also claimed tax privileges on the basis that the guest-house and canteen were "primarily operated for" the discharge of the organization's scientific functions and that the ultimate consumers, i.e., the staff members and guests of the Laboratory, were only indirectly beneficiaries.[658]

The German authorities, on the other hand, advanced a much stricter interpretation, according to which the functions conferred upon the EMBL by Article II of the Establishing Agreement are all of a scientific nature and have no relation to activities which provide alimentary necessities to the staff and the guests of the EMBL. Accordingly, the terms "working accommodation and research facilities" were interpreted as to include laboratory places and the like, but *not* eating facilities, such as the canteen and the cafeteria. In sum, the official activities of the EMBL were argued to be restricted to "all that directly served the achievement of the aims of the EMBL

654 *See* BG.BL. II 1973, 1005.
655 *See* EMBL Award, at 31.
656 *Id.*, at 32.
657 *Id.*, at 33–34.
658 *Id.*, at 35.

whereas antecedent auxiliary functions did not or in any case not by itself count among them"[659] and they should, accordingly, be seen as commercial activities.[660] In further support of their argument, the German authorities argued also that the EMBL had not been charged with the operation of the guest-house and canteen/cafeteria, neither in the Establishing Agreement nor in the Headquarters Agreement. An official activity of the EMBL could only be one which displayed specific characteristics of scientific research or teaching and which could not be carried out just as well by any third person.[661]

In its Award, the Arbitration Tribunal began by pointing out that the determination of the scope of the term 'official activities' is decisive for the classification of the purchase and sale of goods or the use and performance of services in the canteen/cafeteria and the guest-house, such to be carried out on the basis of the text of the Headquarters Agreement in connection with the Establishing Agreement.[662] The latter instrument sets out the purposes of the EMBL in Articles II and IV, referred to above.[663] The Tribunal then concluded that these provisions did not either explicitly include or exclude the operation of the canteen/cafeteria and the guest-house from the official activities of the organization.[664] Equally, faced with the resulting open question of interpretation, the Tribunal found that State practice provided no assistance in interpreting the agreements and that no practice existed in the relationship of the EMBL with Germany. Hence, the Tribunal applied Article 33 of the Headquarters Agreement, which provides that the Agreement is to be interpreted in the light of its primary purpose of enabling the EMBL at its Headquarters in Germany, fully and efficiently to discharge its responsibilities and fulfil its purposes.[665] In the light of this provision, the Tribunal found that activities geared to facilitating scientific

659 *Id.*, at 37.

660 *Id.* at 40.

661 *Id.*, at 37.

662 Thus, the Tribunal distinguished between the cases of official/non-official purchase of goods or services, official/non-official sale of goods or services, and use by the EMBL itself for official/non-official purposes. *Id.*, at 43.

663 The purposes of the EMBL include, *inter alia,* research (Art. II, para. 2(a)–(b)), the provision of working accommodation and research facilities for visiting scientists (Art. II, para. 2(c)), and advanced training and teaching (Art. II, para. 2(d)). Under Art. II, para. 3(1), of the Establishing Agreement, the EMBL may establish and operate the facilities necessary for its scientific programme, including the necessary equipment and buildings to contain the equipment, for the administration and the fulfilment of its functions. *See* EMBL Award, at 43–44.

664 *Id.*, at 44.

665 *Id.*, at 45. *See also* Hahn, at 1015–1016.

events such as courses, seminars, workshops etc. had to be classified as official activities if 'strictly necessary' to the functions of the EMBL. Based upon this reasoning, the Tribunal concluded that the supply of meals and accommodation was part of the EMBL's 'official activities,' but only where *put at the disposal of*, i.e., provided free of charge to, the participants in the course of these activities or used by the EMBL itself for official purposes.[666] Without such a privilege, the Tribunal reasoned that the organization of these activities would be made more difficult because the supply of meals and accommodation is nowadays largely part and parcel of the obvious standard of scientific activities. Also, having regard to the location of the EMBL, the conduct of such activities would be hindered if the participants were not offered any catering facilities.[667] The Tribunal ruled also that the tax privilege disappears when the goods purchased in the course of the official activities are not used by the EMBL itself, but are re-sold, because it is not part of the purposes and functions conferred upon the EMBL to pursue business transactions for profit.[668]

With regard to the expenditures for the renting and the operation of *the official residence of the Director-General*, the EMBL had unsuccessfully claimed reimbursement of value added tax for repairs, restorations, works and the purchase of heating oil. The official residence did not exclusively serve the private use of the Director-General, but constituted a residence put at the disposal of the EMBL's highest staff member by the organization against appropriate remuneration and was used, *inter alia*, for the purpose of representation. Since the EMBL bore a substantial part of the maintenance, operating and rental costs, it argued that they were purchases or services performed in the course of the official activities of the EMBL.[669]

---

666 The Tribunal held that it cannot be deduced from the Establishing Agreement that the functions of the EMBL include the sale of goods or services; therefore, the supply of meals and accommodation *in return for payment* cannot be counted as being among the official activities of the EMBL within the meaning of Article 9 of the Headquarters Agreement. With regard to the supply of meals and accommodation for the EMBL *staff*, the Tribunal applied the criterion of "strictly necessary" employed in Art. 7, para. 2, of the Headquarters Agreement, and found that, under a restrictive interpretation, the canteen/cafeteria and the guest-house appear as *useful* for the staff, but not as *strictly necessary*, since without the canteen the staff would be able to cater for itself and the major part of the staff does not live in the. guest-house anyway. *Id.*, at 46.

667 *Id.*, at 45.

668 *Id.*, at 47–48.

669 *Id.*, at 36. In support of its argument, the EMBL relied also on an analogy with the tax exempt status of the official residence of an ambassador as the head of a State's embassy under diplomatic and sovereign immunity law.

The German authorities did not argue on the merits of the matter of the official residence.

The Arbitration Tribunal found that the renting and maintenance of the official residence of the Director-General, including repairs, alterations and heating, by the EMBL are to be classified as official activities, and as such are exempt from taxation, *to the extent* that the Director-General uses the residence for purposes of representation. If for this purpose the EMBL puts the residence with the maintenance at the disposal of the Director-General *free of charge*,[670] it enjoys the tax privilege under Article 7, paragraph 2, of the Headquarters Agreement *to this extent*. With regard to the private use, the Tribunal held that use *by the EMBL itself for non-official* purposes is subjected to German tax law.[671]

When we embark upon an assessment of this Award, it becomes clear that it is of the utmost importance to lay down in a headquarters agreement or other instrument in as detailed a manner as possible the definition and boundaries of the official activities of an international organization. The various situations and the legal foundations applicable to them should be agreed upon in advance, using terms designed to avoid interpretative conflicts in practice.[672] In the absence of such advance agreement, the parties to an international agreement of the kind under consideration are bound to face disputes of interpretation, which will be difficult to resolve when no objective standards and interpretation mechanism exist. In such situations, the parties will have no other alternative but to resort to third-party settlement of their dispute, and to incur the costs which such a course of action inevitably entails.[673]

---

670 Thus, the Tribunal held that if the EMBL puts the residence with the maintenance at the disposal of the Director-General *in return for payment,* an official activity is no longer present, *not even* in the area in which the Director-General uses the residence for purposes of representation. In other words, renting-out is subjected to German tax law. *Id.*, at 49.

671 *Id.*, at 49.

672 *Compare* the preliminary classification which the Arbitration Tribunal felt it was bound to make, *id.*, at 43.

673 *See, e.g., International Bank for Reconstruction and Development v. District of Columbia,* 171 F.3d 687 (D.C. Cir. 1999), text repr. in 38 ILM 818 (1999), 1999 UN Jurid. Y.B, p. 433, UN Doc. ST/LEG/SER.C/37 (1999). In this case, the U.S. appellate court rejected the argument that an outside private contractor, retained by the World Bank to provide food and beverage services to individuals in the organization's cafeteria on the organization's premises in Washington, D.C., has 'derivate' immunity from the District of Columbia's taxes on the contractor's sales of food and beverages. Focusing on the text of Art. VII, § 9(*a*) of the World Bank's Articles of Agreement ("the Bank, and its

The Tribunal did not apply to an international organization the distinction made in sovereign immunity law between acts *jure imperii* and acts *jure gestionis*.[674] Instead, the Tribunal relied exclusively on the criterion of 'official activity,' including a 'strictly necessary' test. Moreover, the Award made clear that the 'official activities' of an international organization, which the Tribunal found had to be interpreted restrictively, may exempt the organization from national laws where a similar activity, carried out by a sovereign State, would fall within the 'commercial activity' exception applicable to sovereign immunity. Finally, from the Award it may be concluded that the EMBL did not only enjoy the organizational immunities spelled out in the instruments governing the organization's legal position in Germany, but that *any* activity which could be held to come within the realm of 'official activities' would be entitled to immunity.

3.4.2 Determination of 'Official Activity': By Whom?

At this point the question remains to be addressed of who ultimately has the authority to determine whether or not a given activity of an organization can be classified as 'official activity.' This question is likely to arise with greatest frequency in the context of an international organization where an

operations and transactions authorized by this Agreement, shall be immune from all taxation and from all customs duties" and "shall also be immune from liability for the collection or payment of any tax or duty"), the court found that the immunity provision cannot be read to include within its scope activities conducted by any other entity. The court observed that the answer to the question whether the provision of food services is an "operation" of the World Bank, "depends not so much on how essential the [World] Bank believes the activity to be, but on the arrangements the [World] Bank has made to carry it out." An arrangement whereby a separate and independent entity has its own commercial objectives, including making a profit from its contract for the provision of food and beverages services with the international organization, falls outside the immunity provision in the organization's constituent instrument. The situation would be different if the international organization itself had operated its on-site food program. *See* 1999 UN Jurid. Y.B, p. 436, UN Doc. ST/LEG/SER.C/37 (1999).

674 According to Kunz-Hallstein, Privilegien, at 3072, this fact should take away any doubt that might still exist in practice as to the applicability to international organizations of the sovereign immunity distinction, having regard to the well-reasoned and authoritative Award. It should be noted, however, that the Award qualifies as a 'judicial decision,' which, under Art. 38 of the ICJ Statute, is only a *subsidiary* means for the determination of rules of law. In other words, it does not qualify as a direct source of international law, but may only be used *in evidence of* a rule of international law, *i.e.*, of the rules of law falling into one or other of heads (a)–(c) of Art. 38(1) of the ICJ Statute. *See also* J.I. Charney, *Universal International Law*, 87 AJIL 529 (1993).

explicit definition of the term 'official activity' is lacking in an applicable instrument and where a constitutional framework exists which describes the organization's functions and purposes in general terms only.

As Sir Elihu Lauterpacht has pointed out, "this is an area of uncertainty in which one must move with caution."[675] One can take several approaches to resolving this question.

First, one could adopt the view that this determination is the prerogative of *the international organization itself*, acting through its chief administrative officer, without accepting any outside interference. This could be based directly on the fundamental principle of the independence of the international organization as an autonomous international administrative body.[676] It could also be derived by analogy from the practices of international organizations. Accordingly, the United Nations enjoys the right to "freely determine the categories of their personnel whom they consider to be officials, solely within the limits of the relevant charters, constitutions and staff regulations and subject to control only by Member States as collectively represented in the various governing bodies."[677] Similarly, it is the recognized prerogative of the UN Secretary-General, as the organization's chief administrative officer, to determine not only the category of *officials*, but also the official *travel* of these officials. The United States, as the UN's host country, has recognized the Secretary-General's prerogative in this respect and the same is true for all the other UN member States.[678] Also, even in circumstances where the Secretary-General may be under a duty to waive the immunity of any official, Section 20 of the General Convention still reserves to the Secretary-General the discretion to decide when to

675 Lauterpacht, Development, at 428, referring to the decisions of international tribunals.

676 *See* IVRAKIS, at 422.

677 *Personnel Questions: Respect for the Privileges and Immunities of Officials of the United Nations and the Specialized Agencies and Related Organizations, Report of the Secretary General*, at 6, para. 19, UN Doc. A/C.5/44/11 (1989). The chief administrative officer of the UN referred to this independent right in a matter which occurred in 1988, when the Swiss tax authorities decided to apply a global-rate system to the taxable earnings of UN staff members stationed in Geneva and holding short-term contracts, thus taking into account the exempted income earned by such officials in determining the rate of tax on earnings derived from other sources. This decision by the Swiss authorities seemed to be based on the nonrecognition of this category of employees as staff members (officials) of organizations within the UN Family. *See also* 1990 UN Jurid. Y.B, p. 282, UN Doc. ST/LEG/SER.C/28 (1993).

678 *See* Tarassenko & Zacklin, at 12.

exercise this duty. The section provides that the Secretary-General is under a duty to waive immunity only in cases "where, *in his opinion*, the immunity would impede the course of justice and can be waived without prejudice to the interests of the United Nations." (emphasis added)[679] In addition to State practice, legal commentators support the view that the determination of these matters is the prerogative of the international organization.[680] They have based this prerogative on the principle of the independence of the organization[681] or on a general rule according to which institutions of individual States may not evaluate policy acts of international organizations.[682] It also could be inferred by necessary implication from the statement of the International Court of Justice in the *Certain Expenses of the United Nations* Case that "when the Organization takes action which warrants the assertion that it was appropriate for the fulfilment of one of the stated purposes of the United Nations, the presumption is that such action is not *ultra vires* the Organization."[683] Because the Court was clearly referring to an assertion by the organization itself, this statement also may be read to indicate that, when an organization takes action which warrants the assertion that it was appropriate for the fulfilment of its purposes, the presumption is that such activity was an *official* one because *necessary* for the fulfilment of these purposes.[684] One could add that, if the member

---

679 Provisions such as Section 20 of the General Convention have been explained to be the logical extreme of the functional theory. *See* D. Deener, *Some Problems of the Law of Diplomatic Immunity*, 50 AJIL 115, 119 (1956).

680 One authority on organizational immunities, Professor Ignaz Seidl-Hohenveldern, has stated in a private letter to this author that "[m]ost commentators including myself felt that the SG's certificate should be binding on domestic courts," and that it was therefore wrongly decided in the case of *Westchester County v. Ranallo*, 67 N.Y.S.2d 31 (City Ct. of New Rochelle 1946), 13 ILR 168, that a U.S. court was not bound by the certificate of the UN Secretary-General that his driver was on official business, when he got into an accident upon return to his home above the car's garage after having driven the Secretary-General to a reception. Letter from Ignaz Seidl-Hohenveldern to this author (3 Feb. 1993; on file with the author). *See also* Seidl-Hohenveldern, L'immunité, at 163–165; IVRAKIS, at 660–661; BEIER *et al.*, Art. 3, at 21; Zacklin, DUPUY, at 192 n.39.

681 *See* IVRAKIS, at 442, 596.

682 *See* SCHERMERS, at 1070, para. 1600; *see also* Pescatore, in 55 *Annuaire* 214, at 348 (1973).

683 1962 ICJ Rep. 151, 168.

684 *See also* Lauterpacht, Development, at 428–430, who, on the basis of an examination of international jurisprudence, in particular the ICJ's decision in *Effect of Awards*, 1954 ICJ Rep. 47, concludes that "the restraint demonstrated by the Court appears to accord

States of an organization are reluctant to leave the determination of what constitutes an 'official activity' to the organization, acting through its chief administrative officer or main organ, they will have no choice but to define its limits, in as great detail as possible, in the organization's basic instruments. In this regard, Kelsen has argued that, in the absence of an explicit definition of the term 'necessary' as used in Article 105, paragraphs 1–2, of the UN Charter, to be given in a convention pursuant to paragraph 3 of this article, "there is no possibility of imposing upon a Member [State] a definite interpretation of the provisions of Article 105, paragraphs 1 and 2."[685] States should be prevented from having a free hand to interpret unilaterally what is meant by 'necessary' or 'official' in a given case.

If the prerogative of the organization's chief *administrative* or executive organ is unacceptable to member States, the possibility of review by the organization's principal *judicial* organ or even of a special tribunal might be examined by way of an alternative.[686] Such a tribunal would conduct a marginal review of the reasonableness of the organization's decision, by interpreting the basic documents that apply. This practice would ensure that the internal power equilibrium of the organization is not disturbed. Within the United Nations Family, the adoption of definitions of the terms 'official activity' and 'necessary' in agreements and operative rules would result in bringing disputes about whether an activity was 'official,' because a necessary one in the exercise of the organization's functions, into the realm of 'disputes arising out of the interpretation or application' of such rules, and thus into the advisory jurisdiction of the ICJ as

---

with the idea that the Organization is the best judge of what circumstances require and to this extent, therefore, the Court's restraint is directed towards the more effective fulfilment of the objectives of the Organization."

685 KELSEN, at 342. According to Kelsen, a convention would be required instead of a recommendation by the General Assembly, because the latter is not binding. *See also id.*, at 346.

686 *See* Wengler's report on judicial redress against the decisions of international organs, in 47 *Annuaire*, Vol. I, at 5–28, especially at 15–17 (1957), and its discussion in *id.*, Vol. II, at 274–327. *See also* WELLENS, at 9 ("The inherent right of an international organisation unilaterally to qualify its activities is not unlimited, but is instead subject to independent review, which will constitute an important element in the implementation of their accountability") and 25 ("Although determining the purposes of an international organisation is primarily a task for the organisation itself, acting through and jointly with its member states, the remedial perspective emerges if and when an international organisation claims to be the sole judge of what acts are strictly necessary to achieve its purposes and this without external control becoming available").

provided for in, *inter alia*, Section 30 of Article VIII of the 1946 General Convention.[687]

Some writers have mentioned the element of arbitrariness that might be involved in an international organization assigning the 'official' stamp to its own activities.[688] However, one may add that there is nothing arbitrary in the organization adhering to a strict functional necessity rule defined and agreed upon *by the member States* and over which they maintain control.

Alternatively, one could argue, by way of another extreme, that the task of determining the official nature of an organizational activity should be the sole prerogative of *the courts of individual States* and that they should be left with a 'margin of appreciation' on a case-by-case basis. This conclusion could be derived from the absence of any explicit contrary rules in existing instruments. It also could be based, by way of analogy, on the *Asylum* case decided in 1950 by the International Court of Justice.[689] In this case, Colombia sought to grant diplomatic asylum to a Peruvian refugee in the Colombian embassy in Lima (Peru). Basing its claim partly on rules resulting from extradition and asylum agreements and partly on custom, Colombia maintained that, as the State conferring diplomatic asylum, it had a right to unilaterally and definitively determine whether the offence allegedly committed by the refugee qualified for asylum. But the Court stated that the principles of international law, referred to by one such agreement, do not recognize any rule of unilateral and definitive qualification by the State granting diplomatic asylum.[690] According to the Court, "[s]uch a derogation from territorial sovereignty cannot be recognized *unless its legal basis is established in each particular case*."(emphasis added)[691] It involves a competence of an exceptional character which is *not inherent* in the institution of diplomatic asylum, being "a derogation from the equal rights of qualification which, *in the absence of any contrary rule, must be*

---

687 For a general commentary on the judicial review power of the ICJ, see T. Franck, *The "Powers of Appreciation": "Who is the Ultimate Guardian of UN Legality?*, Editorial Comment, 86 AJIL 519 (1992); *see also* Dupuy, in 55 *Annuaire* 214, at 257 (1973); G.R. Watson, *Constitutionalism, Judicial Review, and the World Court*, 34 Harv. Int'l L.J. 1 (1993). For an argument in favor of *not* having the ICJ involved, see Monaco, at 169.

688 *See, e.g.*, Pellet, in [1991] 1 Y.B. Int'l L. Comm'n 178, para. 6, UN Doc. A/CN.4/SER.A/1991.

689 *See Colombian-Peruvian Asylum Case*, 1950 ICJ Rep. 266.

690 *Id.*, at 274.

691 *Id.*, at 275.

attributed to each of the States concerned; it thus aggravates the derogation from territorial sovereignty constituted by the exercise of asylum."(emphasis added)[692] Moreover, the Court was unable to find any constant and uniform usage, accepted as law, with regard to the alleged rule of unilateral and definitive qualification.[693] In other words, customary international law could not be said to support this right either.

When we apply the Court's statements to the issue of whether an organization can make a unilateral and definitive qualification of the nature of its activities, it must be pointed out that the Court in its conclusion relied heavily on the principle of the territorial sovereignty of States and the equal rights enjoyed by these particular subjects of international law. However, international organizations lack sovereignty and have no territory of their own. Because their rights can hardly be said to equal those enjoyed by sovereign States, international organizations need special protection. One element of protection should be the organization's right of unilateral qualification of its activities. This consideration applies also in case the organization has a direct dispute with a private individual instead of with a State, because it will still be the courts, as (independent) organs of States, which would be given the right to ultimately qualify organizational activities, thereby opening themselves up to (frivolous) suits against international organizations.

Contrary to what the International Court of Justice stated with regard to States in the *Asylum* Case, the absence of an explicit provision should not be interpreted to deny an organization's inherent right of unilateral qualification of its activities. The argument of the prevention of abuse does not weigh as heavily in the case of international organizations as it does in that of States, because the former remain under the collective control of the member States and internal mechanisms exist, particularly in the plenary organ of the organization, for member States that insist on a review, on their own initiative or on behalf of their citizens, of a certain practice of the

692 *Id.*, at 275. The Arbitration Tribunal in the EMBL Case seems to have adhered to this equal right of qualification, by holding that a decision by the EMBL as to the official nature of its activities could not be a binding arrangement, but merely an interpretation by *one* of the parties to the headquarters agreement. Since the other party to the agreement, Germany, opposed this unilateral interpretation by the EMBL, the Tribunal concluded that the interpretation was an open question and it arrogated to itself the final determination of it. *See* EMBL Award, at 45.

693 1950 ICJ Rep. 266, 277. The Court referred again to the absence of any relevant provisions in conventions and agreements cited by Colombia.

organization.[694] In the case of an asylum dispute between States, which formed the subject-matter of the *Asylum* Case, the situation is more black and white. These differences militate against an application, by way of analogy, of the Court's statements in the *Asylum* Case to the issue at hand, involving international organizations.

In light of its advisory opinion rendered in the *Cumaraswamy* Case in 1999,[695] it is uncertain whether the International Court of Justice would endorse an organization's inherent right of unilateral and *definitive* qualification of its activities. In that case, the ICJ did not endorse the UN Secretary-General's view that it is for him alone to decide, with conclusive effect on local courts asserting jurisdiction over a UN agent, whether a UN agent is entitled to jurisdictional immunity.[696] The ICJ held that the Secretary-General's immunity finding, together with its documentary expression communicated to the government of the territory in which the court sits, must be given the greatest weight by local courts and creates a presumption in favor of immunity which "can only be set aside [by local

---

694 Moreover, any possible abuse could be prevented through the dispute settlement procedures between international organizations and States parties to general conventions and headquarters agreements, discussed below. It is recalled that "[i]nternational organizations cannot be said to be supreme unto themselves, since their creation, existence, and preservation are subject, not only in fact but also under law, to the dispositions of their members ...." *See* Hahn, at 1049. Although the protective device meant here is, of course, not available to non-member States, these States may in practice assert their influence on the organization through their alliance with Members with which they maintain friendly relations.

695 *Difference Relating to Immunity from Legal Process of a Special Rapporteur of the Commission on Human Rights*, Advisory Opinion, 1999 ICJ Rep. 62.

696 The term 'agent of an international organization' has been defined broadly as meaning "an official or other person or entity, other than an organ, who is charged by the organization with carrying out, or helping to carry out, one of its functions, and thus through whom the organization acts." Art. 2, sub (d), of the 'Draft articles on the responsibility of international organizations.' adopted by the International Law Commission at its sixty-third session, and submitted to the UN General Assembly as part of the ILC's report covering the work of that session, UN Doc. A/66/10 (2011). This definition clearly was inspired by the ICJ's description of 'agent' in its advisory opinion rendered in the *Reparation* Case, 1949 ICJ Rep. 174, 177 ("The Court understands the word 'agent' in the most liberal sense, that is to say, any person who, whether a paid official or not, and whether permanently employed or not, has been charged by an organ of the Organization with carrying out, or helping to carry out, one of its functions—in short, any person through whom it acts"). *See also* R.S.J. Martha, The Financial Obligation in International Law 65–67 (2015).

courts] for the most compelling reasons."[697] Similarly, it could be said that the determination by the chief administrative officer of an international organization that a certain activity constitutes 'official activity' by reference to the functions and purposes of the organization must be given the greatest weight by local courts and creates a presumption in favor of considering an impugned activity as 'official,' which can only be set aside by local courts for the most compelling reasons.

We find it difficult to accept any conclusive role for the courts of individual (member) States, unless it is accepted that the interpretation given by the organization of its practice relating to the disputed nature of an activity can only be set aside by local courts for the most compelling reasons.[698] The courts of individual States could apply the organization's views to an individual case, but would lack competence to substitute their views for those of the international organization absent compelling reasons.[699] Any abuse by the organization of its unilateral position may be obviated by its good faith obligation to co-operate with individual (member) States, in addition to a mutual obligation of consultation.[700] These obligations are dictated by the functional necessity concept.

It follows from the above that, if the member States of an international organization wish to protect the organization against the possibility of judicial scrutiny or review regarding what the organization considers to be 'official activity' in a given case, the member States should consider including in the organization's basic (constituent) instrument or in a protocol on its privileges and immunities or other relevant instrument a provision along the following lines:

> The official activities of the organization shall, for the purposes of this Protocol/Convention, etc., be such as are strictly necessary for the [administrative/technical/etc.] operation of the organization in the exercise of its functions and the fulfilment of its purposes, such to be

---

697 *Difference Relating to Immunity from Legal Process of a Special Rapporteur of the Commission on Human Rights*, Advisory Opinion, 1999 ICJ Rep. 62, at 87, para. 61.

698 *See also* Seyersted, Personality, at 21: "... if the constitutionally competent organs have decided, under the procedure prescribed in the constitution, that the Organization shall perform a specific act in order to attain a purpose within the scope of its constitution, then a court cannot declare the act invalid because, in its view, the aim could have been attained without resorting to that act, or because it otherwise does not consider the act 'esssential' or 'necessary' for the attainment of that aim."

699 *But see* Monaco, at 169–170.

700 *See* SCHERMERS, at 1070, para. 1600.

> determined [ultimately and conclusively and in good faith by the organization itself, acting through its chief administrative officer [or other competent person or body]] / [in good faith by the organization itself, acting through its chief administrative officer [or other competent official or body], and this determination shall create a presumption in favor of considering an activity as official and can be set aside only for the most compelling reasons].

A basic provision of this kind should be supplemented by internal operative rules drawn up by the plenary organ of the organization, including administrative circulars, instructions, guidelines and regulations, which give further content to the 'official activity' formula.[701]

3.5 *Conclusion*

The previous paragraphs on the functional necessity concept established that this concept can be a useful tool for determining what kind of special protection an international organization requires and may demand. Its main advantage is that it provides a framework reflecting the true nature of the international organization, which may be used as a starting-point for the determination of both the *basis* and the *extent* of organizational immunities. The functional concept enables organizational immunities to be granted *when* the interests of the organization's functions and purposes so require and it sets the *limits* beyond which there is no need to grant or enjoy them, simultaneously establishing a close link with the organization's basic instruments, which contain elementary information on the precise functions and purposes of the organization concerned. This shows that the basis-element and the scope-element of the functional necessity concept are closely linked. As Sucharitkul has stated:

> The question of privileges and immunities, ..., was *founded* in the case of international organizations on functional necessity and was thus *limited* in scope by the purposes of the organization concerned.[702] (emphasis added)

701 Such practice would, *e.g.*, be within the purview of Article 105, paragraph 3, of the UN Charter, which envisages that further content could be given to the term "necessary" by the General Assembly. If the Assembly can do so by making recommendations or proposing conventions, it could also use the machinery of adopting internal operative rules that bind the organization.

702 Sucharitkul, in [1983] 1 Y.B. Int'l L. Comm'n 240, para. 20, UN Doc. A/CN.4/SER.A/1983; *see also id.*, in [1977] 1 Y.B. Int'l L. Comm'n 207, paras. 51–52, UN Doc. A/CN.4/SER.A/

In other words, using the functional necessity criterion as a yardstick for determining the extent of organizational immunities will result in immunities that are automatically qualified or limited by the functions and purposes of an organization. One must realize at the same time, however, that the functional concept might not in all cases be able to provide clear-cut answers. This observation applies, in particular, to Steps Two and Three of our analysis, for, as one author has stated, "it is easier to agree in general terms to relate privileges and immunities to functional need than to translate this into the precise details of a scale of appropriate privileges and immunities."[703]

By providing a stringent standard of 'official activity,' incorporating a 'strictly necessary' element, the functional necessity test has the advantage of contributing to the development of a general, 'all-organizational' formula for determining whether a certain activity is essential for the organization to perform its (core) functions, and, therefore, whether the organization is entitled to protection through immunity. A narrow interpretation or formulation of the 'official activity' formula can achieve the same restrictive results as the commercial activity concept of sovereign immunity law, while at the same time avoiding the controversies and puzzling ambiguities that may be caused by a confusion of two different kinds of immunity law, one concerned with sovereign States, the other with international organizations—two fundamentally different subjects of international law. By interpreting the organization's basic functions and purposes narrowly, the test could be made even more stringent. Moreover, there is the additional advantage that the functional necessity concept is practicable. It has very similar consequences whatever the nature and size of the international organization, thereby furnishing a criterion which is generally applicable, being constructive as well as critical. It would both accommodate the interests of private individuals having dealings or doing business with international organizations and the interests of international organizations in avoiding undue interference with their activities. The stringency of such a standard is enhanced by a clear definition of the organization's functions and purposes in its constituent instrument. Good examples which deserve to be followed are provided by Article 3, paragraph 4, of the Protocol on Privileges and Immunities of the European Patent Organization, Articles

---

1977. *See also* AMERASINGHE, at 316 ("Because the basis of such privileges and immunities is functional, organizations are and can expect to be accorded only those privileges and immunities which are necessary for that purpose").

703 SATOW'S GUIDE, at 376, para. 40.17.

7–9 of the EMBL Headquarters Agreement, discussed above, and Articles V(2) and VI of Annex I ('Privileges and Immunities') to the Convention for the establishment of a European Space Agency, as these provisions contain the terms 'strictly necessary' and refer explicitly to the organization's purposes as described in its constituent instrument. Use of the word 'strictly' emphasizes that an activity must relate closely to the statutory purposes and core functions of the organization concerned in order to qualify as 'official' and to come within the legitimate incidence of immunity.[704]

We subscribe to the conclusion formulated by an expert on this subject, according to whom:

> States should not take a restrictive view of the privileges and immunities to be accorded to international organizations which is reminiscent of the times when the grant of privileges and immunities to international organizations was considered as something exceptional and in the nature of a favour or concession. ... Since these privileges and immunities are granted as a result of the recognition of their international personality, States should not grant them in a grudging manner or otherwise subject them to undue national pressures. Various States of the world should banish doubts and misgivings from their minds that any extension in the privileges and immunities of such international organization would lead to their abuse.[705]

The part that follows will examine in greater detail the mechanisms and instruments designed to mitigate the risk of abuse of organizational immunities and methods of counterbalancing such immunities.

3.6 *Methods of Counterbalancing Organizational Immunities*

> "... it might perhaps be advisable to provide against the risk of abuses, since man was still an irrational being."[706]

3.6.1 Introduction

In the previous parts of this study the topic of organizational immunities was given consideration mainly from the perspective of the international organization. Although the organization must be regarded as the

704 *But see* BEIER *et al.*, Art. 3, at 21, where the use of a strict test is criticized.

705 AHLUWALIA, at 208.

706 Malek, in [1983] 1 Y.B. Int'l L. Comm'n 252, para. 36, UN Doc. A/CN.4/SER.A/1983.

main beneficiary of organizational immunities, other interests also are at stake. These other interests may be endangered or jeopardized due to the favorable legal position enjoyed by an international organization cloaked with immunity. Besides the organizations themselves there are two other identifiable groups which are directly interested in the legal position of international organizations:

(1) Third parties with whom international organizations interact: *private individuals* or *corporations*;
(2) The *States* in whose territory international organizations operate or with which they come in contact.

Private interests can be regarded as the most fragile in this regard. Here one is confronted with the dilemma of how to reconcile, on the one hand, the need for protection of, and access to justice by, the *individual* who may be disadvantaged due to the immunity from jurisdiction enjoyed by the organization with which he or she has interacted, and, on the other hand, the necessity of assuring independence to the *organization*, in order to keep it functioning smoothly, free from (undue) outside interference. Our main concern here is the innocent party who suffers loss without any expectation and through no fault of his or her own because of a wrongful or negligent act or omission of an international organization, and not loss caused by normal trading risks inherent in dealing or doing business with an organization.[707] To deprive individuals from all domestic legal remedies, which is the consequence of granting immunity from jurisdiction to an international organization, is regarded as the main argument against organizational immunities. In such cases the only option available to an individual would be to apply for protection by his or her State, which may put pressure on the organization concerned and exercise diplomatic protection or make a

707 *See* Non-Contractual Liability of the European Communities xi (H.G. Schermers, T. Heukels & Ph. Mead eds. 1988)[hereinafter: SCHERMERS, NON-CONTRACTUAL LIABILITY]. The liability which arises from such wrongful loss may be of a contractual or a non-contractual nature. On precedents concerning illegal acts of international organizations, see J. Salmon, *Les accords Spaak-U Thant du 20 février 1965*, 11 AFDI 468 (1965); I. Seidl-Hohenveldern, *Les organisations internationales et les actes illicites des fonctionnaires, in* Science et Action Administratives – Mélanges Georges Langrod 385 (1980); *id.*, Responsibility, at 416–417; E. Lauterpacht, *The Legal Effect of Illegal Acts of International Organizations, in* Cambridge Essays In International Law in Honour of Lord McNair 88 (1965); P. Guggenheim, *La validité et la nullité des actes juridiques internationaux*, 74 RdC 191 (1949 I). *See also Effect of Awards of Compensation Made by the United Nations Administrative Tribunal*, Advisory Opinion, 1954 ICJ Rep. 47.

formal complaint on behalf of its citizen.[708] The problems we see ourselves confronted with in this regard have been recognized by the international community, which has taken several initiatives to tackle them.[709] One of the main solutions has been found in the provision for modes of settlement of disputes in international agreements concerning the legal status, privileges and immunities of international organizations, which will be given specific consideration in this section of our study.

The issue of, or need for, balancing organizational immunity with access to justice is especially pressing in jurisdictions that are subject to the European Convention on Human Rights (ECHR),[710] Article 6, paragraph 1, of which provides, in pertinent part: "In the determination of his/her civil rights and obligations ..., everyone is entitled to a fair and public hearing within a reasonable time by an independent and impartial tribunal established by law."[711] According to the European Court of Human Rights, "Article

---

708 *See* Lalive, at 303.

709 *See, e.g.,* the work by the *Institut de Droit International,* in 47 *Annuaire,* Vol. I, at 274–327 (1951)(*Recours judiciaire à instituer contre les décisions d'organes internationales*).

710 Convention on the Protection of Human Rights and Fundamental Freedoms, signed at Rome, 4 Nov. 1950, 213 U.N.T.S. 2889, p. 221. [hereinafter: ECHR]. *See* M.E. Villiger, Handbook on the European Convention on Human Rights (2023), at 312–350. For most States parties to the ECHR, the ECHR incorporates directly applicable treaty obligations, while in some countries it also enjoys the status of domestic constitutional law (*e.g.,* Austria). In its judgment of 29 September 2022, the Austrian Constitutional Court (*Verfassungsgerichtshof*) declared unconstitutional parts of the headquarters agreement between Austria and OPEC that lacked provisions for the settlement of employment disputes through an independent mechanism, which it found to violate the employees' right to a fair trial enshrined in Article 6 of the ECHR. *X v. Organization of the Petroleum Exporting Countries,* No. SV 1/2021–23, judgment of 29 Sept. 2022. Austria's Constitutional Court ruled that the relevant provisions were no longer to be applied after 30 September 2024, and it imposed a timeframe of two years on the Government of Austria to negotiate an amendment to the Austria-OPEC headquarters agreement in compliance with the ruling. For a discussion of this ruling, see Note, *International Decisions,* 118(2) AJIL 331 (2024)(authored by Philipp Janig). See generally M. Kloth, Immunities and the Right of Access to Court under Article 6 of the European Convention on Human Rights (2010).

711 The International Covenant on Civil and Political Rights contains a similar provision in Article 14: "In the determination of any criminal charge against him, or of his rights and obligations in a suit at law, everyone shall be entitled to a fair and public hearing by a competent, independent and impartial tribunal established by law." International Covenant on Civil and Political Rights, opened for signature 16 Dec. 1966, entry into force 23 Mar. 1976, 999 U.N.T.S. 171 [hereinafter: ICCPR]. In its commentary to the ICCPR, the UN Human Rights Committee notes that a limitation on the right

6 § 1 secures to everyone the right to have any claim relating to his civil rights and obligations brought before a court or tribunal" and "[i]n this way the Article embodies the 'right to a court', of which the right of access, that is, the right to institute proceedings before courts in civil matters, constitutes one aspect only."[712] Acknowledging that "[m]easures taken by a High Contracting Party which reflect generally recognized rules of public international law on State immunity (the Court would add: or to an international organization) cannot in principle be regarded as imposing a disproportionate restriction on the right to access to a court as embodied in Article 6 § 1," the Court went on to state that "[j]ust as the right of access to a court is an inherent part of the fair trial guaranteed in that Article, so some restrictions on access must likewise be regarded as inherent."[713] The Court mentioned as examples of such restrictions "those limitations generally accepted by the community of nations as part of the doctrine of immunity from domestic jurisdiction, whether it concerns the immunity of a foreign sovereign State or that of an international organization …."[714]

The International Court of Justice has framed the issue as an aspect of the principle of equality of the parties, stating that this "principle must now be understood as including access on an equal basis to available appellate or similar remedies unless an exception can be justified on objective and reasonable grounds."[715]

In a ruling issued in a case involving two entities affiliated with the North Atlantic Treaty Organization (NATO) in 2021, the Supreme Court (*Hoge Raad*) of The Netherlands considered that granting immunity from jurisdiction to an international organization constitutes a limitation of a natural and legal person's right of access to judicial redress as meant in Article 6 of the ECHR, and that such a limitation cannot be reconciled with the right

---

expressed in Article 14 that is based on an immunity deriving from international law would not violate Article 14. *General Comment No. 32, Article 14: Right to Equality Before Courts and Tribunals and to a Fair Trial*, UN Doc. CCPR/C/GC/32, 23 Aug. 2007, at para. 18.

712 *See Stichting Mothers of Srebrenica et al. v. The Netherlands*, European Court of Human Rights, App. No. 65542/12, judgment of 11 June 2013, at para. 139.

713 *Id.*, at para. 139 sub (f).

714 *Id.* (case citations omitted).

715 *Judgment No. 2867 of the Administrative Tribunal of the International Labour Organization upon a complaint filed against the International Fund for Agricultural Development*, Advisory Opinion, 2012 ICJ Rep. 10, at 29, para. 44. The author served as counsel to IFAD in the ICJ proceeding.

guaranteed by Article 6 if it does not serve a legitimate purpose or is disproportionate to the purpose served by the limitation.[716] While acknowledging that the granting of privileges and immunities to international organizations has been held to serve a legitimate purpose in the jurisprudence of the European Court of Human Rights,[717] the Dutch Supreme Court observed that, in order to satisfy the proportionality requirement, it must be investigated by the competent court in a particular case whether the person seeking justice has access to reasonable alternative means of redressing the rights conferred by the ECHR.[718] If reasonable alternative means of redress are available, it may be assumed that the granting of organizational immunities does not affect the essence of a person's access to judicial redress and a fair hearing. While the existence of a financial reconciliation mechanism contained in the escrow agreement between the private claimant and one of the NATO-affiliated parties was found in principle to constitute a reasonable alternative means satisfying Article 6 of the ECHR, the Dutch Supreme Court left the door open for subsequent judicial review once the contractually agreed alternative means has taken its

716 *Supreme Site Services GmbH et al v. Supreme Headquarters Allied Powers Europe and Allied Joint Force Command Headquarters Brunssum*, Supreme Court (*Hoge Raad*) of The Netherlands, case no. 20/00937, judgment of 24 Dec. 2021, at para. 3.2.2. For an English case, *see Entico Corporation, Limited, Claimant, against the Secretary of State for Foreign and Commonwealth Affairs, Intervener, and the United Nations Educational, Scientific and Cultural Organization* (*UNESCO*), *Defendant*, High Court of London, judgment of 28 Mar. 2008, paras. 23–29, text repr. in 2008 UN Jurid. Y.B, pp. 477–489, UN. Doc. ST/LEG/SER.C/46 (2008).

717 *See Waite and Kennedy v. Germany*, ECHR, App. No. 26083/94, judgment of 18 Feb. 1999, para. 63 ("the Court finds that the rule of immunity, which the German courts applied to the [European Space Agency] in the present case, has a legitimate objective"); *Beer and Regan v. Germany*, ECHR, App. No. 28934/95, 18 Feb. 1999. These cases concerned staff disputes.

718 *Supreme Site Services GmbH et al v. Supreme Headquarters Allied Powers Europe and Allied Joint Force Command Headquarters Brunssum*, Supreme Court (*Hoge Raad*) of The Netherlands, case no. 20/00937, judgment of 24 Dec. 2021, at para. 3.2.3. *See also Waite and Kennedy v. Germany*, ECHR, Nr. 26083/94, judgment of 18 Feb. 1999, paras. 68 ("For the Court, a material factor in determining whether granting [the European Space Agency] immunity from German jurisdiction is permissible under the Convention is whether the applicants had available to them reasonable alternative means to protect effectively their rights under the Convention") and 72 ("the test of proportionality cannot be applied in such a way as to compel an international organisation to submit itself to national litigation in relation to employment conditions prescribed under national labor law").

course.[719] This arguably creates a tension with the essentially procedural nature of the law of immunity, as stated by the International Court of Justice in a ruling regarding jurisdictional immunities of States issued in 2012:

> Immunity from jurisdiction is an immunity not merely from being subjected to an adverse judgment but from being subjected to the trial process. It is, therefore, necessarily preliminary in nature. Consequently, a national court is required to determine whether or not a foreign State is entitled to immunity as a matter of international law before it can hear the merits of the case brought before it and before the facts have been established.[720]

---

719 *Supreme Site Services GmbH et al v. Supreme Headquarters Allied Powers Europe and Allied Joint Force Command Headquarters Brunssum*, Supreme Court (*Hoge Raad*) of The Netherlands, case no. 20/00937, judgment of 24 Dec. 2021, para. 3.3.2. *See also* [*Plaintiff*] *v. European Patent Organisation*, Supreme Court (*Hoge Raad*) of The Netherlands, case no. 08/00118, judgment of 23 Oct. 2009 (upholding the organization's immunity after finding that the former employee's availability of redress before the ILO Administrative Tribunal satisfied the balancing test under Article 6 of the ECHR); *European Patent Organisation v. Vakbondsunie van het Europees Octrooibureau* (*VEOB*) *and SUEPO* (*Staff Union of the European Patent Office*), Supreme Court (*Hoge Raad*) of The Netherlands, case no. 15/02186, judgment of 20 Jan. 2017, NJ 2017/235 (upholding organization's immunity in suit by trade and staff union after finding that the grant of immunity satisfied the proportionality test in this case); *European Patent Organisation* (*European Patent Office*) *v. Stichting Restaurant De la Tour*, Court of Appeal The Hague, case no. 200.065.887/01, judgment of 21 June 2011 (rejecting organization's immunity in a dispute arising from a tender for catering services after finding that no alternative dispute resolution mechanism was available to the private party and that denying the private party judicial access did not meet the proportionality test under Article 6 of the ECHR, but upholding the organization's immunity from execution shielding it from a judicially imposed fine or penalty for non-compliance with a judgment). In its judgment of 17 May 2024, concerning an employment dispute involving the embassy of the United Arab Emirates in The Hague, the Dutch Supreme Court observed that there exists no rule of customary international law prohibiting the imposition by a court of a fine to induce compliance with a judicial decision on a foreign State in a situation where immunity has been waived. *See United Arab Emirates v.* [*Employee*], case no. 23/01711, Supreme Court (*Hoge Raad*) of The Netherlands, judgment of 17 May 2024, NJ 2024/204, para. 3.2.2. Given that the Dutch Supreme Court refers in its judgment to the immunity of both States and international organizations, this statement can be said to apply to States and international organizations alike. *Id.*, paras. 3.12–3.1.3.

720 *Jurisdictional Immunities of the State* (*Germany v. Italy; Greece intervening*), Judgment, 2012 ICJ Rep. 99, at 136, para. 82.

It is difficult to imagine how the 'ultimate' judicial review reserved by the Dutch Supreme Court could take place without establishing certain facts, particularly the facts concerning the availability of a reasonable and adequate alternative means of redress in a given case.[721] Specifically, the International Court of Justice has stated with regard to the jurisdictional immunities of States that it "can find no basis in the State practice from which customary international law is derived that international law makes the entitlement of a State to immunity dependent upon the existence of effective alternative means of securing redress."[722] In the view of the ICJ, "the application of any such condition, if it indeed existed, would be exceptionally difficult in practice …."[723]

As regards the balancing exercise to be conducted by national courts facing State immunity questions, the ICJ has made the following observation:

> In so far as the argument based on the combined effect of the circumstances is to be understood as meaning that the national court should balance the different factors, assessing the respective weight,

---

721 As an English court has observed: "It would be wholly inimical to the international scheme envisaged [in the 1947 Specialized Agencies Convention] if individual States party arrogated to themselves the power to determine whether the provision made by each specialised agency for the settlement of disputes is adequate, whether considered generally or by reference to the facts of a particular case." *Entico Corporation, Limited, Claimant, against the Secretary of State for Foreign and Commonwealth Affairs, Intervener, and the United Nations Educational, Scientific and Cultural Organization (UNESCO), Defendant,* High Court of London, judgment of 28 Mar. 2008, at para. 17, text repr. in 2008 UN Jurid. Y.B, pp. 477–489, UN. Doc. ST/LEG/SER.C/46 (2008).

722 2012 ICJ Rep. 99, at 143, para. 101. In a case involving the immunity of the United Nations in relation to a peacekeeping mission falling under Chapter VII of the UN Charter, the Supreme Court of The Netherlands invoked this statement by the ICJ to justify exempting the United Nations from the "reasonable alternative means of redress" balancing test that Dutch courts apply to other international organizations, at least in a situation involving the exercise by the UN Security Council of its power to take such action as may be necessary to maintain or restore international peace and security. In this respect, the Dutch Supreme Court referred to Art. 103 of the UN Charter, which reads: "In the event of a conflict between the obligations of the Members of the United Nations under the present Charter and their obligations under any other international agreement, their obligations under the present Charter shall prevail." *Stichting Mothers of Srebrenica et al. v. State of The Netherlands and United Nations,* Supreme Court (*Hoge Raad*) of The Netherlands, case no. 10/04437, judgment of 13 Apr. 2012, NJ 2014/262, at para. 4.3.6.

723 *Jurisdictional Immunities of the State (Germany v. Italy; Greece intervening),* Judgment, 2012 ICJ Rep. 99, at 143, para. 102.

> on the one hand, of the various circumstances that might justify the exercise of its jurisdiction, and, on the other hand, of the interests attaching to the protection of immunity, such an approach would disregard the very nature of State immunity. As explained ... above, according to international law, State immunity, where it exists, is a right of the foreign States. In addition, ..., national courts have to determine questions of immunity at the outset of the proceedings, before consideration of the merits. *Immunity cannot, therefore, be made dependent upon the outcome of a balancing exercise of the specific circumstances of each case to be conducted by the national court before which immunity is claimed.*[724] (emphasis added)

It may be the case that the practice of the courts of European jurisdictions in giving effect to the jurisprudence of the European Court of Human Rights on this issue[725] points to a rule of regional customary international law, with a limited carve-out for the immunities of the United Nations, as evidenced in Dutch case law,[726] given the particular language of the General Convention (granting immunity "from every form of legal process") and because the special conflict/priority rule set forth in Article 103 of the UN

---

724 *Id.*, at 145, para. 106.

725 *See Stichting Mothers of Srebrenica et al. v. The Netherlands*, European Court of Human Rights, App. No. 65542/12, judgment of 11 June 2013, at para. 139. For examples of French court decisions, see *UNESCO v. Boulois*, Tribunal de grande instance de Paris, judgment of 20 Oct. 1997, Rev Arb 575 (1997); *Banque africaine de développement v. M.A. Degboe*, Cour de Cassation, Chambre sociale, judgment of 25 Jan. 2005, 04-41012, 132 *Journal du droit international* 1142 (2005).

726 *See*, e.g., *Stichting Mothers of Srebrenica et al. v. State of The Netherlands and United Nations*, Supreme Court (*Hoge Raad*) of The Netherlands, case no. 10/04437, judgment of 13 Apr. 2012, NJ 2014/262, at para. 4.3.3 (observing that there is no ground for assuming that the European Court of Human Rights in its reference to "international organizations" included the United Nations, at least not insofar as it concerns action taken under Chapter VII of the UN Charter). *See also Behrami and Behrami v. France*, European Court of Human Rights, App. No. 71412/01, judgment of 2 May 2007, and *Saramati v. France, Germany and Norway*, European Court of Human Rights, App. No. 78166/01, judgment of 2 May 2007, at para. 149 ("Since operations established by [UN Security Council] Resolutions under Chapter VII of the UN Charter are fundamental to the mission of the UN to secure international peace and security and since they rely for their effectiveness on support from member states, the [European] Convention [on Human Rights] cannot be interpreted in a manner which would subject the acts and omissions of Contracting Parties which are covered by [UN Security Council] Resolutions and occur prior to or in the course of such missions, to the scrutiny of the Court").

Charter applies to all UN Member States, including those States that are parties to the ECHR, at least in situations falling under Chapter VII of the UN Charter.

In sum, in line with the jurisprudence of the European Court of Human Rights, before Dutch courts will uphold the immunity of an international organization (with the exception of the United Nations in light of the text of the General Convention) in a case in which the private party is entitled to the guaranty enshrined in Article 6, paragraph 1, of the ECHR, they will require that: (1) the essence of the right derived from that treaty provision is not impaired; (2) the organizational immunity serves a legitimate objective, in the sense that it is an essential means of ensuring the proper functioning of the organization free from unilateral interference by individual governments; and (3) the limitation represented by the organization's immunity is proportionate for the purpose of Article 6, paragraph 1, of the ECHR, in the sense that reasonable alternative means of redress are available to the complainant for the effective protection of rights derived from the ECHR.[727] Courts in other jurisdictions have held that the absence of alternative means of dispute resolution is not, in and of itself, determinative of whether an international organization is entitled to immunity.[728]

What is emerging in the case law of national courts, with the exception of the United Nations (especially in connection with activity coming within

727 In its more recent case law, the European Court of Human Rights has considered the right under Article 6(1) of the ECHR also in conjunction with the right to an effective remedy guaranteed by Article 13 of the ECHR. *See*, e.g., *Kudła v. Poland*, App. No. 30210/96, judgment of 26 Oct. 2000. *See also* C. Ryngaert, *The Immunity of International Organizations Before Domestic Courts—Recent Trends*, 7 IOLR 121 (2010).

728 *See*, e.g., *Amaratunga v. Northwest Atlantic Fisheries Organization*, Supreme Court of Canada, judgment of 29 Nov. 2013, 2013 SCC 66, [2013] 3 SCR 866, para. 60 ("The absence of a dispute resolution mechanism or of an internal review process is not, in and of itself, determinative of whether [the Northwest Atlantic Fisheries Organization] is entitled to immunity" before the courts of Canada); *Georges v United Nations*, No. 15-455-cv, judgment of 18 Aug. 2016 (2d Cir. 2016)(dismissing plaintiffs' argument that the availability of alternative dispute settlement is a material condition to international organizations' entitlement to immunity before upholding UN immunity); *but see Gérald René Trempe v. ICAO Staff Association et al. and Gérald René Trempe v. Dirk Jan Goossen et al.*, High Court, Province of Quebec, District of Montreal, judgment of 20 Nov. 2003, at para. 61, English text reproduced in 2003 UN Jurid. Y.B 585, p. 597, UN Doc. ST/LEG/SER.C/41 (2003)(noting that "[t]he only exception [to organizational immunity] would be if an international organization were to be involved in a commercial activity and had not provided for modes of settling disputes in accordance with the provisions of article 33 of the [Canada-ICAO] Headquarters Agreement").

the scope of Chapter VII of the UN Charter), is a shift away from (virtually) absolute immunity granted to international organizations, either through some kind of balancing exercise, or 'margin of appreciation,' by national courts that takes into account the (human) right to access to judicial redress or protection guaranteed by applicable treaties, as evidenced by recent case law of European countries,[729] or by linking organizational immunities to the immunities enjoyed by States, including limitations to the latter immunities.[730] While these various approaches by local courts have given rise to a jurisprudence that is anything but uniform or universal, they have in common that they adopt a more qualified approach to the immunity of international organizations.

As Schermers has pointed out, "[i]f organizations are indifferent to this changing context and fail to 'update' themselves, it is more likely that national courts will do so by rejecting immunity claims."[731] If the existence of a (human) right to judicial redress is widely accepted and is deemed to form part of contemporary international law[732] and is applicable to

729 *See, e.g.*, L. Pasquet, *Litigating the Immunities of International Organizations in Europe: The 'Alternative-Remedy' Approach and its 'Humanizing' Function,* 36(2) Utrecht Journal of International and European Law 192–205 (2021); U.A. Weber and A Reinisch, *In the Shadow of Waite and Kennedy – The Jurisdictional Immunity of International Organizations, the Individual's Right of Access to the Courts and Administrative Tribunals as Alternative Means of Dispute Settlement,* 1(1) IOLR 59, 65–110 (2004); M. Singer, *Jurisdictional Immunity of International Organizations: Human Rights and Functional Necessity Concerns,* 36 Va. J. Int'l L. 53 (1995); E.C. Okeke, *The Tension between the Jurisdictional Immunity of International Organizations and the Right of Access to Court in* The Role of International Administrative Law at International Organizations (P. Quale ed. 2021). *See also* OAS Guide, Guideline 1, Rapporteur's Notes ("Although the meeting of the minds is the principal source of obligations, such agreement must always consider and be interpreted in harmony with other relevant legal aspects, such as human rights law"); Guideline 5, 'Means of dispute resolution' ("International organizations should provide means of dispute resolution in order to ensure access to justice for individuals who are parties to a dispute not covered bu jurisdictional immunity'); Guideline 6 ("Dispute resolution mechanisms established by international organizations to resolve private law disputes should be adequate and effective").

730 *See Jam v. International Finance Corp.*, 139 S. CT. 759 (2019).

731 SCHERMERS, at 1083, para. 1611A. According to Schermers, the changing context is underscored by the fact that "the number and nature of the activities of international organizations have changed significantly" and such activities "may cause damage or harm more often than previously," and "the current *Zeitgeist* is different from that of the immediate post-War era," which saw a wave of international organizations coming into being. *Id.*, at 1087, para. 1612A.

732 *See*, generally, S.Ø. Johansen, The Human Rights Accountability Mechanisms of International Organizations (2020); R. Gulati, Access to Justice and International Organisations—Coordinating Jurisdiction between the National and Institutional Legal Orders (2022); P. Schmitt, Access to Justice and International Organizations: The Case of

intergovernmental organizations as conventional or customary law, it is difficult to take the position that intergovernmental organizations, which are recognized subjects of international law, should be permitted to ignore or circumvent that right, especially in jurisdictions where the organization is located or operates and which are bound to observe the right to judicial redress based on an applicable treaty instrument.[733] However, the question of exactly which human rights obligations apply to a given intergovernmental organization (as opposed to its member States) is not settled,[734] and the means and modalities of reconciling, or balancing, the (human) right to access to justice and organizational immunity must be carefully assessed and determined, and appropriate distinctions must be made among international organizations in light of the principle of speciality, especially in the case of the United Nations given that organization's special powers under Chapter VII ('Action with respect to Threats to the Peace, Breaches of the

---

Individual Victims of Human Rights Violations (2017); C. Ferstman, International Organizations and the Fight for Accountability: The Remedies and Reparations Gap (2017); Access to Justice as a Human Right (F. Francioni ed. 2007). *See also* V. Shikhelman, *Access to Justice in the United Nations Human Rights Committee*, 39(3) MICH J. INT'L L. 453, 457 (2018)(noting that "[a]ccess to justice is not limited to access to official courts, but rather includes a variety of legal institutions such as quasi-judicial institutions, administrative bodies, arbitration, and even tribunal courts that apply local customary laws."). Shikhelman's broad definition of access to justice as meaning "the evaluation of the possibility of an individual to bring his case before an institution and receive a fair process and a just decision that can be implemented at the national level" does not fit most international organizations.

733 In situations where the international organization has declared itself to be bound by a treaty-based right to judicial redress, such a right is binding on the organization as conventional law. In other cases, the international organization may be bound by a corresponding right deriving from customary international law, unless it has consistently declared that it does not consider itself to be bound by a custom-based rule. In a case between a private party and an international organization in which the organization is alleged to be bound by a rule of customary international law, the private party has the burden of proving that such a rule exists and that the organization is bound by it.

734 For example, the 'Draft Articles on the Responsibility of International Organizations,' adopted by the International Law Commission in 2011, provide little or no support for extending to an international organization a human rights obligation of a member State which is not already binding on the international organization itself, the unlikely scenario of coercion by the organization being a possible exception. *See* Art. 16, Draft articles on the responsibility of international organizations. adopted by the International Law Commission at its sixty-third session, and submitted to the UN General Assembly as part of the ILC's report covering the work of that session, UN Doc. A/66/10 (2011).

Peace, and Acts of Aggression') in conjunction with Article 103 of the UN Charter. This issue will be addressed in further detail below.

As regards the interests of the *host State* within whose territory an international organization operates, it has been stressed by a variety of writers that great care should be taken to ensure a proper *balance* between the legitimate interests of the host States, for which jurisdiction and security needs are of crucial importance, and the interests of international organizations, which need privileges and immunities in order to be able to carry out their work efficiently and free from outside interference.[735] Schwebel has pointed out in this regard that such a balance should not only be struck for reasons of equity, but also in order to improve the popular image of international organizations, a matter which in his view should not be lightly discounted.[736] The ILC Draft on 'Relations between States and International Organizations' contains a separate provision, or 'escape' clause, acknowledging a State's security interests. It reads:

Article 17

> None of the provisions of this chapter shall affect the right of each State party (to this Convention) to adopt the necessary precautions and appropriate measures in the interest of its security.[737]

In sum, the privileges and immunities granted to international organizations cannot be regarded as some kind of 'one way ticket' or *carte blanche*; the enjoyment of such privileges and immunities, as of *right*, entails closely

735 *See, e.g., Waite and Kennedy v. Germany*, ECHR, Nr. 26083/94, judgment of 18 Feb. 1999, para. 63 ("the Court points out that the attribution of privileges and immunities to international organisations is an essential means of ensuring the proper functioning of such organisations free from unilateral interference by individual governments"); *Amaratunga v. Northwest Atlantic Fisheries Organization*, Supreme Court of Canada, judgment of 29 Nov. 2013, 2013 SCC 66, [2013] 3 SCR 866, para. 45 ("It bears repeating at this point that immunity is essential to the efficient functioning of international organizations. Without immunity, an international organization would be vulnerable to intrusions into its operations and agenda by the host state and that state's courts"). *See also* Schwebel, in [1977] 1 Y.B. Int'l L. Comm'n 210, para. 19, UN Doc. A/CN.4/ SER.A/1977; Tabibi, in *id.* at 205, para. 28, UN Doc. A/CN.4/SER.A/1977; Koroma, in [1983] 1 Y.B. Int'l L. Comm'n 244, para. 24, UN Doc. A/CN.4/SER.A/1983.

736 *Id.*

737 *See Report of the International Law Commission on the work of its forty-third session*, GAOR Supp. (No. 10) at 316, para. 293 and n.367, UN Doc. A/46/10 (1991).

related moral and legal obligations, or at least accountability, on the part of the organization.

As regards the *moral* obligations, a particular responsibility rests upon international organizations to avoid what Jenks has called "the development of a psychology of privilege."[738] This statement may be interpreted to mean that the enjoyment of certain privileges and immunities by international organizations must always be in accordance with a *genuine* need, i.e., out of a functional requirement, justifying a particular claim for privileges and immunities by the organization concerned, as opposed to blanket protection. Another writer has defined this moral obligation as including a duty on the part of the organization not to "present itself to the populations of its constituent States as something alien, privileged and ceremonious …."[739]

International organizations are under a *legal* obligation as well, the contents of which have been described by Jenks as follows:

> … the beneficiaries of [organizational] immunities, and in particular all those who have any responsibility for the administration of such immunities, have a corresponding obligation, more exacting because it is the counterpart of these immunities, to ensure that the highest standards of good faith are consistently maintained in the exercise and administration of immunities, to guarantee by adequate safeguards that immunities are used only for the functional purposes which they are intended to serve, and to avoid and prevent any form of abuse.[740]

The limits hence are set by the general legal principle of *good faith*, which indeed is "the indispensable foundation of the whole system of international immunities."[741]

---

738 Jenks, at 151. *See also* the final sentences of the Judgments of 27 April 1988 by the English Court of Appeal (Civil Division) in *Maclaine Watson & Co. Ltd. v. Department of Trade and Industry and related appeals; Re International Tin Council; Maclaine Watson & Co. Ltd. v. International Tin Council; Maclaine Watson & Co. Ltd. v. International Tin Council (No. 2)*, Court of Appeal (Civil Division), 27 April 1988, [1989] 1 Ch. 72, 253, 286, 309, [1988] 3 All E.R. 257, [1988] 3 W.L.R. 1033, 1159, 1169, 1190.

739 McKinnon Wood, at 162. According to Eagleton, "responsibility in international law derives historically from the moral sense of obligation recognized by mankind everywhere; it is a necessary principle of social cooperation, and as such has become embodied in all legal systems." C. Eagleton, *International Organization and the Law of Responsibility,* 76 RdC 319, 323 (1950 I).

740 Jenks, at 169–170.

741 *Id.*, at 170. *See Legality of the Threat or Use of Nuclear Weapons*, Advisory Opinion, 1996 ICJ Rep. 226, at para. 102 ("One of the basic principles governing the creation and performance of legal obligations, whatever their source, is the principle of good faith"

In accordance with the obligation of good faith, international organizations in principle are bound to respect the domestic laws of the host State. There appears to be a striking misunderstanding in the views of many populations that an international organization, being the holder of immunities, is above domestic law. On the contrary, "[i]t should be clearly borne in mind that an international organization is immune only from local *jurisdiction* and not local *laws* and is therefore expected to observe those laws." (emphasis added)[742] As stated above, immunity from jurisdiction does not free an international organization from any obligation, so that the *laws* remain applicable; immunity from legal process prevents, however, their *adjudication* in domestic courts and "may frustrate the enforcement of the law."[743] Moreover, the International Court of Justice has pointed out that "the question of immunity from legal process is distinct from the issue of compensation for any damages incurred as a result of acts performed by the United Nations or by its agents acting in their official capacity."[744]

Given the above-mentioned observations, one may conclude with Schermers that:

> Normally, an organization, like a natural person, is liable if its own acts cause injury to others. The existence of immunity for international organizations before national courts (...) does not affect the existence of liability. Immunity is used to prevent international organizations

---

(citing *Nuclear Tests (Australia v. France)*, Judgment, 1974 ICJ Rep. 268, para. 46)). *See*, generally, Bin Cheng, General Principles of Law As Applied by International Courts and Tribunals (repr. 2006).

742 Ahluwalia, at 66; *see also* Kunz, at 838; Lalive, at 302–303; Henderson, at 491; Kelsen, at 339; Jenks, at 42; Sucharitkul, in (1977] 1 Y.B. Int'l L. Comm'n 207, paras. 51–52, UN Doc. A/CN.4/SER.A/1977.

743 *See* Schermers, at 1084, para. 1612; Restatement (Third), § 467, Comment (c), at 495. As subjects of international law, intergovernmental organizations also are bound by the sources of international law. *See* Wellens, at 1; Schermers, at 865–867, paras. 1335–1339, and 1036–1049, paras. 1572–1581; K. Daugirdas, *How and Why International Law Binds International Organizations*, 57 Harv. Int'l L.J. 325 (2016); J. Klabbers, *The Sources of International Organizations' Law: Reflections on Accountability* in The Oxford Handbook of the Sources of International Law 987–1006 (S. Besson & J. d'Aspremont eds. 2017); A. Reinisch, *The Sources of International Organizations' Law: Why Custom and General Principles are Crucial*, in The Oxford Handbook of the Sources of International Law 1007–1024 (S. Besson & J. d'Aspremont eds. 2017).

744 *Difference Relating to Immunity from Legal Process of a Special Rapporteur of the Commission on Human Rights*, Advisory Opinion, 1999 ICJ Rep. 62, at 88, para. 66.

> from being subject to an outside judiciary: it does not affect the rights and obligations of the organization.[745]

There is a danger that organizational immunities may create a legal vacuum, in which States or private individuals are denied a forum for the enforcement of legitimate claims against an international organization, a form of denial of (access to) justice.[746] To fill this vacuum, means must be devised by which the liability or responsibility,[747] or at least the accountability, of an international organization may be established and enforced, creating a legal solution that bears justice upon individuals or groups to whom the organization has caused loss or damage through acts or omissions attributable to the organization.[748]

Certain exceptions and safeguards should, therefore, be provided to protect the legitimate interests of third persons, and, to a lesser degree, of States.[749] These requirements have been met by immunity agreements, which provide for specific procedures concerning the settlement of disputes of a varying nature, as well as other instruments and mechanisms agreed and developed over the past decades. In the subsequent paragraphs we will provide an overview of some major instruments containing such procedures, thereby distinguishing between the special settlement of disputes procedures regarding alleged *abuses* of privileges and immunities, and more *general* procedures for the settlement of disputes with staff and third parties.[750]

---

745 SCHERMERS, at 1050, para. 1583; *see also id.*, *Liability of International Organizations*, 1 LJIL 3, 14 (1988)[hereinafter: Schermers, Liability]. According to Bowett, "(t)he existence of immunities from the jurisdiction of municipal courts should never be allowed to obscure the fact that the organization remains responsible for the consequences of its actions." BOWETT, at 363.

746 Reference may be made here to Council of Europe Report 1969, at 25, para. 39, where the sub-committee observed, by way of example, that persons entitled to succeed to a deceased person's estate might be prejudiced by legacies or gifts to international organizations if any disputes arising in this connection could be withdrawn from the normal jurisdiction of the national courts.

747 Notice incidentally that the objective *existence* of such liability or responsibility is not affected by whatever immunity, although immunity may work to prevent this liability or responsibility from being established in a (local) court of law, thereby blocking its local judicial enforcement.

748 *See also* Tomuschat, in [1990] 1 Y.B. Int'l L. Comm'n 203, para. 22, UN Doc. A/CN.4/SER.A/1990.

749 *See* Council of Europe Report 1969, at 23, para. 32.

750 Notice incidentally that, as WEISSBERG, at 69, has pointed out, "provisions for the settlement of dispute furnish considerable additional proof of the international legal

3.6.2 Settlement of Disputes Concerning Alleged Abuse of Immunities

3.6.2.1 *Introduction*

The Council of Europe Report of 1969, to which reference was made in an earlier part of this book, states that:

> ... every international organisation ... in general should take all appropriate steps available to it to promote the interests of justice. In particular, since privileges and immunities are accorded to an international organisation only in the interests of the organisation, it is incumbent on its representative organs and secretariat in co-operation with the authorities of the host state to ensure that there is no abuse.[751]

The more recent OAS Guide also addresses abuse in a separate guideline as follows:

> International organizations and their staff members have a duty to co-operate at all times with the receiving State to facilitate the proper administration of justice, guarantee the observance of the domestic legal system and *prevent the occurrence of any abuse* in the enjoyment of immunities, exemption, and privileges.[752] (emphasis added)

Before entering into a more detailed examination of some major international agreements, the meaning and extent of the word 'abuse' within the scope of the present study must be addressed. In order for settlement procedures to be applicable, there must at least be a general indication that there might have been abuse on the part of (agents of) the organization, although the final determination whether any such abuse has occurred in a particular case is, of course, one of the main purposes of these procedures.

Since, as we shall see, relatively little use appears to have been made of any of the procedures under present review, no definition of the word can be deduced from existing agreements, jurisprudence or practice. Legal doctrine does not provide much help either, with the exception of Hug.[753]

---

personality of an entity such as the United Nations, this time from the point of view of its procedural capacity."

751 Council of Europe Report 1969, at 21, para. 26.

752 OAS Guide, Guideline 7, 'Observance of the domestic legal system.'

753 HUG, at 155 *et seq.* IVRAKIS, at 654, presents a rather ideological view by arguing that "the privileges and immunities, guaranteed by international instruments, do not present discernible loopholes for possible abuse by the United Nations. *The notion of 'abuse' seems to be out of place here* since the privileges and immunities of the United

Following Hug's suggestions, 'abuse' may within the scope of the topic under present consideration be defined as follows: the false use of privileges and immunities by an international organization, which does not correspond to the original purposes for which they were granted to the organization concerned. We admit that this working definition is of a rather general kind and is, therefore, somewhat vague, but this is mainly because any attempt at defining the term must give sufficient credit to considerations of practicability. According to the aforementioned definition, such activities as the organization's intervention in matters which are essentially within the domestic jurisdiction of the host State,[754] and the operation or stimulation of activities which endanger the security interests of States, clearly do not correspond to the purposes for which immunities are granted to international organizations, and must be classified as being abusive, and, consequently, as lying outside the protective realm of immunity.[755]

The origin in international instruments of provisions regarding alleged abuses of privileges and immunities and embodying the obligation of international organizations to provide means of redress by appropriate international procedures as the counterpart of organizational immunities, can be traced to an 1945 ILO Memorandum referred to in a previous part of the present study,[756] which contained a draft clause, proposing, *inter alia*, as follows:

> 18(1). The International Labour Organisation shall co-operate at all times with the appropriate authorities of the Members of the Organization to facilitate the proper administration of justice, secure the execution of police regulations, and prevent the occurrence of any abuse in connection with the immunities and facilities provided for in this resolution.

The first major instrument containing a reference to abuse of organizational immunities, influenced by the above draft clause, was the *Convention on the*

Nations exist strictly and solely to facilitate the exercise of its administrative functions and the fulfilment of its beneficial, world-wide purposes. They could not be twisted to serve other and perhaps obscure ends since the very reason of their existence and the range of their legitimate applicability are clearly defined and, further, the work of the Organization is carried on in the open for everyone to see."(emphasis added).

754 *See* UN Charter, Art. 2, para. 7.

755 For more examples see HUG, at 156.

756 *International Labour Office, Official Bulletin,* 10 Dec. 1945, Vol. XXVII, No. 2; *see also* JENKS, at 42.

Privileges and Immunities of the United Nations of 1946. Section 21 of this Convention provides as follows:

> The United Nations shall co-operate at all times with the appropriate authorities of Members to facilitate the proper administration of justice, secure the observance of police regulations and prevent the occurrence of any abuse in connection with the privileges, immunities and facilities mentioned in this Article.

Although there is a clear resemblance between the two provisions, it must be noted with Jenks[757] that the scope of Section 21 is narrower than the ILO proposal, as Section 21 is part of Article V dealing only with the privileges and immunities of *officials*. Strictly speaking, the General Convention does, therefore, not contain any explicit provision concerned with the settlement of disputes regarding alleged abuses by the United Nations Organization as such. This does not necessarily mean that the United Nations is not bound on other grounds to settle disputes of this kind.[758] As one commentator has pointed out, "[i]t is possible that the assertion [by an international organization] of privilege or claim to immunity in the case of [an] abuse amounts to, and may be characterized as, an *abus de droit* and, therefore, be a violation of international law"[759] triggering the international responsibility of the organization concerned in the event the violation is attributable to the organization.

The 1947 Specialized Agencies Convention, on the other hand, after addressing in Section 23 the issue of abuse by officials in identical language as Section 21 of the General Convention, contains a separate section dealing explicitly with the issue of abuse by the specialized agencies themselves. Section 24 of the Specialized Agencies Convention provides as follows:

> If any State party to this Convention considers that there has been an abuse of a privilege or immunity conferred by this Convention, consultations shall be held between that State and the specialized agency concerned to determine whether any such abuse has occurred and, if so, to attempt to ensure that no repetition occurs. If such consultations fail to achieve a result satisfactory to the State and the specialized

757 JENKS, at 43.

758 *See, e.g.*, the moral obligation as well as the binding legal principle of good faith referenced above; JENKS, at 169–170.

759 AMERASINGHE, at 351.

> agency concerned, the question whether an abuse of a privilege or immunity has occurred shall be submitted to the International Court of Justice in accordance with section 32. If the International Court of Justice finds that such an abuse has occurred, the State party to this Convention affected by such abuse shall have the right, after notification to the specialized agency in question, to withhold from the specialized agency concerned the benefits of the privilege or immunity so abused.

This rather extensive provision calls for a closer examination, since it incorporates several conditions and restrictions, which might not be altogether apparent on first reading.

Section 24 can be divided into three different phases. The *first phase* consists solely of *consultations* between the State party to the Specialized Agencies Convention and the specialized agency concerned in order to determine whether that agency has abused a privilege or immunity. The purpose of these consultations is twofold: (a) determining whether an abuse has taken place; and (b), if (a) has been answered in the affirmative, to try and prevent repetition of such abuse.[760] Failing the success of such consultations, *phase two* comes into operation and the question is referred to the International Court of Justice for an advisory opinion in accordance with Section 32 of the Specialized Agencies Convention. Should the International Court of Justice find that the alleged abuse did occur, then *phase three* provides the State concerned with a right to withhold from the specialized agency concerned the benefits of the privilege or immunity so abused.

In order for a State to be entitled to withhold privileges and immunities under the Specialized Agencies Convention, the following, necessary and cumulative conditions must, therefore, be satisfied:

(1) consultations between the State and the specialized agency concerned must have failed;

(2) until the International Court of Justice has ruled in its favor, no State party to the Specialized Agencies Convention is entitled to take immediate unilateral action in response to an alleged abuse;

(3) a favorable ruling by the Court creates a right to *withhold* only, not a right of denunciation;

(4) the State may withhold only the *particular* privilege or immunity that was found to have been abused, not the whole scale of privileges and immunities, no matter how strongly related to the abused privilege or immunity;

760 *See* Lalive, at 343; Council of Europe Report 1969, at 21, para. 27.

(5) only the incidental *benefits* of the privilege or immunity abused are subject to withholding; the privilege or immunity as such does *not* become void;[761] and

(6) any right to withhold the benefits of a privilege or immunity is subject to *due notification* by the State to the specialized agency in question.

The conditions and restrictions just referred to call for a further comment.

With regard to the extent of any withholding of privileges or immunities, Section 24 does not specify whether the privilege or immunity in question may be withheld for some particular period of time or indefinitely. It is most difficult to assess the precise time required in order for the organization concerned to be entitled again to the benefits of a particular privilege or immunity being legitimately withheld. This will be subject to negotiations between the international organization and the State concerned, so as to solve any questions concerning the proper use of a particular privilege or immunity, to clarify views on such use, and to come to an understanding in order to restore the original situation and prevent any further abuse. Both parties, i.e., the 'abused' State and the 'abusive' organization, are under an obligation to come to terms with each other, this obligation to be based on the purposes behind the granting of privileges and immunities to international organizations and the general principle of good faith.[762] Accordingly, the period of time during which the State is entitled to withhold any privilege or immunity would be such as is reasonably required to conduct negotiations between this State and the organization concerned to come to terms with each other. This, of course, may differ according to the nature of the abused privilege or immunity in question and the extent of such abuse. In any event, the authorities of a State should inform the organization concerned without delay of any action taken by it in derogation of the privileges and immunities of the organization and, if the circumstances so permit, should first consult with the organization with a view to taking any steps which might be agreed to protect the wider interests of the organization.[763]

From this passage one may conclude that a State has an obligation to consult with the organization *under any circumstances*, i.e., both prior to a favorable judicial ruling as well as after it has legally withheld any privilege or immunity. It seems generally accepted that a privilege or immunity cannot be withheld indefinitely. With Ahluwalia we agree that "[t]he grant of a legal right to a State to withhold indefinitely a privilege or immunity abused

761 *See* Chen, at 904.

762 *See also* AMERASINGHE, at 348.

763 *See* Council of Europe Report 1969, at 21, para. 27, and 28, para. 46.

by a specialized agency [for which we may substitute any international organization] would greatly weaken its juridical régime."[764]

As regards the role of the International Court of Justice, Section 24 refers only to an advisory opinion which "shall" be requested by the specialized agency concerned. The specialized agency, as the only party to the dispute with standing to request an advisory opinion, is, therefore, under a legal obligation to submit the question whether an abuse of a privilege or immunity has occurred to the Court, whose opinion shall be accepted as decisive by the parties.[765] Unless it is agreed upon by the parties to have recourse to another mode of settlement, a State is bound to follow this course of action. The State cannot have recourse to the contentious jurisdiction of the Court, since only two or more States, not international organizations, may be parties to such cases.[766] Consequently, a somewhat peculiar situation arises, to the effect that the claimant, i.e., the State against which the specialized agency concerned has allegedly abused a privilege or immunity, cannot itself ask the Court to pronounce on any such abuse. In view of the technical impossibility just referred to, in combination with the explicit acceptance of the opinion of the Court as decisive in Section 32, reference to which is made in Section 24, the provision under review must, however, be deemed to be satisfactory from a legal point of view.

Although Section 24 of the Specialized Agencies Convention only refers to disputes between a State party to the Convention and a specialized agency, this provision is of use to private individuals and corporate entities as well, since these groups may request the State of which they are citizens, or, as regards corporate entities, under the laws of which they are incorporated and in whose territory they have their registered office,[767] to take up their case against the specialized agency by way of diplomatic protection. However, since the State retains in this respect a discretionary power, it must be viewed as the sole judge to decide whether it will assume a representative role, to what extent it grants diplomatic protection, and when it will cease.[768] In any event, the State can only assert its influence with the specialized agency concerned; it cannot institute proceedings against the agency before the ICJ.

---

764 AHLUWALIA, at 102.

765 *See* Specialized Agencies Convention, S. 32.

766 *See* ICJ Statute, Art. 34, para. 1.

767 *See Barcelona Traction, Light and Power Company, Limited* (*Belgium v. Spain*), Second Phase, Judgment, 1970 ICJ Rep. 3, 42, para. 70.

768 *Id.*, at 44, para. 79.

According to Jennings,[769] the sanction of withholding a privilege or immunity may be disproportionate to the abuse committed. What should the International Court of Justice do once it has to give its opinion on an act by the organization which constitutes an abuse from a technical point of view, but which does not cause serious harm? Should the Court merely ascertain the occurrence of such abuse or should it also examine the extent of it and determine whether the abuse is a sufficient justification for the sanction? The second option would seem to be more harmonious with the seriousness of the matter under present consideration. The uncertainty to which Jennings refers may be addressed by including the elements of 'false intention' (malice) and 'serious damage' in a future definition of the term 'abuse.' It must, however, be added that whatever definition of the term will be adopted, it would necessarily have to remain somewhat vague in order to cover a wide variety of situations. This may be seen as an inherent disadvantage of any such definition, which renders questionable the whole issue whether anything would be served by introducing a definition of the term 'abuse.'

3.6.2.2 *Abuse Procedures: A Classification*

Ahluwalia, presenting a review of existing provisions concerning abuse contained in the legal instruments of a number of international organizations, suggests a threefold classification of the present legal régime concerning the abuse of privileges and immunities by international organizations.[770]

The first category consists of international organizations whose instruments contain somewhat vague provisions, requiring mere 'co-operation' with the competent authorities of the host country in order to prevent abuse of privileges and immunities provided under the respective instruments. Examples of this kind are Article 22 of the ILO Headquarters Agreement, Article 21 of the WMO Headquarters Agreement, Article 26 of the UNESCO Headquarters Agreement, Article 2 of the *General Agreement on privileges and immunities of the Council of Europe*, Article 11 of the OAS Multilateral Agreement, and Article 20 of the *Protocol on Privileges and Immunities of the European Patent Organization.*[771]

The second category is formed by a group of international organizations whose agreements go a step further and prescribe the procedure to be

769 R.Y. Jennings, *Some Aspects of the International Law of the Air*, 75 RdC 509, 579 (1949 II).

770 *See* AHLUWALIA, at 101–103; Dominicé, L'immunité, at 180–182.

771 For a commentary on the latter provision, see BEIER *et al.*, Art. 20, at 66–68. For more examples see, *e.g.*, HUG, at 91 n.472 and at 155 n.746; JENKS, at 43–44.

followed in the event of an alleged complaint by the government of the host country that an abuse of a privilege or immunity has occurred. Article 33(a)–(b) of the FAO Headquarters Agreement and Section 48(a)–(b) of the IAEA Headquarters Agreement fall under this heading.

The final category is characterized by rather far-reaching provisions, including 'withholding,' 'withdrawal,' 'limiting' or 'conditioning' of a particular privilege or immunity allegedly abused by the organization concerned. Examples of this kind are Section 24 of the Specialized Agencies Convention, Section 28 of the ICAO Headquarters Agreement with Canada,[772] and Section 1 of Title 1 of U.S. Public Law 291.[773]

3.6.3 General Settlement of Disputes Procedures

3.6.3.1 *Introduction*

As Jenks has pointed out, "[o]ne major factor which must be taken into account in considering how far the present system of international immunity may be open to abusive application is the extent to which provision has been made for legal process in determining any difference of opinion on the subject between States and international organisations."[774] By this passage the link between general settlement of disputes and alleged abuse procedures, dealt with in the preceding section, is established. The main objection against the grant of immunity to international organizations – denying natural and legal persons their legitimate remedies and denying their right to (access to) justice – has been addressed by the provisions contained in the legal instruments of most organizations. These instruments stipulate that the organizations should provide for appropriate modes of settlement of disputes arising out of a variety of reasons, thereby providing States and private parties with a remedy for their grievances.[775] In this way both the

772 96 U.N.T.S. 155, at 174.

773 Under the latter Act (IOIA), the President of the United States may revoke the designation of an international organization that is considered to be abusing its immunity. *See* P.C. Szasz, *The United Nations Legislates to Limit its Liability,* 81 AJIL 739, 740 n. 1 (1987)[hereinafter: Szasz, Liability]. For a critical comment see EGGER, at 150, who argues that the Presidential powers involved violate the fundamental requirements of the principle *ne impediatur officia,* which is the basis of Article 105 UN Charter to which the U.S. is a party. Moreover, according to Egger these powers create a position of dependence of the organization concerned toward the host State, which he finds unacceptable.

774 JENKS, at 21.

775 *See also* AHLUWALIA, at 200. The purpose of such dispute settlement procedures is to remove what is generally recognized as the serious injustice to private parties which arises when a sovereign State, as Sir Hersch Lauterpacht put it, "screens itself behind

interests of host States, for which, as we have seen, special protection against abuses is provided, and those of private parties are served. Since the latter group is dependent upon the State concerned in the matter of the applicability of abuse procedures, it will particularly benefit from the procedures that we will discuss in this part of our review.

The evolving law regarding the settlement of disputes to which international organizations are parties must be viewed in the context of parallel developments, including the rise in the number of international organizations and hence the potential sources of conflict, the establishment of internal appeals or justice mechanisms within international organizations, the shift away from assistance by governments to the provision of products and services by commercial parties (including in support of UN peacekeeping missions), and the progression of the rule of law, including notions of procedural fairness/due process and of international human rights law, particularly the right to access to justice or courts as guaranteed in a variety of international instruments.[776] The choice of method of dispute settlement will vary depending not only on the nature of the parties involved but also the nature and complexity of the dispute to be settled.

In the past decades, increasing interest has been shown in the development, by way of a counterpart to the privileges and immunities of international organizations, of procedures of judicial and non-judicial redress against acts or omissions[777] of international bodies which cause injury to (host) States or private parties.[778] International instruments on a broad scale now endeavor to mitigate the injurious effects of immunity in several ways, of which *waiver* and *arbitration* are the most important. In the following paragraphs we will highlight some of the major instruments providing for these forms of dispute settlement. We do not pretend to provide a

the shield of immunity in order to defeat a legitimate claim." *See* H. Lauterpacht, *The Problem of Jurisdictional Immunities of Foreign States*, 28 BYBIL 220, 235 (1951). The same reasoning applies to the case of international organizations.

776 *E.g.*, Art. 6 ECHR; Art. 8, American Convention on Human Rights, signed at San José, 22 Nov. 1960, 1144 U.N.T.S. 17955, p. 123. *See also* Pierre Schmitt, Access to Justice and International Organizations: The Case of Individual Victims of Human Rights Violations (2017); Y. Kryvoi, *Procedural Fairness as a Precondition for Immunity of International Organizations*, 13(1) IOLR 255 (2016).

777 *See, e.g.*, J. Klabbers, *Reflections on Role Responsibility: The Responsibility of International Organizations for Failing to Act*, 8 EJIL 1133–1161 (2017). *See also Georges v. United Nations*, No. 15-455-cv, judgment of 18 Aug. 2016 (2d Cir. 2016); *Kling et al. v. World Health Organization*, 532 F.Supp. 3d 141 (S.D.N.Y. 2021).

778 *See*, generally, AMERASINGHE, at 479–511.

detailed or exhaustive analysis of the existing conventional texts in this matter, but will offer a general guide instead.

3.6.3.2 *Waiver of Immunity*

While an organization may waive its immunities, it is in principle under no strict legal duty to do so; the decision is usually left to the discretion of the organization concerned, with certain exceptions.[779] However, an international organization should feel compelled to waive its immunities in situations where the immunity is not strictly necessary for the exercise of the organization's functions in the fulfilment of its purposes[780] and serves the administration of justice.

Waiver of immunity from jurisdiction results in the ability to appear in court in the same manner as all other persons.[781] Waiver can, therefore, be seen as a useful means of counterbalancing the legitimate interests of local life with the exemption from local jurisdiction, which is the logical consequence of the granting of privileges and immunities to international organizations.[782] It has been noted that "[t]he waiver of immunity is a remedy available to organizations to prevent immunity from impeding justice in certain cases" and that "waiver maintains the functional nature of the

779 Section 20 of the General Convention, covering officials of the United Nations, provides as follows: "(...). The Secretary-General shall have the right and *the duty* to waive the immunity of any official in any case where, in his opinion, the immunity would impede the course of justice and can be waived without prejudice to the interests of the United Nations. ...."(emphasis added) Similar wording is used in Section 23 of the General Convention, covering experts on mission. A similar provision covering officials of UN specialized agencies is included in Section 22 of the Specialized Agencies Convention. An obligation to waive immunity is also included in Article 17 of the Protocol on the Privileges and Immunities of the European Union ("Each institution shall be required to waive the immunity accorded to an official or other servant wherever that institution considers that the waiver of such immunity is not contrary to the interests of the Union"). *See* Protocol on the Privileges and Immunities of the European Union, Official Journal of the European Union, 16.12.2004, C 310/261 (2004). Note that this provision concerns the "officials and other servants of the [European] Union" and not the EU itself. *See also* Restatement (Third), § 467, Reporters' Note 7, at 502; BEIER *et al.*, Art. 3, at 24, para. 24.

780 *See also* Pellet, in [1991] 1 Y.B. Int'l L. Comm'n 178, para. 4, UN Doc. A/CN.4/SER.A/ 1991.

781 *See* SCHERMERS, at 1084, para. 1612.

782 *See, e.g.*, OAS Guide, Guideline 10, 'Waiver of jurisdictional immunity' ("International organizations should consider the waiver of their jurisdictional immunity or that of their employees a corollary to their obligation to cooperate with the competent authorities of Member States"). *See also* Kunz, at 839.

immunities" of international organizations.[783] The great majority of international instruments provide that waiver must be *express*[784] and *in a particular case* and that no such waiver shall extend to any measure of *execution*, which means that a ruling against the organization cannot be enforced without its voluntary co-operation.[785]

As regards the requirement that any waiver must be 'in a particular case,' the Office of Legal Affairs of the United Nations Secretariat stated in an internal Memorandum of 1948 with reference to Section 2 of the General Convention, which provides for waiver of immunity, that "it was not the intention of the Preparatory Commission, or of the General Assembly, to extend the right of waiver to waiver in future by the terms of a contract."[786] It is not the policy of the United Nations to enter into agreements, either with private contractors, other international organizations, or

783 OAS Guide, Guideline 10, 'Waiver of jurisdictional immunity,' Rapporteur's Notes.

784 *See also id.* ("a waiver of jurisdictional immunity must be express" and "merely appearing in court does not amount to a waiver if the organization has asserted immunity, unless it puts on a defense with respect to the merits of the case"). For examples of international instruments containing clauses on waiver see HUG, at 85 n.443; the requirement of an express waiver means, *inter alia,* that such waiver cannot be implied by reason of a litigation initiated by the organization, *i.e.,* in case the organization is the plaintiff. *See* JENKS, at 39; AHLUWALIA, at 200; SCHERMERS, at 1085, para. 1602; Zacklin, DUPUY, at 185; Dominicé, L'immunité, at 183; Farrugia, at 513; BEIER *et al.,* Art.8, at 11; *id.,* Art. 3, at 21–22 and nn.22–23; Restatement (Third), § 467, Comment (e), at 495. *But see* AMERASINGHE, at 349 (positing that "an international organization (like a sovereign state) can, expressly or impliedly by its conduct, waive a relevant immunity").

785 *See* OAS Guide, Guideline 10, 'Waiver of jurisdictional immunity' ("waiver of jurisdictional immunity does not include *ipso facto* the waiver of immunity from enforcement"); FOX-WEBB, at 583; Zacklin, DUPUY, at 185. For arbitral awards rendered against intergovernmental organizations and in favor of private parties, this means in the United States (or at least in the District of Columbia Circuit) that "absent waiver, the [organization's] immunity entitles it to ignore an arbitration award against it," unless the underlying contract containing the arbitration agreement includes the words "judgment may be entered upon any award in any court having jurisdiction thereof" or similar wording (so-called entry-of-judgment clause). *See Sacks v. International Monetary Fund,* 26 F.4th 470, 474 (D.C. Cir. 2022). *See also* International Law Commission, Memorandum by the Secretariat, Questionnaire—Replies received from international organizations and entities, at 134, UN Doc. A/CN.4/764 (2024)(reply by the UN Office of Legal Affairs: "In isolated and exceptional cases, immunity has been waived [by the United Nations] for purposes of pursuing enforcement of arbitral awards").

786 *See* [1967] 2 Y.B. Int'l L. Comm'n 225, UN Doc. A/CN.4/SER.A/1967/Add.1. A contrary situation exists within the IMF. *See* IMF Articles of Agreement, An. IX, S. 3, providing for waiver "by the terms of any contract."

with governments of (member) States, whereby it agrees in advance to waive its immunity if specified events occur.[787]

Unless the agreement provides differently, the authority to waive the immunity of an organization is vested normally in the secretary-general or the director(-general) of the organization concerned.[788] In the United Nations, this authority is vested exclusively in the Secretary-General, even though his authority to assert immunity is not settled by the actual terms of the General Convention.[789] In its advisory opinion rendered in the *Cumaraswamy* Case in 1999,[790] the International Court of Justice ruled, in a case where the Special Rapporteur on the Independence of Judges and Lawyers of the UN Commission on Human Rights was facing several lawsuits instituted against him before Malaysian courts, that national governments should immediately notify their competent local courts of any immunity finding by the UN Secretary-General in relation to a local case involving a UN official or expert on mission and that his finding, together with its documentary expression, must be given the greatest weight by local courts and creates a presumption in favor of immunity.[791] In the Court's view, the presumption "can only be set aside for the most compelling reasons."[792] While the ICJ found that in the specific circumstances of the case the UN Special Rapporteur was entitled to immunity under Section 22 (*b*) of the General Convention, as asserted by the UN Secretary-General, and that the Government of Malaysia had the obligation to inform the Malaysian courts of the Secretary-General's assertion of immunity,[793] the ICJ did not endorse the Secretary-General's

787 *See* [1967] 2 Y.B. Int'l L. Comm'n 226, para. 85, UN Doc. A/CN.4/SER.A/1967/Add. 1. For the technical issue of anticipated waiver, *i.e.*, waiver of immunity by the terms of any contract, as opposed to waiver in face of a court, *i.e.*, for the purposes of any legal proceedings, see Dominicé, L'immunité, at 183; HUG, at 85–86.

788 For more detailed information on this issue, see HUG, at 86 n.446; Dominicé, L'immunité, at 183.

789 *See* A.J. Miller, *The Privileges and Immunities of the United Nations*, 6 IOLR 7, 88–95 (2009); Zacklin, DUPUY, at 185; SCHERMERS, at 1085, para. 1612.

790 *Difference Relating to Immunity from Legal Process of a Special Rapporteur of the Commission on Human Rights*, Advisory Opinion, 1999 ICJ Rep. 62.

791 *Id.*, at 87, paras. 60–61.

792 *Id.*, at 87, para. 61.

793 *Id.* The ICJ also found that the Malaysian courts had the obligation to deal with the immunity question as a preliminary issue, and that the UN Special Rapporteur, a national of Malaysia, must be held financially harmless for the costs imposed upon him by the Malaysian courts. The Court also held that the Government of Malaysia was obligated to communicate the Advisory Opinion to the Malaysian courts in order that

view that it is for him alone to decide, with conclusive effect on local courts, whether a United Nations agent is entitled to immunity.[794] Hence, the ICJ left the door open for local courts to disagree with the Secretary-General's assertion of immunity in a given case.[795] The ICJ did not indicate what might be covered under "the most compelling reasons" and it left other relevant questions unaddressed in its ruling.[796]

Moreover, an international organization's secretary-general or director(-general) sometimes is designated in an international agreement as the official who may give the organization's express consent to service of legal process upon the organization, without which the organization cannot be made subject to the jurisdiction of local courts.[797]

In some jurisdictions, the immunities of an intergovernmental organization are subject to a statutory limitation in addition to (express) waiver by the international organization itself.[798] For example, in the United States of

---

Malaysia's international obligations be given effect and the Special Rapporteur's immunity be respected. *Id.*, at 90, para. 67.

794 *See also* FOX-WEBB, at 583 (observing that "an international or national court is unlikely to treat it as conclusive evidence").

795 The Court confirmed that "[t]he Secretary-General, as the chief administrative officer of the Organization, has the authority and the responsibility to exercise the necessary protection where required." 1999 ICJ Rep. 62, at 84, para. 50. In recognition of the fact that the UN "Secretary-General, as the chief administrative officer of the Organization, has the primary responsibility to safeguard the interests of the Organization," the Court explained that "the Secretary-General has the authority and responsibility to inform the Government of a member State of his finding and, where appropriate, to request it to act accordingly and, in particular, to request it to bring this finding to the knowledge of the local courts if acts of an agent [of the Organization] have given or may give rise to court proceedings." *Id.*, at 87, para. 60.

796 *See* P.H.F. Bekker, World Court Decisions at the Turn of the Millennium (1997–2001) (2002), 145–173.

797 *See, e.g.*, Headquarters Agreement between the Republic of Austria and the Organization of the Petroleum Exporting Countries, Article 5(2) of which provides that service of legal process upon OPEC "shall not take place within the headquarters seat except with the express consent of and under the conditions approved by the [OPEC] Secretary General;" *Prewitt Enterprises, Inc. v. OPEC*, 224 F.R.D. 497 (N.D. Ala. 2002)(dismissing lawsuit by an Alabama corporation accusing OPEC of price-fixing agreements on production and export of crude oil in violation of U.S. antitrust laws based on insufficiency of service of process under U.S. law due to the refusal of the OPEC Secretary-General to give his express consent to the service of process by the American plaintiff at OPEC's headquarters in Austria), *aff'd* 353 F.3d 916 (11th Cir. 2003).

798 In determining whether an international organization has waived its immunity, U.S. courts (or at least those seated within the District of Columbia Circuit) ask "whether the particular type of suit would *further* the [organization]'s objectives."

America organizational immunity is subject to specific limitation by the U.S. President acting under the International Organizations Immunities Act, having the effect of withdrawing or curtailing the immunity of an intergovernmental organization falling within the scope of the IOIA.[799] Following the U.S. Supreme Court's 2019 ruling that "the Foreign Sovereign Immunities Act governs the immunity of international organizations,"[800] it remains to be seen how the U.S. President's authority to 'withhold,' to 'withdraw,' to 'condition,' or to 'limit' immunity under the IOIA is affected, because the ruling would seem to give rise to dual-branch review involving both the U.S. President (the Executive Branch) and the U.S. courts (the Judicial Branch). In practice, this would mean that the U.S. President no longer has the ultimate authority to decide whether and to what extent eligible international organizations receive immunity in the United States. If the FSIA, including its restrictions, "governs" the immunity of international organizations, one wonders what areas of immunity are left for the U.S. President to withhold, withdraw, condition or limit. The result of the *Jam* ruling is that

---

Dujardin v. International Bank for Reconstruction and Development, 9 F.App'x 19 (D.C. Cir. 2001)(citing *Atkinson v. Inter-American Dev. Bank*, 156 F.3d, 1335, 1338 (D.C. Cir. 1998). If it does not further the organization's objectives, the organization's immunity should be construed as not waived. *Id.* In contrast, Canada's Supreme Court has rejected this criterion, stating that "the rationale underlying the 'benefits/burden exception' has no bearing in the context of international organization immunity" and "simply has no relevance in this context." *World Bank Group v. Wallace*, Supreme Court of Canada, judgment of 29 Apr. 2016, 2016 SCC 15, at para. 98, text *repr. in* 2016 UN Jurid. Y.B, pp. 430–451, UN Doc. ST/LEG/SER.C/54 (2016).

799 *See* 22 U.S.C. § 288: "The President shall be authorized, *in light of the functions performed by any such international organization*, by appropriate Executive order to withhold or withdraw from any such organization or its officers or employees any of the privileges, exemptions, and immunities provided for in this title (including the amendments made by this title) or to condition or limit the enjoyment by an such organization or its officers or employees of any such privilege, exemption, or immunity" (emphasis added). The words in italics indicate that the U.S. Congress designed the IOIA to ensure *functional* immunity of designated international organizations and entrusted the U.S. President with broad power to withhold or withdraw organizational immunities "in light of" an organization's functions. *See also Dujardin v. International Bank for Reconstruction and Development*, 9 F.App'x 19 (D.C. Cir. 2001); *Mendaro v. The World Bank*, 717 F.2d 610, 613–14 (D.C. Cir. 1983). The IOIA extends statutory immunity only to international organizations "which have been designated by the President through appropriate Executive order as being entitled to enjoy" immunity under that statute. *See* 22 U.S.C. § 288 (setting forth a definition of "international organization" for the purpose of the statute).

800 *Jam v. International Finance Corp.*, 139 S. CT. 759, 772 (2019).

the immunity enjoyed by international organizations in the United States is now governed by two statutory sources, namely, the IOIA and the FSIA. This risks creating interpretative problems. For example, the commercial activity exception enshrined in the FSIA is premised on the distinction between the sovereign acts of States and their private acts, a distinction that is meaningless in the case of international organizations lacking sovereignty. Moreover, the FSIA allows States to waive their immunity "either explicitly or by implication,"[801] whereas international organizations may only waive immunity "expressly" under the IOIA,[802] thereby creating an open conflict. While the FSIA stipulates that its provisions are "[s]ubject to existing international agreements to which the United States is a party at the time of enactment of this Act [i.e., 21 October 1976],"[803] this provision does not alleviate the potential for conflict with subsequent agreements or with U.S. obligations under customary international law. If the FSIA "governs" organizational immunity under the IOIA, the latter would violate any non-self-executing treaties concluded by the United States after 21 October 1976 that provide different immunities for international organizations compared to the FSIA and which are not accompanied by implementing legislation.[804] In a situation where the immunity of an international organization is denied by a U.S. court, the U.S. President lacks authority under the IOIA to "restore" that organization's immunity so as to shield it from a judicial finding of liability.

Practice demonstrates that international organizations have recourse to the instrument of waiver, and that national courts find a waiver by an international organization, in exceptional cases only.[805] With Dominicé it hence may be concluded as follows:

> La renonciation à l'immunité de juridiction ... apparait comme une bonne solution en matière contractuelle, dans le cas de certaines organisations et à l'égard de certains types de contrats. Il nous paraît cependant que c'est relativement exceptionnel, car cela suppose tout de même la réunion de plusieurs conditions: contrat gouverné par le

801 28 U.S.C. § 1605(a)(1).
802 22 U.S.C § 288a(b).
803 28 U.S.C. § 1604.
804 *See, e.g.*, *Medellín v. Texas*, 552 U.S. 491, 504–505 (2008).
805 *See, e.g.*, *Lutcher S.A. Celulose E Papel v. Inter-Am. Dev. Bank*, 382 F.2d 454 (D.C. Cir. 1967); *Osseiran v. International Finance Corp.*, 552 F.3d 836 (D.C. Cir. 2009); *OSS Nokalva, Inc. v. Eur. Space Agency*, civil action no. 08-3169 (MLC) (D.N.J. 4 Aug. 2009), *aff'd* on other grounds, 617 F.3d 756 (3d Cir. 2010).

droit local et exécuté au siège, organisation judiciaire satisfaisante et offrant toute garantie d'impartialité, de rapidité aussi.[806]

3.6.3.3 *International Judicial Settlement; Arbitration*

3.6.3.3.1 Introduction

If the organization is unwilling to waive its immunity and if it has no competent judiciary of its own,[807] recourse will have to be had to some other method of settlement. In this regard disputes can be distinguished according to the nature of the interests involved. A first distinction can be drawn between disputes with staffs, as opposed to disputes with third parties (States and private parties, and possibly other international organizations).

The decision of the International Law Commission to include the topic of settlement of disputes to which international organizations are parties in its current program of work at its seventy-third session in 2022 is a welcome development in this context.[808]

3.6.3.3.2 Settlement of Disputes with Staffs

Most international organizations have their own systems of administration of justice for the settlement of any disputes which may arise in the relations between them and their staff.[809] Employment-related disputes may

806 Dominicé, L'immunité, at 217 and 198.

807 This is the exception rather than the rule. Within the European Union, the Court of Justice, seated at Luxembourg, is the competent organ to hear cases in which the EU is in any way involved.

808 *See Report of the International Law Commission on the work of its seventy-third session*, GAOR, seventy-seventh session, Supp. No. 10, UN Doc. A/77/10, at para. 238.

809 For a more elaborate discussion of this category, *see*. e.g., P. Rossi, International Law Immunities and Employment Claims: A Critical Appraisal (2021); FOX-WEBB, at 460–465; A. Plantey, The International Civil Service – Law and Management 382 *et seq.* (P. Underwood & T. Cook Radmore trans. 1981); C.F. Amerasinghe, The Law of the International Civil Service (As Applied by International Administrative Tribunals) (1988)[hereinafter: AMERASINGHE, CIVIL SERVICE]; I. Seidl-Hohenveldern, *Jurisdiction over Employment Disputes in International Organizations, in* Colleccion de Estudios Juridicos en Homenaje al Prof.Dr.D. José Perez Montero 359 (Vol. III, 1988); *Recent Developments, International Organizations – Immunity – Personnel Decisions of an International Organization are not 'Commercial Activities' and thus May Not Form the Basis for an Action Against the Organization,* 20 Va. J. Int'l L. 913 (1980)(authored by K.R. Lee); M.L. Nash, *Contemporary Practice of the United States Relating to International Law (Privileges and Immunities – World Bank)*, 74 AJIL 917 (1980); *Recent Developments, International Organizations: Immunity – Broadbent v. Organization of American States,* 21 Harv. Int'l L.J. 552 (1980)(authored by M. Gordon); Note,

concern the alleged unfair or wrongful termination of employment or remuneration issues, as well as issues of work-floor discrimination or harassment.[810] As the International Court of Justice has stated with regard to the United Nations:

> It was inevitable that there would be disputes between the Organization and staff members as to their rights and duties. The Charter contains no provision which authorizes any of the principal organs of the United Nations to adjudicate upon these disputes, and Article 105 secures for the United Nations jurisdictional immunities in national courts. It would, in the opinion of the Court, hardly be consistent with the expressed aim of the Charter to promote freedom and justice for individuals and with the constant preoccupation of the United Nations Organization to promote this aim that it should afford no judicial or

Restricting the Immunity of International Organizations in Labor Disputes: Reforming an Obsolete Shibboleth, 25 Va. J. Int'l L 1007 (1985) (authored by J.C. Griffith); R.J. Oparil, *Immunity of International Organizations in U.S. Courts: Absolute or Restrictive?,* 24 VANDERBILT J. TRANSNAT'L L. 689 (1991); Farrugia; Dominicé, L'immunité, at 184–192, and 216; Seidl-Hohenveldern, Eurocontrol; A. Bleckmann, Internationale Beamtenstreitigkeiten vor nationalen Gerichten (1981); A. Reinisch, International Organizations Before National Courts (2000); D. Sarooshi, Remedies and Responsibility for the Actions of International Organizations (2014); K. Wellens, Remedies against International Organisations (2002); Challenging Acts of International Organizations Before National Courts (A. Reinisch ed. 2010).

810 *See* 'Administration of Justice in the Organizations of the United Nations Common System: Grievance, Disciplinary and Appeals Procedures,' UN Doc. ICSC/29/R.8 (1988). According to the information contained in footnote 2 at page 45 of this report, 86 cases which occurred between 1928 and 1985 in 21 countries are listed in "Lawsuits against international organizations: Cases in national courts involving staff and employment," World Bank Legal Dep't, 1 July 1985. For a comprehensive analysis of disputes involving non-staff personnel, including individual contractors and consultants, for the United Nations system, see the 2017 UN Secretary-General's Report on the administration of justice at the United Nations, UN Doc. A/72/204, annex II. As is pointed out in the OAS Guide, "[a] gap … in the UN and OAS agreements on privileges and immunities is that the availability of dispute resolution remedies is limited to staff members who enjoy immunity, and does not cover employees who have been hired under the national laws of the country in which they are serving" and "there are multiple differences between the remedies available to local staff and officials, even when both categories commonly perform similar duties." OAS Guide, Guideline 5, 'Means of dispute resolution,' Rapporteur's Notes.

> arbitral remedy to its own staff for the settlement of any disputes which may arise between it and them.[811]

To settle disputes with their officials and experts, a number of international organizations have established administrative tribunals,[812] which have developed a separate and independent body of international administrative law. The jurisdiction of these tribunals has often been extended to the staffs of several other organizations.[813] The ILO Memorandum of 1945[814] already referred to this class of disputes, by stating as follows:

811 *Effect of Awards of Compensation made by the United Nations Administrative Tribunal*, Advisory Opinion, 1954 ICJ Rep. 47, 57. In a more recent advisory opinion, the ICJ observed that "a contract of employment entered into between an individual and an international organization is a source of rights and duties for the parties to it" and that "staff regulations and rules of the organization in question 'constitute the legal basis on which the interpretation of the contract must rest'," *Judgment No. 2867 of the Administrative Tribunal of the International Labour Organization upon a complaint filed against the International Fund for Agricultural Development*, Advisory Opinion, 2012 ICJ Rep. 10, at 41, para. 76 (citing *Judgments of the Administrative Tribunal of the ILO upon Complaints Made against UNESCO*, Advisory Opinion, 1956 ICJ Rep. 77, at 94).

812 The most important examples are the United Nations Administrative Tribunal (UNAT), which was replaced with the UN Dispute Tribunal (UNDT) and the UN Appeals Tribunal (UNAT) as part of the new United Nations Internal Justice System with effect from 1 July 2009, the Administrative Tribunal of the International Labour Organization (ILOAT) and the Administrative Tribunal of the International Bank for Reconstruction and Development. *See also* O. Elias and M. Thomas, *Administrative Tribunals of International Organizations in* The Rules, Practice, and Jurisprudence of International Courts and Tribunals (C. Giorgetti ed. 2012); A. Reinisch, *The Immunity of International Organizations and the Jurisdiction of Their Administrative Tribunals*, 7(2) Chinese Journal of International Law 285 (2008); SCHERMERS, at 485–491; AMERASINGHLE, CIVIL SERVICE, at 49 *et seq.* On other remedial options available to employees of international organizations, see Farrugia, at 520–524; AMERASINGHE, CIVIL SERVICE, at 29 *et seq.*

813 The jurisdiction of the UNAT, for example, extends over all personnel of the United Nations and that of certain other organizations within the UN Family. The jurisdiction of the ILOAT even extends beyond the UN Family. The jurisdiction of the Administrative Tribunal of the Council of Europe (ATCE), which replaced the Appeals Board in 1994, extends to the Central Commission for the Navigation of the Rhine, the Hague Conference on Private International Law and the Intergovernmental Organization for International Carriage by Rail, in addition to being competent to hear complaints of serving and former staff members of the Council of Europe and its Development Bank against their employer. The new Statute of the ATCE entered into force on 1 January 2023. *See* the website of the ATCE, https://www.coe.int/en/web/tribunal/home. *See also* H.G. Schermers, *International Organizations, Legal Remedies Against Acts of Organs, in* [Installment] 5 Encyclopedia of Public International Law 146 (1983); G. Vandersanden, *Administrative Tribunals, Boards and Commissions in International*

> The International Labour Organisation shall make provision for the determination by an appropriate international tribunal of:
>
> ...
>
> (c) disputes concerning the terms of appointment of members of the staff and their rights under the applicable staff and pension regulations.

Moreover, the Memorandum pointed out in an explanatory note:

> There are ... well grounded objections to the permanent exemption of substantial numbers of international officials from any jurisdictional control of their official acts and from any such control of their private affairs except in so far as their immunities are waived by their official superiors. It would therefore seem necessary to organise an international jurisdictional control over the official acts of international civil servants and any of their private affairs in respect of which the jurisdiction of an international authority may seem preferable to a waiver of immunity in favour of the jurisdiction of one State.[815]

The extension of the jurisdiction of the ILO Administrative Tribunal to staff members of an international organization having a housing arrangement with another organization confronted the International Court of Justice with challenging procedural equality issues in a special advisory proceeding involving the Global Mechanism of the United Nations Convention to Combat Desertification in Those Countries Experiencing Serious Drought and/or Desertification, Particularly in Africa, initiated by the International Fund for Agricultural Development in 2010.[816] In that case, IFAD sought review of a judgment of the ILO Administrative Tribunal, the jurisdiction of which IFAD has accepted, rendered in favor of a staff member performing work for the Global Mechanism, an organization hosted by IFAD at its headquarters in

---

Organizations, in 1 [Installment] Encyclopedia of Public International Law 1 (providing further references)(1981).

814 *See International Labour Office, Official Bulletin,* 10 Dec. 1945, Vol. XXVII, No. 2. For an early precedent, see McKinnon Wood, at 148.

815 *Id., quoted in* JENKS, at 42.

816 *Judgment No. 2867 of the Administrative Tribunal of the International Labour Organization upon a complaint filed against the International Fund for Agricultural Development,* Advisory Opinion, 2012 ICJ Rep. 10. The present author served as counsel to IFAD in the ICJ proceeding.

Rome. The ILO Administrative Tribunal had attributed a decision not to renew the fixed-term employment contract of a Global Mechanism staff member to IFAD, the Global Mechanism's housing body, in light of the housing arrangement between IFAD and the Global Mechanism and applicable employment documentation. The ICJ considered that the principle of the equality of the parties "must now be understood as including access on an equal basis to available appellate or similar remedies unless an exception can be justified on objective and reasonable grounds."[817] Acknowledging that it is not in a position to reform the existing system of challenges against administrative tribunal decisions, the ICJ sought to ensure equality in the proceedings before it by ordering the IFAD President to transmit to the Court any statement setting forth the views of the staff member which she might wish to bring to the attention of the Court and it fixed the same time-limits for her as for IFAD for the filing of written statements in the first round of written pleadings and comments in the second round of the written phase of the proceedings. The ICJ also decided to dispense with oral proceedings in this case in light of the fact that individuals have no standing before the Court under its Statute.[818] The procedural adjustments applied by the ICJ in the *Global Mechanism* Case, which the Court justified as being "required by its inherent judicial character and by the good administration of justice,"[819] likely will have a chilling effect on the review mechanism and the Court's observations and the outcome of this case will need to be taken into account in future inter-organization housing arrangements.

Within the United Nations, internal dispute settlement is governed by the *Staff Regulations and Staff Rules* and administrative issuances.[820] The UN General Convention does not deal with the settlement of disputes with staff but only with disputes in which the act of any UN official is

817 *Id.*, at 29, para. 44.

818 *Id.*, at 30, para. 45.

819 *Id.*, at 30, para. 47. The ICJ placed on record its "concern about the inequality of access to the Court arising from the review procedure under Article XII of the Annex to the Statute of the ILOAT." *Id.*, at 31, para. 48.

820 *See Staff Regulations and Staff Rules, including provisional Staff Rules, of the United Nations*, UN Doc. ST/SGB/2023/1/Rev. 1 (2023). Until 2009, cases could on appeal come before the United Nations Administrative Tribunal, whose judgments were subject to a final review by the International Court of Justice as the principal judicial organ of the United Nations until the UN General Assembly decided in December 1995 to remove the provision for review of UNAT decisions by the ICJ with effect from 1 January 1996. *See* General Assembly resolution 50/54 of 11 Dec. 1995, UN Doc. A/RES/50/54). Reviews from UNAT decisions were sought in only a handful of cases between 1955 and 1995. The last "binding" advisory opinion to be given by the ICJ pursuant to

implicated.[821] UN staff members are subject to the UN's Internal Justice System, which was approved by the UN General Assembly and became effective on 1 July 2009.[822] The main components of the UN's Internal Justice System are the following: (1) Office of Administration of Justice (OAJ); (2) Office of Staff Legal Assistance (OSLA); (3) United Nations Dispute Tribunal (UNDT); and (4) United Nations Appeals Tribunal (UNAT) (replacing the UN Administrative Tribunal). The overall coordination of the various components of the Internal Justice System is entrusted to the Office of Administration of Justice (OAJ). The OAJ is an independent office based at the UN Secretariat in New York. It is headed by an Executive Director appointed by the Secretary-General of the United Nations. The OAJ also includes staff members serving in the Registries of the UNDT and UNAT as part of its role of providing administrative, substantive and technical support to both tribunals. The OAJ is also charged with ensuring that the Office of Staff Legal Assistance (OSLA) functions independently in providing legal advice and assistance to UN staff members.

The two-tier system of formal judicial settlement of UN staff disputes comprises the UNDT and the UNAT, each having their own Statute that defines its legal framework and governs its judicial work and each having its own Rules of Procedure guiding its legal procedures. The UNDT is the first-instance tribunal and it is competent to hear and decide cases initiated by or on behalf of current and former staff members seeking review of administrative decisions alleged to be in non-compliance with their terms of appointment or contract of employment, or cases arising from disciplinary action, following management evaluation of the impugned decision. The management evaluation constitutes a mandatory preliminary step in the formal system, unless the impugned decision was taken pursuant to advice from technical bodies or in disciplinary matters. The UNAT, comprising a total of seven judges, is the final-instance tribunal to which either party may lodge an appeal from a decision issued by the UNDT. The UNAT's decisions, which usually are rendered by a panel of three judges, are final and binding on the parties.

In addition to the aforementioned components of the *formal* conflict resolution system within the United Nations, the UN's Internal Justice System

---

article 11 of the Statute of the UN Administrative Tribunal was *Application for Review of Judgment No. 333 of the United Nations Administrative Tribunal* (1987 ICJ Rep. 18).

821 *See* General Convention, Art. VIII, S. 29 sub (b).

822 For an overview, *see* https://www.un.org/en/internaljustice/overview/ (last visited 1 December 2024). *See also* P. Vargiu, *From Advisory Opinions to Binding Decisions: The New Appeal Mechanism of the UN System of Administration of Justice*, 7(2) IOLR 261 (2010).

also supports *informal* conflict resolution through the United Nations Ombudsman and Mediation Services (UNOMS). UNOMS includes ombudsman and mediation services for the UN Secretariat and UN funds and programs. The UNDT may refer a dispute that is subject to its jurisdiction for mediation, if the parties agree.

3.6.3.3.3 Settlement of Disputes with Third Persons

International organizations are parties to *contracts* as is any other subject of law. In order to satisfy the daily needs stemming from their operational activities, organizations need to rent buildings, purchase supplies and office equipment, etc. All these matters are incidental to the performance of functions by the organization.[823] This may, however, lead to conflicts with governments, individual parties or corporate entities, which are parties to such contracts, whenever a dispute arises and the immunity from jurisdiction of the organization comes into operation. To protect the interests of third persons, most international instruments provide for some appropriate mode of settlement of disputes. The disputes that we are concerned with at this point concern disputes arising out of contracts or disputes which are of a private law character.[824]

The Preparatory Commission of the United Nations stated its view that, whenever the United Nations or the specialized agencies conclude contracts with private individuals or corporations, they should include in these contracts a provision to the effect that disputes arising from such contracts shall be submitted to arbitration. According to the Preparatory Commission, the United Nations and the specialized agencies should have recourse to this practice if they are reluctant to go before the courts.[825]

The general multilateral immunities conventions normally oblige the international organizations concerned to make arrangements for appropriately resolving contract or other disputes of a private law nature to which the organizations are parties. The UN General Convention provides as follows in Article VIII, Section 29 under (a):

---

823 *See* AHLUWALIA, at 70.

824 On non-contractual liability, see, *e.g.*, Schermers, Non-Contractual Liability; Szasz, Liability; 1976 UN Jurid. Y.B 176, UN Doc. ST/LEG/SER.C/14 (1978); WHITEMAN, 13 DIGEST, at 24–28. *See also* Art. 268, TEEU (designating the Court of Justice of the European Union as the court with exclusive competence regarding non-contractual liability). See further section 3.6.4 below.

825 *See Report of the Preparatory Commission of the United Nations*, at 62, UN Doc. PC/20 (1945).

> The United Nations shall make provision for appropriate modes of settlement of: (a) Disputes arising out of contracts or other disputes of a private law character to which the United Nations is a party.

In order to comply with this provision, non-national courts or tribunals usually are made available for the settlement of any disputes arising out of contracts or other disputes of a private law character.[826] The latter type of dispute may arise from tort or delict claims of a private law character by third parties for personal injury, illness or death, as well as for property loss or damage resulting from, or attributable to, the international organization's operations in the performance of its official duties or sustained at the organization's premises.[827] They also may involve claims of intellectual property infringement, including when an international organization is alleged to have used third-party owned materials without appropriate licenses or in breach of a license.

The United Nations has regularly made provision in its contracts, including contracts for the procurement of products or services concluded with individual contractors or consultants, for recourse to *arbitration* in cases in which agreement cannot be reached by direct negotiations, i.e., through diplomatic procedure or settlement discussions, as the case may be.[828] In such

826 It has been held that the UN's fulfilment of its obligation under Section 29 of the General Convention is not a condition precedent to its immunity under Section 2 of the General Convention, because the immunity granted under Section 2 is unconditional and by its wording is subject only to express waiver by the UN. *See Georges v. United Nations*, No. 15-455-cv, judgment of 18 Aug. 2016 (2d Cir. 2016).

827 For a brief description of the relevant practice of the United Nations, see International Law Commission, Questionnaire—Replies received from international organizations and entities, at 75–76, UN Doc. A/CN.4/764 (2024)(reply by the UN Office of Legal Affairs). *See also* D.U. Picard, *The United Nations' Obligation to Provide Access to Remedies to Third-Party Claimants Under International* Law, 20(3) IOLR 330, 335–352 (2023); Y. Okada, *Interpretation of Article VIII, Section 29 of the Convention on the Privileges and Immunities of the UN—Legal Basis and Limits of a Human Rights-based Approach to the Haiti Cholera Case*, 15 IOLR 39 (2018)(describing the content and scope of the Section 29 obligation to provide alternative means of dispute resolution in the context of UN peacekeeping operations).

828 *See* International Law Commission, Questionnaire—Replies received from international organizations and entities, p. 51 *et seq.*, UN Doc. A/CN.4/764 (2024); [1967] 2 Y.B. Int'l L. Comm'n 296, UN Doc. A/CN.4/SER.A/1967/Add. 1. According to a legal opinion of the UN Secretariat, the governing procedures for contracts concluded by the UN Office in Geneva, by contrast to UN Headquarters, provide for such negotiations through the appointment of an expert who gives his opinion prior to the

cases, the organization agrees to submit to binding arbitration before an *ad hoc* international tribunal.[829]

United Nations contracts usually do not contain choice of *law* clauses[830] but incorporate standard clauses relating to settlement of contractual *disputes*. For contracts with commercial vendors, the United Nations General Conditions of Contracts for the Provision of Goods and Services[831] provide the following standard dispute settlement clause:

> 17.1 AMICABLE SETTLEMENT: The Parties shall use their best efforts to amicably settle any dispute, controversy, or claim arising out of the Contract or the breach, termination, or invalidity thereof. Where the Parties wish to seek such an amicable settlement through conciliation, the conciliation shall take place in accordance with the Conciliation Rules then obtaining of the United Nations Commission on International Trade Law ("UNCITRAL"), or according to such other procedure as may be agreed between the Parties in writing.
>
> 17.2 ARBITRATION: Any dispute, controversy, or claim between the Parties arising out of the Contract or the breach, termination, or

---

institution of any judicial proceedings. *See* 1976 UN Jurid. Y.B 159, 162–163 n.21, UN Doc. ST/LEG/SER.C/14 (1976). In addition to negotiations, the possible resort to the Committee on Relations with the Host Country, as well as the use of good offices, mediation and conciliation, also may be contemplated as peaceful means of settlement. *See* Rao, in [1987] 1 Y.B. Int'l L. Comm'n 204, para. 53, UN Doc. A/CN.4/SER.A/1987. *See also* Institut de Droit International, 'Contracts Concluded by International Organizations with Private Persons,' resolution adopted on 6 September 1977, 57 *Annuaire de l'Institut de Droit International*, p. 33 (recommending that contracts "provide for the settlement of disputes arising out of such contracts by an independent body," which may include an arbitral tribunal (Arts. 7–8), and suggesting that an international organization either waive immunity or agree on an alternative dispute settlement method such as arbitration (Art. 9)).

829 For a more detailed review of the instrument of – *ad hoc* and institutional – arbitration, see P. Bekker, Arbitration of International Disputes in New York (2024), 183–184; Dominicé, L'immunité, at 180–205, 217.

830 *See* 1994 UN Jurid. Y.B, p. 449, UN Doc.ST/LEG/SER.C/32 (1994)(noting that contractual clauses referring to local law "could be construed as a waiver of immunity of the United Nations from the jurisdiction of the courts, since national laws regulate, *inter alia*, arbitral proceedings and provide for interim measures and regulate execution of awards, in addition to making provisions for the substantive rules").

831 Text available at https://www.un.org/Depts/ptd/sites/www.un.org.Depts.ptd/files/files/attachment/page/pdf/general_condition_goods_services.pdf (last visited 1 December 2024)

> invalidity thereof, unless settled amicably under Article 17.1 above, within sixty (60) days after receipt by one Party of the other Party's written request for such amicable settlement, shall be referred by either Party to arbitration in accordance with the UNCITRAL Arbitration Rules then obtaining. The decisions of the arbitral tribunal shall be based on general principles of international commercial law. The arbitral tribunal shall be empowered to order the return or destruction of goods or any property, whether tangible or intangible, or of any confidential information provided under the Contract, order the termination of the Contract, or order that any other protective measures be taken with respect to the goods, services or any other property, whether tangible or intangible, or of any confidential information provided under the Contract, as appropriate, all in accordance with the authority of the arbitral tribunal pursuant to Article 26 ("Interim measures") and Article 34 ("Form and effect of the award") of the UNCITRAL Arbitration Rules. The arbitral tribunal shall have no authority to award punitive damages. In addition, unless otherwise expressly provided in the Contract, the arbitral tribunal shall have no authority to award interest in excess of the London Inter-Bank Offered Rate ("LIBOR") then prevailing, and any such interest shall be simple interest only. The Parties shall be bound by any arbitration award rendered as a result of such arbitration as the final adjudication of any such dispute, controversy, or claim.[832]

From the private party's perspective, it is recommended to replace the words "be referred by either Party to arbitration" in the above standard clause with "be exclusively and unconditionally referred by either Party to

832 *See* International Law Commission, Memorandum by the Secretariat, Questionnaire—Replies received from international organizations and entities, at 118–119, UN Doc. A/CN.4/764 (2024). *See also* [1967] 2 Y.B. Int'l L. Comm'n 209, para. 6, UN Doc. A/CN.4/SER.A/1967/Add. 1; 1976 UN Jurid. Y.B 159, 168–169, UN Doc. ST/LEG/SER.C/14 (1978); 1990 UN Jurid. Y.B 287–288, UN Doc. ST/LEG/SER.C/28(1993); Ehrenfeld, at 93. We are concerned in this study with certain *procedural* aspects of the legal position of IGOs (in other words, their 'standing') rather than with the *substantive law* applicable to agreements entered into by IGOs. For an excellent early survey of the application of different systems of substantive law to IGOs, see F. Seyersted, *Applicable Law in Relations between Intergovernmental Organizations and Private Parties*, 122 RdC 427 (1967 III).

arbitration." The additional words 'exclusively and unconditionally' should prevent any argument that the international organization's contractual consent to arbitration does not constitute an implied waiver of jurisdictional immunity, including of arbitral jurisdiction, in a given case.

In light of U.S. case law, it is recommended that the following language be added to the above clause in situations involving intergovernmental organizations that are based, or conduct activities, in the United States: "Judgment upon any award rendered by the arbitral tribunal may be entered in any court having jurisdiction thereof." This additional sentence will prevent an international organization from invoking its immunity from suit in post-award enforcement proceedings before a U.S. court, because the UNCITRAL Arbitration Rules do not contain an entry-of-judgment provision and, in any event, U.S. courts have held that, even if the parties have incorporated arbitration rules containing an entry-of-judgment provision by reference in their arbitration agreement, the international organization cannot be deemed to have issued an express waiver of immunity from suit, especially where the parties' contract specifically preserves the organization's immunity "notwithstanding anything to the contrary" in the contract.[833]

The omission of entry-of-judgment language in an arbitration clause that is embedded in a contract between a private party and an international organization arguably creates an imbalance in the contractual relationship between the private contracting party and the international organization: if the private party were to prevail in an arbitration, the international organization would be able to block an action to enforce the arbitral award commenced by the private party in a national court by invoking the organization's immunity before the national court and thereby render the arbitral

---

833 *See, e.g.*, *Sacks v. International Monetary Fund*, 26 F.4th 470 (D.C. Cir. 2022). *See also* International Law Commission, Memorandum by the Secretariat, Questionnaire—Replies received from international organizations and entities, at 134, UN Doc. A/CN.4/764 (2024)(reply by the UN Office of Legal Affairs: "In isolated and exceptional cases, immunity has been waived [by the United Nations] for purposes of pursuing enforcement of arbitral awards"). The reply by the UN Office of Legal Affairs suggests that the UN Secretary-General occasionally waives the UN's immunity in order to pursue enforcement of an arbitral award rendered in favor of the UN, but that he does not waive the UN's immunity when defending against enforcement of arbitral awards rendered against the UN.

award unenforceable,[834] but if the international organization were to prevail in an arbitration with the private party, it could waive its immunity and could seek enforcement of the arbitral award in a local court as an award creditor based on the United Nations Convention on the Recognition and Enforcement of Foreign Arbitral Awards[835] in the event the private party does not voluntarily comply with the arbitral award. For this reason, it would appear to be reasonable if a national court not only were to treat an international organization's agreement to arbitrate as an implied waiver of its immunity from jurisdiction enabling arbitral jurisdiction,[836] but also would consider the organization's agreement to arbitrate as enabling a national court to assume jurisdiction in a post-award enforcement proceeding to confirm an arbitral award rendered against an international organization, while respecting the organization's immunity from execution in such a proceeding.[837] For the foregoing reasons, it is recommended that possible post-award enforcement measures be precisely described in an arbitration agreement with an international organization.

Based on the U.S. Supreme Court's ruling in *Jam v. International Finance Corporation* that "the Foreign Sovereign Immunities Act governs the immunity of international organizations" in the United States, organizations covered by the International Organizations Immunities Act will be subject to the arbitration exception contained in Section 1605(a)(6) of the FSIA, which reads as follows:

> A foreign state shall not be immune from the jurisdiction of courts of the United States or of the States in any case—

834 *See, e.g., Sacks v. International Monetary Fund*, 26 F.4th 470, 476 (D.C. Cir. 2022)("absent waiver, the [organization]'s immunity from suit entitles it to ignore an arbitration award against it").

835 United Nations Convention on the Recognition and Enforcement of Foreign Arbitral Awards, done at New York, 10 June 1958, entry into force 7 June 1959, 330 U.N.T.S. 3 (1958). For the text and updated status, *see* https://uncitral.org.

836 *But cf.* A.J. Miller, *The Privileges and Immunities of the United Nations*, 6 IOLR 7, 94 (2009)(arguing that "[t]he existence of an arbitration clause can hardly be an implied waiver of immunity because this would mean that, by complying with the express terms of Article 29 [of the General Convention] and providing an alternate remedy, the UN would be taken to have waived its immunity").

837 *See* SCHERMERS, at 1084, para. 1612 ("a decision against the organization cannot be enforced, as international organizations enjoy immunity from execution"). For an early arbitration case addressing an organization's duty to arbitrate, see *A (organisation internationale) v. B (société)*, Award of 14 May 1972, ICC Case No. 2091, *Revue de l'Arbitrage* 252 (1975).

> …
>
> (6) in which the action is brought, either to enforce an agreement made by the foreign state with or for the benefit of a private party to submit to arbitration all or any differences which have arisen or which may arise between the parties with respect to a defined legal relationship, whether contractual or not, concerning a subject matter capable of settlement by arbitration under the laws of the United States, or to confirm an award made pursuant to such an agreement to arbitrate, if (A) the arbitration takes place or is intended to take place in the United States, (B) the agreement or award is or may be governed by a treaty or other international agreement in force for the United States calling for the recognition and enforcement of arbitral awards, (C) the underlying claim, save for the agreement to arbitrate, could have been brought in a United States court under this section or section 1607, or (D) paragraph (1) of this subsection is otherwise applicable.[838]

UN entities are known to resist a reference to a place of arbitration in the arbitration clause embedded in a contract out of concern that such a designation might be interpreted to imply a submission to the local courts and a designation of local procedural law.[839] For this reason, they might prefer to include the following language: "The venue of in-person hearings shall be New York, N.Y., U.S.A." However, it should be kept in mind that an arbitral tribunal can be expected to determine the formal place of arbitration at the outset of the arbitral proceedings if the parties have not previously agreed on the place of arbitration.[840]

---

838 28 U.S.C. 1605(a)(6). Note that the legal position of the United Nations is governed by the General Convention, which as a self-executing treaty is binding in U.S. courts. *See Brzak v. United Nations*, 597 F.3d 114 (2d Cir. 2010).

839 *See* International Law Commission, Memorandum by the Secretariat, Questionnaire—Replies received from international organizations and entities, at 120, UN Doc. A/CN.4/764 (2024)(reply by the UN Office of Legal Affairs: "[T]he United Nations takes the position that its arbitrations are delocalized in nature, without a seat of arbitration that would entail its submission to the jurisdiction of national courts or the application of any local procedural law, which would be inconsistent with the Organization's privileges and immunities").

840 *See, e.g.*, UNCITRAL Arbitration Rules (2021), Art. 18(1) ("If the parties have not previously agreed on the place of arbitration, the place of arbitration shall be determined by the arbitral tribunal having regard to the circumstances of the case"). The location of the international organization that is a party to the arbitration, the contractual selection of a certain venue to hold in-person hearings, and the choice of the law of a

As regards choice of *law* clauses in connection with an arbitration agreement involving an intergovernmental organization, it is recommended that a broad reference to "generally accepted principles of international commercial law" be avoided, because an arbitral tribunal can be expected to struggle with defining the status and content of such principles in a given case. It is preferable to refer to a specific jurisdiction (e.g., the (substantive) laws of the State of New York) or, if this is not acceptable to both parties, to "the UNIDROIT [International Institute for the Unification of Private Law] Principles of International Commercial Contracts (2010) and, with respect to issues not covered by such Principles, by generally accepted principles of international commercial law."[841]

As regards interest, LIBOR has been replaced worldwide with effect from 1 July 2023. A possible alternative benchmark for the determination of interest in an arbitration could be the SOFR (Secured Overnight Financing Rate) reference rate (subject to an appropriate spread adjustment in the coupon calculation in order to account for the value transfer in switching from LIBOR to SOFR, an overnight rate).

Practice demonstrates that the United Nations has only had recourse to arbitral proceedings in a limited number of cases, mostly arising out of disputes with commercial vendors supporting UN peacekeeping missions, and that very few cases involving commercial contracts to which the UN was a party have come before municipal courts.[842]

---

certain jurisdiction (e.g., New York) may serve as *indicia* for determining the formal place of arbitration by the arbitral tribunal.

841 *See* International Law Commission, Memorandum by the Secretariat, Questionnaire—Replies received from international organizations and entities, at 120, UN Doc. A/CN.4/764 (2024)(reply by the UN Office of Legal Affairs: "the standard United Nations contract is governed by its own terms and not by any national law, whether substantive or procedural"). *See also* P. Bekker, Arbitration of International Disputes in New York (2024), 187–197.

842 *See* 1976 UN Jurid. Y.B, p. 170, UN Doc. ST/LEG/SER.C/14 (1978); International Law Commission, Memorandum by the Secretariat, Questionnaire—Replies received from international organizations and entities, at 85 and 96, UN Doc. A/CN.4/764 (2024) (reply by the UN Office of Legal Affairs, p. 85: "In general, the majority of disputes are settled amicably, without going to arbitration; and, of the claims that do go to arbitration, the majority are settled amicably before going through the full arbitration process and concluding with an arbitration award")((reply by the UN Office of Legal Affairs, p. 96: "Over the past three decades, around 40 arbitrations were initiated by commercial vendors in which the Office of Legal Affairs acted as counsel for the United Nations, of which approximately 30 per cent involved United Nations Funds and Programmes").

The Permanent Court of Arbitration (PCA), an intergovernmental organization that is seated at the Peace Palace in The Hague, The Netherlands, has offered 'Optional Rules for Arbitration between International Organizations and Private Parties' in addition to 'Optional Rules for Arbitration between International Organizations and States' since 1996.[843] For example, the Headquarters Agreement between France and the International Criminal Police Organization (INTERPOL) incorporates a reference to these Optional Rules for the resolution of disputes between INTERPOL and private parties.[844]

The Specialized Agencies Convention contains substantially the same provision as Section 29 of the General Convention. According to Article IX, Section 31(a):

> Each specialized agency shall make provision for appropriate modes of settlement of:
>
> (a) Disputes arising out of contracts or other disputes of private character to which the specialized agency is a party.[845]

Although considerable variation exists, the majority of contracts entered into by specialized agencies provide for the settlement of disputes by arbitration, following recourse to direct negotiations or consultations. Section 31 (a), although applicable to all specialized agencies, cannot, however, be said to have created a uniform system of settlement of disputes. For example, most contracts concluded by the International Labour Organization include

---

843 Text available on the website of the PCA, www.pca-cpa.org. These Optional Rules have been updated and consolidated in the PCA Arbitration Rules of 2012, which are based on the 2012 UNCITRAL Arbitration Rules. Through 2024, the PCA had administered more than 45 arbitrations involving international organizations with a wide range of counterparties arising from disputes spanning various sectors.

844 Art. 24, para. 1, Agreement between the International Criminal Police Organization and the Government of the French Republic regarding INTERPOL's Headquarters in France, adopted on 24 Apr. 2008, entry into force 1 Sept. 2009. *See* R.S.J, Martha, C. Grafton and S. Bailey, The Legal Foundations of INTERPOL 299–300 (2020).

845 The formula "Disputes arising out of contracts or other disputes of a private law character" used in Sections 29 and 31 of the General and Specialized Agencies Conventions, respectively, does not apply to agreements which are of a public international law nature, such as treaties. The latter usually contain their own specific provisions concerning the settlement of disputes.

a provision whereby all disputes in which the ILO is involved are to be referred to the ILO Administrative Tribunal for decision.[846] Another exception is found in the IBRD, IDA and IFC, which have developed a distinct body of practice with regard to the settlement of disputes.[847]

The headquarters agreements of most specialized agencies commonly provide for the settlement of disputes arising out of contracts or which are of a private law character.[848]

As regards *regional* organizations, reference may be made to Article 21 of the *General Agreement on privileges and immunities of the Council of Europe*, providing for arbitration in "any dispute between the Council and private persons regarding supplies furnished, services rendered or immovable property purchased on behalf of the Council,"[849] as well as to Article 12 of the OAS Multilateral Agreement.[850]

3.6.3.3.4 Differences Arising out of the Interpretation of a Certain Instrument

A final category of disputes consists of differences arising out of the interpretation or application of international immunities instruments. This category is not so much concerned with private interests, but with differences of opinion between an international organization and one of its member States, or between two member States (inter-State disputes) and possibly another intergovernmental organization.

The position within the United Nations framework is that all differences between governments and international organizations concerning the interpretation or application of immunities agreements are justiciable by some organized procedure, usually consisting of international judicial settlement or arbitration.[851]

Section 30 of Article VIII of the General Convention provides as follows:

> All differences arising out of the interpretation or application of the present convention shall be referred to the International Court of Justice, unless in any case it is agreed by the parties to have recourse to

846 *See* [1967] 2 Y.B. Int'l L. Comm'n 300, para. 5, UN Doc. A/CN.4/SER.A/1967/Add. 1.

847 *See id.*, at 300, paras. 7–8.

848 For examples see UN Docs. ST/LEG/SER.B/10 & 11; International Law Commission, Questionnaire—Replies received from international organizations and entities, at 51–135, UN Doc. A/CN.4/764 (2024).

849 250 U.N.T.S. 14 *reprinted in* UN Doc. ST/LEG/SER.B/11 (1961), at 390, 395.

850 Pan American Union, Law and Treaty Series, No. 31, *reprinted in* UN Doc. ST/LEG/SER.B/11 (1961), at 377, 381.

851 *See* JENKS, at 25.

> another mode of settlement. If a difference arises between the United Nations on the one hand and a Member on the other hand, a request shall be made for an advisory opinion on any legal question involved in accordance with Article 96 of the Charter and Article 65 of the Statute of the Court. The opinion given by the Court shall be accepted as decisive by the parties.[852]

The first sentence of Section 30 thus deals with inter-State disputes, which are to be submitted to the International Court of Justice as contentious cases. As the Court has explained in its advisory opinion rendered in *Applicability of Article VI, Section 22, of the Convention on the Privileges and Immunities of the United Nations* (*Mazilu* Case) on 15 December 1989:

> The first sentence of the Section provides for the case where a difference arises out of the interpretation or application of the General Convention between States parties to it, and contains two elements. The first is the treaty obligation to refer the difference to the Court, unless another mode of settlement is decided upon by the parties; the second is the object of the reference to the Court, namely to settle the difference.[853]

Disputes between the United Nations and a member State are to be submitted, in accordance with the second sentence of Section 30, for an advisory opinion by the Court which will be binding on both parties. The reason for inserting this particular sentence, as the Court has observed, was the fact that the United Nations is itself intimately, and for the most part directly, concerned with the operation of the General Convention.[854] A distinction must be made, because, as pointed out above in the discussion in relation to Section 24 of the Specialized Agencies Convention, a State itself cannot request an advisory opinion, neither can an organization bring a contentious case before the ICJ.[855]

---

852 On the latter aspect, see R. Ago, *'Binding' Advisory Opinions of the International Court of Justice*, 85 AJIL 439 (1991), and the response by Bowett, in 86 AJIL 342–343 (1992). *See also* C.N. Brower and P.H.F. Bekker, *Understanding 'Binding' Advisory Opinions of the International Court of Justice in Liber Amicorum* Judge Shigeru Oda 351–368 (N. Ando, E. McWhinney & R. Wolfrum eds. 2002).

853 1989 ICJ Rep. 177, at 189, para. 32.

854 *Id.*, at 189, para. 33.

855 *See* UN Charter Art. 96 and ICJ Statute Arts. 34, para. 1, and 65.

In cases arising under the second sentence of Section 30 of the General Convention, it is worth mentioning that the UN General Assembly, the Security Council, other UN organs and specialized agencies at any time so authorized by the General Assembly, may avoid the invocation of any reservations made by a member State to that Section, by simply not referring to Section 30 in the resolution requesting the advisory opinion. As the Court indicated in the *Mazilu* Case, in any such case the request is not made under Section 30, and the Court does not therefore need to determine the effect of any reservation to that provision, provided that the "'content and extent of the obligations entered into by States' – and, in particular, by [the State making the reservation] – 'when they consented to be bound by the Convention'" are not modified by the request and by the advisory opinion in question.[856] Moreover, as advisory opinions are intended for the guidance of the United Nations or another requesting organization, the consent of States parties to a dispute, which normally is the basis of the Court's jurisdiction in contentious cases, is not a condition precedent to the competence of the Court to give advisory opinions.[857] In such cases, therefore, the Court has jurisdiction under the 'ordinary' clause contained in Article 96 of the UN Charter and Article 65 of the Statute of the Court.[858]

Practice shows that differences which have so far arisen regarding the interpretation or application of the General Convention have always been settled by means of negotiation and discussion.[859] The advisory opinion rendered by the International Court of Justice in the *Cumaraswamy* Case in 1999, constituted the first time in the Court's history that it had responded to a request for an advisory opinion premised explicitly on Article VIII, Section 30, of the General Convention.[860] The request in the *Cumaraswamy*

856 1989 ICJ Rep. 177, at 190, para. 35.

857 *Id.*, at 188–189, para. 31.

858 *Id.*, at 177, 190, para. 34; *ICJ Pleadings, Applicability of Article VI, Section 22, of the Convention on the Privileges and Immunities of the United Nations,* at 249–250 (Reply by the UN Legal Counsel to the Question put by Judge Guillaume). Notice incidentally that in such cases the advisory opinion will be non-binding.

859 *See* [1967] 2 Y.B. Int'l L. Comm'n 296, para. 389, UN Doc. A/CN.4/SER.A/1967/Add. 1. The *Mazilu* Opinion by the ICJ, 1989 ICJ Rep. 177, might be called an exception, although the case was brought under Article 96 UN Charter and not under the settlement mechanism of the General Convention.

860 *Difference Relating to Immunity from Legal Process of a Special Rapporteur of the Commission on Human Rights*, Advisory Opinion, 1999 ICJ Rep. 62. For a description of the facts of the *Cumaraswamy* Case and the Court's ruling, see International Decisions, 93 AJIL 913 (1999)(case report authored by P.H.F. Bekker). *See also* P.H.F. Bekker,

Case was made by the United Nations Economic and Social Council (ECOSOC) and it pertained to the immunity of the Special Rapporteur on the Independence of Judges and Lawyers of the UN Commission on Human Rights.[861]

Bilateral immunities agreements normally provide for arbitration, usually before a panel of three arbitrators. This is a normal feature of United Nations headquarters and host agreements. The 1947 *Agreement between the United Nations and the United States of America regarding the Headquarters of the United Nations* provides in Section 21(a):

> Any dispute between the United Nations and the United States concerning the interpretation or application of this agreement or of any supplemental agreement, which is not settled by negotiation or other agreed mode of settlement,[[862]] shall be referred to a tribunal of three arbitrators, one to be named by the Secretary-General, one to be named by the Secretary of State of the United States, and the third to be chosen by the two, or, if they should fail to agree upon a third, then by the President of the International Court of Justice.

In addition to this general arbitration clause, reference is also made in the Agreement to a request for an advisory opinion by the ICJ, pending the arbitration procedure. In this regard, Section 21 provides under (b):

The Independence of UN Special Rapporteurs: Dispute Resolution under the Convention on Privileges and Immunities, in International Administration – Law and Management Practices in International Organisations, Suppl. VII, at III.2/1–29 (C. de Cooker ed. 2001).

861 For a comprehensive analysis of the advisory opinion rendered in the *Cumaraswamy* Case, including its referral (ante-adjudicative) and implementation (post-adjudicative) aspects, see C.N. Brower & P.H.F. Bekker, *Understanding 'Binding' Advisory Opinions of the International Court of Justice, in Liber Amicorum* Judge Shigeru Oda 351–368 (N. Ando, E. McWhinney & R. Wolfrum, eds., 2002). As explained by the authors, "[t]he 'binding' quality of Section 30 opinions incorporates two elements: (1) an ante-adjudicative element, consisting of the treaty obligation to request an advisory opinion of the [International] Court [of Justice] (to be undertaken by an organ which itself may not be a party to the difference underlying the request); and (2) a post-adjudicative element, consisting of the treaty obligation of the parties to the difference to accept the advisory opinion as 'decisive', i.e., as final and binding (directed toward two parties to the difference that did not submit the request themselves"). *Id.*, at 365.

862 For the general modes of pacific settlement of disputes see Art. 33, para. 1, of Chapter VI of the UN Charter.

> The Secretary-General or the United States may ask the General Assembly to request of the International Court of Justice an advisory opinion on any legal question arising in the course of such proceedings. Pending the receipt of the opinion of the Court, an interim decision of the arbitral tribunal shall be observed by both parties. Thereafter, the arbitral tribunal shall render a final decision, having regard to the opinion of the Court.

Most United Nations headquarters agreements do not explicitly refer to the possibility of a request for an advisory opinion by the ICJ and contain only a provision which is drafted in the same manner as paragraph (a) of the UN-U.S. Agreement, with slight differences as to the appointment of the third arbitrator. In this regard, the 1946 *Interim Arrangement on Privileges and Immunities of the United Nations concluded between the Secretary-General of the United Nations and the Swiss Federal Council* provided in Section 27 of Article VIII that the third, presiding arbitrator shall be appointed directly by the President of the ICJ in every case.[863]

As regards the *specialized agencies*, the constituent instruments of most agencies provide for either a reference to the International Court of Justice or a decision by the executive organs of the respective agencies or by arbitration.[864] When two or more member States of a specialized agency differ as to the exact interpretation or application of the constituent instrument in question, they may bring their inter-State dispute before the ICJ as a contentious case. In case of a difference between a specialized agency, on the one hand, and a member State, on the other hand, the agency concerned is under a legal obligation to make a request to the ICJ for an advisory opinion on any legal questions involved. Section 32 of Article IX of the Specialized Agencies Convention is drafted in substantially the same terms as its corresponding section in the General Convention, Section 30. Finally, a specialized agency may, of course, if authorized to do so, ask the ICJ for an advisory opinion on questions relating to the interpretation or application of its constituent instrument. In such cases, there is no official dispute and the second sentence of Section 32 of the Specialized Agencies Convention does not apply; in this particular case the agency concerned is under no legal obligation to ask such questions.

The headquarters agreements concluded by the specialized agencies also contain provisions for arbitration or reference to the International Court of

863 For more examples see JENKS, at 22.

864 *See* Chen, at 904 n.18, and further references therein.

Justice. Reference may be made to the 1951 Agreement between the International Civil Aviation Organization and the Government of Canada regarding the Headquarters of the International Civil Aviation Organization, Article VII, Section 31 of which provides for a mode of settlement drafted in substantially the same terms as the corresponding provision of the UN-U.S. Agreement, Section 21.[865]

3.6.4 Additional Procedures; Liability

Besides the devices of waiver, arbitration and international judicial settlement by the International Court of Justice or by an administrative tribunal, still other methods for counteracting the negative effects of organizational immunities have been employed or suggested.

Bilateral agreements between States and international organizations frequently provide that the State party thereto will, on its own account, defend any action that normally could be brought against the international organization concerned.[866] The United Nations in particular makes use of this method, and has included such clauses in various conference agreements, *ad hoc* agreements for seminars, symposia and workshops and other meetings convened and arranged by the UN Secretariat away from an established headquarters, as well as in technical assistance agreements.[867]

As regards conferences held under the auspices of the United Nations, the UN introduced a 'Model conference agreement' in 1987.[868] Article X of this Model provides as follows:

> *Liability*
>
> 1. The Government shall be responsible for dealing with any action, claim or other demand against the United Nations or its officials and arising out of:
>
> (a) Injury to persons or damage to or loss of property in the premises [referred to in article III] that are provided by or are under the control of the Government;
>
> (b) Injury to persons or damage to or loss of property caused by, or incurred in using, the transport services [referred to in article VI] that are provided by or are under the control of the Government;

865 For more examples see JENKS, at 23 and UN Docs. ST/LEG/SER.8/10 & 11.

866 *See also* Szasz, Immunities, at 159.

867 *See also* DUFFAR, at 264.

868 UN Doc. ST/AI/342 of 8 May 1987.

> (c) The employment for the Conference of the personnel provided by the Government under article VIII.
> 2. The Government shall indemnify and hold harmless the United Nations and its officials in respect of any such action, claim or other demand.

The underlying rationale for the insertion of the liability clause is that the government, and not the United Nations, should bear such risks as may be involved in the provision of premises, transportation, employment of local personnel, etc. The clause is based on paragraph 10 of General Assembly resolution 2609(XXIV),[869] which has been reaffirmed on a number of occasions.[870] By resolution 2609, it was decided that sessions of UN bodies may be held away from their established headquarters when the government issuing the invitation for a session to be held within its territory has agreed to defray, after consultation with the UN Secretary-General as to their nature and possible extent, the actual additional costs directly or indirectly incurred. The effect of the liability clause is, therefore, to ensure that the government concerned, not the United Nations, will be liable for any claims as may arise from injury to persons or damage to or loss of property in the premises, or caused by the local transport services or from the employment of local personnel, which are considered to constitute indirect additional costs to the United Nations.[871] In the absence of any such arrangement regarding liability claims, the United Nations could be regarded as being implicitly liable and might as a result incur a financial risk which it is impossible for the organization to assume.

The following indemnification provision is used by the United Nations Development Programme (UNDP) in its Standard Basic Assistance Agreement:

> Assistance under this Agreement being provided for the benefit of the Government and people of ..., the Government shall bear all risks of operations arising under this agreement. It shall be responsible for dealing with claims which may be brought by third parties against the UNDP or an Executing Agency, their officials or other persons

869 24 GAOR Supp. (No. 30) at 86, 87, UN Doc. A/7630 (1970).

870 *E.g.*, GA Res. 40/23, Part I, para.5, 40 GAOR Supp. (No. 53) at 284, UN Doc. A/40/53 (1986).

871 *See* GA Res. 31/140, 31 GAOR Supp. (No. 39) at 155, UN Doc. A/31/39 (1977).

> performing services on their behalf and shall hold them harmless in respect of claims or liabilities arising from operations under this Agreement. The foregoing provision shall not apply where the Parties and the Executing Agency have agreed that a claim or liability arises from the gross negligence or wilful misconduct of the above-mentioned individuals.

There have, however, been deviations from the practice referred to. The most usual deviation is to exempt the government concerned in the event of "gross negligence or wilful misconduct by United Nations personnel," or a clause of similar wording. An example is found in the final sentence contained in the above provision used by the UNDP. Another deviation is the non-inclusion of a liability clause in the agreement. Such non-inclusion commonly is compensated for by an undertaking in writing by the host country regarding the assumption of liability. In such cases, the normal way of dealing with the liability issue is for the host country to insure itself against the risks involved.

In connection with the increase in peacekeeping operations conducted by the United Nations and the rise in third-party liability claims against that organization resulting from such operations, the United Nations has assumed its liability for damage caused by members of its forces in the performance of their duties. For this reason, paragraph 51 of the model status-of-forces agreement for peacekeeping operations of the United Nations includes an undertaking by the United Nations to settle by means of a three-member 'standing claims commission' any claims resulting from damage caused by members of the force in the performance of their official duties and which as a result of the immunity enjoyed by the United Nations and its member States cannot be submitted to national courts. In conformity with Section 29 of the General Convention, paragraph 51 provides as follows:

> Except as provided in paragraph 53, any dispute or claim of a private law character to which the United Nations peace-keeping operation or any member thereof is a party and over which the courts of [host country/territory] do not have jurisdiction because of any provision of the present Agreement, shall be settled by a standing claims commission to be established for that purpose. One member of the commission shall be appointed by the Secretary-General of the United Nations, one member by the Government and a chairman jointly by the Secretary-General and the Government. If no agreement as to the

> chairman is reached within thirty days of the appointment of the first member of the commission, the President of the International Court of Justice may, at the request of either the Secretary-General of the United Nations or the Government, appoint the chairman. Any vacancy on the commission shall be filled by the same method prescribed for the original appointment, provided that the thirty-day period prescribed shall start as soon as there is a vacancy in the chairmanship. The commission shall determine its own procedures, provided that any two members shall constitute a quorum for all purposes (except for a period of thirty days after the creation of a vacancy) and decisions shall require the approval of any two members. The awards of the commission shall be final and binding, unless the Secretary-General of the United Nations and the Government permit an appeal to a tribunal established in accordance with paragraph 53. The awards of the commission shall be notified to the parties and, if against a member of the United Nations peace-keeping operation, to the Special Representative/Commander or the Secretary-General of the United Nations shall use his best endeavours to ensure compliance.[872]

The Secretary-General of the United Nations has stated that the undertaking in paragraph 51 evidences "the recognition on the part of the United Nations that liability for damage caused by members of United Nations forces is attributable to the Organization."[873]

---

872 'Comprehensive Review of the Whole Question of Peace-keeping Operations in All Their Aspects, Model status-of-force agreement for peace-keeping operations,' Report of the Secretary-General, UN Doc. A/45/594 (1990). Paragraph 53 provides, in pertinent part: "Any other dispute between the United Nations peace-keeping operation and the Government, and any appeal that both of them agree to allow from the award of the claims commission established pursuant to paragraph 51 shall, unless otherwise agreed by the parties, be submitted to a tribunal of three arbitrators." While the UN's model status-of-forces agreement provides for a standing claims commission, and while a provision of this kind has been included in all of the UN's status-of-forces agreements and certain status-of-mission agreements, it has been reported that a standing claims commission has never been actually established in the practice of United Nations peacekeeping operations. *See* International Law Commission, Questionnaire—Replies received from international organizations and entities, at 122, UN Doc. A/CN.4/764 (2024)(reply by the UN Office of Legal Affairs). *See also* FOX-WEBB, at 585; M. Zwanenburg, *UN Peace Operations Between Independence and Accountability*, 5(1) IOLR 23, 27–29, 46 (2008).

873 'Administrative and budgetary aspects of the financing of the United Nations peacekeeping operations: financing of the United Nations peacekeeping operations,' Report

In its resolution 52/247, adopted at the eighty-eighth plenary meeting held on 26 June 1998, the General Assembly of the United Nations stipulated temporal and financial limitations applicable to third-party claims against the United Nations for personal injury, illness or death, and for property loss or damage (including non-consensual use of premises) resulting from, or attributable to, the activities of members of United Nations peacekeeping operations in the performance of their official duties,[874] as follows:

> 8. *Decides* that, where the liability of the Organization is engaged in relation to third-party claims against the Organization resulting from peacekeeping operations, the Organization will not pay compensation in regard to such claims submitted after six months from the time the damage, injury or loss was sustained, or from the time it was discovered by the claimant, and in any event after one year from the termination of the mandate of the peacekeeping operation, provided that in exceptional circumstances, such as described in paragraph 20 of the report of the Secretary-General, the Secretary-General may accept for consideration a claim made at a later date.
>
> 9. *Decides also*, in respect of third-party claims against the Organization for personal injury, illness or death resulting from peacekeeping operations, that:
>
> (*a*) Compensable types of injury or loss shall be limited to economic loss, such as medical and rehabilitation expenses, loss of earnings, loss of financial support, transportation expenses associated with the injury, illness or medical case, legal and burial expenses;
>
> (*b*) No compensation shall be payable by the United Nations for non-economic loss, such as pain and suffering or moral anguish, as well as punitive or moral damages;

---

of the Secretary-General, UN Doc. A/51/389 of 20 Sept. 1996, at p. 4, para. 8. The report addresses the scope of United Nations liability for activities of United Nations forces, procedures for the handling of third-party claims and limitations of liability.

874 The third-party claims addressed in resolution 52/247 do not include claims arising within the context of a contractual or other direct legal relationship between the claimant and the United Nations, claims arising from off-duty acts or activities of members of a peacekeeping operation not relating to official duties, and claims arising from accidents involving official United Nations vehicles, the latter being covered by the United Nations worldwide insurance policy against third-party liability.

(*c*) No compensation shall be payable by the United Nations for home-maker services and other such damages that, in the sole opinion of the Secretary-General, are impossible to verify or are not directly related to the injury or loss itself;

(*d*) The amount of compensation payable for injury, illness or death of any individual, including for the types of loss and expenses described in subparagraph (*a*) above, shall not exceed a maximum of 50,000 United States dollars, provided, however, that within such limitation the actual amount is to be determined by reference to local compensation standards;

(*e*) In exceptional circumstances, the Secretary-General may recommend to the General Assembly, for its approval, that the limitation of 50,000 dollars provided for in subparagraph (d) above be exceeded in a particular case if the Secretary-General, after carrying out the required investigation, finds that there are compelling reasons for exceeding the limitation;

10. *Decides further* in respect of third-party claims against the Organization for property loss or damage resulting from peacekeeping operations that:

(*a*) Compensation for non-consensual use of premises shall either: (i) be calculated on the basis of the fair rental value, determined on the basis of the local rental market prices that prevailed prior to the deployment of the peacekeeping operation as established by the United Nations pre-mission technical survey team; or (ii) not exceed a maximum ceiling amount payable per square metre or per hectare as established by the United Nations pre-mission survey team on the basis of available relevant information; the Secretary-General will decide on the appropriate method for calculating compensation payable for non-consensual use of premises at the conclusion of the pre-mission technical survey;

(*b*) Compensation for loss or damage to premises shall either: (i) be calculated on the basis of the equivalent of a number of months of the rental value, or a fixed percentage of the rental amount payable for the period of United Nations occupancy; or (ii) be set at a fixed percentage of the cost of repair; the Secretary-General will decide on the appropriate method for calculating compensation payable for loss or damage to premises at the conclusion of the pre-mission technical survey;

> (*c*) No compensation shall be payable by the United Nations for loss or damages that, in the sole opinion of the Secretary-General, are impossible to verify or are not directly related to the loss of or damage to the premises;
>
> 11. *Decides* that:
>
> (*a*) Compensation for loss or damage to personal property of third parties arising from the activities of the operation or in connection with the performance of official duties by its members shall cover the reasonable costs of repair or replacement;
>
> (*b*) No compensation shall be payable by the United Nations for loss or damages that, in the sole opinion of the Secretary-General, are impossible to verify or are not directly related to the loss of or damage to the personal property; ....[875]

In his report underlying resolution 52/247, the Secretary-General of the United Nations provided the following rationale for the limitation on the liability of the United Nations in respect of peacekeeping operations:

> The limitation on the liability of the Organization as a means of allocating the risks of peacekeeping operations between the United Nations and host States is premised on the assumption that consensual peacekeeping operations are conducted for the benefit of the country in whose territory they are deployed, and that having expressly or implicitly agreed to the deployment of a peacekeeping operation in its territory, the host country must be deemed to bear the risk of the operation and assume, in part at least, liability for damage arising from such an operation. As a practical matter, limiting the liability of the Organization is also justified on the ground that the funds from which

875 'Third-party liability: temporal and financial limitations,' UN General Assembly resolution 52/247, adopted on 26 June 1998, UN Doc. A/RES/52/247 (1998). The resolution endorsed proposals of the Secretary-General. *See* 'Administrative and budgetary aspects of the financing of the United Nations peacekeeping operations: financing of the United Nations peacekeeping operations,' Report of the Secretary-General, UN Doc. A/51/903 of 21 May 1997 (with claim form annexed). For the definition of 'economic loss,' the term employed in paragraph 9 sub (a) of the resolution, see United Nations Headquarters regulation No. 4 on 'Limitations of damages in respect of acts occurring within the Headquarters district,' adopted by the UN General Assembly in its resolution 41/210 of 11 Dec. 1986, UN Doc. A/RES/41/210 (1986).

> third-party claims are paid are public funds contributed by the States Members of the United Nations for the purpose of financing activities of the Organization as mandated by those Member States. To the extent that funds are used to pay third-party claims, lesser amounts may be available to finance additional peacekeeping or other United Nations operations. In limiting the liability of the Organization with regard to third-party claims arising from peacekeeping operations it is expected that the host Government will assume responsibility for providing any additional compensation that may appear warranted under the circumstances.[876]

Paragraph 6 of resolution 52/247 endorses the view of the Secretary-General that liability is not engaged in relation to third-party claims resulting from, or attributable to, the activities of members of peacekeeping operations arising from "operational necessity," i.e., "where damage results from necessary actions taken by a peacekeeping force in the course of carrying out its operations in pursuance of its mandates."[877]

---

876 'Administrative and budgetary aspects of the financing of the United Nations peacekeeping operations: financing of the United Nations peacekeeping operations,' Report of the Secretary-General of 21 May 1997, UN Doc. A/51/903 (1997), at p. 5, para. 12. In its resolution on 'The Legal Consequences for Member States of the Non-fulfilment by International Organizations of their Obligations toward Third Parties' adopted in 1995, the *Institut de Droit International* expressed the view that, in the absence of specific rules of an international organization, "there is no general rule of international law whereby States members are, due solely to their membership, liable concurrently or subsidiarily, for the obligations of an international organization of which they are members." Institut de Droit International, 'The Legal Consequences for Member States of the Non-fulfilment by International Organizations of their Obligations toward Third Parties,' resolution adopted on 1 Sept. 1995, 1995 *Annuaire de l'Institut de Droit International*, vol. 66(II), p. 445. *Cf.* O. Murray, *Piercing the Corporate Veil: The Responsibility of Member States of an International Organization*, 8(2) IOLR 291 (2011); J. d'Aspremont, *Abuse of the Legal Personality of International Organizations and the Responsibility of Member States*, 4(1) IOLR 91 (2007). *See also Special Issue: International Organizations and Member State Responsibility – Critical Perspectives*, 12(2) IOLR (2015).

877 'Administrative and budgetary aspects of the financing of the United Nations peacekeeping operations: financing of the United Nations peacekeeping operations,' Report of the Secretary-General, UN Doc. A/51/389 of 20 Sept. 1996, at p. 5, para. 13. The report also describes what factors must be taken into account in deciding upon the "operational necessity" of any given measure. *Id.*, para. 14. The report points out that the scope of third-party liability for combat-related activities (as opposed to peacekeeping operations) is to be determined by the principles and rules of international humanitarian law or the laws of war. *Id.*, at p. 6, para. 16.

Paragraph 7 of resolution 52/247 further indicates that "third-party claims resulting from gross negligence or wilful misconduct of the personnel provided by troop-contributing States for peacekeeping operations" are excluded from the temporal and financial limitations to third-party liability of the United Nations addressed in the resolution. With regard to such claims, the Secretary-General of the United Nations has stated as follows:

> If such claims are established, the Organization would assume liability to compensate a third party, retaining the right to seek recovery from the individual or the troop-contributing State concerned. In the view of the Secretary-General, the Organization cannot limit its responsibility when a member of a peacekeeping operation, while performing his duties, has committed a wrongful act wilfully or with a criminal intent or because of gross negligence. But it is precisely because of that element of gross fault or wilful or criminal intent that the Organization is justified in seeking recovery from the individual or the troop-contributing State concerned. This approach is consistent with the prevailing practice in other fields of international law where limited liability is recognized for negligence, but is not applicable in cases of gross negligence.[878]

Yet another option is the conclusion of insurance agreements, granting those harmed by the international organization a direct right of redress.[879] In fact, cases involving third-party liability insurance, as in contracts of insurance for motor vehicles, constitute the main situation in which the United Nations has been willing to waive its immunity. By General Assembly resolution 22 E(I) of 13 February 1946, the Secretary-General was instructed "to ensure that the drivers of all official motor-cars of the United Nations and all members of the staff, who own or drive motor-cars, shall be properly insured against third party risks." In such cases, insurance is procured and the insurance company is required to defend suits arising under the policy.[880] Before the insurers can do so, however, the United Nations

---

878 'Administrative and budgetary aspects of the financing of the United Nations peacekeeping operations: financing of the United Nations peacekeeping operations,' Report of the Secretary-General of 21 May 1997, UN Doc. A/51/903 (1997), at p. 5, para. 14.

879 *See* HUG, at 90; Szasz, Liability, at 739–744.

880 *See Resolutions Adopted by the General Assembly During the First Part of its First Session,* UN Doc. A/64 (1946), at 33; Szasz, Immunities, at 159; 1976 UN Jurid. Y.B 176, UN Doc. ST/LEG/SER.C/14 (1978).

must waive its immunity, in accordance with the terms of Section 2 of the General Convention. In this respect, the UN Office of Legal Affairs observed in a memorandum issued in 1949:

> As it is really not feasible to take out insurance without permitting the insurance carrier the right to defend any suits which might be brought against the United Nations, the Secretary-General clearly has the power to waive immunity of the United Nations for the purpose of permitting such suits to be brought.[881]

In all other cases, however, the United Nations submits to arbitration rather than waive its immunity.

Another instrument of note in this context is an independent accountability mechanism (IAM) established within an intergovernmental organization and charged with carrying out independent administrative reviews of the organization's acts or omissions under its operational policies and procedures on the basis of third-party complaints. The first IAM was established by the World Bank when it created the Inspection Panel for the IBRD and the IDA in 1993.[882] Another example is the Office of the Compliance Advisor/Ombudsman (CAO) established within the IFC.[883] IAM bodies, which have been established by multiple intergovernmental organizations since 1993, are administrative systems addressing accountability issues raised by external parties affected by an organization's operations, for example, local communities affected by a project financed by a multilateral development bank. While they can hold organizations answerable for their acts or omissions through reports or findings following a compliance investigation, they do not engage in judicial review and they do not provide legal remedies to complainants. They cannot establish an

881 [1967] 2 Y.B. Int'l L. Comm'n 226, UN Doc. A/CN.4/SER.A/1967/Add. 1; *see also* Restatement (Third), § 467, Reporters' Note 7, at 503.

882 *See* Ibrahim Shihata, The World Bank Inspection Panel: In Practice (2000); E.C. Okeke, *Assessing the Accountability Mechanism of Multilateral Development Banks Against Access to Justice: The Case of the World Bank*, King's Law Journal Online 1–18 (2023); A. Orakhelashvili, *The World Bank Inspection Panel in Context: Institutional Aspects of the Accountability of International Organizations*, 2(1) IOLR 57 (2005). *See also* World Bank Inspection Panel website at https://www.inspectionpanel.org/panel-cases.

883 *See* https://www.cao-ombudsman.org. *See also* B.M. Saper, *The International Finance Corporation's Compliance Advisor/Ombudsman (CAO): An Examination of Accountability and Effectiveness from a Global Administrative Law Perspective*, 44 NYU J. Int'L & Pol. 1279 (2012)

organization's legal liability or international responsibility with binding effect in a given case.

Finally, it also should be mentioned that suggestions have been made for the setting up of a claims court within or without an international organization, but other than the provision for a standing claims commission in United Nations status-of-forces agreements this suggestion still awaits implementation.[884] Also, preliminary problems arising in a given case might be entrusted to a special (expert) committee or international 'tribunal of first instance,' to which grievants would have direct access, and then to have the International Court of Justice or a special chamber of the Court adjudge on the unsolved and disputed legal issues by way of appeal and under the normal system of adjudication.[885] However, given the standing restrictions that currently prevail before the ICJ and the procedural equality issues highlighted in the *Global Mechanism* Case before the ICJ,[886] this system would require certain substantial procedural and material amendments of the UN Charter, the ICJ Statute and the Rules of Court.[887]

3.6.5 Responsibility of Intergovernmental Organizations

In the previous section, in which the provision of a standing claims commission in United Nations status-of-forces agreements and the United Nations' third-party liability resulting from peacekeeping operations conducted by that organization were discussed, reference was made to the views of the Secretary-General and the General Assembly of the United Nations with regard to third-party liability in connection with United Nations peacekeeping operations. In one of his reports underlying General Assembly resolution 52/247, the Secretary-General of the United Nations made the following

---

884 *See* Ehrenfeld, at 94 n.21, referring, *inter alia,* to a proposal made by C.W. Jenks in 1943 to create a single 'World Administrative Tribunal,' associated with the PCIJ, and competent in cases in which some official act performed by or on behalf of an international organization is alleged to have violated a private right. *See also* Chen, at 904; Dominicé, L'immunité, at 202.

885 *Cf.* Jenks, in 47 *Annuaire,* Vol. I, at 30 (1957); McKinnon Wood, at 163; Pellet, in [1990] 1 Y.B. Int'l L. Comm'n 216, paras. 20–21, UN Doc. A/CN.4/SER.A/1990.

886 *Judgment No. 2867 of the Administrative Tribunal of the International Labour Organization upon a complaint filed against the International Fund for Agricultural Development,* Advisory Opinion, 2012 ICJ Rep. 10.

887 On this point, see the discussions held in 1957 at the Amsterdam Session of the *Institut de Droit international, reprinted in* 47 *Annuaire,* Vol. II, at 307 (bottom)-314 (1957). *See also* WHITEMAN, 13 DIGEST, at 23.

important statement linking the various elements of the legal position of the United Nations:

> The international responsibility of the United Nations for the activities of United Nations forces is an attribute of its international legal personality and its capacity to bear international rights and obligations. It is also a reflection of the principle of State responsibility – widely accepted to be applicable to international organizations – that damage caused in breach of an international obligation and which is attributable to the State (or to the Organization), entails the international responsibility of the State (or of the Organization) and its liability in compensation.[888]

The International Court of Justice did not address the issue of the responsibility of an intergovernmental organization in its advisory opinion rendered in the *Reparation* Case in 1949, because it had no occasion to do so based on the wording of the request for advisory opinion in that case. In an advisory opinion issued in 1980, the Court did note, however, that, as subjects of international law, international organizations "are bound by any obligations upon them under general rules of international law, under their constitutions or under agreements to which they are parties."[889] As one commentator has explained, "the greater degree of autonomy enjoyed by international organisations in their decision-making and operational activities, especially since the end of the Cold War, has been matched by a growing awareness that they have to account for their acts, actions and omissions."[890]

It is a well-established norm in international law that every internationally wrongful act entails the international responsibility of the entity

888 'Administrative and budgetary aspects of the financing of the United Nations peacekeeping operations: financing of the United Nations peacekeeping operations,' Report of the Secretary-General of 20 Sept. 1996, UN Doc. A/51/389 (1996), at p. 4, para. 6.

889 *Interpretation of the Agreement of 25 March 1951 between the WHO and Egypt*, Advisory Opinion, 1980 ICJ Rep. 73, at 89–90, para. 36. For a discussion of the application of the sources of international law to international organizations, see SCHERMERS, at 1036–1047, paras. 1572–1579, and n.743 above. As Martha has pointed out, "financial obligations that may emanate from the operation of the internal law of international organizations are special obligations under international law, which thus by definition cannot be governed by the municipal law of any State." R.S.J. Martha, The Financial Obligation in International Law 52 (2015).

890 WELLENS, at 2.

engaging in conduct consisting of an action or omission that is attributable to such entity under international law and constitutes a breach of an international obligation of that entity.[891] This norm, which belongs to the category of primary rules, can be said to apply to States and intergovernmental organizations alike.[892] The legal consequence that international law attaches to international responsibility (belonging to the category of secondary rules) is, *inter alia*, an obligation to make full reparation for the injury caused by the internationally wrongful act either through "[r]estitution in kind, or, if this is not possible, payment of a sum corresponding to the value which a restitution in kind would bear".[893]

In its advisory opinion rendered in the *Cumaraswamy* Case in 1999, the International Court of Justice pointed out that "the question of immunity from legal process is distinct from the issue of compensation for any damages incurred as a result of acts performed by the United Nations or by its agents acting in their official capacity."[894] In a 2012 ruling, the Court

891 Articles on the Responsibility of States for Internationally Wrongful Acts, Report of the International Law Commission, arts. 1–2, GAOR, sixty-sixth session, Suppl. 10, UN Doc. A/66/10, 54 *et seq.*, text annexed to UN General Assembly resolution 56/83 of 12 Dec. 2001 [hereinafter: ARSIWA]. *See* J. Crawford, The International Law Commission's Articles on State Responsibility: Introduction, Text and Commentaries (2002); R. Jennings & A. Watts, Oppenheim's International Law, Vol. 1, Part 1, 499–554 (9th ed. 1996).

892 *See also* BROWNLIE, at 686 ("If an organization has a legal personality distinct from that of the member states, and functions which in the hands of states may create responsibility, then it is in principle reasonable to impute responsibility to the organization") and 696 ("The correlative of legal personality and a capacity to present international claims is responsibility"); 'Financing of the United Nations Protection Force, the United Nations Confidence Restoration Operation in Croatia, the United Nations Preventive Deployment Force and the United Nations Peace Forces Headquarters,' Report of the Secretary-General of 20 Sept. 1996, paras. 6–8, UN Doc. A/51/389 (1996).

893 *Factory at Chorzów, Merits, 1928 PCIJ Ser. A, No. 17*, at 47; ARSIWA, Art. 31, para. 1. *See also LaGrand* (*Germany v. United States of America*), *Judgment*, 2001 ICJ Rep. 466, at 485, para. 48 (finding that "[w]here jurisdiction exists over a dispute on a particular matter, no separate basis for jurisdiction is required by the Court to consider the remedies a party has requested for the breach of the obligation (*Factory at Chorzów, P.C.I.J., Series A, No. 9*, p. 22)").

894 *Difference Relating to Immunity from Legal Process of a Special Rapporteur of the Commission on Human Rights*, Advisory Opinion, 1999 ICJ Rep. 62, at 88, para. 66. This statement has been cited approvingly by the European Court of Human Rights. *See Stichting Mothers of Srebrenica et al. v. The Netherlands*, App. No. 65542/12, judgment of 11 June 2013, at para. 155.

observed that the law of immunity "regulates the exercise of jurisdiction in respect of particular conduct and is thus entirely distinct from the substantive law which determines whether that conduct is lawful or unlawful"[895] and is compensable. As was explained above, the objective existence of liability (under domestic law) or responsibility (under international law) is not affected by whatever immunity, although immunity may work to prevent this liability or responsibility from being established (adjudicated) in a court of law, thereby blocking its judicial enforcement.[896]

While compensation, or more broadly reparation, is an aspect (legal consequence) of the international responsibility of intergovernmental organizations, the International Court of Justice has observed that "[t]he duty to make reparation is a rule which exists independently of those rules which concern the means by which it is to be effected" and "the law of ... immunity concerns only the latter; a decision that [an entity] is immune no more conflicts with the duty to make reparation than it does with the rule prohibiting the original wrongful act."[897] The Court's statement that "whether a State is entitled to immunity before the courts of another State is a question entirely separate from whether the international responsibility of that State is engaged and whether it has an obligation to make reparation"[898] can be said to apply with equal force to international organizations.

While a detailed discussion of the complex question of the responsibility of intergovernmental organizations under international law goes beyond the scope of this book, it is important to refer to certain key developments in this field, including especially the adoption by the International Law Commission of a set of *Articles on the Responsibility of International*

---

895 *Jurisdictional Immunities of the State* (*Germany v. Italy; Greece intervening*), Judgment, 2012 ICJ Rep. 99, at 124, para. 58, and 140, para. 93 (observing that the rules of immunity "do not bear upon the question whether or not the conduct in respect of which the proceedings are brought was lawful or unlawful").

896 *See also Sayag a.o. v. Leduc a.o.*, Court of Justice of the European Communities, Judgment of 11 July 1968, Case C-5/68 (emphasizing that "the designation of an act with regard to immunity from legal proceedings, and any decision taken by the competent institution with regard to waiver of the immunity, do not prejudge any liability on the part of the Community, this being governed by special rules designed for a purpose separate from that of the provisions of the Protocol on the Privileges and Immunities.").

897 *Jurisdictional Immunities of the State* (*Germany v. Italy; Greece intervening*), Judgment, 2012 ICJ Rep. 99, at 141, para. 94.

898 *Id.*, at 143, para. 100, and 145, para. 108 ("The question whether Germany still has a responsibility towards Italy, or individual Italians, in respect of war crimes and crimes against humanity committed by it during the Second World War does not affect Germany's entitlement to immunity. Similarly, the Court's ruling on the issue of immunity can have no effect on whatever responsibility Germany may have.").

Organizations (ARIO), comprising 67 articles spread over six Parts, in 2011.[899] These Articles are modelled after, albeit are different from, the Articles on the Responsibility of States for Internationally Wrongful Acts (ARSIWA), which were adopted by the ILC a decade earlier, in 2001.[900] In addition, the International Law Association (ILA) adopted its Final Report on 'Accountability of International Organizations' and a resolution on 'Rules and Recommended Practices on Liability/Responsibility of International Organizations' in 2004.[901]

Article 2 sub (a) ARIO defines 'international organization' as "an organization established by a treaty or other instrument governed by international law and possessing its own international legal personality," thereby making international legal personality on the part of a given organization a threshold condition for responsibility. As was explained earlier in the present study, an organization's international legal personality is not always expressed in its constituent instrument or other instrument, and this circumstance could give rise to applicability issues in this context.[902]

---

899 Draft articles on the responsibility of international organizations, adopted by the International Law Commission at its sixty-third session, and submitted to the UN General Assembly as part of the ILC's report covering the work of that session, UN Doc. A/66/10 (2011). For a scholarly discussion of the ARIO, including the criticism it has attracted, see M. Möldner, *Responsibility of International Organizations – Introducing the ILC's DARIO*, *in* Max Planck Yearbook of United Nations Law Vol. 16, 281–328 (A. von Bogdandy & R. Wolfrum eds. 2012). As of this writing, the question of the form that might be given to the ARIO remained pending in the UN General Assembly. *See* P. Palchetti, *Is It Time to Take a Decision on the Final Form of ARIO?*, 20(2) IOLR 103 (2023).

900 As one commentator has remarked, "[w]hat the ILC has done is essentially to take the ILC's previous, and highly successful, effort to delineate articles of state responsibility and do a 'global search and replace' so that anywhere the word 'state' appeared in the old articles, the word 'international organization' now appears." J.E. Alvarez, *Governing the World: International Organizations as Lawmakers*, 31(3) Suff. Transnat'l L.R. 591, 612 (2008). *See also* SCHERMERS, at 1060–1061, para. 1590B, and 1064, para. 1590C (positing that "the ILC has sufficiently taken into account the special nature of these organizations").

901 'Accountability of International Organizations,' Final Report and Resolution No. 1/2004, Berlin Conference (2004), *International Law Association Reports of Conference*, vol. 71 (2004), at 164–234, text available on the website of the ILA, https://www.ila-hq.org. *See also* Study Group on the Responsibility of International Organizations, Final Report, Sofia Conference (2012), *International Law Association Reports of Conference*, vol. 75 (2012), at 880.

902 As one commentator has pointed out, "it remains nebulous why an entity could only be held responsible if it possesses a formal quality in a legal order which generally declines any insistence on formal qualities." J. Klabbers, *Book Review*, 17 IOLR 683, 684 (2020).

Article 3 ARIO stipulates that "[e]very wrongful act of an international organization entails the international responsibility of that organization." According to Article 4 ARIO, "[t]here is an internationally wrongful act of an international organization when conduct consisting of an action or omission: (a) is attributable to that organization under international law; and (b) constitutes a breach of an international obligation of that organization." The latter element underscores that the breach must concern an international obligation that is binding on the international organization itself. Moreover, Article 11 ARIO makes clear that "[a]n act of an international organization does *not* constitute a breach of an international obligation unless *the organization is bound by the obligation* in question at the time the act occurs." (emphasis added)

Article 33 ARIO limits the scope of international obligations set out in Part Three ('Content of the international responsibility of an international organization') to obligations "owed to one or more States, to one or more other organizations, or to the international community as a whole, depending in particular on the character and content of the international obligation and on the circumstances of the breach," and it states that Part Three "is without prejudice to any right, arising from the international responsibility of an international organization, which may accrue directly to *any person or entity other than a State or an international organization*."(emphasis added) In this respect, Article 65 ARIO provides that "[t]he applicable rules of international law continue to govern questions concerning the responsibility of an international organization or a State for an internationally wrongful act to the extent that they are not regulated by these draft articles." These provisions make clear that the ARIO do not address the potential remedies that private parties may have *vis-à-vis* an international organization.

In recognition of the fact that an international organization interacts or cooperates with other subjects of international law, particularly States, Part Five of the ARIO addresses the responsibility of a State in connection with the conduct of an international organization, including through aid or assistance, direction and control, or coercion (Articles 58–60 ARIO). As regards member States, Article 61 ARIO provides for international responsibility of a member State "if, by taking advantage of the fact that the organization has competence in relation to the subject-matter of one of the State's international obligations, it circumvents that obligation by causing the organization to commit an act that, if committed by the State, would have constituted a breach of the obligation," regardless of whether the act in question is internationally wrongful for the international organization. According to Article

62 ARIO, a member State also is responsible for an internationally wrongful act of an organization to which it belongs "if: (a) it has accepted responsibility for that act towards the injured party; or (b) it has led the injured party to rely on its responsibility," with such State responsibility being presumed to be subsidiary.

According to Articles 66–67, constituting the final two provisions of the ARIO, the articles are without prejudice to "any question of the individual responsibility under international law of any person acting on behalf of an international organization or a State" and "the Charter of the United Nations."

Notably, the ARIO do not differentiate between the various categories of international organization, including regional economic integration organizations such as the European Union that display unique supranational elements, thereby ignoring the key principle of the speciality of international organizations.[903] There is little or no trace of 'functional' terminology in the ARIO. Article 2 sub (d) defines 'agent of an organization' as meaning "in particular, an official or other person or entity, other than an organ, who is charged by the organization with carrying out, or helping to carry out, one of its *functions* and thus through whom the organization acts."(emphasis added) In addressing the conduct of organs or agents in the context of attribution of conduct to an international organization, Article 6, paragraph 2, stipulates that "[t]he rules of the organization apply in the determination of the *functions* of its organs and agents."(emphasis added) Article 8, which addresses excess of authority or contravention of instructions as part of Chapter II ('Attribution of conduct to an international organization') of Part Two of the ARIO, provides that "[t]he conduct of an organ or agent of an international organization shall be considered an act of that organization under international law if the organ or agent acts in an official capacity and

903 *See Legality of the Use by a State of Nuclear Weapons in Armed Conflict*, Advisory Opinion, 1996 ICJ Rep. 66, at 78–79, para. 25 ("International organizations are governed by the 'principle of speciality', that is to say, they are invested by the States which create them with powers, the limits of which are a function of the common interests whose promotion those States entrust to them."). *See also* J.E. Alvarez, *Governing the World: International Organizations as Lawmakers*, 31(3) Suff. Transnat'l L.R. 591, 614 (2008) (noting that "the premise that a blanket approach to legal responsibility can be found to apply to all [intergovernmental organizations], irrespective of the differing structures and purposes of such organizations, seems fatally flawed"); J. Klabbers, *Book Review*, 12 IOLR 279, 280 (2015)(noting "the lament that organizations differ substantively in their structures and in particular in their operations, and thus a one-size-fits-all regime will not work").

within the overall *functions of that organization*, even if the conduct exceeds the authority of that organ or agent or contravenes instructions."(emphasis added) Articles 6 and 8 are the only ARIO provisions referring to the functions *of the organization.*

The ARIO also do not address the position of private parties in their dealings with intergovernmental organizations, including their remedies. Article 64 ('*Lex specialis*') of the ARIO highlights a key limitative, but also flexible, aspect by making it clear that "[t]hese draft articles do not apply where and to the extent that the conditions for the existence of an internationally wrongful act or the content or implementation of the international responsibility of an international organization, or of a State in connection with the conduct of an international organization, are governed by special rules of international law," including those contained in the rules of the organization applicable to the relations between an international organization and its members.

The aspect of the attribution of internationally wrongful conduct taking the form of an act or omission to an international organization can be said to be the most controversial (and complex) one in the debate regarding the proper regime for the responsibility of international organizations as opposed to States.[904] The national and international legal proceedings stemming from the massacre at the Srebrenica municipality in eastern Bosnia under the watch of (the Dutch battalion forming part of) the United Nations Protection Force (UNPROFOR), which had as their root a dispute between the claimants and the United Nations based on the use by the UN Security Council of its powers under Chapters VII of the UN Charter, as well as the International Tin Council proceedings before the English courts that are discussed in Chapter 3 of this book underscore the legal complexities that can arise in this context.[905]

---

904 *See, e.g.*, R.S.J. Martha, *Attribution of Conduct After the Advisory Opinion on the Global Mechanism, in* Responsibility of International Organizations—Essays in Memory of Sir Ian Brownlie 275–287 (M. Ragazzi ed. 2013).

905 *See, e.g.*, *Stichting Mothers of Srebrenica et al. v. The Netherlands*, European Court of Human Rights, App. No. 65542/12, judgment of 11 June 2013; *Stichting Mothers of Srebrenica et al. v. State of The Netherlands*, Supreme Court (*Hoge Raad*) of The Netherlands, case no. 17/04567, judgment of 19 July 2019, NJB 2019/1862; *Stichting Mothers of Srebrenica et al. v. State of The Netherlands and United Nations*, Supreme Court (*Hoge Raad*) of The Netherlands, case no. 10/04437, judgment of 13 April 2012. For a discussion of these cases, *see* G. den Dekker, *Absolute Validity, Absolute Immunity: Is There Something Wrong with Article 103 of the UN Charter?, in* What's Wrong with International Law? *Liber Amicorum* A.H.A. Soons 247–264 (C. Reyngaert et al., eds. 2015).

It has been pointed out that an international organization "may also be held responsible for damage or injury resulting from its activities, though whether this [organizational] liability excludes the concurrent liability of its Member States is a complex and controversial question."[906] While it is correct to state generally that "international organizations are liable if their acts cause injury to others" and that "[t]he fact that they generally have immunity before national courts does not affect that liability,"[907] the (extent of the) responsibility of international organizations remains surrounded by controversy. The system of primary and secondary rules regarding the responsibility of intergovernmental organizations, and the broader notion of the accountability (political, legal, administrative, fiscal, reputational and otherwise[908]) of these entities and transparency in their decision-making and operations, can be expected to continue to evolve in tandem with the law of organizational immunities, infused by the relevant practice of intergovernmental organizations and contributions made by learned bodies and scholars.[909] In light of the evolving nature of the

---

906 SATOW, at 290, para. 21.7. *See also* ARIO, Arts. 18–19, 48 and 61–63. It is the longstanding view of the Office of Legal Affairs of the United Nations that "once the Organization incurs a legal liability, it is legally obligated to pay that liability" and "[i]t is for the appropriate financial officials of the Organization to take the necessary steps to do so" and that "[a]s matter of international law, it is clear that the Organization can incur liabilities of a private law nature and is obligated to pay in regard to such liabilities." 2001 UN Jurid. Y.B, pp. 384–385, UN Doc. ST/LEG/SER.C/39 (2001). *See also* A. Nollkaemper et al., *Guiding Principles on Shared Responsibility in International Law*, 31(1) EJIL 15 (2020).

907 SCHERMERS, at 1088, para. 1613.

908 *See, e.g.*, WELLENS, at 8; K. Boon and F. Mégret, *New Approaches to the Accountability of International Organizations*, 16 IOLR 1 (2019); K. Daugirdas, *Reputation and Accountability: Another Look at the United Nations' Response to the Cholera Epidemic in Haiti*, 16(1) IOLR 11 (2019); K. Daugirdas, *Reputation and the Responsibility of International Organizations*, 25 EJIL 991–1018 (2015).

909 *See, e.g.*, T. Henquet, The Third-Party Liability of International Organizations—Towards a 'Complete Remedy System' Counterbalancing Jurisdictional Immunity (2023); D. Nauta, The International Responsibility of NATO and its Personnel during Military Operations (2017); Remedies and Responsibility for the Actions of International Organizations (D. Sarooshi ed. 2014); SCHERMERS, at 1049–1063, para. 1582–1590C; AMERASINGHE, at 384–406 (2005); P. Klein, La Responsabilité des Organisations Internationales dans les Ordres Juridiques Internes et en Droit des Gens (1998); M. Hirsch, The Responsibility of International Organizations Toward Third Parties: Some Basic Principles (1995); K. Boon, *Rethinking the Accountability-Immunity Axis through Remedies: Lessons from National Militaries*, 16 IOLR 137 (2019); Special Issue: International Organizations and Member State Responsibility—Critical Perspectives, 12(2) IOLR (2015); M. Zwanenburg, *UN Peace Operations Between Independence and*

international responsibility of intergovernmental organizations, especially of the relevant practice regarding certain aspects of that responsibility, the ARIO can be said to represent a progressive development of the law rather than a codification.[910] It must be remembered that "'functional necessity' is not only the *raison d'être* of the immunity rules of international organizations, but also the rationale of an adequate accountability regime."[911] However, what is 'adequate' for a given organization is not settled. What is clear is that "a well-functioning accountability regime increases the efficiency of international organisations and is thus also indispensable to them in terms of assisting them to serve their purpose."[912] In the end, as one commentator has rightly stated:

> The fundamental question, ..., is whether the mechanisms specifically put in place by international organisations to deal with claims against them or permanent mechanisms for serving other purposes as well, and the actual outcome of their utilization by a variety of potential claimants, have indeed satisfactorily assured the accountability of international organisations.[913]

While, generally speaking, the "remedies for the implementation of accountability of international organisations should correspond to the kind and nature of the complainants addressed to them,"[914] they also should correspond to the purposes and functions of a given international organization, as dictated by the international law principle of speciality. While sovereign States are more or less the same,[915] justifying a uniform regime of primary and secondary rules regarding their responsibility under international law, the same cannot be said about intergovernmental organizations and this calls,

---

Accountability, 5(1) IOLR 23 (2008); G. Hafner, *Accountability of International Organizations—A Critical Review in* Towards World Constitutionalism 585 (R.St. J Macdonald & D.M. Johnston eds. 2005).

910 In the General Commentary to the ARIO, the ILC acknowledged that "[t]he fact that several of the present draft articles are based on limited practice moves the border between codification and progressive development in the direction of the latter." General Commentary, note 1, para. 5.

911 SCHERMERS, at 1087, para. 1612A.

912 WELLENS, at 9.

913 *Id.*, at 2.

914 *Id.*, at 8.

915 *See* Art. 2, para. 1, UN Charter ("The Organization is based on the principle of the sovereign equality of all its Members").

therefore, for a more nuanced approach.[916] It must be kept in mind that, "[i]n contrast to the situation of states there is, generally, no one single comprehensive system governing all relevant questions" when it comes to intergovernmental organizations and their responsibility.[917]

3.6.6 Conclusion

After having reviewed the most significant organizational immunity instruments dealing with settlement of disputes of a wide variety, some conclusions may be drawn as to the use and satisfactory application of these procedures.

The words written by Jenks in 1961, that "[l]ittle if any use appears to have been made of all these provisions for international judicial settlement or arbitration" no longer apply, thereby underscoring the rapid developments that have taken place in this regard since the 1960s.[918] The study prepared by the United Nations Secretariat in 1967[919] and supplemented in 1985[920] on the practice of the United Nations Family concerning its status, privileges and immunities, as well as the more recent replies by States and intergovernmental organizations to a questionnaire forming part of the ILC's study of the settlement of disputes to which international organizations are parties,[921] provide evidence of the increasing practical significance of the aforementioned procedures. Jenks did immediately add, however, that "the fact that it does not appear to have been necessary to have recourse to them does not reduce their significance."[922] The mere existence of these provisions and their increased use are indeed evidence of the fact that international organizations cannot rely unrestrictively on the privileges and

916 *See also* BROWNLIE, at 686 (cautioning that "regard must be had to each set of circumstances" in this context); WELLENS, at 21 ("the governance of primary rules over states is, in principle, uniform, whereas the functional variety of international organisations substantially reduces the range and number of guidelines, rules, norms and standards that may be considered commonly applicable"). For a succinct comparison of remedies against States with those against international organizations, listing both distinctive and common features, *see* WELLENS, at 19 *et seq.*

917 WELLENS, at 8.

918 JENKS, at 25.

919 [1967] 2 Y.B. Int'l L. Comm'n 296, para. 389, and 321, para. 179, UN Doc. A/CN.4/ SER. A/1967/Add. 1.

920 UN Doc. A/CN.4/L.383 and Add. 1–3 (1985) *reprinted in* [1985] 2 Y.B. Int'l L. Comm'n 145, 209, UN Doc. A/CN.4/SER.A/1985/Add. 1 (Part 1/Add. 1).

921 *See* International Law Commission, Memorandum by the Secretariat, Questionnaire, UN Doc. A/CN.4/764 (2024).

922 JENKS, at 25.

immunities to which they are entitled.[923] This is what we meant when we stated earlier that organizational immunities are in no way to be regarded as some kind of 'one way ticket' or *carte blanche*.

With regard to the direct relationship between the organization and the host State, Jenks has rightly observed that the procedures with which we have dealt in this section:

> afford valuable safeguards to both governments and international organisations. Governments are protected against abuse and the organisations against the chiselling away of arrangements which have been made on grounds of high international policy to protect their independence and freedom of action. Both safeguards are equally necessary to a balanced and rational régime of international immunities.[924]

With respect to the special interests of third parties, reference may be made to another authority on organizational immunities, who concluded:

> The arrangement provided by the organizations for the settlement of disputes arising out of contracts or other disputes which are of a private law character is commendable. Such an arrangement inspires public confidence and makes it clear that the organization in question does not occupy an unfairly privileged status.[925]

From the above analysis we venture to draw the conclusion that, with regard to the procedures for the settlement of disputes concerning the privileges and immunities of international organizations and claims against organizations that have been developed over the past decades, the law of organizational immunities constitutes a more or less balanced régime, the significance of which is underscored by the mere reference to such procedures in existing agreements and the constant fine-tuning of dispute settlement procedures, including through an organization's internal mechanisms and inter-organizational arrangements. Although the practice relating to these procedures is still evolving, this fact in itself cannot be a ground for regarding the régime just referred to as not being satisfactory from the point of view of interests other than those of the organizations themselves,

923 *See also* HUG, at 155.
924 JENKS, at 25.
925 AHLUWALIA, at 72.

including the interests of shareholders and of stakeholders. The interests of private parties would be served even more by further developing procedures to which they have direct access, rather than having to rely on their States' discretion to grant diplomatic protection or to complain on their behalf. As a general rule, international organizations should insert arbitration clauses in their contracts with private parties that are readily enforceable in practice and they should offer redress in the form of an independent accountability mechanism or grievance system to which external parties may submit claims for independent administrative review in appropriate cases. The rapid development of such mechanisms within multiple intergovernmental organizations, especially multilateral development banks, since the mid-1990s is an encouraging development, one which can be expected to continue in future years.

Similar to what the International Court of Justice held with regard to diplomatic immunity law in the case concerning *United States Diplomatic and Consular Staff in Tehran*,[926] the rules of organizational immunity law constitute a self-contained régime which, on the one hand, lays down the host State's obligations regarding the facilities, privileges and immunities to be accorded to international organizations and, on the other hand, foresees their possible abuse by these organizations and specifies the means at the disposal of any aggrieved party to counter any such abuse, despite an absence of strict reciprocity.

With regard to the future development and evaluation of the topic under present review, we refer again to Jenks, who concluded in 1961, subject to the condition that international organizations remain faithful to certain basic principles, that:

> there is every justification for maintaining the essentials of the present system of international immunities until the further development of world organisation has so bridled national sovereignty that the collective instrumentalities of the world community no longer need special protection from its encroachments to secure their freedom and independence, preserve their constitutional responsibility to their membership as a whole acting through the appropriate bodies against unilateral interference by particular members, and permit the impartial, efficient and economical discharge of the responsibilities

926 *United States Diplomatic and Consular Staff in Tehran*, 1980 ICJ Rep. 3, 40, para. 86.

> entrusted to them by the community as a whole. At that stage international immunities will have served their purpose and the whole matter can be reconsidered in the light of a changed situation .... But let us create an effective international system before we dismantle the main existing legal bulwark of the freedom and independence of the organs of that system.[927]

Some writers consider that the appropriate moment for such a reconsideration has already arrived.[928] Although we admit that since 1961, when Jenks made the remarks just referred to, world organization has undergone a tremendous development, we are still confronted with an international community in which the exigencies of daily life call for the special protection of international bodies which lack sovereignty. We must face the fact that the danger of interference by sovereign States and their courts with the activities of international organizations will constantly be lurking, no matter what stage the development of world organization has reached. In this regard one must keep in mind that "the need for immunities must be gauged not by the extent to which they are necessary or useful in every day life in a well-ordered capital but by their potential importance in emergencies"[929]

927 JENKS, at 170–171.

928 *See, e.g.*, E. Gaillard and I. Pingel-Lenuzza, *International organizations and immunity from jurisdiction: to restrict or to bypass*, 51 ICLQ 1–15 (2002); Note, *Jurisdictional Immunities of Intergovernmental Organizations,* 91 Yale L.J. 1167, 1184 n.149 (1982), and, to a certain extent, O'Toole, at 16. *See also* J. Henquet, The Third-Party Liability of International Organisations—Towards a 'Complete Remedy System' Counterbalancing Jurisdictional Immunity (2023); OAS Guide, Guideline 1, 'Legal basis for the jurisdictional immunities of international organizations,' Rapporteur's Notes ("Although the meeting of the minds is the principal source of obligations, such agreement must always consider and be interpreted in harmony with other relevant legal aspects, such as human rights law. Therefore, it is advisable for the States and the organizations to update the applicable legal framework in order to bring it into line with current needs and challenges."). *But see* SCHERMERS, at 1087, para. 1612A ("there does not seem to be a need for a complete overhaul of the existing immunity rules of international organizations; it is rather their implementation that should be improved").

929 JENKS, at xxxvi. Attempts by U.S. plaintiffs to hold the World Health Organization liable for the COVID-19 pandemic in U.S. court are an apt example. *See*, e.g., *Kling et al. v. World Health Organization*, 532 F.Supp. 3d 141 (S.D.N.Y. 2021)(upholding the WHO's immunity from suit alleging the WHO's liability in connection with the spread of the COVID-19 virus in 2019–2020).

and that, in the majority of cases, international organizations still have not too much but too little authority. Relating these considerations to the present stage of development, we can safely say that international organizations still have a legitimate need for protection by way of certain functional privileges and immunities.

CHAPTER 3

The Functional Concept Applied: The International Tin Council

1 Introducing: The Tin Crisis

The landmark English litigation surrounding the International Tin Council (ITC) is an apt case study for demonstrating how the three steps of the functional necessity analysis operate to determine whether an international organization has a legitimate need for privileges and immunities.[1] This is due to the fact that the nature of the ITC as an international organization involves aspects which are in the 'grey area' of activities *jure imperii* and activities *jure gestionis*, were one to use sovereign immunity terminology.

24 October 1985 marked the collapse of the Sixth International Tin Agreement (ITA), an international commodity agreement originally concluded in 1956.[2] Trading in tin was suspended following an announcement by the ITC that it had run out of funds and that it was no longer able to meet its obligations. As a consequence, it became impossible for the ITC to pursue its basic objective, namely, the regulation of the world production and consumption of tin through the stabilization of tin prices on world markets, especially on the London Metal Exchange (LME).[3]

1 Moreover, as one commentator has stated, "[t]he relevance of the Tin Council's collapse on the study of the responsibility of international organizations can hardly be underestimated." J. Klabbers, *Schermers' Dilemma*, 31(2) EJIL 565, 580, n.74 (2020).

2 Similar ones to the ITC exist for other commodities, such as sugar, cocoa, coffee, rubber, and wheat; on international commodity agreements in general see R.N. Gariepy, *International Commodity Agreements*, 25 ICLQ 677 (1976); G. Fischer, *Les associations de pays exportateurs de produits de base*, 22 AFDI 528 (1976); U. Wassermann, *Tin and Other Commodities in Crisis*, 20 J.W.T.L. 232 (1986)[hereinafter: Wassermann, Tin]; W.A. Kewenig, *Der Internationale Zinnrat – Ein Lehrstück des Völkerrechts*, 10 RIW 781 (1990)[hereinafter: Kewenig].

3 Under the aegis of UNCTAD, a number of international commodity agreements on different commodities have been concluded between consumer and producer States aimed at stabilizing export earnings for developing countries. In 1976, UNCTAD adopted the 'Integrated Programme for Commodities,' which covers some eighteen commodities, including tin. *See* UN Doc. TD/Res. 93(IV)(1976). As an operational arm of the Programme, UNCTAD concluded in 1980 the 'Agreement Establishing the Common Fund for Commodities,' with

 DOI:10.1163/9789004724211_004

In order to avoid excessive fluctuations in price and earnings and to balance supply and demand of tin, the ITC was equipped to operate a buffer stock, designed to maintain the tin price within a fixed bracket of floor and ceiling prices.[4] Under this mechanism, the ITC – through the Buffer Stock Manager (BSM) – would purchase tin whenever prices dropped below the fixed floor price. Reducing prices would increase demand, and in turn would lead to a rise in prices on the world market. Conversely, the BSM would sell tin from the buffer stock when prices were rising, in order to create a downward pressure on prices through an increase in the supply of tin.[5] The success of this price-regulation mechanism depends on a long-term balance between demand and supply of tin, which, in turn, requires a regulation of the production. However, practice showed a stagnating demand causing over-production, which led to the crisis after a dramatic decline in the U.S. dollar exchange rate in early 1985. Other factors which caused the tin price to collapse were the development of cheaper substitutes such as aluminum, the continued operation of expensive and inefficient producers, diminished consumption, the smuggling onto the market by ITC members and a vast increase in supply by non-signatory tin producers.[6] By early 1985, however, the BSM had already contracted with commodity brokers to purchase large quantities of tin in an ultimate effort to keep the price of tin up; the BSM had financed these transactions by concluding loan agreements with banks. The ITC defaulted on its contracts with the brokers and failed to repay the loans made by the banks, thus creating debts estimated at around one billion Pounds Sterling.[7] This situation triggered a spate of proceedings, especially before the English courts, involving a wide range of complex legal issues.[8] It must be kept in mind that

its Secretariat in Amsterdam, The Netherlands. *See* UN Doc. TD/IPC/CONF./L.15; UN Doc. A/46/372 (1991).

4 *See* M.E. MacGlashan, *The International Tin Council: Should a Trading Organisation Enjoy Immunity?*, 46 C.L.J. 193, 193 (1987)[hereinafter: MacGlashan]. The ITC had the additional power to borrow to finance the buffer stock operations.

5 *See* C. Greenwood, *Put Not Your Trust In Princes: The Tin Council Appeals*, 48 C.L.J. 46, 46 (1989)[hereinafter: Greenwood].

6 *See* D. Thompson, *The International Tin Council Litigation*, 22 J.W.T.L. 103, 105 (1988)[hereinafter: Thompson]; Wassermann, Tin, at 232–33; MacGlashan, at 193.

7 *See* Wassermann, Tin, at 233; Seidl-Hohenveldern, Tin, at 44.

8 The main question before the courts was to what extent (if at all) the member States of the ITC could be held liable, whether primarily or secondarily, for the debts of the ITC (the 'direct actions'). *See* House of Lords Judgment of 26 October 1989 in *Maclaine Watson & Co. Ltd. v. Department of Trade and Industry and related appeals; Maclaine Watson & Co. Ltd. v. International Tin Council*, [1990] 2 App.Cas. 418, [1989] 3 All E.R. 523, [1989] 3

these English court proceedings were governed by English law, not international law.

2 Step One: The Status of the ITC as an Organization

The first step in applying the functional concept is identifying the entity concerned. The entity's basic instruments provide the primary source for embarking upon this examination of its legal status.

The most recent operative agreement was the Sixth International Tin Agreement (ITA6), which was signed in Geneva on 26 June 1981 following the United Nations Tin Conference, held under the auspices of UNCTAD.[9] Membership included 23 States and the European Economic Community.[10]

In the preamble, the parties to ITA6 recognize, *inter alia*:

> (a) The significant assistance to economic growth, especially in developing producing countries, that can be given by commodity agree-

---

W.L.R. 969, *reprinted in* 29 ILM 670, 695 (1990) [hereinafter: *Maclaine Watson*]; *see also* Schermers, Liability, at 4. For a summary of the litigation, involving 'direct actions' by banks and brokers, a winding-up action, a receivership action and a discovery of assets action, *see* Greenwood, at 47–53; *see also* P.M. Eisemann, *Crise du Conseil International de L'Etain et Insolvabilité d'une Organisation Intergouvernementale,* 31 AFDI 730 (1985); E. McFadden, *The Collapse of Tin: Restructuring a Failed Commodity Agreement,* 80 AJIL 811 (1986); Thompson, at 107–110; D.N. Hutchinson, *Decisions of British Courts During 1987 Involving Questions of Public International Law,* 58 BYBIL 399, 399–429 (1987)[hereinafter: Hutchinson]; M. Herdegen, *Bemerkungen zur Zwangsliquidation und zum Heffungsdurchgriff bei internationalen Organisationen,* 47 ZaöRV 537 (1987); G. Hoffmann, *Der Durchgriff auf die Mitgliedstaaten von internationalen Organisationen für deren Schulden,* 41 NJW 585 (1987); Seidl-Hohenveldem, Responsibility; *id.,* Tin; *id.,* Communautés; C.F. Amerasinghe, *Liability to Third Parties of Member States of International Organizations: Practice, Principle and Judicial Precedent,* 85 AJIL 259 (1991); AMERASINGHE, at 407–446; Ebenroth. The creditors and the member States entered into a settlement of the ITC case after the House of Lords Judgment. The creditors received around forty percent of their original claims. *See* THE FINANCIAL TIMES, 3 Nov. 1989. This study's discussion will concentrate on immunity aspects of the ITC litigation.

9 Entered into force on 1 July 1982, Misc. No. 13 (1982), Cmnd. 8546; *Multilateral Treaties Deposited with the Secretary-General – Status as at 31 December 1986,* UN Doc. ST/LEG/SER.E/5 (1987), at 677–678; *see also* U. Wassermann, *UNCTAD: Sixth International Tin Agreement,* 15 J.W.T.L. 557, 557–558 (1981)[hereinafter: Wassermann, UNCTAD];

10 For a list of member States see *Maclaine Watson v. Dept. of Trade,* (Kerr, L.J.) [1988] 3 All E.R. 257, 271; I. Cheyne, *The International Tin Council,* 38 ICLQ 417, 417 n.2 (1989) [hereinafter: Cheyne]. The member States are divided into producers and consumers according to their selection at the time of ratification, acceptance or accession. Article 5 of ITA6 refers to these two categories, which are defined in Article 2.

> ments in helping to secure stabilization of prices and steady development of export earnings and of primary commodity markets;
>
> ...
>
> (c) The exceptional importance of tin to numerous countries whose economy is heavily dependent upon favourable and equitable conditions for its production, consumption or trade;
>
> (d) The need to protect and foster the health and growth of the tin industry, especially in the developing producing countries, and to ensure adequate supplies of tin to safeguard the interests of consumers;
>
> (e) The importance to tin producing countries of maintaining and expanding their import purchasing power; and
>
> (f) The desirability of improving efficiency in the use of tin in both the developing and industrialized countries, as an aid to the conservation of world tin resources.[11]

Article 1 of Chapter I of ITA6 sets out the objectives of the member States. These objectives indicate that the International Tin Agreements were effected to adjust and stabilize tin prices, increase export earnings from tin, provide a long-term equilibrium between production and consumption, prevent un(der)-employment, increase the use of tin, make arrangements in case of a shortage or a surplus in tin, and promote the development of the tin market in the developing producing countries.[12]

Article 3 of ITA6 maintained the International Tin Council (ITC) as the administering body of the ITO.[13] Article 7 provides that the ITC:

> (a) Shall have such powers and perform such functions as may be necessary for the administration and operation of this Agreement;
>
> (b) Shall have the power to borrow for the purposes of the Administrative Account established under article 17, or of the Buffer Account in accordance with article 24; ....[14]

11 Preamble, ITA6, Cmnd. 8546.

12 While frequent reference is made in Article 1 to developing countries, it should be noted that out of the 23 member States only six are generally regarded as such.

13 The ITC had originally been established by Article IV of ITA1, *see Maclaine Watson,* 29 ILM 670, 680 (1990).

14 A distinction is drawn between the administration account and the buffer stock account, *see* ITA6, Art. 17 *et seq.; Maclaine Watson,* 29 ILM 670,684 (1990).

This provision is clearly drafted along the lines of the functional concept.

The legal status of the ITC is regulated by Article 16, paragraph 1, of ITA6, which provides as follows: "1. The Council shall have legal personality. It shall in particular have the capacity to contract, to acquire and dispose of movable and immovable property and to institute legal proceedings."[15]

In order to implement Article 3, paragraph 3, of ITA6, which selected London as the seat of the ITC, and Article 16(4), a Headquarters Agreement was entered into between the United Kingdom and the ITC, signed in London on 9 February 1972.[16] Article 3 of this agreement is drafted in the same terms as Article 16 of ITA6. Moreover, both provisions were given effect by the *International Tin Council (Immunities and Privileges) Order* of 1972,[17] made under the terms of the *International Organisations (Immunities and Privileges) Act* of 1968.[18]

These provisions and the general language in the basic instruments indicate that the member States had by treaty agreed to establish the ITC as the administrative body of an intergovernmental organization with a legal personality distinct from those of its member States.[19] One fundamental question the House of Lords addressed in *Maclaine Watson*[20] was whether on the true construction of the Order in Council of 1972 the ITC was vested with a separate personality distinct from its constituent members as a matter of domestic English law.[21] The House of Lords, *per* Lord Oliver of Aylmerton, answered this question in the affirmative, holding that:

> the effect of the Order in Council was to create the I.T.C. (which, as an international legal persona, had no status under the laws of the United Kingdom) [as] a legal person in its own right, independent of its members. In engaging in the contracts on which the claims of the brokers and the banks are based, it was the contracting party. Its members were not. It was to the I.T.C. and not to its members that credit was extended and it is elementary that the only persons liable and entitled under a contract, in the absence of trust or agency, are the parties to the contract.[22]

15 ITA6, Art. 16, para. 1, Cmnd. 8546.

16 834 U.N.T.S. 287.

17 S.I. 1972 No. 120; Art. 5; *see also* Hutchinson, at 400 n.6.

18 *Halsbury's Statutes of England,* Vol. 6, at 1051 (3rd ed. 1969) and Vol. 18, at 821 (4th ed. 1977). For the relevant provisions of this Act *see Maclaine Watson,* 29 ILM 670,689 (1990).

19 *See Maclaine Watson,* 29 ILM 670, 673 (1990).

20 *Maclaine Watson,* 29 ILM 670 (1990).

21 *Id.*, at 695.

22 *Id.*, at 700; *see also* Lord Templeman, *id.,* at 674.

Significantly, the ITC derived its legal personality from *international law* and the Order of 1972 merely gave effect to that international personality in domestic law.[23] Without the recognition of the existence of separate legal personality, the immunities conferred upon the ITC would be meaningless, a fact already stressed by the ICJ in its advisory opinion rendered in the *Reparation* Case in 1949.[24]

Article 1 would seem to indicate that the major part of ITA6, with its emphasis on matters of high economic policy, belongs to the sovereign or *jure imperii* sphere of the member States. It has, however, been argued, that the essential *modus operandi* of the ITC – its principal method of giving effect to those *prima facie* sovereign objectives – was to enter into ordinary commercial contracts for the purchase and sale of tin on the London and Penang markets.[25] In fact, buying and selling tin was the ITC's principal activity, which, if viewed *in isolation*, is a *jure gestionis* activity.[26] The ITC hence seems to have pursued sovereign aims by commercial means, thus creating a discrepancy between objectives and operation. The English Court of Appeals (Civil Division) mentioned this discrepancy in the general introduction to its judgment in the case of the International Tin Council Appeals rendered on 27 April 1988:

> In the traditional terms of international law the objectives of the members of the ITC fall to be regarded as *jure imperii*. But the attainment of its objectives also necessarily involved trading – on the LME and the Tin Market in Penang – and loan transactions on a massive scale which would in themselves be regarded as operations conducted *jure gestionis*.[27]

Schermers has argued that "[w]hen governments create an international organization to perform a governmental task, be it to regulate international

23 *See* Greenwood, at 49–50; Seidl-Hohenveldem, Tin, at 45.

24 *See* 1949 ICJ Rep. 174, 179. For the relationship between legal status and immunities see Chapter 2 above, and, *inter alia*, Greenwood, at 49; Lalive, at 304, 314; AHLUWALIA, at 208; BOWETT, at 339, 341; Calero Rodriques, in [1985] 1 Y.B. Int'l L. Comm'n 292, para. 25, UN Doc. A/CN.4/SER.A/1985.

25 *See* Greenwood, at 51.

26 *See* Seidl-Hohenveldern, Tin, at 48, 50.

27 *Maclaine Watson & Co. Ltd. v. Department of Trade and Industry and related appeals; Re International Tin Council; Maclaine Watson & Co. Ltd. v. International Tin Council; Maclaine Watson & Co. Ltd. v. International Tin Council (No. 2)*, Court of Appeal (Civil Division), 27 April 1988, [1989] 1 Ch. 72, 253, 286, 309, [1988] 3 All E.R. 257, [1988] 3 W.L.R. 1033, 1159, 1169, 1190 [hereinafter: *ITC Civil Division Appeals*].

traffic or to stabilize commodity prices, they do so in a public function and not for the sake of raising capital or for trading."[28] U.S. case law has recognized that a State's right to regulate its natural resources, such as tin, is a uniquely sovereign function, or a sovereign prerogative, and that the control over its mineral resources is a basic attribute of State sovereignty.[29] Nonetheless, it is a different question whether an international organization still has a legitimate need for privileges and immunities when it becomes involved in trading on capital markets by means of commercial contracts, especially when such activities overshadow the organization's (quasi-) sovereign purposes. One might suggest 'lifting the veil' and regarding the ITC as an ordinary trading organization, with a less compelling need for certain privileges and immunities. Seidl-Hohenveldern has proposed distinguishing between international organizations, properly so-called, established by member States '*jure imperii*,' and common inter-State enterprises, which are created *jure gestionis* and which are subject to domestic law instead of international law.[30] Since the latter entities have no right to perform sovereign acts, one might argue that they do not require any international legal personality nor privileges and immunities.[31] Schermers has, however, pointed at the fundamental differences that exist between an

---

28 Schermers, Liability, at 9; *see also* Lord Oliver of Aylmerton in *Maclaine Watson*, 29 ILM 670, 712 (1990), who maintained that "[t]he creation and regulation by a number of sovereign states of an international organisation for their common political and economic purposes was an act jure imperii;" Seidl-Hohenveldern, Tin, at 47, 50.

29 For 'natural resource' decisions to this effect see, e.g., *Mol, Inc. v. People's Republic of Bangladesh*, 736 F.2d 1326 (9th Cir. 1984); *In Re SEDCO, Inc.*, 543 F.Supp. 561,566 (S.D. Tex. 1982), *vac.* in part, 610 F.Supp. 306 (S.D. Tex. 1984), *rem.*, 767 F.2d 1140 (5th Cir. 1985); *IAM v. OPEC*, 477 F.Supp. 553, 569 (C.D. Calif. 1979), *aff'd* on other grounds, 649 F.2d 1354 (9th Cir. 1981), *cert. den.*, 454 U.S. 1163 (1982); *Carey v. National Oil Corp.*, 453 F.Supp. 1097 (S.D.N.Y. 1978), *aff'd*, 592 F.2d 673 (2d Cir. 1979); *Internat'l Ass'n of Machinists and Aerospace Workers (IAM) v. Organization of the Petroleum Exporting Countries*, 477 F.Supp. 553, 569 (C.D. Cal. 1979)(dismissing case brought against OPEC and its member countries by an American labor association alleging that the price-setting activities of OPEC and its member countries violated U.S. antitrust laws, on the basis of (the collective) sovereign immunity of the OPEC member countries, while observing that "[t]he action of sovereign nations coming together to agree on how each will perform certain sovereign acts [pertaining to natural resources located within their territory] can only, itself, be a sovereign act"), *aff'd* 649 F.2d 1354 (9th Cir. 1981)(affirming lower court's dismissal based on the alternate ground of 'Act of State' doctrine). *See* G.B. Born & D. Westin, International Civil Litigation in United States Courts – Commentary & Materials 364–387 (1989). The Texas court in *In Re SEDCO, Inc.* made an exception to this general rule, however, in the case of the actual sale of a State's mineral resources on the world market.

30 Seidl-Hohenveldern, Corporations, at 109 *et seq.*

31 *Id.*, at 112.

international organization properly so-called, and an ordinary company or enterprise; these differences include those of purpose, method of budgeting, and structure and method of management.[32] These fundamental differences militate against comparing the ITC, which was not run for commercial profit, with an ordinary enterprise.[33] According to Seidl- Hohenveldern "States opt to co-operate in an enterprise which is capable of performing *jure gestionis* acts only, because they want to solve the problems concerned on lines as similar as possible to those used by private persons."[34] However, as Lord Templeman noted, "[t]he Order of 1972 is inconsistent with any intention on the part of Parliament that creditors and courts should regard the I.T.C. as a partnership between 23 sovereign states and the E.E.C. trading in the United Kingdom like any private partnership."[35]

The previous analysis invoked standard sovereign immunity concepts. However, Part Two of the present study demonstrated that the same result can be achieved through another route, which avoids any ambiguous sovereign immunity terminology. Unlike States, international organizations enjoy limited international legal status only, and the legal régime of these limitations is defined by the special purposes for which the organization was established.[36] To determine the nature and extent of an organization's activities, the key sources are its basic instruments, which contain its purposes, functions and powers. Herein lies the basic difference between States and international organizations: whereas in sovereign immunity law the purpose of a certain act is irrelevant,[37] that purpose constitutes the ultimate justification for every activity of an international organization.

In Chapter 2 we pointed out also that the purposes and functions of an international organization may very well require the performance of commercial activities, while still remaining within the organization's 'official

32 Schermers, Liability, at 6.

33 Millet J. in *In re International Tin Council*, (1987] 2 W.L.R. 1229, (1987] 1 All E.R. 890, Ch.D., *quoted in* Hutchinson, at 412, addressed this discussion at 1246 a-d; 903 f-h, observing that the member States had clearly chosen the medium of an international organization instead of a collective enterprise.

34 Seidl-Hohenveldern, Corporations, at 112.

35 Lord Templeman in *Maclaine Watson*, 29 ILM 670, 674 (1990).

36 *See also* Díaz González, *Second Report*, UN Doc. A/CN.4/391 and Add. 1 *reprinted in* [1985] 2 Y.B. Int'l L. Comm'n 103, 110, para. 61, UN Doc. A/CN.4/SER.A/1985/Add. 1 (Part 1).

37 *See also* Foreign Sovereign Immunities Act, S. 1603(d), which provides that the "commercial character of an activity shall be determined by reference to the nature of the course of conduct or particular transaction or act, rather than by reference to its purpose."

activities' framework, and, therefore, within the legitimate incidence of immunity.[38] Immunity may apply to every activity of an international organization, as long as that activity is required by the organization's purposes and functions.[39] In the tin case, the trading in which the ITC was involved was functionally necessary to attain the ITC's objectives. As the English Court of Appeals remarked:

> One of the main functions of the ICT throughout its history was to engage in trade in connection with its buffer stock operations in order to keep the world price of tin between the Floor and Ceiling prices laid down from time to time. Inevitably, therefore, the ITC was bound to enter into contracts for the purchase and sale of tin on a very large scale, primarily in this country on the LME, and other commercial transactions, such as heavy borrowings, were also likely.(emphasis added)[40]

What might have been dubbed 'commercial activities' if undertaken by an individual State were inevitable outcomes of official activity by an intergovernmental organization.[41]

A judgment of the Court of Justice of the European Communities (as it then was) may further illustrate this point. This judgment provides an apt example of a judicial refusal to accord 'commercial activity' status to the activities of an intergovernmental organization.

The Belgian *Cour de Cassation* had referred to the Luxemburg Court for a preliminary ruling under Article 177 of the EEC Treaty the question whether the European Organization for the Safety of Air Navigation (Eurocontrol) constitutes an 'undertaking' within the meaning of Articles 86 and 90 of the Treaty of Rome of 25 March 1957 establishing the European Economic

38 *See* the text accompanying *supra* note 571 *et seq.*

39 *See* AHLUWALIA, at 66; Hutchinson, at 400.

40 *ITC Civil Division Appeals,* [1988] 3 All E.R. 257.

41 In any event, the member States apparently had answered in the affirmative the preliminary question whether the ITC had a legitimate need for certain privileges and immunities, as an examination of the basic documents in Step Two will demonstrate; *see also* BEIER *et al.*, at 15, mentioning the fact that, during the drafting conference of the Protocol on the Privileges and Immunities of the EPO, the British delegation had proposed to classify the EPO as a 'quasi-commercial' entity, not having a special need for immunities. The conference refused, however, to accept this proposal and agreed that the EPO would have to carry out tasks that were regarded as within the public function of States.

Community.[42] This question had arisen in the course of proceedings which Eurocontrol had brought before the Belgian courts against SAT, an airline company governed by German law, seeking the recovery of route charges payable by SAT for air navigation services provided by Eurocontrol in connection with flights made by SAT during a certain period. In order to justify its refusal to pay the charges, SAT maintained that Eurocontrol had infringed Articles 86 and 90 of the EEC Treaty and it claimed that Eurocontrol is an 'undertaking' within the meaning of these provisions and that the procedures followed by it constitute an abuse of a dominant market position.[43] SAT argued that the research and coordination activities carried out by Eurocontrol and the collection of route charges do not fall within the definition of '*jus imperii*,' but constitute economic activities that could be carried out by bodies governed by private law. According to SAT, even air navigation control is an economic activity, pointing to the fact that in some States it is private undertakings that exercise such control. It also put forward an alternative claim, alleging that the collection of charges by Eurocontrol is a commercial activity. In support of its contention, SAT relied on the fact that Eurocontrol has brought actions for recovery before national courts.[44]

The arguments advanced by SAT were rejected by the governments of several member States of Eurocontrol, who argued that air navigation control is a supervisory activity intended to ensure public safety and that the collection of route charges is an activity carried out on behalf of the Contracting States, with the charges merely constituting the consideration for the air navigation services provided by those States.[45] They based their denial of Eurocontrol's characterization as an 'undertaking' on the public character of this organization's activities and they pointed in support of their argument to the case law of the European Court, according to which Eurocontrol must be regarded as a public authority acting in the exercise of its powers.[46]

The European Court, in a relatively short judgment, rejected SAT's arguments and ruled that Articles 86 and 90 of the EEC Treaty are to be interpreted as meaning that an international organization such as Eurocontrol

---

42 *SAT Fluggesellschaft mbH and European Organization for the Safety of Air Navigation*, Decision of 19 Jan. 1994, Nr. C-364/92 (1994).

43 *See id.*, paras. 6 & 15.

44 *See id.*, para. 15.

45 *See id.*, para. 16.

46 *Id.*

does not constitute an undertaking within the meaning of those articles.[47] Most important, the Court stressed at the outset that "[i]n order to determine whether Eurocontrol's activities are those of an 'undertaking' within the meaning of Articles 86 and 90 of the Treaty, it is necessary to establish the nature of those activities,"[48] which are financed by the contributions of the participating States. The Court observed that Eurocontrol is a regionally-oriented international organization established by the Convention of 13 December 1960, as substantially amended by the Protocol of 12 February 1981, in which some 14 European States participate,[49] and whose aim and function is, according to Article 2 of the amended Convention, to strengthen co-operation between the Contracting States in the field of air navigation and to develop joint activities in this field, making due allowance for defence needs and providing maximum freedom for all air space users consistent with the required level of safety.[50] According to the 1981 Protocol, the operational exercise of air navigation control is limited since Eurocontrol can only carry out this activity at the request of the Contracting States.[51] In particular, it is Eurocontrol's function to establish and collect for and on behalf of the Contracting States the route charges levied on users of air navigation services, based on rates the amount of which is not fixed or even influenced by Eurocontrol, but by each of the Contracting States for the use of its air space.[52] On this point, the European Court rejected SAT's contention referred to above, holding that "Eurocontrol's collection of route charges, ..., cannot be separated from the organization's other activities. Those charges are merely the consideration, payable by users, for the obligatory and exclusive use of air navigation control facilities and services. ... Eurocontrol must, in collecting the charges, be regarded as a public authority acting in the exercise of its powers."[53]

---

47 Before it reached this conclusion on the substance of the case, the Court rejected Eurocontrol's claim that "as an international organization, whose relations with the Community are governed by the rules of public international law, it is outside the jurisdiction of the Court." *See id.*, para. 8. It based this rejection on the fact that the Belgian court had referred to it a question concerning the interpretation of the EEC Treaty rather than one concerning the interpretation of the instruments governing the functioning of Eurocontrol. *See id.*, paras. 9–11.

48 *See id.*, para. 19.

49 *See id.*, para. 3.

50 *See id.*, paras. 4 & 21–22.

51 *See id.*, para. 24.

52 *See id.*, paras. 4 & 23.

53 *See id.*, para. 28.

On the basis of the above considerations, the Court concluded that Eurocontrol "carries out, on behalf of the Contracting States, tasks in the public interest aimed at contributing to the maintenance and improvement of air navigation safety"[54] and that "[t]aken as a whole, Eurocontrol's activities, by their nature, their aim and the rules to which they are subject, are connected with the exercise of powers relating to the control and supervision of air space which are typically those of a public authority."[55] In contrast to SAT's contention, the Court left out any reference to the term *'jus imperii'* and held instead that the activities carried out by Eurocontrol do not qualify as economic or commercial activity, which results in the inapplicability of the competition rules laid down in the Treaty of Rome.[56]

The Eurocontrol Case demonstrates that an intergovernmental organization's activities as a cashier for the States which participate in it do not necessarily constitute 'economic' or 'commercial' activity by the organization, as long as they are not carried out for profit. In the case of Eurocontrol, the route charges levied on users of air space are collected by Eurocontrol on behalf of the member States to which they are paid over, after deduction of a proportion of the revenue intended to cover collection costs. The collection of these charges, an activity carried out by Eurocontrol without any aim of making a profit for itself or its member States, is merely ancillary to Eurocontrol's principal task, namely, the control and supervision of air space, which clearly lies in the sphere of 'public authority.'

The above analysis of Step One of the functional necessity concept as applied to the ITC demonstrates that the ITC's operations as a trading organization entering into commercial contracts do not constitute grounds for denying it the privileges and immunities that an intergovernmental organization traditionally enjoys; instead, the ITC emerges from this preliminary analysis as a *prima facie* candidate for organizational immunities.[57] Indeed, to deny this reality would be to deny a long-standing practice of the member States. The ITC's trading operations may, however, be of importance in

54 *See id.*, para. 27.

55 *See id.*, para. 30.

56 *Id.* In para. 18, the Court explained that it follows from its case law that the concept of an undertaking in Community competition law relies on an entity being engaged in an economic activity, which is determined regardless of the legal status of the entity and the way in which it is financed.

57 *See also* Millett J. in *In re International Tin Council*, [1987] 2 W.L.R. 1229, [1987] 1 All E.R. 890, Ch.D., at 1249 a; 906 a, *quoted in* Hutchinson, at 417, who concluded: "In respect of its commercial activities, therefore, the ITC enjoys complete immunity from the court's adjudicative jurisdiction."

the Second and Third Steps of the functional necessity inquiry. Those steps deal more specifically with the privileges and immunities which are actually (to be) accorded to the ITC.

3 Step Two: The Immunities of the ITC

Step Two of the functional necessity inquiry examines the privileges and immunities which have been granted to the ITC. Three instruments form the immediate background to this examination.

The first is *ITA6*, the ITC's most recent constituent instrument. The privileges and immunities of the ITC are regulated by Article 16 of this agreement:

> 2. The Council shall have in the territory of each member, to the extent consistent with its law, such exemption from taxation on the assets, income and other property of the Council, as may be necessary for the discharge of its functions under this agreement.
>
> 3. The Council shall be accorded in the territory of each member such currency exchange facilities as may be necessary for the discharge of its functions under this agreement.[58]

Second, the 1972 *Headquarters Agreement* between the United Kingdom and the ITC, made pursuant to paragraph 4 of Article 16 of ITA6, regulates the immunities régime of the ITC in more detail. Article 8 of this agreement provides for the ITC's immunity from jurisdiction and execution and it is characterized by a set of narrow exceptions:

> (1) The Council shall have immunity from jurisdiction and execution except:
>
> (a) to the extent that the Council shall have expressly waived such immunity in a particular case;
>
> (b) in respect of a civil action by a third party for damage arising from an accident caused by a motor vehicle belonging to or operated on behalf of the Council or in respect of a motor traffic offence involving such vehicle; and

58 Art. 16 ITA6, Cmnd. 8546.

(c) in respect of an enforcement of an arbitration award made under either article 23 or article 24.

(2) The Council's property and assets wherever situated shall be immune from any form of requisition, confiscation, expropriation, sequestration or acquisition. They shall also be immune from any form of administrative or provisional judicial constraint except insofar as may be temporarily necessary in connection with the prevention of, and investigation into, accidents involving motor vehicles belonging to, or operated on behalf of, the Council.[59]

In addition to immunity from jurisdiction and execution, Articles 4 and 5 of the Headquarters Agreement provide for the inviolability of the archives[60] and premises of the ITC, whereas Articles 9–13 grant the ITC basic exemption from taxes and customs duties as well as freedom to transfer and hold funds, currency, and securities. Finally, Articles 14 and 15 provide for freedom of communications and circulation of publications by the ITC.

The third instrument is the British Order in Council of 1972 made under the *International Organisations (Immunities and Privileges) Act* of 1968. Article 6 is drafted in similar language as Article 8 of the Headquarters Agreement. Under the 1972 Order the Council's official archives and premises are inviolable, whereas Articles 8 and 10–13 provide for exemptions from rates, customs duties and taxes.[61]

These three sources demonstrate that the ITC was accorded the most basic organizational immunities, as defined by *Restatement (Third) of Foreign Relations Law of the United States*:

§ 467. Privileges and Immunities of International Organizations

(1) Under international law, an international organization generally enjoys such privileges and immunities from the jurisdiction of a member

59 Art. 8, ITC Headquarters Agreement, 834 U.N.T.S. 287, at 292–294.

60 On litigation involving the inviolability of the ITC's archives and documents, see the House of Lords Judgment of 3 Dec. 1987 in *Shearson Lehman Bros. Inc. v. Maclaine Watson & Co. Ltd. (ITC intervening)(No. 2)*, [1988] 1 All E.R. 116; [1988] 1 W.L.R. 16, H.L. (E), *quoted in* Cheyne, at 420, n.19; *see also* I. Cheyne & C. Warbrick, *The International Tin Council*, 36 ICLQ 931, 934 (1987)[hereinafter: Cheyne & Warbrick]; J.K. Bentil, *Suing an International Organisation for Debt Payment*, 134 Sol. J. 475, 476–77 (27 Apr. 1990)[hereinafter: Bentil]; Thompson, at 107–08; Greenwood, at 53.

61 There are also a number of articles dealing with the privileges and immunities of the ITC's officers, experts, and the representatives of member States.

> state as are necessary for the fulfilment of the purposes of the organization, including immunity from legal process, and from financial controls, taxes, and duties.
>
> ...
>
> § 468. Immunity of Premises, Archives, Documents, and Communications of International Organizations
>
> An international organization enjoys immunity from any exercise of jurisdiction by a member state that would interfere with official use by the organization of its premises, archives, documents, or communications. [62]

The inclusion of paragraph (b) of Article 8 of the Headquarters Agreement, dealing with traffic accidents, is specific evidence of the basic, rather skeletal immunities régime of the ITC, a régime which has not gained currency to the same extent in the immunities agreements of other international organizations.[63]

The exemptions granted by Articles 8 and 10–13 of the 1972 Order in each case refer to the 'official activities' of the ITC as mentioned in Article 2:

> 2-(1) For the purposes of this Order, the official activities of the International Tin Council shall include its administrative activities and those undertaken pursuant to the Fourth International Tin Agreement or any succeeding agreement.[64]

Through the closing words of Article 2, one is referred expressly to ITA6, the ITC's constituent instrument, which contains the organization's basic purposes and functions. This approach should be adopted by every international organization, because it demonstrates the interplay between (the extent of) an organization's immunities and its limited, functional legal status, as defined in the organization's basic instruments. As was mentioned earlier in this study, it is advisable to define the organization's 'official activities' in precise terms, in order to avoid interpretative issues arising in practice, especially before courts and tribunals, as becomes apparent from the discussion of the EMBL Award discussed above and Step Three in general.

62 Restatement (Third), § 467, at 493, and § 468, at 505.

63 *See* Council of Europe report 1969, at 25, para. 40.

64 S.I. 1972 No. 120, Art. 2.

4 Step Three: The Extent of the Immunities of the ITC

The third and final step in our analysis deals with the extent to which international organizations should be, or have been, accorded specific organizational immunities. This phase typically presents issues of interpretation: What is the exact reach of an organizational immunity?

The practical operation of this approach is illustrated by the English case of *Standard Chartered Bank v. International Tin Council and Others*, decided by the High Court of Justice (Queen's Bench Division) on 17 April 1986.[65] In this case, the ITC applied to set aside the writ and service of writ in proceedings commenced against it by Standard Chartered Bank. The basic issue was the ITC's immunity from the jurisdiction of the English court. The ITC could, of course, only rely on its immunity insofar as it had not waived it by special clauses inserted in contracts. In the case at hand, the ITC had accepted a so-called facility letter, in which the Bank offered to lend the ITC a certain amount of Pounds Sterling and which included the following provision:

> 7. Governing Law and Jurisdiction.
>
> This facility letter shall be governed by and interpreted in accordance with English law and *you hereby irrevocably submit to the nonexclusive jurisdiction of the High Court of Justice in England* and consent to the giving of any relief and/or the issue of any process for enforcement or otherwise against you.(emphasis added)

Following the ITC's default in repayment of the loan and interest, the Bank instituted proceedings against the ITC on 11 March 1986. The issue before Mr. Justice Bingham of the High Court of Justice was whether the ITC's acceptance of this clause constituted an express waiver of immunity in this particular case and it involved an interpretation of Article 6 of the 1972 Order, which provided that the ITC would be immune from suit and legal process except "(a) to the extent that the Council shall have expressly waived such immunity in a particular case."[66] The case contains a string of

---

65 High Court of Justice (Queen's Bench Division) Judgment in *Standard Chartered Bank v. International Tin Council and Others*, [1986] 3 All E.R. 257, [1987] 1 W.L.R. 641, (Bingham J.), 17 April 1986 *reprinted in* 25 ILM 650 (1986)[hereinafter: High Court of Justice, 25 ILM 650 (1986)]; *see also* Hutchinson, at 400.

66 S.I. 1972 No. 120; Art. 6.

interesting arguments pro and con upholding the immunity of the ITC, only the most important of which can be considered here.

The question under review can be described as follows: Is a contractual obligation to waive immunity in regard to a specific transaction concluded in advance of a particular dispute concerning that transaction a waiver "in a particular case" or must the waiver be made expressly for the purpose of a particular dispute when proceedings are instituted in respect of that dispute?[67]

The ITC submitted, *inter alia*, that the relevant instruments, in particular the 1972 Order, excluded any anticipatory waiver and, instead, required an express waiver "in a particular case." The 1972 Order was argued to have contemplated only specific waivers, made after proceedings had begun, or at the very earliest after a particular dispute had arisen.[68] The ITC found support for its argument in a study by the Office of Legal Affairs of the United Nations Secretariat.[69] In that study, Section 2 of the Convention on the Privileges and Immunities of the United Nations, which contains an exception "in so far as in any particular case it shall have waived its immunity," was compared with Article IX, Section 3, of the Articles of Agreement of the International Monetary Fund, providing for waiver of immunity either for the purposes of any proceedings *or by the terms of any contract*. The study concluded from this difference in wording that the San Francisco drafters had not intended to extend the right to waiver in future by contractual terms.[70] The ITC submitted that the same reasoning should apply to the case at hand.

In his ruling, Mr. Justice Bingham made it clear at the outset, however, that he would take an entirely different approach, choosing to protect the injured private party rather than the international organization. The court's entire reasoning seems to reflect a teleological interpretation of the provisions in dispute, with the ultimate aim of ensuring the aforesaid protection. Consider the following excerpt from his ruling: "as here, the obligation appears on its face to be plain and the creditor may have no means of

67 *See* JENKS, at 39; for an earlier British case see *Duff Development Co. Ltd. v. Government of Kelantan*, [1924] App.Cas. 797, [1924] All E.R. 1, H.L., quoted in JENKS, at 39 n.16.

68 *See* High Court of Justice, 25 ILM 650, 657 (1986); *see also* Hutchinson, at 401.

69 *See* [1967] 2 Y.B. Int'l L. Comm'n 225, paras. 82–83, UN Doc. A/CN.4/SER.A/167/Add. 1; for a follow-up study see UN Doc. A/CN.4/L.383/Add. 1 (1985), at 31–33, *reprinted in* [1985] 2 Y.B. Int'l L. Comm'n 145, UN Doc. A/CN.4/SER.A/1985/Add. 1 (Part/Add. 1).

70 *See* [1967] 2 Y.B. Int'l L. Comm'n 225, para. 83, UN Doc. A/CN.4/SER.A/1967/Add. 1.

obtaining judgment save in the proceedings which he is said to be precluded from bringing."[71] Although this may seem a sound concern, it may also be said that this approach overlooks the basic provisions of the legal instruments concerning the ITC, especially Article 2 of the Headquarters Agreement:

> This Agreement shall be interpreted in the light of the primary objective of enabling the Council at its Headquarters in the United Kingdom fully and efficiently to discharge its responsibilities and fulfil its purposes and functions.[72]

Had the High Court of Justice adhered strictly to this provision, which embodies an interpretation rule of *effet utile*, it might not have concluded so easily that the clause in the facility letter should be construed as a plain waiver. Consequently, the High Court of Justice gave effect to the waiver in accordance with its terms, thereby rejecting the ITC's claim to jurisdictional immunity.

It may well be that considerations from Step One, namely, that the ITC was a trading organization, operating (*quasi*) commercially, were of direct influence to the Court's interpretation, but were not expressly relied upon.[73] Regarding the requirement that any waiver must be "in a particular case,"

---

71 *See* High Court of Justice, 25 ILM 650, 651 (1986).

72 834 U.N.T.S. 287, at 290; Art. 2. For a similar arrangement, see EMBL Award at 2, quoting an agreement between the German Government and the EMBL, which reads: "A. The Parties noted 2. that the interpretation of the Headquarters Agreement should be guided by the principle that the Laboratory is enabled to fully and efficiently discharge its responsibilities and fulfil its purposes (Art. 33)." Based on this provision, the Tribunal concluded as follows: "The Parties are in agreement that the privileges and immunities of the EMBL under the HQA [Headquarters Agreement, PB] must not be restrictively interpreted. As far as the interpretation is concerned, the Arbitration Tribunal observes that generally, the HQA is to be interpreted according to the rules of public international law, i.e., according to Articles 31–33 of the two Vienna Conventions on the Law of Treaties of 23 May 1969 and on the Law of Treaties between States and International Organisations or between International Organizations of 21 March 1986." See EMBL Award, at 18, para, 4; *see also* Hahn, at 1015–1016; Lauterpacht, Development, at 417. For an early precedent, see UN-U.S. Headquarters Agreement, Art. IX, S. 27.

73 *See* Millett J. who, in giving judgment in *In re International Tin Council*, [1987] 2 W.L.R. 1229, [1987] 1 All E.R. 890, Ch.D., *quoted in* Hutchinson, at 425 n.106, stated at 1713 g: "The ITC, it must be said, has behaved more like a disreputable private debtor concerned only to hinder and delay his creditors than the responsible international organisation that it claims to be."

Mr. Justice Bingham indicated that an "obviously fair and sensible" interpretation of these words meant no more than that the waiver must relate to a specific transaction, such as the loan agreement which was the subject-matter of the facility letter.[74] It stands in contrast to the United States courts, which have generally held more narrowly that "courts should be reluctant to find that an international organization has inadvertantly waived immunity."[75] Moreover, having observed that "this is a field in which it is the duty of the English courts so far as possible to keep in step with the settled practice of other nations,"[76] Mr. Justice Bingham's interpretation would appear to diverge from the practice of other States that he sought to follow. The judge had every reason to conclude that he could not bring himself "to suppose that the responsible officers of the ITC who accepted the terms of the facility letter on its behalf then conceived clause 7 to have the nugatory effect now contended for."[77] It does not make sense to accept an express clause in a contract which would be without effect; such practice is, it would seem, misleading. The question arises, however, as to who must accept the consequences. The choice here is between the creditor and the international organization.

As regards the creditor, Schermers has pointed out with regard to traders that they usually know the competences of the organizations they deal with and the risks they take in their trade.[78] Hence, "the risk of the [organization] making errors is a calculated risk and the loss caused by such errors is part of business and compensated by the prices charged."[79] In such cases, Schermers argues, fairness does not really require compensation for all the damage caused through the fault of the organization. Reference may also be made to the House of Lords judgment in the *Maclaine Watson* case discussed above, which mentions the case of *Salomon v. A. Salomon & Co.*

---

74 See High Court of Justice, 25 ILM 650, 658 (1986).

75 Farrugia, at 514, citing *Boimah v. United Nations General Assembly*, 664 F.Supp. 69, 72 (E.D.N.Y. 1987); *see also Broadbent v. Organization of American States*, 628 F.2d 27, 34 (D.C. Cir. 1980)(emphasizing the relevance of the unique nature of international organizations in determining the extent of organizational immunity and possible waiver of that immunity). Farrugia concludes that the reliance placed on express waiver by the *Boimah* court implies that courts should be reluctant to restrict organizational immunities.

76 High Court of Justice, 25 ILM 650, 659 (1986).

77 *Id.*

78 Schermers, Non-Contractual Liability, at xi.

79 *Id.*

Ltd.[80] Lord Templeman noted that since the *Salomon* case, traders and creditors have known that they do business with a corporation at their peril if they do not require guarantees from members of the corporation or adequate security. However, one may argue that the facility letter constituted such a guarantee in the instant case. This argument seems sound, albeit with the reservation that it was an *invalid* guarantee under a strict interpretation of the provisions of the Headquarters Agreement and the 1972 Order. Moreover, contrary to Article 23 of the Headquarters Agreement, which deals with contracts, the loan agreement between Standard Chartered Bank and the ITC did not contain an arbitration clause. Under *Salomon*, the bank may be held responsible for the omission of this clause, although it may be argued that the ITC had an even greater good faith obligation, stemming from the fact that the omission constituted a breach by the ITC of the Headquarters Agreement.[81] It may then be asked whether Standard Chartered Bank could and should have known in advance that the ITC was in no position to accept the clause in the facility letter, by consulting the relevant legal provisions. Can one require such an inquiry from a private party? An affirmative answer will leave the private party with empty hands, while denying such a mandatory inquiry will cause interference by the judiciary of a sovereign State with the work of the organization. However, is not the obligation to pay one's debts a basic rule of law,[82] independent of considerations of unhampered exercise of an organization's functions? Indeed, it is, but it is not so much the obligation itself with which we are concerned, but its *enforcement*."[83] Schermers has suggested that "the rights of individuals to have their debts paid should outweigh a

---

80 *Salomon v. A. Salomon & Co. Ltd.*, [1897] App.Cas. 22, [1895–9] All E.R. Rep. 33, H.L. On the notion of 'commercial plausibility,' which is involved here, see Seidl-Hohenveldern, Tin, at 50.

81 *See also* High Court of Justice, 25 ILM 650, 657 (1986)("The omission of this clause may at most have involved an oversight by the Bank, but the omission whether deliberate or inadvertent was a breach by the ITC of its Headquarters Agreement with the United Kingdom government."); Seidl-Hohenveldern, Tin, at 49. As Hutchinson, at 406, has pointed out, under the ITC's reading, if the ITC failed to insert an arbitration clause in a contract in breach of its duty under Art. 23 of the Headquarters Agreement, the plaintiff might not be able to sue the ITC without the latter's consent, despite the presence in the contract of an agreement to waive that immunity. In such case, the ITC would benefit from its own wrong in respect of the plaintiff's loan agreement.

82 *See* Schermers, Liability, at 5.

83 Although immunity does not imply absence of liability, anyone contracting with the organization would on that basis have *no enforceable remedy* under their contracts; see SCHERMERS, at 1084, para. 1612; *id.*, Liability, at 14; BOWETT, at 362–363.

presumed right of an international organization to claim immunity against the execution of an international court decision or arbitral award which orders the payment of a debt."(emphasis added)[84] Here we are concerned, however, with adjudication before a national court. It is a basic rationale of organizational immunity law to prevent an international organization from having to defend itself before the various jurisdictions of its member States, in order to prevent the independence and international character of the organization from being fragmented and destroyed.[85] On the other hand, basic notions of good faith and fairness plead against denying a private creditor its cause of action, especially under the facts of the *Standard Chartered Bank* case.[86]

Although the final outcome of the case may, therefore, be satisfying, when "guided by a general sense of justice and equity,"[87] the legal route which the High Court of Justice took in order to achieve this result gives rise to criticism. This criticism is heightened by the Court's frequent reliance on sovereign immunity law, whereas the Court itself admits that "[w]hatever the merits of this doctrine as between personal sovereigns or sovereign states, it is not obviously apt to be applied to a body such as the ITC of which sovereign states are no more than members …."[88] The High Court of Justice used the interpretation which has been given by authorities on waivers in sovereign immunity law to demonstrate that in the case before it a waiver of organizational immunity had been effected.[89] It is, however, settled doctrine that waivers in sovereign immunity law and organizational immunity law differ fundamentally in that in the latter a waiver cannot be

84 Schermers, Liability, at 11. *See also* Art. 6, para. (1) sub (c) of the 1972 Order in Council, S.I. 1972 No. 120.

85 *See* Millett J. in *In re International Tin Council*, [1987] 2 W.L.R. 1229, [1987] 1 All E.R. 890, Ch.D., at 1246 a-d; 903 f-h, *quoted in* Hutchinson, at 412; this consideration loses much of its strength if the organization has accepted under the terms of a contract the national law of a particular State as the governing law.

86 *See* JENKS, at 169–170, describing the limits set by the general legal principle of good faith on organizations which have been granted certain privileges and immunities. Seidl-Hohenveldern, Corporations, at 85, has argued that the protection of the good faith of the third party should be the overriding consideration. On the facts of the case, it may be seriously doubted whether the ITC in this specific case had any longer a functionally determined need for immunity. From this fact may stem an implicit duty to waive its immunity.

87 UN Doc. A/CN.4/L.383/Add. 1 (1985), at 31, para. 17, *reprinted in* [1985] 2 Y.B. Int'l L. Comm'n 145, 162, para. 17, UN Doc. A/CN.4/SER.A/1985/Add. 1 (Part 1/Add. 1).

88 High Court of Justice, 25 ILM 650, 659 (1986); *see also* Hutchinson, at 402–404.

89 *See* High Court of Justice, 25 ILM 650, 658–660 (1986).

implied as easily as in the former.[90] This fundamental difference militates against any far-reaching comparison between the two. In any case, by doing so, the High Court of Justice joined forces with a number of courts in confusing different kinds of immunity.

It is interesting to compare the cases involving the International Tin Council discussed above, with the Interim Award Regarding Jurisdiction rendered in 1984 by the Arbitral Tribunal acting under the auspices of the International Chamber of Commerce in *Westland Helicopters Ltd. v. The Arab Organization far Industrialization, the United Arab Emirates, the Kingdom of Saudi Arabia, the State of Qatar, the Arab Republic of Egypt and the Arab British Helicopter Company*.[91] The *Westland* Interim Award concerned the question of whether an arbitration clause included in an agreement between an international organization and a private party is binding, first, on the *international organization* with whom the private party (in this case Westland) has concluded an agreement, and, second, on the *participating States*. The case did not involve, as did *Standard Chartered Bank*, the question of the consequences to a private party of the *omission* of an arbitration clause.

With regard to the reliance by the *participating States* on their sovereign immunity, the Arbitral Tribunal held that the conclusion of an arbitration agreement or clause implies the waiver of immunity, reasoning that the participating States, in creating the organization whose obligations were binding on themselves, "could not have overlooked the possibility of being proceeded against at law in respect of these obligations."[92] The Tribunal

90 *See, e.g.*, JENKS, at 39; AHLUWALIA, at 200, and further references therein.

91 Award of 5 March 1984, Case No. 3879/AS, *reprinted in* 23 ILM 1071 (1984). The Arab Industrialization Organization was established by treaty of 29 April 1975 between the United Arab Emirates, Saudi Arabia, Qatar and the Arab Republic of Egypt with the aim of developing an arms industry for the benefit of the four founding States. After the organization and Westland Helicopters Limited, an English private company, concluded a Shareholders Agreement which created a 'joint stock company' ("The Arab British Helicopter Company") between the two parties, the organization was dissolved with effect from 1 July 1979 as a consequence of the Camp David Accords between Egypt and Israel. Subsequently, Westland sought to enforce the agreement it had entered into with the organization, relying on the arbitration Clause 12 of the Shareholders Agreement. According to Clause 12, "[a]ny controversy or dispute which may arise between the parties in connection with the interpretation, application or effect of this Agreement which cannot be resolved amicably shall be finally settled under the Rules of Conciliation and Arbitration of the International Chamber of Commerce by one or more arbitrators appointed in accordance with the said Rules" *See id.*, at 1079.

92 *See id.*, at 1089 sub VII.

rejected the argument, raised by one of the respondents, that, on the ground of the organization being a legal entity separate from its founding member States, an arbitration clause included in a contract between the organization and a private party cannot bind the founding member States, who are no more than third parties and who themselves never signed any contract with the private party concerned. In other words, the Tribunal 'lifted the veil' of the organization to find that it had jurisdiction *as against the participating States*.[93] Similar to Mr. Justice Bingham's reasoning in *Standard Chartered Bank*, the Arbitral Tribunal observed that the private claimant would not have entered into the transaction without the necessary guarantees from the participating States and that "the latter could not help but be aware of the implications of their actions."[94] The Arbitral Tribunal also relied on considerations of equity to establish its jurisdiction over the dispute, pointing out that "[i]t would be wrong if the disagreement which arose between the 4 States, in May 1979, were to be prejudicial to Westland, rendering all the guarantees worthless."[95] The Arbitral Tribunal reasoned that, if Westland were not in a position to sue the participating States, "there would be a real denial of justice," adding that "[e]quity, in common with the principles of international law, allows the corporate veil to be lifted, in order to protect third parties against an abuse which would be to their detriment."[96] Accordingly, the Arbitral Tribunal considered that it had competence to deal with the dispute.

With regard to the *organization* itself, the Arbitral Tribunal identified, by way of a first step, that it possessed supranational status, enjoyed legal personality, full administrative and financial independence and the right of ownership, disposition and litigation.[97] However, the Arbitral Tribunal did

93 The Arbitral Tribunal held that the "question whether the 4 States are bound by the arbitration clause concluded by the AOI in its own name (Shareholders Agreement concluded with Westland, Clause 12.1) is exactly the same as the substantive law question whether the 4 States are bound in general by the obligations contracted by the AOI." *See id.*, at 1080. Moreover, it stated that "[f]inally, one must admit that in reality, in the circumstances of this case, the AOI is one with the States." *See id.*, at 1085 sub (c).

94 *See id.*, at 1085, final paragraph.

95 *See id.*, at 1086, sub G.

96 *See id.*, at 1087.

97 At the same time, the Arbitral Tribunal hastened to point out that the designation of an organization as "legal person" and the attribution to it of an independent existence do not provide any basis for a conclusion as to whether or not those who compose it are bound by obligations undertaken by it, even if the organization's founding documents are silent on this point. This led the Arbitral Tribunal into a short, but not insignificant discussion of the merits of the case, concerning the question of the possible liability of the founding States for the acts of the organization which they had created.

not rely on a line of reasoning that Mr. Justice Bingham borrowed from the law of sovereign immunity and applied in *Standard Chartered Bank*, but simply upheld the binding nature of the written arbitration clause on the ground that Westland's submissions were clearly in connection with the application or effect of the Shareholders Agreement of 27 February 1978, and thus triggered the right of recourse to arbitration contained in Clause 12 of the Agreement.[98]

Both the decision in *Standard Chartered Bank* and the Interim Award in *Westland* are evidence of a tendency on the part of arbitral and judicial tribunals to protect the interests of private parties who have contracted with international organizations in situations where the international organizations, or possibly their member States, seek to avoid liability under the contracts by hiding behind the organization's structure. They have done so on pragmatic grounds, using the instrument of teleological interpretation or basing their decisions on considerations of equity or on general principles of law such as good faith. These decisions differ, however, in the reasons they use to reach a result that favors the injured private party. We believe that in *Standard Chartered Bank*, Mr. Justice Bingham wrongly relied on the law of sovereign immunity to reach what is probably the right or 'just' result, whereas in *Westland* too little attention was paid to the position of the international organization in this respect and too much emphasis was placed, instead, on the position of the States that created the organization, with a view to lifting the veil of the organization and holding against the participating States on the matter of jurisdiction. We simply submit that it would have been salutory if these cases had relied more on considerations of functional necessity, especially in implying a waiver, so as to do justice to the special nature of the international organization as distinguished from sovereign States.

Consequently, despite its observation that "[i]n making this appraisal, the Arbitral Tribunal does not at this stage intend to rule upon the substance of the Request," *see id.*, at 1086, the Arbitral Tribunal went beyond the boundaries of a discussion of its jurisdiction and touched upon the subject matter of the litigation surrounding the International Tin Council, which, as pointed out above, lies outside the scope of the present book.

98 *See id.*, at 1079, sub III.1. A possible explanation for this difference in reasoning may be that, in contrast to *Standard Chartered Bank* before an English court, the *Westland Case* before an arbitral tribunal did not involve issues of organizational immunity of the organization concerned, but rather concerned the question of the binding force of an arbitration clause.

CHAPTER 4

General Conclusion

In the preceding parts of this book an effort was made to demonstrate the generalized operation of the three-step functional necessity analysis of the legal position of intergovernmental organizations, including by reference to examples from the practice of international organizations. The discussion of Step One introduced the role of functional necessity in determining the fundamental aspect of legal position, namely, the legal status, or personality, capacities and powers, of international organizations. It was shown that this aspect of an organization's legal position can be explained by using functional terminology linking their existence and operation to the purposes and functions of the organization. By using this functional approach, an attempt was made to demonstrate that the elements of the legal position of international organizations, in their application by international and domestic legal systems, are more flexible and deserve wider systematic consideration than is sometimes assumed in legal doctrine and in judicial decisions.

The identification process of Step One of the functional necessity analysis is a prerequisite to the examination of the privileges and immunities of international organizations, represented by Steps Two and Three. As shown by the selection process of Step Two, functional necessity provides for certain immunities in order to enable a particular organization to give effect to what the member States had agreed would be its mission, and not in order to place the organization above the law for reasons of mere prestige. A summary was provided of the basic considerations behind the granting of organizational immunities and of their fundamental legal sources, both written and unwritten, to demonstrate that international organizations enjoy certain protections as of right. While organizational immunity remains overwhelmingly conventional in nature, customary international law may also provide a basis for organizational immunities, even though its contribution toward explaining the extent of these immunities remains uncertain and subject to debate, especially as it concerns non-member States.

Step Three demonstrates that the functional necessity test is an appropriate yardstick for determining the extent of the immunities that a given organization must enjoy in order to fulfil its mission (*ratione materiae*). It was shown that the exception of 'commercial activity' applied in State, or foreign sovereign, immunity law has no place in the law of organizational

 | DOI:10.1163/9789004724211_005

immunities and that the test of 'official activity' is a more appropriate one. With regard to the official activity criterion, which is at the core of the functional necessity analysis, the test, especially in the context of international organizations that engage in '(*quasi*-)commercial activities' as that term is traditionally understood, should be whether the organization concerned not only participates in the marketplace by concluding agreements with private contractors but also acts as a supplier and trader of goods or services for profit, thereby exposing itself to the ordinary forces of market competition. In the former case, immunities may attach, but not, or to a lesser extent, in the latter case. The grant of immunity for 'official activities,' in order to meet the 'strictly necessary' test, should be limited to activities carried out by an organization *in the course of the actual exercise of* its functions in the fulfilment of its purposes and should be a *normal consequence* of the organization's purposes and functions to such an extent that they could be said to *logically arise from*, and have a direct causal relationship with, its purposes and functions, rather than being merely 'useful' to the pursuit of the latter.

The discussion of the Arbitral Award rendered in the dispute between the EMBL and Germany underscores the viability of the application in practice of a functional necessity analysis that uses 'official activity' as its core criterion. The EMBL Award deserves the widest dissemination as it constitutes an important precedent in the development of a new law of organizational immunities, one that is freed from the shackles of State or 'sovereign' immunity.

Our analysis of the issue of who is to determine what constitutes 'official activity' in a particular case revealed that this should be the prerogative of the international organization itself, acting through its chief administrative officer or possibly an international judicial or arbitral organ, rather than entrusting this task to the authorities of individual States, including their courts. This determination may only be set aside for the most compelling reasons in a given case. A clear definition of what constitutes 'official activity,' complete with examples of what is *not* included, and of what constitutes 'compelling reasons' in an immunity or other instrument would help to avoid, or at least limit, interpretative disputes in practice.

In the final section of the discussion of Step Three, a review of the most significant organizational immunity instruments dealing with settlement of disputes of a wide variety showed that the law of organizational immunities has developed into a balanced and self-contained régime, although the application of the recourse procedures contained in these instruments is still evolving and could profit from further development and refinement.

This applies especially to the issues of the liability and the responsibility of intergovernmental organizations.

The analysis of the legal position of the International Tin Council, presented in Chapter 3 by way of an example of the operation in practice of the three steps of functional necessity, besides stressing the importance of the inclusion of an unequivocal arbitration clause in contracts between international organizations and private parties or States, demonstrates that a possible reconsideration of the immunities of international organizations should be carried out along the lines of the functional necessity concept described in this book. This is the most suitable approach for doing justice to the special nature of the international organization as distinguished from sovereign States and to the international law principle of speciality applicable to intergovernmental organizations.

However, a word of caution is appropriate here. Notwithstanding the great advantages of a consistent functional necessity approach, which defines organizational immunities and their limits, this approach should be regarded, first and foremost, as providing a *general framework* for seeking solutions to the problems posed by the legal position of international organizations rather than providing clear-cut answers. It should be borne in mind that, in the end, the answers to the questions posed by the functional necessity concept underlying organizational immunities depend upon an interpretation of the various elements of the concept: whether there was in a particular case a 'functional' need or requirement, whether a certain privilege or immunity was 'strictly necessary,' and whether the activity concerned came within the realm of an organization's 'official activity.' Indeed, the functional necessity concept as such "can never predetermine specific answers" and "opinions differ as to what precisely is necessary for the independent exercise of its functions by an international organization."[1]

For this reason, and for purposes of interpretation, a given organization's objectives and functions, which are at the basis of its immunities, should be specified in as great detail as possible in an international instrument. Other documents that spell out specific privileges and immunities should be similarly precise. Most important, the 'official activities' of an organization should be defined as clearly and strictly as possible, using a justified functional need for organizational immunities as a yardstick. The outcome of an individual case will depend upon interpreting these questions either narrowly or liberally, which, in turn, will be determined by a preference for

1 SCHERMERS, at 269, para. 324.

protecting the often conflicting interests of either the organization concerned or those of injured parties with which the organization has interacted. The facts of the English cases involving the International Tin Council discussed in Chapter 3 provide a practical example of this conflict of interests, and while the final results adopted in those cases may be salutory, the reasoning used in achieving these results often conflicts with the functional necessity concept as applied to international organizations.

Despite the disadvantages outlined above, the functional necessity concept set forth in the present study may provide more appropriate answers than one which borrows wholesale certain concepts developed in different branches of immunity law.

Finally, it has been aptly observed in the literature that the changing context in which international organizations operate in the twenty-first century "requires both modern, forceful and effective explanations of the need and function of immunities of international organizations (in academia and in practice), as well as modern, forceful and effective ways in which the injurious effects of these immunities are mitigated," which ultimately is "in the long-term self-interest of these organizations and their members, since they will not be able, at the end of the day, to perform their functions if they continue to deal with immunity and accountability questions today in the same way as yesterday, not sufficiently adapting themselves to modern times."[2] The present book seeks to make a modest contribution to providing a structured explanation of the legal position of intergovernmental organizations, including their immunities, one that is in keeping with international institutional law as a sub-field of public international law, especially the international institutional law principle of speciality.

2 *Id.*, at 1087, para. 1612A.

Selected Bibliography

The text between square brackets indicates the short form through which a book or article is referred to in the footnotes in the present study.

Books

Ahluwalia, K., The Legal Statzus, Privileges and Immunities of the Specialized Agencies of the United Nations and Certain Other International Organizations (1964). [AHLUWALIA]

Alvarez, J.E., International Organizations as Law-makers (2005).

Amerasinghe, C.F., Principles of the Institutional Law of International Organizations (2nd ed. 2005). [AMERASINGHE]

Akehurst, M., A Modern Introduction to International Law (6th ed. 1987).

Amerasinghe, C.F., The Law of the International Civil Service (As Applied by International Administrative Tribunals) (1988). [AMERASINGHE, CIVIL SERVICE]

Archer, C., International Organizations (2nd ed. 1992). [ARCHER]

Beier, F.-K., Härtel, K. & Schricker, G., eds., Europäisches Patentübereinkommen, Münchner Gemeinschaftskommentar, [various Articles] (1984). [BEIER et al.]

Bekker, P.H.F., World Court Decisions at the Turn of the Millennium (1997–2001) (2002).

Bekker, P., Arbitration of International Disputes in New York (2024).

Bernhardt, R., ed., Encyclopedia of Public International Law (various installments).

Bleckmann, A., Internationale Beamtenstreitigkeiten vor nationalen Gerichten. Materialen zum Recht der internationalen Organisationen und zur Immunität. Rechts-gutachten für die Union Syndicale, Section Eurocontrol (Schriften zum Völkerrecht 68)(1981).

Blokker, N.M. & Schrijver, N.J., eds., Immunity of International Organizations (2015).

Born, G.B., & Weston, D., International Civil Litigation in United States Courts, Commentary & Materials (1989).

Bos, M., A Methodology of International Law (1984). [BOS, METHODOLOGY]

Bowett, D.W., The Law of International Institutions (4th ed. 1982). [BOWETT]

Brower, C.N. & Brueschke, J.D, The Iran-United States Claims Tribunal (1998).

Brownlie, I., Principles of Public International Law (5th ed. 1998). [BROWNLIE]

Cahier, P., Étude des accords de siège conclus entre les organisations internationales et les états où elles résident (1959).

Carroz, J. & Probst, Y., Personnalité juridique internaţionale et capacité de conclure des traités de 1'O.N.U. et des institutions specialisées (1953).

Chiu, H., The Capacity of International Organizations to Conclude Treaties, and the Special Legal Aspects of the Treaties so concluded (1966).

Clark, R.C., Corporate Law (1986).

Claude, Jr., I.L., Swords into Plowshares. The Problems and Progress of International Organization (3rd ed. 1964). [CLAUDE]

Cooker, De, C., International Administration – Law and Management Practices in International Organisations (1990).

Damian, H., Staatenimmunität und Gerichtszwang: Grundlagen und Grenzen der völkerrechtlichen Freiheit fremder Staaten von inländischen Gerichtsbarkeit in Verfahren der Zwangsvollstreckung oder Anspruchssicherung. [State Immunity and Judicial Coercion] (Beiträge zum ausländischen öffentlichen Recht und Völkerrecht 89)(1985). [DAMIAN]

Duffar, J., Contribution à 1'étude des privilèges et immunités des organisations internationales (1982). [DUFFAR]

Egger, M., Die Vorrechte und Befreiungen zugunsten internationalen Organisationen und ihrer Funktionäre (1954). [EGGER]

Ferstman, C., International Organizations and the Fight for Accountability: The Remedies and Reparations Gap (2017).

Fox, H. & Webb, Ph., The Law of State Immunity (3rd ed. 2013). [FOX-WEBB]

Franciono, F., ed., Access to Justice as a Human Right (2007).

Giorgetti, C., ed., The Rules, Practice, and Jurisprudence of International Courts and Tribunals (2012).

Goodrich, L., & Hambro, E., Charter of the United Nations, Commentary and Documents (1946). [GOODRICH & HAMBRO]

Gore-Booth, Lord, ed., Satow's Guide to Diplomatic Practice (5th ed. 1979). [SATOW'S GUIDE]

Groom, A.J.R., & Taylor, P., eds., Functionalism: Theory and Practice in International Relations (1975).

Guggenheim, P., Traité de droit international public (Vol. I, 1953). [GUGGENHEIM]

Gulati, R., Access to Justice and International Organisations—Coordinating Jurisdiction between the National and Institutional Legal Orders (2022).

Henquet, J., The Third-Party Liability of International Organisations—Towards a 'Complete Remedy System' Counterbalancing Jurisdictional Immunity (2023).

Higgins, R., Problems and Process – International Law and How We Use It 93 (1994)

Higgins, R., Webb, P., Akande, D., Sivakumaran, S., & Sloan, J., eds., Oppenheim's International Law: United Nations (2017).

Hirsch, M., The Responsibility of International Organizations Toward Third Parties: Some Basic Principles (1995).

Hug, D., Die Rechtsstellung der in der Schweiz niedergelassenen internationalen Organisationen (1984). [HUG]

Ivrakis, S.C., Privileges and Immunities of the United Nations – Precedents and Present-Day Developments (1954). [IVRAKIS]

Jackson, J.H., World Trade and the Law of GATT (1969).

Jenks, C.W., The Headquarters of International Institutions – A Study of their Location and Status (1945).

Jenks, C.W., International Immunities (1961). [JENKS]

Jenks, C.W., The Proper Law of International Organizations (1962).

Jennings, R. & Watts, A., Oppenheim's International Law (9th ed. 1996).

Johansen, S.Ø., The Human Rights Accountability Mechanisms of International Organizations (2020).

Kelsen, H., The Law of the United Nations, A Critical Analysis of its Fundamental Problems (5th pr. 1966). [KELSEN]

Kennedy, D.W., International Legal Structures (1987). [KENNEDY]

Klabbers, J., An Introduction to International Organizations Law (2022).

Klabbers, J., ed., The Cambridge Companion to International Organizations Law (2022).

Klein, P., La Responsabilité des Organisations Internationales dans les Ordres Juridiques Internes et en Droit des Gens (1998).

Kloth, M., Immunities and the Right of Access to Court under Article 6 of the European Convention on Human Rights (2010).

Lauterpacht, H., International Law and Human Rights (1950).

Martha, R.S.J., The Financial Obligation in International Law (2015).

Martha, R.S.J., Grafton, C., & Bailey, S., The Legal Foundations of Interpo (2020).

Matte, N.M., Aerospace Law. From Scientific Exploration to Commercial Utilization (1977).

McCormick Croswell, C., Protection of International Personnel Abroad. Law and Practice Affecting the Privileges and Immunities of International Organization (1952). [CROSWELL]

Megzari, A., The Internal Justice of the United Nations—A Critical History 1945–2015 (2015).

Michaels, D.B., International Privileges and Immunities. A Case for a Universal Statute (1971). [MICHAELS]

Mitrany, D., A Working Peace System (1943; 1966).

Muller, A.S., International Organizations and Their Host States—Aspects of Their Legal Relationship (1995).

Nauta, D., The International Responsibility of NATO and its Personnel during Military Operations (2017).

Nijman, J.E., The Concept of International Legal Personality: An Inquiry into the History and Theory of International Law (2004)

Okeke, E.C., Jurisdictional Immunities of States and International Organizations (2018). [OKEKE]

Plantey, A., The International Civil Service – Law and Management (P. Underwood & T. Cook-Radmore trans. 1981).

Ragazzi, M., ed., Responsibility of International Organizations—Essays in Memory of Sir Ian Brownlie (2013).

Ramcharan, B., The International Law Commission – Its Approach to the Codification and Progressive Development of International Law (1965).

Reinisch, A., ed., The Conventions on the Privileges and Immunities of the United Nations and its Specialized Agencies: A Commentary (2016).

Reuter, P., International Institutions (1958). [REUTER, INSTITUTIONS]

Roberts, Sir Ivor, ed., Satow's Diplomatic Practice (2009). [SATOW]

Rossi, P., International Law Immunities and Employment Claims: A Critical Appraisal (2021).

Ryngaert, C., Dekker, I.F., Wessel, R.A., & Wouters, J., Judicial Decisions on the Law of International Organizations (2016).

Sarooshi, D., ed., Remedies and Responsibility for the Actions of International Organizations (2014).

Schermers, H.G., & Blokker, N.M., International Institutional Law – Unity within Diversity (2018). [SCHERMERS]

Schermers, H.G., Heukels, T., & Mead, Ph., eds., Non-Contractual Liability of the European Communities (1988). [SCHERMERS, NON-CONTRACTUAL LIABILITY]

Schmitt, P., Access to Justice and International Organizations: The Case of Individual Victims of Human Rights Violations (2017).

Seidl-Hohenveldern, I., Die Immunität internationaler Organisationen in Dienstrechts-streitfällen, Rechtsgutachten für Eurocontrol (Schriften zum Völkerrecht 71)(1981). [SEIDL-HOHENVELDERN, EUROCONTROL]

Seidl-Hohenveldern, I., Das Recht der Internationalen Organisationen einschliesslich der Supranationalen Gemeinschaften (4th ed. 1984). [SEIDL-HOHENVELDERN, RECHT]

Seidl-Hohenveldern, I., Corporations In and Under International Law (Hersch Lauterpacht Memorial Lectures)(1987). [SEIDL-HOHENVELDERN, CORPORATIONS]

Shihata, I., The World Bank Inspection Panel: In Practice (2000).

Simma, B., Khan, D., Nolte., G., & Paulus, A., eds., The Charter of the United Nations: A Commentary (2012).

Simmonds, K.R., adv. ed., Sweet & Maxwell's European Community Treaties – Including the European Communities Act 1972 (1972).

Steiner, H., Vagts, D., & Koh, H.H., Transnational Legal Problems – Materials and Text (4th ed. 1994).

St. John MacDonald, R., & Johnston, D.M., eds., Towards World Constitutionalism – Issues in the Legal Ordering of the World Community (2005).

Sucharitkul, S., State Immunities and Trading Activities in International Law (1959).

Villiger, M.E., Customary International Law and Treaties – A Study of their Interactions and Interrelations with Special Consideration of the 1969 Vienna Convention on the Law of Treaties (1985).

Villiger, M.E., Commentary on the 1969 Vienna Convention on the Law of Treaties (2009).

Villiger, M.E., Handbook on the European Convention on Human Rights (2023).

Wallace, R.M.M., International Law (1986). [WALLACE]

Wellens, K., Remedies against International Organisations (2002). [WELLENS]

Wenckstern, M., Die Immunität internationaler Organisationen (1991). [WENCKSTERN]

Weissberg, G., The International Status of the United Nations (1961). [WEISSBERG]

Whiteman, M.M., Digest of International Law, Vol. 13 (1968). [WHITEMAN, 13 DIGEST]

Wolf, F., Le droit aux privilèges et immunités des Institutions spécialisées reliées aux Nations Unies (1948).

Articles and Periodicals

Abbott, K.W., and Snidal, D., *Why States Act through Formal International Organizations*, 42 J. Conflict Resol. 3 (1998).

Ago, R., *'Binding' Advisory Opinions of the International Court of Justice*, 85 AJIL 439 (1991).

Alvarez, J.E., *Governing the World: International Organizations as Lawmakers*, 31(3) Suff. Transnat'l L.R. 591 (2008).

Amerasinghe, C.F., *Liability to Third Parties of Member States of International Organizations: Practice, Principle and Judicial Precedent*, 85 AJIL 259 (1991).

Aufricht, H., *The Expansion of the Concept of Sovereign Immunity: With Special Reference to International Organizations*, 46 Proc. Am. Soc'y Int'l L. 85 (1952). [Aufricht]

Bekker, P.H.F., *The Work of the International Law Commission on 'Relations between States and International Organizations' Discontinued: an Assessment*, 6 LJIL 3 (1993). [Bekker]

Bekker, P.H.F., *The Independence of UN Special Rapporteurs: Dispute Resolution under the Convention on Privileges and Immunities, in* International Administration – Law and Management Practices in International Organisations, Suppl. VII, at III.2/1–29 (C. de Cooker ed. 2001).

Bentil, J.K., *Suing an International Organisation for Debt Payment,* 134 Sol. J. 475 (April 27, 1990). [Bentil]

Bernhardt, R., *Customary International Law,* in [Installment] 7 Encyclopedia of Public International Law 61 (1984).

Bianchi, A., Book Review, 88 AJIL 212–214 (1994) (reviewing S. de Bellis, *L'immunità delle organizzazioni dalla giurisdizione* (1992)).

Blokker, N.M., *Jurisdictional Immunities of International Organisations – Origins, Fundamentals and Challenges, in* The Cambridge Handbook of Immunities and International Law (T. Ruys, N. Angelet & L. Ferro, eds., 2019).

Boon, K., & Mégret, F., *New Approaches to the Accountability of International Organizations,* 16 IOLR 1 (2019).

Boon, K., *Rethinking the Accountability-Immunity Axis through Remedies: Lessons from National Militaries,* 16 IOLR 137 (2019).

Bouchez, L.J., *The Nature and Scope of State Immunity from Jurisdiction and Execution,* 10 N.Y.I.L. 3 (1979).

Brandon, M., *The Legal Status of the Premises of the United Nations,* 28 BYBIL 90 (1951). [Brandon]

Brower, C.N., & Bekker, P.H.F., *Understanding 'Binding' Advisory Opinions of the International Court of Justice, in Liber Amicorum* Judge Shigeru Oda 351–368 (N. Ando, E. McWhinney & R. Wolfrum, eds., 2002).

Cassese, A., *L'immunité de juridiction civile des organisations internationales dans la jurisprudence italienne,* 30 AFDI 556 (1984). [Cassese]

Charney, J.I., *Universal International Law,* 87 AJIL 529 (1993).

Chen, K., *The Legal Status, Privileges and Immunities of the Specialized Agencies,* 42 AJIL 900 (1948). [Chen]

Cheyne, I., & Warbrick, C., *The International Tin Council,* 36 ICLQ 931 (1987). [Cheyne & Warbrick]

Cheyne, I., *The International Tin Council,* 38 ICLQ 417 (1989). [Cheyne]

d'Aspremont, J., *Abuse of the Legal Personality of International Organizations and the Responsibility of Member States,* 4(1) IOLR 91 (2007)

Daugirdas, K., *Reputation and the Responsibility of International Organizations,* 25 EJIL 991 (2015).

Daugirdas, K., *How and Why International Law Binds International Organizations,* 57 Harv. Int'l L.J. 325 (2016).

Daugirdas, K., *Reputation and Accountability: Another Look at the United Nations' Response to the Cholera Epidemic in Haiti,* 16(1) IOLR 11 (2019).

Deener, D., *Some Problems of the Law of Diplomatic Immunity*, 50 AJIL 115 (1956).

Den Dekker, G., *Absolute Validity, Absolute Immunity: Is There Something Wrong with Article 103 of the UN Charter?, in* What's Wrong with International Law? *Liber Amicorum* A.H.A. Soons 247–264 (C. Reyngaert et al. eds. 2015)

Dinh, N.Q., *Les privilèges et immunités des organismes internationaux d'après les jurisprudences nationales depuis* 1945, 3 ADFI 262 (1957). [Dinh]

Dominicé, Chr., *L'immunité de juridiction et d'exécution des organisations internationales*, 187 RdC 145 (1984 IV). [Dominicé, L'immunité]

Dominicé, Chr., *La nature et l'étendue de l'immunité de juridiction des organisations internationales, in* Law of Nations, Law of International Organizations, World's Economic Law, *Liber Amicorum* Honouring Ignaz Seidl-Hohenveldern 77 (K.-H. Böckstiegel, H.-A. Folz, J.M. Mössner & K. Zemanek, eds., 1988). [Dominicé, LIBER SEIDL]

Eagleton, A., *International Organization and the Law of Responsibility*, 76 RdC 319 (1950 I).

Ebenroth, C.T., *Shareholders' Liability in International Organizations – The Settlement of the International Tin Council Case*, 4 LJIL 171 (1991). [Ebenroth]

Ehrenfeld, A., *United Nations Immunity Distinguished From Sovereign Immunity*, 52 Proc. Am. Soc'y Int'l L. 88 (1958). [Ehrenfeld]

Eifler, R.K., *International Law – Privileges and Immunities of UN Delegates and Officials – The International Organizations Immunities Act*, 46 Mich. L. Rev. 381 (1984).

Eisemann, P.M., *Crise du Conseil International de l'Etain et Insolvabilité d'une Organisation Intergouvernementale*, 31 AFDI 730 (1985).

El-Erian, A., *La Conférence et la Convention sur la Représentation des Etats dans leurs relations avec les organisations internationales (un aperçu général)*, 21 AFDI 445 (1975). [El-Erian, AFDI]

El-Erian, A., *Vienna Convention on the Representation of States in Their Relations with International Organizations of a Universal Character, in* [Installment] 5 Encyclopedia of Public International Law 392 (1983). [El-Erian, ENCYCLOPEDIA]

El-Erian, A., *International Organizations and International Relations, in* A Handbook on International Organizations 625 (R.-J. Dupuy ed. 1984). [El-Erian, DUPUY]

Engel, S., *'Living' International Constitutions and the World Court (The Subsequent Practice of International Organs under their Constituent Instruments)*, 16 ICLQ 865 (1967). [Engel]

Farrugia, A.A., *Boimah v. United Nations General Assembly: International Organizations Immunity is Absolutely Not Restrictive*, 15 Brooklyn J. Int'l L. 497 (1989). [Farrugia]

Fatouros, A.A., *On the Hegemonic Role of International Functional Organization*, 23 GYIL 9 (1980). [Fatouros]

Fedder, E.H., *The Functional Basis of International Law and Organization*, 9 Am. U.L. Rev. 60 (1960). [Fedder]

Fennesy, J.G., *The 1975 Vienna Convention on the Representation of States in their Relations with International Organizations of a Universal Character*, 70 AJIL 62 (1976). [Fennessy]

Fischer, G., *Les associations de pays exportateurs de produits de base*, 22 AFDI 528 (1976).

Franck, T., *The 'Powers of Appreciation': Who is the Ultimate Guardian of UN Legality?*, 86 AJIL 595 (1991).

Fry, J.D., *Rights, Functions, and International Legal Personality of International Organizations*, 36 B.U. Int'l L.J. 221 (2018).

Gaillard, E., & Pingel-Lenuzza, I., *International organizations and immunity from jurisdiction: to restrict or to bypass*, 51 ICLQ 1 (2002).

Gariepy, R.N., *International Commodity Agreements*, 25 ICLQ 677 (1976).

Glenn, G.H., Kearney, M.M. & Padilla, D.J., *Immunities of International Organizations*, 22 Va. J Int'l L. 247 (1982). [Glenn *et al.*]

Graefrath, B., *The International Law Commission Tomorrow: Improving its Organization and Methods of Work*, 85 AJIL 595 (1991). [Graefrath]

Greenwood, C., *Put Not Your Trust In Princes: The Tin Council Appeals*, 48 C.L.J. 46 (1989). [Greenwood]

Grütters, D.M., *NATO, International Organizations and Functional Immunity*, 13(2) IOLR 211 (2016).

Guggenheim, P., *La validité et la nullité des actes juridiques internationaux*, 74 RdC 191 (1949 I).

Hafner, G., *Accountability of International Organizations—A Critical Review*, *in* Towards World Constitutionalism 585 (R. St. J Macdonald & D.M. Johnston eds. 2005).

Hahn, H.J., *Euratom: The Conception of an International Personality*, 71 Harv. L.R. 1001 (1958). [Hahn]

Hammerskjöld, A., *Les immunités des personnes investies de fonctions internationales*, 56 RdC 107 (1936 II).

Hardy, M.J.L., *Claims by International Organizations in Respect of Injuries to their Agents*, 37 BYBIL 516 (1961).

Henderson, F.W., *How Much Immunity for International Organizations?: Mendaro v. World Bank*, 10 N.C.J. Int'L L. Comm. Reg. 487 (1985). [Henderson]

Herdegen, M., *Bemerkungen zur Zwangsliquidation und zum Heffungsdurchgriff bei internationalen Organisationen*, 47 ZaöRV 537 (1987).

Hexner, E.P., *Interpretation by Public International Organizations of their Basic Instruments*, 53 AJIL 341 (1959).

Higgins, R., *The Role of Resolutions of International Organizations in the Process of Creating Norms in the International System, in* International Law and the International System 21 (W.E. Butler ed. 1987).

Hoffmann, G., *Der Durchgriff auf die Mitgliedstaaten von internationalen Organisationen für deren Schulden,* 41 NJW 585 (1987).

Hutchinson, D.N., *Decisions of British Courts During 1987 Involving Questions of Public International Law,* 58 BYBIL 399 (1987). [Hutchinson]

Jenks, C.W., *Some Constitutional Problems of International Organizations,* 22 BYBIL 11 (1945).

Jenks, C.W., The Legal Personality of International Organizations, 22 BYBIL 267 (1945). [Jenks, Personality]

Jennings, R.Y., *Some Aspects of the International Law of the Air,* 75 RdC 509 (1949 II).

Kewenig, W.A., *Der Internationale Zinnrat – Ein Lehrstück des Wirtschaftsvölkerrechts,* 10 Recht der Internationalen Wirtschaft 781 (1990). [Kewenig]

Klabbers, J., *Presumptive Personality: The European Union in International Law,* in International Law Aspects of the European Union 231–253 (M. Koskenniemi ed. 1998).

Klabbers, J., *The Emergence of Functionalism in International Institutional Law: Colonial Inspirations,* 25 EJIL 645 (2014).

Klabbers, J., *The EJIL Foreword: The Transformation of International Organizations Law,* 26 EJIL 9 (2015).

Klabbers, J., *Book Review,* 12 IOLR 279 (2015).

Klabbers, J., *Reflections on Role Responsibility: The Responsibility of International Organizations for Failing to Act,* 8 EJIL 1133 (2017).

Klabbers, J., *The Sources of International Organizations' Law: Reflections on Accountability, in* The Oxford Handbook of the Sources of International Law 987–1006 (S. Besson & J. d'Aspremont, eds., 2017).

Klabbers, J., *Schermers' Dilemma,* 32 EJIL 565 (2020).

Klabbers, J., *Towards a Political Economy of International Organizations Law,* 20 IOLR 82 (2023).

Köck, H.F., *Multinational Diplomacy and Progressive Development of International Law, The Vienna Convention of March 14, 1975,* 28 ZaöRV 51 (1977). [Köck]

Köck, H.F., *Die 'implied powers' der Europäischen Gemeinschaften als Anwendungsfall der 'implied powers' internationaler Organisationen überhaupt, in* Law of Nations, Law of International Organizations, World's Economic Law, *Liber Amicorum* Honouring Ignaz Seidl-Hohenveldern 279 (K.-H. Böckstiegel, H.- A. Folz, J.M. Messner. & K. Zemanek eds. 1988).

Kryvoi, Y., *Procedural Fairness as a Precondition for Immunity of International Organizations,* 13 IOLR 255 (2016).

Kunz, J.L., *Privileges and Immunities of International Organizations*, 41 AJIL 828 (1947). [Kunz]

Kunz-Hallstein, H.P., *Privilegien und Immunitäten internationaler Organisationen im Bereich nicht hoheitlicher Privatrechtsgeschäfte*, 48 NJW 3069 (1992). [Kunz-Hallstein, Privilegien]

Lalive, J.F., *L'immunité de juridiction des états et des organisations internationales*, 84 RdC 205 (1953 III). [Lalive]

Lauterpacht, E., *The Development of the Law of International Organization by the Decisions of International Tribunals*, 152 RdC 377 (1976 IV). [Lauterpacht, Development]

Lauterpacht, E., *The Legal Effect of Illegal Acts of International Organizations, in* Cambridge Essays in International Law in Honour of Lord McNair 88 (1965).

Lauterpacht, H., *The Problem of Jurisdictional Immunities of Foreign States*, 28 BYBIL 220 (1951).

Liang, Y.-L., *The Legal Status of the United Nations in the United States*, 2 Int'l L.Q. 577 (1948).

MacGlashan, M.E., *The International Tin Council: Should a Trading Organisation Enjoy Immunity?*, 46 C.L.J. 193 (1987). [MacGlashan]

Makarczyk, J., *The International Court of Justice on the Implied Powers of International Organizations, in* Essays in International Law in Honour of Judge Manfred Lachs 502 (J. Makarczyk ed. 1984).

Mann, F.A., *The 'Interpretation' of the Constitutions of the International Financial Organizations*, 42 BYBIL 1 (1968–69).

McCaffrey, S., *Current Developments: The Forty-Second Session of the International Law Commission*, 84 AJIL 930 (1990).

McCaffrey, S., *Current Developments: The Forty-Third Session of the International Law Commission*, 85 AJIL 708 (1990).

McFadden, E., *The Collapse of Tin: Restructuring a Failed Commodity Agreement*, 80 AJIL 811 (1986).

McKinnon Wood, H., *Legal Relations between Individuals and a World Organization of States*, 30 Transactions of the Grotius Society 141 (1944,1962). [McKinnon Wood]

Michalek, S.J., *The League of Nations and the United Nations in world politics: a plea for comparative research and universal international organizations*, 15 Int'l Studies Q. 387 (1971).

Miller, A.J., *The Privileges and Immunities of the United Nations*, 6 IOLR 7 (2009).

Miller, A.J., *Privileges and Immunities of United Nations Officials*, 4(2) IOLR 169 (2008).

Miller, A.J., *United Nations Experts on Mission and their Privileges and Immunities*, 4(1) IOLR 11 (2007).

Möldner, M., *Responsibility of International Organizations – Introducing the ILC's DARIO*, *in* Max Planck Yearbook of United Nations Law Vol. 16, 281–328 (A. von Bogdandy & R. Wolfrum, eds., 2012).

Monaco, R., *Le caractère constitutionnel des actes institutifs d'organisations internationales*, *in* Mélanges Offerts à Charles Rousseau – La Communauté Internationale 153 (1974). [Monaco]

Monaco, R., *Les principes régissant la structure et le fonctionnement des organisations internationales*, 156 RdC 79 (1977 III).

Murray, O., *Piercing the Corporate Veil: The Responsibility of Member States of an International Organization*, 8(2) IOLR 291 (2011).

Nash, M.L., *Contemporary Practice of the United States Relating to International Law (Privileges and Immunities – World Bank)*, 74 AJIL 917 (1980).

Nollkaemper A., et al., *Guiding Principles on Shared Responsibility in International Law*, 31(1) EJIL 15 (2020).

Note, *Federal Jurisdiction over International Organizations*, 61 Yale L.J. 111 (1952).

Note, *Recent Developments – International Agreements: United Nations Headquarters Agreement – Dispute over the United States' Denial of a Visa to Yasir Arafat*, 30 Harv. Int'l L.J. 536 (1989) (authored by S. Sadiq Reza).

Note, *Jurisdictional Immunities of Intergovernmental Organizations*, 91 Yale L.J. 1167 (1982) (authored by Kathleen Cully).

Note, *Restricting the Immunity of International Organizations in Labor Disputes: Reforming an Obsolete Shibboleth*, 25 Va. J. Int'l L. 1007 (1985) (authored by J.C. Griffith).

Note, *International Decisions*, 118(2) AJIL 331 (2024)(authored by Philipp Janig).

Okada, Y., *Interpretation of Article VIII, Section 29 of the Convention on the Privileges and Immunities of the UN—Legal Basis and Limits of a Human Rights-based Approach to the Haiti Cholera Case*, 15 IOLR 39 (2018).

Okeke, E.C., *Assessing the Accountability Mechanism of Multilateral Development Banks Against Access to Justice: The Case of the World Bank*, King's Law Journal Online 1 (2023).

Okeke, E.C., *The Tension between the Jurisdictional Immunity of International Organizations and the Right of Access to Court*, in The Role of International Administrative Law at International Organizations (P. Quale ed. 2021).

Oparil, R.J., *Immunity of International Organizations in U.S. Courts: Absolute or Restrictive?*, 24 Vanderbilt J. Transnat'l L. 689 (1991).

Orakhelashvili, A., *Responsibility and Immunities: Similarities and Differences between International Organizations and States*, 11(1) IOLR 114 (2014).

Orakhelashvili, A., *The World Bank Inspection Panel in Context: Institutional Aspects of the Accountability of International Organizations*, 2(1) IOLR 57 (2005).

O'Toole, T.J., *Sovereign Immunity Redivivus: Suits against International Organizations*, 4 Suff. Transnat'l L.J. 1 (1980). [O'Toole]

Osieke, E., *Ultra Vires Acts in International Organizations – The Experience of the ILO*, 48 BYBIL 259 (1976–77).

Osieke, E., *The Legal Validity of* Ultra Vires *Decisions of International Organizations*, 77 AJIL 239 (1983).

Ostrihansky, R., *The 'Mazilu' Opinion of the International Court of Justice and its Contribution to the Clarification of International Law*, 18 Pol. Y.B Int'l L. 1989 (1992).

Palchetti, P., *Is It Time to Take a Decision on the Final Form of ARIO?*, 20(2) IOLR 103 (2023).

Pasquet, L., *Litigating the Immunities of International Organizations in Europe: The 'Alternative-Remedy' Approach and its 'Humanizing' Function*, 36(2) Utrecht Journal of International and European Law 192 (2021).

Pescatore, P., *Les relations extérieures des Communautés européennes: Contribution à la doctrine de la personnalité des Organisations internationales*, 103 RdC 198 (1961 II).

Phan, H.D., *The Association of Southeast Asian Nations: International Legal Personality and Its Treaty-Making Power*, 13(2) IOLR 273 (2016).

Picard, D.U., *The United Nations' Obligation to Provide Access to Remedies to Third-Party Claimants Under International Law*, 20(3) IOLR 330 (2023).

Preuss, L., *The International Organizations Immunities Act*, 40 AJIL 332 (1946). [Preuss]

Rama-Montaldo, M., *International Legal Personality and Implied Powers of International Organizations*, 44 BYBIL 111 (1970).

Recent Developments, *International Organizations: Immunity – Broadbent v. Organization of American States*, 21 Harv. Int'l L.J. 552 (1980) (authored by Mark Gordon).

Recent Developments, *International Organizations – Immunity – Personnel Decisions of an International Organization are not 'Commercial Activities' and thus May Not Form the Basis for an Action Against the Organization*, 20 Va. J. Int'l L. 913 (1980) (authored by Kenneth R. Lee).

Reinisch, A., *The Sources of International Organizations' Law: Why Custom and General Principles are Crucial*, *in* The Oxford Handbook of the Sources of International Law 1007–1024 (S. Besson & J. d'Aspremont, eds., 2017).

Reinisch, A., *The Immunity of International Organizations and the Jurisdiction of Their Administrative Tribunals*, 7(2) Chinese J. Int'l L. 285 (2008).

Ritter, J.-P., *La Conférence et la Convention sur la représentation des états dans leurs relations avec les organisations internationales – Quelques questions particulières*, 21 AFDI 471 (1975). [Ritter]

Ryngaert, C., *The Immunity of International Organizations Before Domestic Courts—Recent Trends*, 7 IOLR 121 (2010).

Salmon, J., *Les accords Spaak – U Thant du février 1965*, 11 AFDI 468 (1965).

Saper, B.M., *The International Finance Corporation's Compliance Advisor/Ombudsman (CAO): An Examination of Accountability and Effectiveness from a Global Administrative Law Perspective*, 44 NYU J. Int'l L. & Pol. 1279 (2012).

Sari, A., *Status of Forces and Status of Mission Agreements under the ESDP: the EU's Evolving Practice*, 19 EJIL 67 (2008);

Sari, A., *The Conclusion of International Agreements by the European Union in the context of the ESDP*, 57 ICLQ 53 (2008);

Schermers, H.G., *International Organizations – Legal Remedies Against Acts of Organs, in* [Installment] 5 Encyclopedia of Public International Law 145 (1983).

Schermers, H.G., *Liability of International Organizations*, 1 LJIL 3 (1988). [Schermers, Liability]

Schermers, H.G., *The International Organizations, in* International Law: Achievements and Prospects 67 (M. Bedjaoui ed. 1991). [Schermers, Organizations]

Schroer, F., *De l'application de l'immunité juridictionnelle des états étrangers aux organisations internationales*, 75 R.G.D.I.P. 712 (1971).

Schroer, F., *On the Application of State Immunity from Enforcement Measures to International Organizations*, 30 R.E.D.I. 76 (1974).

Seidl-Hohenveldern, I., *The Legal Personality of International and Supranational Organizations*, 21 R.E.D.I. 35 (1965). [Seidl-Hohenveldern, Personality]

Seidl-Hohenveldern, I., *L'immunité de juridiction et d'exécution des Etats et des organisations internationales, in* Droit International 1, Cours et Travaux de l'Institut des hautes études internationales de Paris 109–174 (1979/1980). [Seidl-Hohenveldern, L'immunité]

Seidl-Hohenveldern, I., *Dienstrechtliche Klagen gegen Internationalen Organisationen, in* Festschrift für Hans-Jürgen Schlochauer 615 (I. von Münch ed. 1981).

Seidl-Hohenveldern, I., *Responsibility of Member States of an International Organization for Acts of that Organization, in* International Law at the Time of its Codification, Essays in honour of Roberto Ago 415 (Vol. Ill, 1987). [Seidl-Hohenveldern, Responsibility]

Seidl-Hohenveldern, I., *Jurisdiction over Employment Disputes in International Organizations, in Liber Amicorum*: Coleccion de Estudios Juridicos en Homenaje al Prof.Dr.D. José Perez Montero 359 (Vol. Ill, 1988).

Seidl-Hohenveldern, I., *Piercing the Corporate Veil of International Organizations: The International Tin Council Case in the English Court of Appeals*, 32 GYIL 43 (1989). [Seidl-Hohenveldern, Tin]

Seidl-Hohenveldern, I., *L'immunité de juridiction des Communautés européennes*, 338 Rev. Marché Commun 475 (1990). [Seidl-Hohenveldern, Communautés]

Sette-Camara, J., *U.N. and International Law-Making: the Vienna Convention on the Representation of States in their Relations with International Organizations, in* UN Law/Fundamental Rights Two Topics in International Law 91 (A. Cassese ed. 1979). [Sette-Camara]

Seyersted, F., *United Nations Forces, Some Legal Problems,* 37 BYBIL 351 (1961). [Seyersted, UN Forces]

Seyersted, F., *International Personality of Intergovernmental Organizations. Do Their Capacities Really Depend upon Their Constitutions?,* 4 Indian J. Int'l L. 1 (1964). [Seyersted, Personality]

Seyersted, F., *Is the International Personality of Intergovernmental Organizations valid vis-à-vis non-Members?,* 4 Indian J. Int'l L. 233 (1964).

Seyersted, F., *Applicable Law in Relations between Intergovernmental Organizations and Private Parties,* 122 RdC 427 (1967 III).

Shikhelman, V., *Access to Justice in the United Nations Human Rights Committee,* 39(3) Mich J. Int'l L. 453 (2018).

Sinclair, Sir Ian, *The Law of Sovereign Immunity,* 167 RdC 113 (1980 II).

Singer, M., *Jurisdictional Immunity of International Organizations: Human Rights and Functional Necessity Concerns,* 36 Va. J. Int'l L. 53 (1995).

Skubiszewski, K., *Implied Powers of International Organizations, in* International Law at a Time of Perplexity – Essays in Honour of Shabtai Rosenne 855 (1989).

Sucharitkul, S., *Immunities of Foreign States before National Authorities,* 149 RdC 87 (1976 I).

Sucharitkul, S., *The Role of the International Law Commission in the Decade of International Law,* 3 LJIL 15 (1990).

Szasz, P.C., *International Organizations, Privileges and Immunities, in* [Installment] 5 Encyclopedia of Public International Law 152 (1983). [Szasz, Immunities]

Szasz, P.C., *The United Nations Legislates to Limit its Liability,* 81 AJIL 739 (1987). [Szasz, Liability]

Tarassenko, S., & Zacklin, R., *Independence of International Civil Servants (Privileges and Immunities), in* International Administration – Law and Management Practices in International Organisations III.1/1–15 (C. de Cooker ed. 1990). [Tarassenko & Zacklin]

Thompson, D., *The International Tin Council Litigation,* 22 J.W.T.L 103 (1988). [Thompson]

Treichl, C., & Reinisch, A., *Domestic Jurisdiction over International Financial Institutions for Injuries to Project-Affected Individuals: The Case of* Jam v International Finance Corporation, 16 IOLR 105 (2019).

Vandersanden, G., *Administrative Tribunals, Boards and Commissions in International Organizations, in* [Installment] 1 Encyclopedia of Public International Law 1 (1981).

Van Vollenhoven, C., *Diplomatic Prerogatives of Non-Diplomats*, 19 AJIL 469 (1925).

Vargiu, P., *From Advisory Opinions to Binding Decisions: The New Appeal Mechanism of the UN System of Administration of Justice*, 7(2) IOLR 261 (2010).

Virally, M., *De la classification des organisations internationales*, *in* Miscellanea Ganshof van der Meersch 365 (Vol. I, 1972). [Virally, Classification]

Virally, M., *La notion de fonction dans la théorie de l'organisation internationale*, *in* Mélanges Offerts à Charles Rousseau – La Communauté Internationale 277 (1974). [Virally, Fonction]

Virally, M., *Definition and Classification of International Organizations*, *in* The Concept of International Organizations 50 (G. Abi-Saab ed. 1981).

Voskuil, C.C.A., *The International Law of State Immunity, As Reflected in the Dutch Law of Execution*, 10 N.Y.I.L. 245 (1979).

Wassermann, U., *UNCTAD: Sixth International Tin Agreement*, 15 J.W.T.L. 557 (1981). [Wassermann, UNCTAD]

Wassermann, U., *Tin and other Commodities in Crisis*, 20 J.W.T.L. 232 (1986). [Wassermann, Tin]

Watson, G.R., *Constitutionalism, Judicial Review, and the World Court*, 34 Harv. Int'l L.J. 1 (1993).

Weber, U.A., & Reinisch, A., *In the Shadow of Waite and Kennedy – The Jurisdictional Immunity of International Organizations, the Individual's Right of Access to the Courts and Administrative Tribunals as Alternative Means of Dispute Settlement*, 1(1) IOLR 59 (2004).

Wessel, R.A., *Immunities of the European Union*, 10(2) IOLR 395 (2013).

Wolfrum, R., *International Organizations Headquarters*, *in* [Installment] 5 Encyclopedia of Public International Law 140 (1983).

Wood, M., *Do International Organizations Enjoy Immunity under Customary International Law?*, 10 IOLR 287 (2013).

Wright, Q., *The Jural Personality of the United Nations*, 43 AJIL 509 (1949). [Wright]

Yasseen, M.K., *La personnalité juridique des organisations internationales*, *in* A Handbook on International Organizations 43 (R.-J. Dupuy ed. 1988). [Yasseen]

Zacklin, R., *Diplomatic Relations: Status, Privileges and Immunities*, *in* A Handbook on International Organizations 179 (R.-J. Dupuy ed. 1988). [Zacklin, DUPUY]

Zwanenburg, M., *UN Peace Operations Between Independence and Accountability*, 5(1) IOLR 23 (2008).

Documents, Official Publications, Cases

Note: Listings are in chronological order.

Council of Europe Documents

Privileges and Immunities of International Organisations, Resolution (69)29, adopted by the Committee of Ministers of the Council of Europe, 26 September 1969 and Explanatory Report (1969);

Convention for the Protection of Human Rights and Fundamental Freedoms, done at Rome on 4 Nov. 1950, entry into force 3 Sept. 1953, 213 U.N.T.S. 2889, p. 221;

European Convention on State Immunity, done at Basle on 16 May 1972, entry into force 11 June 1976, Eur. Treaty Series No. 074.

European Space Agency Documents

Convention for the establishment of a European Space Agency (as amended), Annex I—'Privileges and Immunities,' entry into force 30 Oct. 1980.

European Union Documents

Treaty establishing a Constitution for Europe, signed in Rome on 29 Oct. 2004, Official Journal of the European Union, 16.12.2004, No. C 310 (did not enter into force);

Protocol on the privileges and immunities of the European Union, Official Journal of the European Union, 16.12.2004, No. C 310/261 (2004);

Treaty of Lisbon amending the Treaty on European Union and the Treaty establishing the European Community, signed at Lisbon on 13 Dec. 2007, entry into force on 1 Dec. 2009, Official Journal of the European Union, 17.12.2007, No. C 306;

(Consolidated Version of the) Treaty on the Functioning of the European Union, Official Journal of the European Union, 26.10.2012, No. C 326/47.

Institut de Droit International Documents

47 Annuaire (1957)(Recours judiciaire d'instituer contre les décisions d'organes internationales)(Judicial Redress against the Decisions of International Organs), available at www.idi-iil.org (tab 'Resolutions');

55 Annuaire (1973)(L'application des règles du droit international général des traités aux accords conclus par les Organisations internationales);

57 Annuaire (1977)(Contracts Concluded by International Organizations with Private Persons);

66 Annuaire (1995)(The Legal Consequences for Member States of the Nonfulfilment by International Organizations of their Obligations toward Third Parties).

International Law Association Documents

'Accountability of International Organizations,' Final Report and Resolution No. 1/2004, Berlin Conference (2004), *International Law Association Reports of Conference*, vol. 71 (2004), pp. 164–234;

Study Group on the Responsibility of International Organizations, Final Report, Sofia Conference (2012), *International Law Association Reports of Conference*, vol. 75 (2012), p. 880.

Netherlands Advisory Committee on Issues of Public International Law (Commissie van advies inzake volkenrechtelijke vraagstukken) Documents

Advice No. 13, 'Aansprakelijkheid tijdens vredesoperaties' [Responsibility during peacekeeping operations], 13 Feb. 2002;

Advice No. 27, 'Aansprakelijkheid van internationale organisaties' [Responsibility of international organizations], 23 Dec. 2015;

Advice No. 47, 'Beslechting van geschillen waarbij een internationale organisatie partij is' [Resolution of disputes to which an international organization is a party], 13 Aug. 2024.

Organization of American States Documents

American Convention on Human Rights, done at San Jose 22 Nov. 1960, 1144 U.N.T.S. 17955, p. 123;

Practical Application Guide on the Jurisdictional Immunities of International Organizations. [OAS Guide]

United Nations Documents

Documents of the United Nations Conference on International Organization, Vol. XIII, Commission IV, Judicial Organization (1945);

Report of the Preparatory Commission of the United Nations, UN Doc. PC/20 (1945);

Handbook on the Legal Status, Privileges and Immunities of the United Nations, UN Doc. ST/LEG/2 (1952);

Repertory of United Nations Practice, UN Sales No. 1955.V.2 (Vol. V, 1955) and Supplements 1–5;

Legislative Texts and Treaty Provisions concerning the Legal Status, Privileges and Immunities of International Organizations, UN Docs. ST/LEG/SER.B/10 (1959) & ST/LEG/SER.B/11 (1961);

International Covenant on Civil and Political Rights, opened for signature 16 Dec. 1966, entry into force 23 Mar. 1976, 999 U.N.T.S. 171;

The Practice of the United Nations, the specialized agencies and the International Atomic Energy Agency concerning their status, privileges and immunities, UN Doc. A/CN.4/L.118 and Add. 1–2 (1967); Id. \ supplementary study prepared by the Secretariat, UN Doc. A/CN.4/L.383 and Add. 1–3 (1985);

Official Records of the United Nations Conference on the Representation of States in Their Relations with International Organizations, Vienna, 4 February-14 March 1975, Vol. I (Summary records of the plenary meetings and of the meetings of the Committee of the Whole), UN Doc. A/CONF.67/18 (1976);

Id., Vol. II (Documents of the Conference), UN Doc. A/CONF.67/18/Add.l (1976);

UN Doc. TD/Res. 93(IV)(1976);

Headquarters regulation No. 4 on 'Limitations of damages in respect of acts occurring within the Headquarters district,' adopted by the UN General Assembly in its resolution 41/210 of 11 Dec. 1986, UN Doc. A/RES/41/210 (1986);

Multilateral Treaties Deposited with the Secretary-General - Status as at 31 December 1986, Un Doc. ST/LEG/SER.E/5 (1987);

Economic co-operation and integration among developing countries: compilation of the principal legal instruments, UNCTAD Doc. TD/B/609/Add. 1 (5 Vols.);

The Work of the International Law Commission, UN Sales No. E.88. V. 1 (4th ed. 1988);

Personnel Questions: Respect for the Privileges and Immunities of Officials of the United Nations and the Specialized Agencies and Related Organizations, Report of the Secretary-General, UN Doc. A/C.5/44/11 (1989);

'Comprehensive Review of the Whole Question of Peace-keeping Operations in All Their Aspects, Model status-of-force agreement for peace-keeping operations,' Report of the Secretary-General, UN Doc. A/45/594 (1990);

Multilateral Treaties Deposited with the Secretary-General - Status as at 31 December 1992, UN Doc. ST/LEG/SER.E/11 (1993);

Report of the Committee on Relations with the Host Country, UN Doc. A/48/614 (1993);

Topical summary of the discussion held in the Sixth Committee of the General Assembly during its forty-seventh session, prepared by the Secretariat, UN Doc. A/CN.4/446 (1993);

'Financing of the United Nations Protection Force, the United Nations Confidence Restoration Operation in Croatia, the United Nations Preventive Deployment Force and the United Nations Peace Forces Headquarters,' Report of the Secretary-General of 20 Sept. 1996, UN Doc. A/51/389 (1996);

'Administrative and budgetary aspects of the financing of the United Nations peacekeeping operations: financing of the United Nations peacekeeping operations,' Report of the Secretary-General of 21 May 1997, UN Doc. A/51/903 (1997);

'Third-party liability: temporal and financial limitations,' UN General Assembly resolution 52/247, adopted on 26 June 1998, UN Doc. A/RES/52/247 (1998);
Articles on the Responsibility of States for Internationally Wrongful Acts, Report of the International Law Commission, GAOR, sixty-sixth session, Suppl. 10, UN Doc. A/66/10, 54 *et seq.*, text annexed to UN General Assembly resolution 56/83 of 12 Dec. 2001, UN Doc. A/RES/56/83 (2001);
United Nations Convention on Jurisdictional Immunities of States and Their Property, adopted by UN General Assembly resolution A/59/38 of 2 Dec. 2004, not yet in force;
UN Human Rights Committee, *General Comment No. 32, Article 14: Right to Equality Before Courts and Tribunals and to a Fair Trial*, UN Doc. CCPR/C/GC/32, 23 Aug. 2007;
Draft articles on the responsibility of international organizations, adopted by the International Law Commission at its sixty-third session, and submitted to the UN General Assembly as part of the ILC's report covering the work of that session, UN Doc. A/66/10 (2011);
Staff Regulations and Staff Rules, including provisional Staff Rules, of the United Nations, UN Doc. ST/SGB/2023/1/Rev. 1 (2023);
1974 UN Jurid. Y.B, UN Doc. ST/LEG/SER.C/12 (1976);
1976 UN Jurid. Y.B, UN Doc. ST/LEG/SER.C/14 (1978);
1980 UN Jurid. Y.B, UN Doc. ST/LEG/SER.C/18 (1983);
1990 UN Jurid. Y.B, UN Doc. ST/LEG/SER.C/28 (1993);
1994 UN Jurid. Y.B, UN Doc. ST/LEG/SER.C/54 (1994) ;
1999 UN Jurid. Y.B, UN Doc. ST/LEG/SER.C/37 (1999) ;
2001 UN Jurid. Y.B, UN Doc. ST/LEG/SER.C/39 (2001);
2003 UN Jurid. Y.B, UN Doc. ST/LEG/SER.C/41 (2003);
2004 UN Jurid. Y.B, UN Doc. ST/LEG/SER.C/42 (2004);
2008 UN Jurid. Y.B, UN Doc. ST/LEG/SER.C/46 (2008);
2016 UN Jurid. Y.B, UN Doc. ST/LEG/SER.C/54 (2016).

International Cases

Permanent Court of International Justice

Competence of the International Labour Organization to Regulate, Incidentally, the Personal Work of the Employer, 1926 PCIJ (ser. B), No. 13 [ser. A/B, No. 19];
Interpretation of the Greco-Turkish Agreement of December 1st, 1926 (Final Protocol, Article IV), 1926 PCIJ (ser. B), No. 16 [ser. A/B, No.31];
Factory at Chorzów, Merits, 1928 PCIJ (ser. A), No. 17;
Jurisdiction of the European Commission of the Danube between Galath and Braila, 1927 PCIJ (ser. B), No. 14 [ser. A/B, No.25].

International Court of Justice

Reparation for Injuries Suffered in the Service of the United Nations, Advisory Opinion, 1949 ICJ Rep. 174;

Colombian-Peruvian Asylum Case, Judgment, 1950 ICJ Rep. 266;

Effect of Awards of Compensation made by the United Nations Administrative Tribunal, Advisory Opinion, 1954 ICJ Rep. 47;

Certain Expenses of the United Nations (Article 17, paragraph 2, of the Charter), Advisory Opinion, 1962 ICJ Rep. 151;

North Sea Continental Shelf Cases (FRG/Den.; FRG/Neth.), Judgment, 1969 ICJ Rep. 3;

Barcelona Traction, Light and Power Company, Limited, Second Phase, Judgment, 1970 ICJ Rep. 3;

Legal Consequences for States of the Continued Presence of South Africa in Namibia (South West Africa) notwithstanding Security Council Resolution 276 (1970), Advisory Opinion, 1971 ICJ Rep. 16;

United States Diplomatic and Consular Staff in Tehran, Judgment, 1980 ICJ Rep. 3;

Application for Review of Judgment No. 333 of the United Nations Administrative Tribunal, Advisory Opinion, 1987 ICJ Rep. 18;

Applicability of the Obligation to Arbitrate under Section 21 of the United Nations Headquarters Agreement of 26 June 1947, Advisory Opinion, 1988 ICJ Rep. 12;

Applicability of Article VI, Section 22, of the Convention on the Privileges and Immunities of the United Nations, Advisory Opinion, 1989 ICJ Rep. 177;

Arbitral Award of 31 July 1989 (Guinea-Bissau v. Senegal), Judgment, 1991 ICJ Rep. 53;

Application of the Convention on the Prevention and Punishment of the Crime of Genocide (Bosnia and Herzegovina v. Yugoslavia (Serbia and Montenegro)), 1993 ICJ Rep. 3 (Provisional Measures, Order of 8 April 1993);

Legality of the Use by a State of Nuclear Weapons in Armed Conflict, Advisory Opinion, 1996 ICJ Rep. 66;

Legality of the Threat or Use of Nuclear Weapons, Advisory Opinion, 1996 ICJ Rep. 226;

Difference Relating to Immunity from Legal Process of a Special Rapporteur of the Commission on Human Rights, Advisory Opinion, 1999 ICJ Rep. 62;

LaGrand (Germany v. United States of America), Judgment, 2001 ICJ Rep. 466;

Arrest Warrant of 1 April 2000 (Democratic Republic of the Congo v. Belgium), Judgment, 2002 ICJ Rep. 3;

Pulp Mills on the River Uruguay (Argentina v. Uruguay), Judgment, 2010 ICJ Rep. 14;

Judgment No. 2867 of the Administrative Tribunal of the International Labour Organization upon a complaint filed against the International Fund for Agricultural Development, Advisory Opinion, 2012 ICJ Rep. 10;

Jurisdictional Immunities of the State (Germany v. Italy; Greece intervening), Judgment, 2012 ICJ Rep. 99.

Court of Justice of the European Communities/European Union

Sayag a.o. v. Leduc a.o., Judgment of 11 July 1968, Case C-5/68;

ERTA Case, Commission of the EC v. Council of the EC, Case 22/70, Decision of 31 March 1971, [1971] ECR 273; 1971 CMLR 335;

Opinion 1/76, European Laying-Up Fund for Inland Waterway Vessels, Decision of 26 April 1977, [1977] ECR 754; 1977 CMLR 279;

Zwartveld, Decision of 13 July 1990, Nr. C-2/88 (1990);

SAT Fluggesellschaft mbH and European Organization for the Safety of Air Navigation (Eurocontrol), Decision (preliminary ruling) of 19 Jan. 1994, Nr. C-364/92 (1994).

Société générale d'entreprise électro-mécaniques (SGEEM) and R. Etroy v. European Investment Bank, Court of Justice of the European Communities, Case C-370/89, Jur. 1992–10, I-6233, ECR 1992 I-06211.

European Court of Human Rights

Waite and Kennedy v. Germany, App. No. 26083/94, judgment of 18 Feb. 1999;

Beer and Regan v. Germany, App. No. 28934/95, judgment of 18 Feb. 1999;

Kudła v. Poland, App. No. 30210/96, judgment of 26 Oct. 2000;

Behrami and Behrami v. France, App. No. 71412/01, judgment of 2 May 2007;

Saramati v. France, Germany and Norway, App. No. 78166/01, judgment of 2 May 2007;

Stichting Mothers of Srebrenica and others v. The Netherlands, App. No. 65542/12, judgment of 11 June 2013.

Arbitrations

A (*organisation internationale*) v. B (*société*), Award of 14 May 1972, ICC Case No. 2091, *Revue de l'Arbitrage* 252 (1975) ;

Texaco Overseas Petroleum et al. v. Libyan Arab Republic, Arbitral Award of 19 Jan. 1977, 17 ILM 1 (1978);

Westland Helicopters Ltd. v. The Arab Organization for Industrialization, the United Arab Emirates, the Kingdom of Saudi Arabia, the State of Qatar, the Arab Republic of Egypt and the Arab British Helicopter Company, International

Chamber of Commerce Court of Arbitration, Interim Award Regarding Jurisdiction of 5 March 1984, Arbitral Tribunal, Case No. 3879 (1984), 23 ILM 1071 (1984);

European Molecular Biology Laboratory v. Germany, Arbitration Award of 29 June 1990, 105 ILR 1 (1997).

National Cases

Austria

Firma Baumeister Ing. Richard L v. O…, Supreme Court of Austria, judgment of 14 Dec. 2004, English translated text in 2004 UN Jurid. Y.B, p. 394, UN Doc. ST/LEG/SER.C/42 (2004);

X v. Organization of the Petroleum Exporting Countries, No. SV 1/2021–23, Austrian Constitutional Court (*Verfassungsgerichtshof*), judgment of 29 Sept. 2022.

Belgium

Scimet v. African Development Bank, Court of First Instance of Brussels, 1997, 128 ILR 582, 584 (1997).

Canada

Gérald René Trempe v. ICAO Staff Association et al. and Gérald René Trempe v. Dirk Jan Goossen et al., High Court, Province of Quebec, District of Montreal, judgment of 20 Nov. 2003, at para. 58, English text reproduced in 2003 UN Jurid. Y.B. 585, at 596, UN Doc. ST/LEG/SER.C/41 (2003);

Amaratunga v. Northwest Atlantic Fisheries Organization, Supreme Court of Canada, judgment of 29 Nov. 2013, 2013 SCC 66, [2013] 3 SCR 866.

France

ECOWAS v. BCCI, Cour d'Appèl, Paris, judgment of 13 Jan. 1993, 113 ILR 473 (1993);

UNESCO v. Boulois, Tribunal de grande instance de Paris, judgment of 20 Oct. 1997, REV ARB 575 (1997);

Banque africaine de développement v. M.A. Degboe, Cour de Cassation, Chambre sociale, judgment of 25 Jan. 2005, 04-41012, 132 Journal du droit international [JDI] 1142 (2005), 110 R.G.D.I.P. 217 (2006).

Italy

Branno v. Ministry of War, Italian Court of Cassation, judgment of 14 June 1954, 1955 ILR 756, *Giurisprudenza Italiana*, 1954, I, 904.

The Netherlands

U.N.R.R.A. v. Daan, Supreme Court (Hoge Raad) of The Netherlands, Decision of 19 May 1950, NJ 1951, 150, 1949 ILR 337 (case 114);

A.S. v. Iran-United States Claims Tribunal, Court of First Instance (Kantongerecht) The Hague, judgment of 8 June 1983, *De Praktijkgids* (1983) No. 2022;

Iran-United States Claims Tribunal v. A.S., District Court (Rechtbank) The Hague, judgment of 9 July 1984, *De Praktijkgids* (1984) No. 2206;

Spaans v. Iran-United States Claims Tribunal, Supreme Court (Hoge Raad) of The Netherlands, case nr. 12627, judgment of 20 Dec. 1985, NJ 438, 1691–1702 (1985), ILR 327 (1994);

Russian Federation v. Pied-Rich B.V., Supreme Court (Hoge Raad) of The Netherlands, case no. 15162 judgment of 28 May 1993, RvdW 1993 Nr. 116–117, 625;

In re Euratom, Supreme Court (Hoge Raad) of The Netherlands, case no. S 01984/07 CW, judgment of 13 Nov. 2007, NJ 2008, 147;

[Plaintiff] v. European Patent Organisation, Supreme Court (Hoge Raad) of The Netherlands, case no. 08/00118, judgment of 23 Oct. 2009;

European Patent Organisation (European Patent Office) v. Stichting Restaurant De la Tour, Court of Appeal (Gerechtshof) The Hague, case no. 200.065.887/01, judgment of 21 June 2011;

Stichting Mothers of Srebrenica et al. v. State of The Netherlands and United Nations, Supreme Court (Hoge Raad) of The Netherlands, case no. 10/04437, judgment of 13 April 2012, NJ 2014/262;

European Patent Organisation v. Vakbondsunie van het Europees Octrooibureau (VEOB) and SUEPO (Staff Union of the European Patent Office), Supreme Court (Hoge Raad) of The Netherlands, case no. 15/02186, judgment of 20 Jan. 2017, NJ 2017/235;

Stichting Mothers of Srebrenica et al. v. State of The Netherlands, Supreme Court (Hoge Raad) of The Netherlands, case no. 17/04567, judgment of 19 July 2019, NJB 2019/1862;

Supreme Site Services GmbH et al v. Supreme Headquarters Allied Powers Europe and Allied Joint Force Command Headquarters Brunssum, Supreme Court (Hoge Raad) of The Netherlands, case no. 20/00937, judgment of 24 Dec. 2021;

United Arab Emirates v. [Employee], case no. 23/01711, Supreme Court (Hoge Raad) of The Netherlands, judgment of 17 May 2024, NJ 2024/204.

United Kingdom

Salomon v. A. Salomon & Co. Ltd., [1897] App.Cas. 22, [1895–9] All E.R. Rep. 33, H.L.;

Duff Development Co. Ltd. v. Government of Kelantan, [1924] App.Cas. 797, [1924] All E.R. 1, H.L.;

Standard Chartered Bank v. International Tin Council and Others, High Court of Justice (Queen's Bench Division), [1986] 3 All E.R. 257, [1987] 1 W.L.R. 641, (Bingham J.), 17 April 1986, 25 ILM 650 (1986);

In re International Tin Council, [1987] 2 W.L.R. 1229, [1987] 1 All E.R. 890, Ch.D.;

Shearson Lehmann Bros. Inc. v. Maclaine Watson & Co. Ltd. (ITC intervening) (No. 2), House of Lords, [1988] 1 All E.R. 116; [1988] 1 W.L.R. 16, HL (E);

Maclaine Watson v. Dept, of Trade, (Kerr, L.J.) [1988] 3 All E.R. 257, 271;

Maclaine Watson & Co. Ltd. v. Department of Trade and Industry and related appeals; Re International Tin Council; Maclaine Watson & Co. Ltd. v. International Tin Council;

Maclaine Watson & Co. Ltd. v. International Tin Council (No. 2), Court of Appeal (Civil Division), 27 April 1988, [1989] 1 Ch. 72, 253, [1988] 3 All E.R. 257, [1988] 3 W.L.R. 1033;

Maclaine Watson & Co. Ltd. v. Department of Trade and Industry and related appeals; Maclaine Watson & Co. Ltd. v. International Tin Council, House of Lords, 26 October 1989, [1990] 2 App.Cas. 418, [1989] 3 All E.R. 523, [1989] 3 W.L.R. 969, 29 ILM 670 (1990);

Entico Corporation, Limited, Claimant, against the Secretary of State for Foreign and Commonwealth Affairs, Intervener, and the United Nations Educational, Scientific and Cultural Organization (UNESO), Defendant, High Court of London, judgment of 28 Mar. 2008, paras. 23–29, text repr. in 2008 UN Jurid. Y.B, pp. 477–489, UN. Doc. ST/LEG/SER.C/46 (2008).

United States of America

Westchester County v. Ranollo, 67 N.Y.S.2d 31 (City Ct. of New Rochelle 1946), 13 ILR 168;

People v. Carcel, 2 Misc.2d 827, 833, 150 N.Y.S.2d436 (City Magist.Ct. 1956), *rev'd*, 3 N.Y.2d 327, 165 N.Y.S.2d 113, 115, 144 N.E.2d 81, 83 (1957);

Victory Transport Inc. v. Comisaria General de Abastecientos y Transportes, 336 F.2d 354 (2d Cir. 1964);

Lutcher S.A. Celulose e Papel v. Inter-Am. Dev. Bank, 382 F.2d 454 (D.C. Cir. 1967);

Carey v. National Oil Corp., 453 F.Supp. 1097 (S.D.N.Y. 1978), *aff'd*, 592 F.2d 673 (2d Cir. 1979);

Int'l Ass. of Mach. v. OPEC, 477 F.Supp. 553, 569 (C.D. Calif. 1979), *aff'd* on other grounds, 649 F.2d 1354 (9th Cir. 1981), *cert. den.*, 454 U.S. 1163 (1982);

Broadbent v. Organization of American States, 628 F.2d 27 (D.C. Cir. 1980);

In Re SEDCO, Inc, 543 F.Supp. 561 (S.D. Tex. 1982), vac. in part, 610 F.Supp. 306 (S.D. Tex. 1984), *rem.*, 767 F.2d 1140 (5th Cir. 1985);

Mendaro v. World Bank, 717 F.2d.610 (D.C. Cir. 1983);

Mol, Inc. v. People's Republic of Bangladesh, 736 F.2d 1326 (9th Cir. 1984);

Boimah v. United Nations General Assembly, 664 F.Supp. 69 (E.D.N.Y. 1987);
Boos v. Barry, 485 U.S. 312 (1988);
Jungquist v. Sheikh Sultan Bin Khalifa Al Nahyan, 115 F.3d 1020 (D.C. Cir. 1997);
Atkinson v. Inter-American Development Bank, et al., 156 F.3d 1335 (D.C. Cir. 1998);
International Bank for Reconstruction and Development v. District of Columbia, 171 F.3d 687 (D.C. Cir. 1999), text repr. in 38 ILM 818 (1999), 1999 UN Jurid. Y.B, p. 433, UN Doc. ST/LEG/SER.C/37 (1999);
Prewitt Enterprises, Inc. v. OPEC, 224 F.R.D. 497 (N.D. Ala. 2002);
Medellín v. Texas, 552 U.S. 491 (2008);
Osseiran v. International Finance Corp., 552 F.3d 836 (D.C. Cir. 2009);
Polak v. International Monetary Fund, 657 F.Supp. 2d 116 (D.D.C. 2009);
Brzak v. United Nations, 597 F.3d 114 (2d Cir. 2010);
OSS Nokalva Inc. v Eur. Space Agency, civil action no. 08-3169 (MLC) (D.N.J. 4 Aug. 2009), *aff'd* on other grounds, 617 F.3d 756 (3d Cir. 2010);
OBB Personenverkehr AG v. Sachs, 577 U.S. 27 (2015);
Georges v. United Nations, No. 15-455-cv, judgment of 18 Aug. 2016 (2d Cir. 2016);
Jam v. International Finance Corp., 139 S. CT. 759 (2019);
Jam v. International Finance Corp., 442 F.Supp. 3d 162 (D.D.C. 2020);
Kling et al. v. World Health Organization, 532 F.Supp. 3d 141 (S.D.N.Y. 2021);
Sacks v. International Monetary Fund, 26 F.4th 470 (D.C. Cir. 2022);
Rodriguez v. Pan American Health Organization, 29 F.4th 706 (D.C. Cir. 2022);
John Does 1–7 v. Taliban, et al.; International Monetary Fund; International Bank for Reconstruction and Development, judgment of 26 Apr. 2024 (D.C. Cir. 2024).

Index of Subjects